4 BARUCH
(PARALEIPOMENA JEREMIOU)

Society of Biblical Literature

Writings from the Greco-Roman World

John T. Fitzgerald, General Editor

Editorial Board

David Armstrong
Elizabeth Asmis
Brian E. Daley, S.J.
David G. Hunter
David Konstan
Margaret M. Mitchell
Michael J. Roberts
Johan C. Thom
James C. VanderKam

Number 22

4 Baruch
(Paraleipomena Jeremiou)

Volume Editor
Abraham J. Malherbe

4 BARUCH
(PARALEIPOMENA JEREMIOU)

Translated with an Introduction and Commentary

by

Jens Herzer

Society of Biblical Literature
Atlanta

4 BARUCH (PARALEIPOMENA JEREMIOU)

Copyright © 2005 by the Society of Biblical Literature

All rights reserved. No part of this work may be reproduced or transmitted in any form or by any means, electronic or mechanical, including photocopying and recording, or by means of any information storage or retrieval system, except as may be expressly permitted by the 1976 Copyright Act or in writing from the publisher. Requests for permission should be addressed in writing to the Rights and Permissions Office, Society of Biblical Literature, 825 Houston Mill Road, Atlanta, GA 30329 USA.

Library of Congress Cataloging-in-Publication Data

Paralipomena Jeremiae. English & Greek.
    4 Baruch (Paraleipomena Jeremiou) / translated with an introduction and commentary by Jens Herzer.
       p. cm. — (Writings from the Greco-Roman world ; 22)
    Includes critical ed. of Greek and English translation.
    Includes bibliographical references.
    ISBN-13: 978-1-58983-173-5 (paper binding : alk. paper)
    ISBN-10: 1-58983-173-X (paper binding : alk. paper)
  I. Title: Four Baruch (Paraleipomena Jeremiou). II. Herzer, Jens. III. Title. IV. Series.
  BS1830.P22A3 2005
  229'.911—dc22   2005016700

13 12 11 10 09 08 07 06 05   5 4 3 2 1
Printed in the United States of America on acid-free, recycled paper conforming to ANSI/NISO Z39.48-1992 (R1997) and ISO 9706:1994 standards for paper permanence.

Contents

Preface	vii
Abbreviations	ix
Introduction	xv
Sources and Literary Character	xvi
4 Baruch and the Syriac Apocalypse of Baruch (2 Baruch)	xvi
4 Baruch and the Pesiqta Rabbati	xxiii
4 Baruch and the Apocryphon of Jeremiah	xxiv
Conclusions: 4 Baruch and Its Traditional Setting	xxvii
Author, Location, and Date	xxx
Text Transmission	xxxvi
List of Manuscripts	xxxviii
Manuscripts with Similar Characteristics	xli
The Critical Apparatus	xlii
4 Baruch: Text and Translation	1
Chapter 1	2
Chapter 2	4
Chapter 3	6
Chapter 4	10
Chapter 5	12
Chapter 6	18
Chapter 7	24
Chapter 8	30
Chapter 9	32
Commentary	41
Chapter 1	43
Chapter 2	53
Chapter 3	59
Chapter 4	73
Chapter 5	81

Chapter 6	101
Chapter 7	119
Chapter 8	131
Chapter 9	141
S<small>ELECT</small> B<small>IBLIOGRAPHY</small>	159
I<small>NDICES</small>	
Index of Biblical Literature	177
Index of Ancient Literature	187
Index of Modern Authors	202
Index of Ancient Names and Places	207
Index of Subjects	209
Index of Greek Terms	212

Preface

The book of *4 Baruch* has been my constant companion for almost fifteen years, ever since my teacher Christian Wolff asked me to write my Diploma thesis on a Jewish writing that I had never heard of before. When I started to work on my dissertation on *4 Baruch* a few years later, I realized that only a few scholars were engaged in interpreting this short story. Today the situation has changed, and *4 Baruch* has become the focus of an extremely stimulating international discussion in which I have been involved in several ways.

Despite my own work on *4 Baruch* over the years, this commentary could not have been written without the assistance of a number of people who helped me to prepare the manuscript. Thus, I would like to thank Stephen Mace for translating my difficult scholarly German into English; Christoph Reichl, who typeset the entire Greek text so that I could work with it on the computer; Susanne Schuster, who spent hours and hours revising the layout of the manuscript according to the detailed standards of the *SBL Handbook of Style;* and Thorsten Klein, Joram Luttenberger, Jörg Briesowski, Kathrin König, and my secretary Roswitha Köhler for proofreading the manuscript. I also thank Bob Buller for his immense and thorough work copyediting the manuscript, volume editor Abraham Malherbe, who improved the English translation, and, finally, series editor John Fitzgerald for asking me to write this commentary for Writings from the Greco-Roman World, for which I feel greatly honored. I am particularly grateful for John's helpful suggestions, which broadened the horizon of the commentary toward the Greco-Roman World.

The Christian redactor of *4 Baruch* closes the story by mentioning a mysterious stone called "the ally of Jeremiah." In the end, I surely know who my "allies" have been while writing this book.

Jens Herzer
Leipzig, Germany
August 2005

Abbreviations

The abbreviations used for the citation of ancient texts and modern scholarly literature follow, in general, the guidelines of the Society of Biblical Literature as published in *The SBL Handbook of Style* (1999). Those used in this volume include the following:

1 Clem.	*1 Clement*
1 En.	*1 Enoch*
1 Apol.	Justin, *First Apology*
2 Apol.	Justin, *Second Apology*
4QapocrJer	*Apocryphon of Jeremiah* from Qumran Cave 4
AB	Anchor Bible
ABD	*Anchor Bible Dictionary.* Edited by D. N. Freedman. 6 vols. New York, 1992.
'Abot R. Nat.	*'Abot de Rabbi Nathan*
Acts Thom.	*Acts of Thomas*
Ag. Ap.	Josephus, *Against Apion*
AGJU	Arbeiten zur Geschichte des antiken Judentums und des Urchristentums
ALGHJ	Arbeiten zur Literatur und Geschichte des hellenistischen Judentums
Alleg. Interp.	Philo, *Allegorical Interpretation*
AnBib	Analecta biblica
ANRW	*Aufstieg und Niedergang der römischen Welt: Geschichte und Kultur Roms im Spiegel der neueren Forschung.* Edited by H. Temporini and W. Haase. Berlin, 1972–.
Ant.	Josephus, *Jewish Antiquities*
AOAT	Alter Orient und Altes Testament
Ap. John	*Apocryphon of John*
Apoc. Ab.	*Apocalypse of Abraham*
Apoc. Mos.	*Apocalypse of Moses*
Apoc. Paul	*Apocalypse of Paul*

Apocr. Ezek.	*Apocrypon of Ezekiel*
Apocr. Jer.	*Apocrypon of Jeremiah*
Aris. Ex.	Aristeas the Exegete
As. Mos.	*Assumption of Moses*
ASTI	Annual of the Swedish Theological Institute
b.	Babylonian Talmud
B. Bat.	Baba Batra
BEATAJ	Beiträge zur Erforschung des Alten Testaments und des antiken Judentums
Ber.	*Berakot*
BFCT	Beiträge zur Förderung christlicher Theologie
BG	Berolinensis Gnosticus
BTZ	*Berliner Theologische Zeitschrift*
BWANT	Beiträge zur Wissenschaft vom Alten und Neuen Testament
BZ	Biblische Zeitschrift
BZAW	Beihefte zur Zeitschrift für die alttestamentliche Wissenschaft
Caes.	Plutarch, *Caesar*
CBQ	*Catholic Biblical Quarterly*
CBQMS	Catholic Biblical Quarterly Monograph Series
Comm. Isa.	Jerome, *Commentariorum in Isaiam libri XVIII*
CSJH	Chicago Studies in the History of Judaism
Der. Er. Rab.	*Derek Eretz Rabbah*
Det.	Philo, *Quod deterius potiori insidari soleat*
DHA	*Dialogues d'histoire ancienne*
Dial.	Justin, *Dialogue with Trypho*
Ecl.	Clement of Alexandria, *Eclogae propheticae*
EgT	*Église et Théologie*
EncJud	*Encyclopaedia Judaica*. 16 vols. Jerusalem, 1972.
Exc.	Clement of Alexandria, *Excerpts from Theodotus*
Exod. Rab.	*Exodus Rabbah*
FJB	*Frankfurter judaistische Beiträge*
FRLANT	Forschungen zur Religion und Literatur des Alten und Neuen Testaments
Fug.	Philo, *De fuga et inventione*
GCS	Die griechische christliche Schriftsteller der ersten [drei] Jahrhunderte
Git.	*Gittin*
Gos. Truth	*Gospel of Truth*
Haer.	Hippolytus, *Refutation of All Heresies*

Haer.	Irenaeus, *Against Heresies*
Ḥag.	*Ḥagigah*
HAT	Handbuch zum Alten Testament
Her.	Philo, *Quis rerum divinarum heres sit*
Herm. *Sim.*	Shepherd of Hermas, *Similitude*
Herm. *Vis.*	Shepherd Hermas, *Vision*
Hier.	Eusebius, *Against Hierocles*
Hist.	Herodotus, *Histories*
Hist.	Tacitus, *Histories*
HSS	Harvard Semitic Studies
HUCA	Hebrew Union College Annual
Is. Os.	Plutarch, *De Iside et Osiride*
JAOS	*Journal of the American Oriental Society*
JBL	*Journal of Biblical Literature*
JCP	Jewish and Christian Perspectives Series
JE	*The Jewish Encyclopedia.* Edited by I. Singer. 12 vols. New York, 1925.
JJS	*Journal of Jewish Studies*
Jos. Asen.	*Joseph and Aseneth*
JQR	*Jewish Quarterly Review*
JSHRZ	*Jüdische Schriften aus hellenistisch-römischer Zeit*
JSJ	*Journal for the Study of Judaism in the Persian, Hellenistic, and Roman Periods*
JSP	*Journal for the Study of the Pseudepigrapha*
JTS	*Journal of Theological Studies*
Jub.	*Jubilees*
Jud	*Judaica*
J.W.	Josephus, *Jewish War*
KEK	Kritisch-exegetischer Kommentar über das Neue Testament (Meyer-Kommentar)
KlPauly	*Der kleine Pauly*
L.A.B.	*Liber antiquitatum biblicarum* (Pseudo-Philo)
L.A.E.	*Life of Adam and Eve*
Lam. Rab.	*Lamentations Rabbah*
LCL	Loeb Classical Library
Liv. Pro.	*Lives of the Prophets*
LSJ	Liddell, H. G., R. Scott, and H. S. Jones, *A Greek-English Lexicon.* 9th ed. with revised supplement. Oxford, 1996.
LXX	Septuagint
m.	Mishnah

Mart. Ascen. Isa.	*Martyrdom and Ascension of Isaiah*
Mek. de Rabbi Ishmael	*Mekilta de Rabbi Ishmael*
MGWJ	Monatschrift für Geschichte und Wissenschaft des Judentums
Midr. Petirat Moshe	*Midrash Petirat Moshe*
Midr. Pss.	*Midrash Psalms*
Mor.	Plutarch, *Moralia*
Mos.	Philo, *De vita Mosis*
MS(s)	manuscript(s)
MT	Masoretic Text
Mut.	Philo, *De mutatione nominum*
Nat.	Pliny the Elder, *Natural History*
NEchtB	Neue Echter Bibel
Neg.	*Nega'im*
NHC	Nag Hammadi Codices
NHS	Nag Hammadi Studies
NovT	*Novum Testamentum*
NRSV	New Revised Standard Version
NS	new series
NTOA	Novum Testamentum et Orbis Antiquus
NTS	*New Testament Studies*
OBO	Orbis biblicus et orientalis
Odes Sol.	*Odes of Solomon*
OTP	*Old Testament Pseudepigrapha*. Edited by J. H. Charlesworth. 2 vols. New York, 1983.
Pesiq. Rab Kah.	*Pesiqta de Rab Kahana*
Pirqe R. El.	*Pirqe Rabbi Eliezer*
PL	Patrologia latina [= Patrologiae cursus completus: Series latina]. Edited by J.-P. Migne. 217 vols. Paris, 1844–1864.
Pr. Man.	*Prayer of Manasseh*
Praep. ev.	Eusebius, *Preparation for the Gospel*
Pre. Pet.	*Preaching of Peter*
Ps.-Clem.	*Pseudo-Clementines*
Pss. Sol.	*Psalms of Solomon*
PTMS	Pittsburgh Theological Monograph Series
PW	Pauly, A. F. *Paulys Realencyclopädie der classischen Altertumswissenschaft*. New edition G. Wissowa. 49 vols. Munich: Druckenmüller, 1980.
QD	Quaestiones disputatae
Qidd.	*Qiddušin*

RAC	*Reallexikon für Antike und Christentum.* Edited by T. Kluser et al. Stuttgart, 1950–.
RB	*Revue biblique*
RechBib	Recherches bibliques
REJ	*Revue des études juives*
RHPR	*Revue d'histoire et de philosophie religieuses*
Roš Haš.	Roš Haššanah
RST	Regensburger Studien zur Theologie
S. Olam Rab.	*Seder Olam Rabbah*
Sacr.	Philo, *De sacrificiis Abelis et Caini*
Sanh.	Sanhedrin
SBLBMI	Society of Biblical Literature The Bible and Its Modern Interpreters
SBLMS	Society of Biblical Literature Monograph Series
SBLSCS	Society of Biblical Literature Septuagint and Cognate Studies
SBLSP	*Society of Biblical Literature Seminar Papers*
SBLTT	Society of Biblical Literature Texts and Translations
SBS	Stuttgarter Bibelstudien
Sem	*Semitica*
Šeqal	Šeqalim
SHANE	Studies in the History of the Ancient Near East
Sib. Or.	*Sibylline Oracles*
Sipre Num.	Sipre Numbers
SJLA	Studies in Judaism in Late Antiquity
SNTU.A	*Studien zum Neuen Testament und seiner Umwelt,* series A
Spec. Laws	Philo, *On the Special Laws*
STDJ	Studies on the Texts of the Desert of Judah
StPB	Studia post-biblica
Strom.	Clement of Alexandria, *Stromata*
SVTP	Studia in Veteris Testamenti pseudepigraphica
t.	Tosefta
T. Ab.	*Testament of Abraham*
T. Ash.	*Testament of Asher*
T. Gad	*Testament of Gad*
T. Job	*Testament of Job*
T. Jud.	*Testament of Judah*
T. Levi	*Testament of Levi*
T. Reu.	*Testament of Reuben*
T. Sim.	*Testament of Simeon*

T. Zeb.	Testament of Zebulun
Taʻan.	Taʻanit
Tanḥ. B	Midrasch Tanchuma: Ein Agadischer Commentar zum Pentateuch von Rabbi Tanchuma ben Rabbi Abba. Edited by Salomon Buber. Wilna: Wittwe & Gebrüder, 1885.
TDNT	Theological Dictionary of the New Testament. Edited by G. Kittel and G. Friedrich. Translated by G. W. Bromiley. 10 vols. Grand Rapids, 1964–1976.
TDOT	Theological Dictionary of the Old Testament. Edited by G. J. Botterweck and H. Ringgren. Translated by J. T. Willis, G. W. Bromiley, and D. E. Green. 8 vols. Grand Rapids, 1974–.
ThA	Theologische Arbeiten
TF	Theologische Forschung
ThStKr	Theologische Studien und Kritiken
TZ	Theologische Zeitschrift
TLZ	Theologische Literaturzeitung
TRE	Theologische Realenzyklopädie. Edited by G. Krause and G. Müller. Berlin, 1977–.
TSAJ	Texte und Studien zum antiken Judentum
TU	Texte und Untersuchungen
TUGAL	Texte und Untersuchungen zur Geschichte der altchristlichen Literatur
VT	Vetus Testamentum
VTSup	Supplements to Vetus Testamentum
WBC	Word Biblical Commentary
WMANT	Wissenschaftliche Monographien zum Alten und Neuen Testament
WUNT	Wissenschaftliche Untersuchungen zum Neuen Testament
y.	Jerusalem Talmud
Yeb.	Yebamot
ZAW	Zeitschrift für die alttestamentliche Wissenschaft
ZNW	Zeitschrift für die neutestamentliche Wissenschaft und die Kunde der älteren Kirche
ZRGG	Zeitschrift für Religions- und Geistesgeschichte
ZWT	Zeitschrift für wissenschaftliche Theologie

Introduction

The *Paraleipomena Jeremiou* has been variously named. The variant mostly preferred is taken from the Greek tradition: τὰ παραλειπόμενα Ἰερεμίου τοῦ προφήτου.[1] In the Ethiopic translation this early Jewish writing is known as "The Rest of the Words of Baruch."[2] In the context of the remaining Baruch literature, English-speaking research uses the name *4 Baruch* rather than *Paraleipomena Jeremiou*.[3]

These various titles are bound up with assessments of the significance of the two main characters: Jeremiah and Baruch. Both play a major role, though in different ways. Jeremiah is the prophet of the fall of Jerusalem and the confidant of God, the priest who intercedes for the people, the one who accompanies it into exile, becoming there its teacher, and, finally, the one who accompanies the people back to the city. Baruch is the one who waits behind, lamenting the destroyed city of Jerusalem, who finally sends the news of the end of the exile to Jeremiah in Babylon. Later on, another figure appears within the story, binding together the time of the exile and the time of the return, a figure closely related to the Jeremiah tradition: Abimelech the Ethiopian. He becomes a symbol for the people in exile. Before the destruction of the city, Jeremiah sends him to a vineyard, where he sleeps for sixty-six years and then returns to the city still lying in ruins. The preservation of Abimelech and the figs he gathered stand for the exiled people, signifying that their exile also has an end, that the (terrible) dream has passed: the return is announced and prepared for. This theme makes

---

1. The title of the writing in manuscripts A, B, and C.
2. See August Dillmann, "Liber Baruchi," in *Chrestomathia Aethiopica* (ed. A. Dillmann; Leipzig: Weigel, 1866), 1–15, here 8. See also J. Rendel Harris, *The Rest of the Words of Baruch: A Christian Apocalypse of the Year 136 A.D.* (London: Clay, 1889).
3. Bar = the biblical book of Baruch; *2 Bar.* = the *Syriac Apocalyse of Baruch*; *3 Bar.* = the *Greek Apocalypse of Baruch*. Kaufmann Kohler, "The Pre-Talmudic Haggada: B—The Second Baruch or Rather the Jeremiah Apocalypse," *JQR* 5 (1893): 407–19, uses *2 Bar.* for *4 Bar.* Robert Doran names it "The Rest of the Words of Jeremiah" (Robert Doran, "Narrative Literature," in *Early Judaism and Its Modern Interpreters* [ed. Robert A. Kraft and George W. E. Nickelsburg; SBLBMI 2; Atlanta: Scholars Press, 1986], 294).

it possible to date *4 Baruch* (see below on "Author, Location, and Date"), but it also legitimates reading the story of return not just on the collective level on the surface of the text but also on an individual level. On this level a theological perspective of hope is revealed that individuals need to recognize for themselves.[4] The fate and hope of the people are bound up in a special way with the fate and hope of the individual members of that people, including not only the individuals within the story itself but also every reader of the story at any time and place. At the same time, the possibility that individual hopes can exceed those of the people also becomes clear. This sheds specific light on the theological constellations of the time and the context in which *4 Baruch* was written.

Sources and Literary Character

The nine comparatively short chapters of *4 Baruch* contain a number of theological ideas and literary motifs that must be taken into account in any attempt to identify the sources and literary character of the work.[5]

The most important source for *4 Baruch* is *2 Baruch*. This work, which in its literary frame also addresses the events and results of the destruction of the temple in 70 C.E. against the background of the biblical traditions surrounding 587 B.C.E., served as a template for the author of *4 Baruch*. Only thus are the commonalities as well as the characteristic differences between the two works best explained.[6]

4 Baruch and the Syriac Apocalypse of Baruch (2 Baruch)

In the course of the following commentary, I will discuss in detail similarities in content between *4 Baruch* and *2 Baruch*. Because I propose that *4 Baruch* depends on *2 Baruch*, this assumption needs to be made clear first by way of an overview of the similar narrative structures of the two works.[7]

The following table provides an overview of the clear parallels between the two works.[8]

---

4. See Christian Wolff, "Irdisches und himmlisches Jerusalem—Die Heilshoffnung in den Paralipomena Jeremiae," *ZNW* 82 (1991): 147–58.

5. See Jean Riaud, *Les Paralipomènes du Prophète Jérémie: Présentation, texte original, traduction et commentaires* (Cahiers du Centre Interdisciplinaire de Recherches en Histoire, Lettres et Langues 14; Angers: Université Catholique de l'Ouest, 1994); Jens Herzer, *Die Paralipomena Jeremiae: Studien zu Tradition und Redaktion einer Haggadah des frühen Judentums* (TSAJ 43; Tübingen: Mohr Siebeck, 1994).

6. Herzer, *Paralipomena Jeremiae*, passim.

7. Ibid., 38–39.

8. Most commentators note only the most obvious parallels in their comparison; this list seeks to be complete. See Pierre-Maurice Bogaert, *Apocalypse de Baruch: Introduction, Traduction du*

INTRODUCTION xvii

4 Baruch	*2 Baruch*
1:1, 3, 7; 4:6	1:1–2:1; 77:10
1:2	2:2
1:5; 4:7	5:1; 7:1–2; 80:3
2:3	85:1–2
2:4	35:2
3:1–8, 14	6:3–10; see 80:2
3:11–12; 4:5	10:1–5; see 33:2
4:1–2	6:1, 5; 8:1–5
4:3–4	10:18
4:9	11:4–5
4:11	21:1
5:21; 7:32	44:3–45:2
6:7	13:3; 25:1; 76:2
6:8–23	77:12–19
7:1–12	77:20–26
7:8, 30	87:1

This list provides a basis for agreeing with P.-M. Bogaert's claim that most points of contact between *4 Baruch* and *2 Baruch* are found in the so-called "cadre narratif"[9] and in the conclusion of *2 Baruch* (*2 Bar.* 1–12 and 77; cf. *4 Bar.* 1–4 and 6–7). However, there are also numerous parallels outside this frame of reference. With regard to *4 Baruch*, it is particularly interesting to note that there are few if any points of contact with *2 Baruch* in *4 Bar.* 2, 5, 8, and 9, and even these few, as will be seen, can only to a limited extent be regarded as genuine parallels.

Not only the content but also the structure of the narrative frame reveals significant similarities. After the announcement of the destruction of Jerusalem, explained in terms of the sin of the people and its leaders (*2 Bar.* 1:1–5), Baruch

---

Syriaque et Commentaire (2 vols.; Paris: Cerf, 1969), 1:186–90, here 107–13. See also Jean Riaud, "Les Paralipomena Jeremiae dépendent-ils de 2 Baruch?" *Sileno* 9 (1983): 105–28; idem, *Paralipomènes du Prophète Jérémie*, 40–48; Robert H. Charles, *The Apocalypse of Baruch Translated from the Syriac* (London: Black, 1896), xviii–xix, here xix. See also George W. E. Nickelsburg, "Narrative Traditions in the Paralipomena of Jeremiah and 2 Baruch," *CBQ* 35 (1973): 60–68, here 60.

9. Bogaert, *Apocalypse de Baruch*, 1:186.

is required in *2 Bar.* 2, together with Jeremiah "and all those of your kind" (2:1), to leave the city. Baruch's objection (*2 Bar.* 3) and God's answer (*2 Bar.* 4) follow, the latter concluding with God once again requiring Baruch and the others to leave the city (4:8). Finally, Baruch, Jeremiah, and the others accept their fate (*2 Bar.* 5), and the fall of the city follows (*2 Bar.* 6–8). Jeremiah heads to Babylon with the people, while Baruch remains (10:1–5) and sings a lament. Only then does *2 Baruch* provide in a variety of forms a full reflection on what has happened. These prayers, laments, and visions have as their pinnacle the promise of salvation to the people in terms of a return to Jerusalem. These reflections form the main body of *2 Baruch* (10:6–77:26). Although the return itself is not reported, Baruch's message to the exiles concerning the end of the exile is a clear hint of this expectation (*2 Bar.* 77–79).

One notes a similar structure in *4 Baruch*. After an introduction of the situation, one encounters the announcement and the explanation of the destruction of the city, and Jeremiah is required to leave the city together with Baruch (1:1–3). Jeremiah's objection and God's answer follow (1:4–6, 7–11), then Jeremiah and Baruch's acceptance of God's will (*4 Bar.* 2). Finally, *4 Bar.* 4 describes the destruction and conquest of the city. Jeremiah heads to Babylon with the people (3:11; 4:5), while Baruch remains in Jerusalem and sings a lament (4:6–11).

These structural similarities are clear from the following overview.

4 Baruch	*2 Baruch*
1:1 Introduction, dating Word of the Lord to Jeremiah	1:1 Introduction, dating Word of the Lord to Baruch
1:1 Announcement and explanation of the destruction of the city	1:2–5 Announcement and explanation of the destruction of the city
1:1 Demand that the city be left	2:1–2 Demand that the city be left
1:4–6 Jeremiah's objection	3:1–9; 5:1 Baruch's objection
1:7–11 God's answer	4:1–5; 5:2–4 God's answer
2:1–10 Acceptance of God's will	5:5–6 Acceptance of God's will
3:1–4:5 Fall of the city	6:1–8:5 Fall of the city
4:6–11 Baruch's lament	10:5–19 Baruch's lament
6:8–7:32 Letters by Baruch and Jeremiah	77:11–87:1 Letters by Baruch

Further comparison reveals that the commonalities between *4 Baruch* and *2 Baruch* go beyond their narrative frames to their contents.[10] Not all modern scholars, however, agree that the author of *4 Baruch* used *2 Baruch* as a literary source. Other possibilities for understanding the relationship between these two works have been suggested, and these merit discussion. The four competing theories are as follows: (1) *4 Baruch* is earlier than *2 Baruch* and was used by its author; (2) *2 Baruch* is earlier than *4 Baruch* and was used by its author; (3) *2 Baruch* used an earlier, now-unknown version of *4 Baruch;* and (4) *2 Baruch* and *4 Baruch* drew from a common source.[11]

4 Baruch is earlier than *2 Baruch* and was used by its author

Kaufmann Kohler argued for the dependence of *2 Baruch* on *4 Baruch*, though without offering any support for this thesis.[12] Jean Riaud sought to counter this view by pointing to an earlier date for *2 Baruch*.[13] However, his objection fails due to the controversial question regarding the dating of *2 Baruch*, for which dates from 63 B.C.E.[14] through the 132–135 C.E. Bar Kokhba War[15] have been suggested. Even Pierre-Maurice Bogaert, who initially

---

10. Herzer, *Paralipomena Jeremiae*, 40–77.
11. Riaud, "Paralipomena Jeremiae," 106–25. See also his *Paralipomènes du Prophète Jérémie*, 40–48.
12. Kohler, "Pre-Talmudic Haggada," 408; Riaud, "Paralipomena Jeremiae," 106.
13. Riaud, "Paralipomena Jeremiae," 106–7.
14. So Jean Hadot, "La Datation de l'Apocalypse Syriaque de Baruch," *Sem* 15 (1965): 79–95. Hadot was of the opinion that *2 Baruch* reflected the events of Pompey's conquest of Jerusalem in 63 B.C.E.: "il est nécessaire de montrer que le contenu de notre ouvrage répond jusque dans ses moindres détails aux événements que se sont produits autour de 63 av. J.-C. au sein du peuple juif" (95). However, he fails to provide the evidence. Without arguing here the case at length, the fact that in *2 Baruch* the city walls are destroyed stands contrary to this thesis (*2 Bar.* 7:1–3; 8:1: Pompey entered Jerusalem together with his army without destroying the walls). Cf. Josephus, *Ant.* 14.54–63. See also Pierre-Maurice Bogaert, "Le Nom de Baruch dans la Littérature Pseudépigraphique: l'Apocalypse Syriaque et le Livre Deutéronomique," in *La Littérature Juive entre Tenach et Mischna* (ed. Willem Cornelis van Unnik; RechBib 9; Leiden: Brill, 1974), 56–72.
15. Primarily Frederick J. Murphy, "The Temple in the Syriac Apocalypse of Baruch," *JBL* 106 (1987): 671–83. See also Herbert Schmid, "Baruch und die ihm zugeschriebene apokryphe und pseudepigraphe Literatur," *Jud* 30 (1974): 54–70, here 63, who views the years between 132–135 as the terminus ad quem; so also Otto Eissfeldt, *The Old Testament: An Introduction, Including the Apocrypha and Pseudepigrapha, and Also the Works of Similar Type from Qumran—The History of the Formation of the Old Testament* (trans. Peter R. Ackroyd; New York: Harper & Row, 1965), 630. See Albertus F. J. Klijn, "Die syrische Baruch-Apokalypse," *JSHRZ* 5.2 (1976): 107–84: after 100 C.E. and before 130 C.E. In his "2 (Syriac Apocalypse of) Baruch (early Second Century A.D.): A New Translation and Introduction," *OTP* 1:615–52, here 617, he dates it "around A.D. 100."

argued for 96 C.E.,[16] later suggested the period between 70 C.E. and 135 C.E.[17] That means that *4 Baruch* and *2 Baruch* could be dated very near one another. Literary analysis has had the decisive role in these dating questions.[18]

2 Baruch is earlier than *4 Baruch* and was used by its author

Bogaert has been the leading representative[19] of the view that *4 Baruch* is dependent on *2 Baruch*.[20] Riaud's argument against this view makes reference only to three parallels (*4 Bar.* 1:6 // *2 Bar.* 4:2; *4 Bar.* 4:3–4 // *2 Bar.* 10:18; *4 Bar.* 7:8–12 // *2 Bar.* 77:20–26[21]), but a critique based on these three texts is insufficient. Although Bogaert's discussion of the thesis can be shown in some regards insufficient and unconvincing, it basically remains correct: the commonalities and differences between the two works are best explained by assuming that *4 Baruch* depends on *2 Baruch*. Certainly the link from *4 Baruch* to *2 Baruch* is not clear at every point, and often one must evaluate arguments concerning specific shortenings or lengthenings differently. However, one must maintain that parallel passages and their assessment have to fit into the context of the whole, on the basis of which less-certain passages are to be judged.

---

16. Bogaert, *Apocalypse de Baruch*, 1:295; idem,"Le Nom de Baruch," 58. See further Robert Henry Charles, "II Baruch. The Syriac Apocalypse of Baruch. Introduction," in *The Apocrypha and Pseudepigrapha of the Old Testament in English, with Introductions and Critical Explanatory Notes to the Several Books* (ed. Robert Henry Charles; 2 vols.; Oxford: Clarendon, 1913), 2:470–80, here 470; Leonhard Rost, *Einleitung in die alttestamentlichen Apokryphen und Pseudepigraphen einschließlich der großen Qumran-Handschriften* (Heidelberg: Quelle & Meyer, 1971), 97; Riaud, "Paralipomena Jeremiae," 107; Gwendolyn B. Saylor, *Have the Promises Failed? A Literary Analysis of 2 Baruch* (SBLMS 72; Chico, Calif.: Scholars Press, 1984), 103–5.

17. Bogaert, "Nom de Baruch," 58. See also Irene Taatz, *Frühjüdische Briefe: Die paulinischen Briefe im Rahmen der offiziellen religiösen Briefe des Frühjudentums* (NTOA 16; Fribourg: Universitäts-Verlag, 1991), 60.

18. On dating questions, see below the discussion of "Author, Location, and Date."

19. Bogaert, *Apocalypse de Baruch*, 1: Introduction. See further Harris, *Rest of the Words of Baruch*, 20. Charles, *Apocalypse of Baruch* (1896), xviii–xix; Bruno Violet, *Die Apokalypsen des Esra und des Baruch in deutscher Gestalt* (GCS 32; Leipzig: Hinrichs, 1924), lxiv–lxv; Gerhard Delling, *Jüdische Lehre und Frömmigkeit in den Paralipomena Jeremiae* (BZAW 100; Berlin: Töpelmann, 1967), 4–6; Albert-Marie Denis, *Introduction aux Pseudépigraphes Grecs d'Ancien Testament* (SVTP 1; Leiden: Brill, 1970), 75; Christian Wolff, *Jeremia im Frühjudentum und Urchristentum* (TU 118; Berlin: Akademie, 1976), 45–46; Klijn, "2 Baruch," *OTP* 1:620. For others, see Riaud, "Paralipomena Jeremiae," 105 n. 2.

20. However, Nickelsburg ("Narrative Traditions," 62 n. 15) notes critically that Bogaert only twice makes a point of referring to the use of *2 Baruch* in *4 Baruch*. Riaud ("Paralipomena Jeremiae," 107) rightly notes that most are satisfied merely to state the dependence of *4 Baruch* on *2 Baruch*.

21. Riaud, *Paralipomènes du Prophète Jérémie*, 41.

2 Baruch used an earlier, now-unknown version of *4 Baruch*

Léon Gry assumed that an earlier, more primitive form of *4 Baruch* was used by the author of *2 Baruch*.[22] His starting point was the observation that Jeremiah plays a subordinate role in *2 Baruch*.[23] That the pupil is more significant than the master, he argued, indicates a later date for *2 Baruch*.[24] Riaud rightly counters that Jeremiah also plays an important role in *2 Baruch*,[25] even if one must allow that it is not as crucial as Riaud proposes. However, the fact that Jeremiah plays a much more significant role in *4 Baruch* than in *2 Baruch* strongly supports the view that *4 Baruch* built on *2 Baruch*, consciously correcting and revising the specific relationship between Jeremiah and Baruch presented in *2 Baruch*.[26] It is hard to explain the other view, that *2 Baruch* would have consciously attempted to eliminate Jeremiah. Hence the existence of an earlier edition of *4 Baruch* remains highly uncertain and improbable, not least because there are no indications of the existence of such a text.[27]

2 Baruch and *4 Baruch* drew from a common source

Based on J.-M. Rosenstiehl's work,[28] Riaud has argued that *4 Baruch* and *2 Baruch* used one or more sources on which both are dependent.[29] Characterizing this source collection as "un cycle légendaire de Jérémie,"[30] Riaud describes

---

22. Léon Gry, "La ruine du temple par Titus: Quelques traditions juives plus anciennes et primitives à la base de *Pesikta Rabbathi* XXVI," *RB* 55 (1948): 215–26, here 220. See also Riaud, "Paralipomena Jeremiae," 113; Jean Riaud, "La figure de Jérémie dans les Paralipomena Jeremiae," in *Mélanges bibliques et orientaux en l'honneur de M. Henri Cazelles* (ed. André Caquot; AOAT 212; Kevelaer: Butzon & Bercker, 1981), 373–85, here 373; S. E. Robinson, "4 Baruch: A New Translation and Introduction," *OTP* 2:413–25, here 416–17, suggested a similar possibility, assuming that there was an independent original version of *4 Baruch*, which was edited after *2 Baruch* and which has been overworked by a Jewish redactor, in order to harmonize it with *2 Baruch*.

23. Gry, "La ruine du temple par Titus," 220: "L'auteur de Bar.syr., on le sait, cherche à éliminer la personnalité trop importante du Jérémie." See also Nickelsburg, "Narrative Traditions," 66.

24. Gry, "La ruine du temple par Titus," 220.

25. Riaud, "Paralipomena Jeremiae," 114.

26. Against Nickelsburg, "Narrative Traditions," 66, who mentions this explanation, yet rejects it. On the significance of Jeremiah in *4 Baruch*, see Riaud, "La figure de Jérémie," 373.

27. Riaud, "Paralipomena Jeremiae," 115. Also against Nickelsburg, "Narrative Traditions," 66.

28. Jean-Marc Rosenstiehl, "Histoire de la Captivité de Babylone I–V" (Ph.D. diss., Strasbourg, n.d.), referred to in Riaud, "Paralipomena Jeremiae," 115. See also Riaud, *Paralipomènes du Prophète Jérémie*, 53–63.

29. Riaud, "Paralipomena Jeremiae," 115–17. Similarly Robinson, "4 Baruch," 417, who however qualifies his considerations as "speculative suggestions" (417). Berndt Schaller, "Paralipomena Jeremiou," *JSHRZ* 1.8 (1998): 659–777, here 673, expressly develops this thesis.

30. Riaud, "Paralipomena Jeremiae," 115–17.

which elements the author of *4 Baruch* took from it.³¹ This presentation characterizes, however, only part of this cycle and leaves it largely unclear. Therefore, it is hardly possible to verify this hypothesis. If the legend cycle's hypothetical form renders it unlikely, two further considerations make it even less so. The motifs that Riaud claims were taken from the legend cycle are basically parallel passages, which simply shows that such views were also found in other early Jewish works: Jeremiah as the new Moses,³² Jeremiah as spokesman,³³ Jeremiah and the temple vessels,³⁴ Jeremiah and the temple keys,³⁵ Jeremiah and the Yom Kippur sacrifice,³⁶ Jeremiah's death,³⁷ Abimelech's sleep.³⁸ It is impossible to prove the plausibility of the existence of a legend cycle on the basis of such limited evidence. A second consideration refers to *2 Baruch,* which is also claimed to have taken material from this cycle.³⁹ One must explain why Jeremiah slips into the background behind Baruch in *2 Baruch,*⁴⁰ if Jeremiah were the main figure in the supposed legend cycle.⁴¹

Nickelsburg added an argument not taken into account by Riaud: the parallels between *4 Bar.* 3:8, 2 Macc 2:7, and *Liv. Pro.* 2:11 regarding the temple vessels.⁴² In all three cases, Nickelsburg rightly notes: "The eschatological terminus at which the vessels will be restored is the 'gathering together' of God's people."⁴³ From this parallel Nickelsburg concludes: "The author of Par Jer knows a form of this tradition which dates back at least to the 1st century B.C. In this respect, he has preserved elements of the tradition more primitive than

---

31. For details see Riaud, *Paralipomènes du Prophète Jérémie,* 53–63.
32. Riaud, "Paralipomena Jeremiae," 116–20. See also Riaud, *Paralipomènes du Prophète Jérémie,* 53–54; Wolff, *Jeremia im Frühjudentum und Urchristentum,* 79–83.
33. Riaud, "Paralipomena Jeremiae," 120–21; Wolff, *Jeremia im Frühjudentum und Urchristentum,* 83–89.
34. Riaud, "Paralipomena Jeremiae," 122–23; idem, *Paralipomènes du Prophète Jérémie,* 54–55; Wolff, *Jeremia im Frühjudentum und Urchristentum,* 61–71.
35. Riaud, "Paralipomena Jeremiae," 123–24; idem, *Paralipomènes du Prophète Jérémie,* 55–56; Wolff, *Jeremia im Frühjudentum und Urchristentum,* 76–79.
36. Riaud, *Paralipomènes du Prophète Jérémie,* 56.
37. Riaud, "Paralipomena Jeremiae," 124–25; idem, *Paralipomènes du Prophète Jérémie,* 56–58; Wolff, *Jeremia im Frühjudentum und Urchristentum,* 89–95.
38. Riaud, *Paralipomènes du Prophète Jérémie,* 58–63.
39. Riaud, "Paralipomena Jeremiae," 115, 125; Schaller, "Paralipomena Jeremiou," 673.
40. See further Bogaert, *Apocalypse de Baruch,* 1:100–119.
41. See even Riaud, "Paralipomena Jeremiae," 125, on Syriac Baruch: "Baruch est le personnage principal de son Œvre, et Jérémie, son comparse muet."
42. Nickelsburg, "Narrative Traditions," 64. According to Felix Böhl ("Die Legende vom Verbergen der Lade," *FJB* 4 [1976]: 63–80), *Liv. Pro.* 2 is dependent on 2 Macc 2.
43. Nickelsburg, "Narrative Traditions," 64. See also Böhl, "Legende," 66–68.

those in *2 Baruch*."⁴⁴ However, Nickelsburg fails to prove this claim; merely noting the parallel in 2 Macc 2:7 does not suffice.⁴⁵ Against Nickelsburg's argument stands the significantly different wording of the two passages.⁴⁶ The important word in *4 Bar.* 3:8 ἠγαπημένος is missing in 2 Macc 2:7, whereas the language in 3:8 is similar to *2 Bar.* 21:21–23.⁴⁷ That *2 Bar.* 6:7 (as 2 Macc 2:4–5) mentions both the temple vessels and furniture, whereas only the vessels are of concern in *4 Baruch*, is further proof for Nickelsburg that *4 Baruch* used an older tradition.⁴⁸ However, it is hard to imagine what this tradition could have looked like. Even with regard to the relationship between *2 Bar.* 6:3–10 and *4 Bar.* 3:1–8, the links are so clear⁴⁹ that dependence of *4 Baruch* on *2 Baruch* represents a more likely solution that requires no additional hypotheses.⁵⁰ The 2 Macc 2 tradition should thus probably be seen as the basis on which the author of *4 Baruch* combined the prophet Jeremiah and the motif of the hiding of the temple instruments.

4 Baruch AND THE *Pesiqta Rabbati*

Pesiqta Rabbati 26⁵¹ contains a number of passages that are quite similar

---

44. Nickelsburg, "Narrative Traditions," 64. See also Harris, *Rest of the Words of Baruch*, 23; Robinson, "4 Baruch," 417; Craig R. Koester, *The Dwelling of God: The Tabernacle in the Old Testament, Intertestamental Jewish Literature and the New Testament* (CBQMS 22; Washington, D.C.: Catholic Biblical Association of America, 1989), 50.

45. Nickelsburg incorrectly refers to Delling, *Paralipomena Jeremiae*, 65 n. 63, who while referring to 2 Macc 2:7 does not draw conclusions concerning *4 Baruch* from it.

46. Nickelsburg, "Narrative Traditions," 64 n. 25, concedes this point.

47. See the commentary on 3:8 below.

48. Nickelsburg, "Narrative Traditions," 64–65. On the use of 2 Macc 2:4–6 in *Liv. Pro.* 2:9–11, see Anna Maria Schwemer, "Die Verwendung der Septuaginta in den Vitae Prophetarum," in *Die Septuaginta zwischen Judentum und Christentum* (ed. M. Hengel and A. M. Schwemer; WUNT 72; Tübingen: Mohr Siebeck, 1994), 62–91, here 79.

49. See below the commentary on 3:1–8.

50. After his very impressive argument for the dependence of *4 Baruch* and *2 Baruch* on common earlier tradition, Nickelsburg's final sentence is incomprehensible (Nickelsburg, "Narrative Traditions," 68): "That the author of Par Jer knew of an apocalyptic Baruch tradition is evident from 4:11..., and it is not impossible that he knew *2 Baruch*. However, we have argued above that our author also knew some older Jeremiah traditions." S. E. Robinson's assumption (Robinson, "4 Baruch," 417) that a later Jewish editor sought to harmonize *4 Baruch* with *2 Baruch* is also to be rejected: *4 Baruch* has an independence that distinguishes it from *2 Baruch* and leaves no recognizable traces of harmonization.

51. Leo Prijs, *Die Jeremia-Homilie Pesikta Rabbati Kapitel 26: Eine synagogale Homilie aus nachtalmudischer Zeit über den Propheten Jeremia und die Zerstörung des Tempels: Kritische Edition nebst Übersetzung und Kommentar* (Stuttgart: Kohlhammer, 1966), 11 n. 1, suspects that *Pesiqta Rabbati* was written in the second half of the ninth century; on introductory questions, see Hermann L. Strack

to *4 Baruch*.⁵² It tells the story of Jeremiah's life from his birth to the destruction of Jerusalem episodically and thus distinguishes itself from other parts of *Pesiqta Rabbati*, in which a biblical verse typically provides the starting point for an exposition.⁵³ Jeremiah's life is interpreted in the light of the destruction of Jerusalem, and this interpretation concludes with a prophetic vision. A far broader picture is painted here than in *4 Baruch*. However, Jeremiah is the main figure in both works, in contrast to *2 Baruch*. Baruch, who is involved in the passages relevant for comparison, does not appear in *Pesiqta Rabbati*.

A direct relation between *4 Baruch* and *Pesiqta Rabbati* is not demonstrable, however; rather, the commonalities are best explained in terms of a common use of *2 Baruch*,⁵⁴ though whether *Pesiqta Rabbati* is directly or indirectly literarily dependent on *2 Baruch* can hardly be established with certainty.⁵⁵ The various positions offered thus far are highly hypothetical and almost always reckon with intermediary texts for which there is no evidence.⁵⁶ It is important to note that *Pesiqta Rabbati* orients itself much more to the biblical tradition and so seeks to harmonize passages from *2 Baruch* that depart from the biblical text.

4 Baruch and the *Apocryphon of Jeremiah*

Several scholars cite the so-called *Apocryphon of Jeremiah*⁵⁷ as providing a

---

and Günther Stemberger, Introduction to the Talmud and Midrash (trans. Markus Bockmuehl; 7th ed.; Edinburgh: T&T Clark, 1991), 322–29. On the history of the text, see Prijs, *Jeremia-Homilie*, 11–19. The German text of the *Pesiqta Rabbati* is taken from the edition by Prijs, *Jeremia-Homilie*, 25–77. The Hebrew text is also found there: Prijs, *Jeremia-Homilie*, 81–96 (= Codex Parma Nr. 1240[3122]; see Prijs, *Jeremia-Homilie*, 14–16; cf. K.-E. Grözinger and H. Hahn, "Die Textzeugen der Pesiqta Rabbati," *FJB* 1 [1973]: 63–104, here 91–95). For the English translation, see Leo Nemoy, ed., *Pesikta Rabbati: Discourse for Feasts, Fasts and Special Sabbaths* (trans. W. G. Braude; New Haven: Yale University Press, 1968), 525–38. On problems concerning the assessing of textual witnesses for Pesiqta Rabbati, see Grözinger and Hahn, "Textzeugen," 91–95.

52. For a detailed comparison, see Herzer, *Paralipomena Jeremiae*, 79–86.

53. Strack and Stemberger, *Introduction to the Talmud and Midrash*, 326, therefore suspect that *Pesiq. Rab.* 26 has a different origin.

54. Gry, "La ruine du temple par Titus," 200.

55. On the influence of apocalyptic ideas on rabbinic writings, see ibid., passim; Clemens Thoma, "Jüdische Apokalyptik am Ende des ersten nachchristlichen Jahrhunderts," *Kairos* 11 (1969): 134–44, here 139; Beate Ego, *Im Himmel wie auf Erden: Studien zum Verhältnis von himmlischer und irdischer Welt im rabbinischen Judentum* (WUNT 2/34; Tübingen: Mohr Siebeck, 1989), passim.

56. On this, see the summary in Bogaert, *Apocalypse de Baruch*, 1:240–41.

57. The *Apocryphon of Jeremiah* is a text that has come to us in Garshuni, an Arabic language that employs Syriac letters. In the most likely secondary Coptic tradition it bears the same name as *4 Baruch*. The Garshuni version has been edited with an English translation by Alphonse Mingana and J. Rendel Harris, "A New Jeremiah Apocryphon," Woodbrooke Studies I.2, *John Rylands Library Bulletin* 11 (1927): 125–91, 192–233 (with an introduction by J. R. Harris [125–38]).

further basis for postulating a Jeremiah legend cycle.[58] Although some of the material in this apocryphal work concerning Jeremiah, Baruch, and Abimelech is related to *4 Baruch*,[59] there are also important reasons for doubting such a claim.

Like *Pesiqta Rabbati*, the *Apocryphon of Jeremiah* covers much more of Jeremiah's story than does *4 Baruch*, especially as regards Jeremiah's activity before Jerusalem's fall.[60] It relies primarily on Old Testament traditions, elements of which are taken to shape the narrative, such as the lengthy conflict with Zedekiah, to whom Jeremiah is sent, Abimelech's activity (150:1–160:2[61]), and the conflict with Hananiah (152:4–18).[62] A further tradition used is that of the archangel Michael, first named expressly in *4 Bar.* 9:5, whom God gives the task in the *Apocryphon of Jeremiah* of requiring Nebuchadnezzar to conquer Jerusalem (161:26–163:19), after the sins of King Zedekiah have been described at length (159:18–20).

Still, one can observe some similarities between the *Apocryphon of Jeremiah* and *4 Baruch*.[63] Particularly of note is that, in contrast to *2 Baruch* and *Pesiqta Rabbati*, the *Apocryphon of Jeremiah* shares the story of Abimelech with *4 Baruch* (*4 Bar.* 5:1–6:8; *Apocr. Jer.* 167:3–30; 185:8–187:26). In contrast to *4 Baruch*, however, the story is divided in two so that the story of Abimelech's falling asleep and his awakening is separated by the story of the fall of the city, the deportation, the captivity, and the return of the people (167:31–185:7).[64] In *4 Baruch*, an ellipse is purposely created by consciously leaving out these events,[65] which

---

The Arabic version was published in French by Emile Amélineau, *Contes et Romans de l'Égypte Chrétienne* (Collections des Contes et Chançons populaires 13–14; 2 vols.; Paris: Leroux, 1888), 2:97–151. See also K. H. Kuhn, "A Coptic Jeremiah-Apocryphon," *Muséon* 83 (1970): 95–135, 291–350. The original language was probably Greek. See Mingana and Harris, "New Jeremiah Apocryphon," 127, 149; Wolff, *Jeremia im Frühjudentum und Urchristentum*, 53; René-Georges Coquin, "Quelle était la langue originelle du pseudépigraphe conservé en Copte sous le titre de Paralipomènes de Jérémie et en Arabe sous le titre Captivité des fils d'Israel à Babylone?" *Apocrypha* 6 (1995): 79–82; Schaller, "Paralipomena Jeremiou," 673 n. 53.

58. Riaud, *Paralipomènes du Prophète Jérémie*, 49–51; Schaller, "Paralipomena Jeremiou," 673–74.

59. Schaller, "Paralipomena Jeremiou," 674.

60. Wolff, *Jeremia im Frühjudentum und Urchristentum*, 54–55; Riaud, *Paralipomènes du Prophète Jérémie*, 49.

61. Numbering according to page and line number in Mingana's edition used in Mingana and Harris, "New Jeremiah Apocryphon."

62. See further Wolff, *Jeremia im Frühjudentum und Urchristentum*, 54–56.

63. Space does not permit a full treatment of these similarities. See the list in ibid., 53 n. 7; Riaud, *Paralipomènes du Prophète Jérémie*, 49–50.

64. On the story of Abimelech in *4 Baruch*, see below the commentary on chapter 5.

65. See below the introduction to chapter 5.

are supplied in the *Apocryphon of Jeremiah* in detail on the basis of the biblical tradition, especially Ezra-Nehemiah (*Apocr. Jer.* 176:21–23).

The numerous similarities (as well as differences) between *4 Baruch* and the *Apocryphon of Jeremiah* have given rise to theories positing a common source.[66] However, the preceding overview makes it readily apparent that this is unnecessary. It is clear that the editor of the *Apocryphon of Jeremiah* used Old Testament traditions quite freely, and its relationship to *4 Baruch* is to be understood similarly: *4 Baruch* was not a literary model for the *Apocryphon of Jeremiah* but a known tradition freely used, shaped, and combined with others. For example, the "vineyard of Agrippa" (*4 Bar.* 3:10, 15; 5:25[67]) becomes "the garden of his master" (e.g., *Apocr. Jer.* 167:8, 11), probably because the connotations of the former were no longer comprehensible to the author of the *Apocryphon of Jeremiah*. The reference here is also to a vineyard, for Abimelech picks not only figs but grapes, too (e.g., 167:10, 23; 185:10, 18). Likewise, the sixty-six years of sleep (*4 Bar.* 5:1) become seventy (*Apocr. Jer.* 167) in order to fit the biblical tradition.[68] There are also reasons in the text for assuming that other stories of such sleeps were also known to the author of the *Apocryphon of Jeremiah*, from which certain motifs were borrowed. The motif of the mountain, for example, that "covered" Abimelech (167:25–26) can be compared with *b. Ta'an.* 23a,[69] as can the remark that Abimelech slept until "Jerusalem was destroyed and then rebuilt afresh" (167:28–29[70]), which refers back to *y. Ta'an.* 3:9 IVB: "He remained asleep for seventy years, until the Temple was destroyed and it was rebuilt a second time."[71]

Thus, the *Apocryphon of Jeremiah* cannot be used to defend the hypothesis of a Jeremiah legend cycle. Further, it is impossible to demonstrate literary dependence between the *Apocryphon of Jeremiah* and *4 Baruch*.[72] Rather, the similarities and differences between the two works are best explained by assuming that the author of the *Apocryphon of Jeremiah* knew the *4 Baruch* tradition (as well as others).[73]

---

66. Among others, Riaud, *Paralipomènes du Prophète Jérémie*, 49–51; Schaller, "Paralipomena Jeremiou," 674.

67. See below the commentary on 5:25.

68. See below the commentary on 5:1.

69. Wolff, *Jeremia im Frühjudentum und Urchristentum*, 56 n. 3. See below the "Excursus on *4 Baruch* in the Context of Ancient Sleep Narratives."

70. See the contradiction in 185:21–22 and the attempted solution in 185:26–30.

71. Quoted from Jacob Neusner, *The Talmud of the Land of Israel: A Preliminary Translation and Explanation*, vol. 18: *Besah and Taanit* (Chicago Studies in the History of Judaism; Atlanta: Scholars Press, 1987), 226. See below the "Excursus on *4 Baruch* in the Context of Ancient Sleep Narratives."

72. As rightly Schaller, "Paralipomena Jeremiou," 674.

73. See Mingana and Harris, "New Jeremiah Apocryphon," 133; Bogaert, *Apocalypse de Baruch*, 1:180; Wolff, *Jeremia im Frühjudentum und Urchristentum*, 53; Hans Harald Mallau,

CONCLUSIONS: *4 BARUCH* AND ITS TRADITIONAL SETTING

The hypothesis of a Jeremiah legend cycle, postulating the cycle as the single source for various texts (including *4 Baruch*),[74] creates more problems than it solves and is much too complicated to be convincing.[75] In fact, *4 Baruch* uses the story framework as well as individual motifs of *2 Baruch* found outside its frame that serve the development of the story in *4 Baruch*, being molded to fit the intended purpose of the book. Although *4 Baruch* is a shorter text than *2 Baruch*, *4 Baruch* goes beyond it, narratively speaking. Whereas *2 Baruch* reflects theological issues relating to the fall of Jerusalem and the destruction of temple, ending with Baruch's letter (*2 Bar.* 78–86), *4 Baruch* continues the story up to the return of the people.

In order to make this ending possible, the new story of Abimelech is woven into the story taken from *2 Baruch*. Abimelech is introduced in *4 Bar.* 3 by way of an allusion to the Abimelech tradition of Jer 39 (LXX 46):16–18. This promise

---

"Baruch, Baruchschriften: Paralipomena Jeremiae," *TRE* 5 (1980): 269–76, here 272. L. Vegas-Montaner, "Paralipomenos de Jeremias," in *Apocrifos del Antiguo Testamento* (ed. Alejandro Diez Macho et al.; 2 vols.; Madrid: Cristiandad, 1983), 2:353–83, here 360. That the *Apocryphon of Jeremiah* is probably to be dated in the third/fourth century C.E. further speaks for this argument: Mingana and Harris, "New Jeremiah Apocryphon," 149; Arthur Marmorstein, "Die Quellen des neuen Jeremia-Apocryphons," *ZNW* 27 (1928): 327–37, here 337; Heinrich Schützinger, "Die arabische Jeremia-Erzählung und ihre Beziehungen zur jüdischen Überlieferung," *ZRGG* 25 (1979): 1–19, here 11; Wolff, *Jeremia im Frühjudentum und Urchristentum*, 54. There are, however, some Qumran fragments that also seem to refer to a Jeremiah legend and thus are called *4Q Apocryphon of Jeremiah*. If this is related to the already known *Apocryphon of Jeremiah* as discussed above, it would witness to a much earlier date of the legend in the second century B.C.E.; see Devorah Dimant, *Qumran Cave 4.XXI: Parabiblical Texts, Part 4: Pseudo-Prophetic Texts* (DJD 30; Oxford: Clarendon: 2001), 91–260. In support of this hypothesis, see also Lutz Doering, "Jeremia in Babylon und Ägypten: Mündliche und schriftliche Toraparänese für Exil und Diaspora nach *4QApocryphon of Jeremiah C**," in *Frühjudentum und Neues Testament im Horizont biblischer Theologie* (ed. K.-W. Niebuhr und W. Kraus; WUNT 162; Tübingen: Mohr Siebeck, 2003), 50–79. The main argument of Dimant and Doering is that 4Q385a frg.18:I, a–b (Dimant, *Qumran Cave 4.XXI*, 159—one of the biggest and best-preserved fragments) seemingly speaks of Jeremiah being led with the people to Babylon and teaching them the commandments of God. However, not a single word that this reading relies on is preserved in the fragment; rather, it has to be hypothetically added. Thus, the reconstruction of this fragment as well as of others related to it is far from convincing and gives no certain hint to the emergence of the Jeremiah-Babylon legend. According to 4Q385a 18:II (Dimant, *Qumran Cave 4.XXI*, 163), Jeremiah is not in Babylon, but—as in the Old Testament tradition—in Egypt, and 4Q389 (Dimant, *Qumran Cave 4.XXI*, 220) seems to assume a letter from Jeremiah to the exiles.

74. Rosenstiehl, *Histoire de la Captivité de Babylone*. See Riaud, *Paralipomènes du Prophète Jérémie*, 39–80.

75. Herzer, *Paralipomena Jeremiae*, 75–76, 87–88.

to the "Ethiopian" provides the basis for the story of his preservation. Similarly, the motif of the figs is taken from Jer 24, which in the context of the sleeping story is of great moment: the figs stand both for individual hopes of salvation and for the hopes of the people. After thus setting up *4 Bar.* 5, the writer takes the motif of sleep from a tradition concerning Honi the Circle Drawer, found in written form in *y. Ta'an.* 3:9. This story, probably already in existence in the second half of the first century,[76] was probably present in an oral form that was used by both *4 Baruch* and *y. Ta'an.* 3, also appearing later in *b. Ta'an.* 23a. The basic thought running through all these traditions is that found in Ps 126, that the exile passes like a short dream. The interpretation of the psalm found in the Honi story is applied to Abimelech, who is known in the biblical tradition as one who did good to Jeremiah (see also *4 Bar.* 3:9). In contrast to the rabbinic tradition, the psalm is not mentioned in *4 Baruch* because its aim is not merely the exposition of the psalm but rather the development of an eschatological dimension to an already-established exposition. Thus the Abimelech story exemplifies the creation of a new tradition as it draws together originally unconnected and quite different traditions into a new concept.

The *content* of the correspondence between Jeremiah and Baruch does not seem to have any literary sources. Rather, *4 Bar.* 6 and 7 take up the *motif* of a letter from Baruch to Gola in *2 Baruch,* from which book the eagle motif is also taken, and *4 Baruch* molds this motif against the background of the biblical Noah tradition found in Gen 8.

The section dealing with mixed marriages and the founding of Samaria by those disobedient to Jeremiah relies on biblical traditions (2 Kings, Ezra, Nehemiah), the positive attitude of the author toward the Samaritans having parallels in Jewish traditions of his time.[77] The mention of Samaria makes it clear that the Samaritan question was important with regard to the future of the people of Israel and thus required reflection, since reference to Samaria would in other respects not have been necessary for his theological conception. In fact, *4 Bar.* 8 views the Samaritans as belonging to Israel, even if (as yet) separated from Israel by disobedience, but the promise of a heavenly Jerusalem counts for them as well (8:9). That the Ezra-Nehemiah tradition had already raised the issue of mixed marriage in the postexilic period gave the author of *4 Baruch* a starting point for his own presentation.

---

76. Ibid., 92 n. 264.

77. 2 Macc 5:22–23; *m. Kutim* 2:28 (from Aqiba's time; see Lazar Gulkowitsch, "Der kleine Talmudtraktat über die Samaritaner, übersetzt und erklärt, " *ΑΓΓΕΛΟΣ: Archiv für neutestamentliche Zeitgeschichte und Kulturkunde I.1.2* [ed. Johannes Leipoldt et al.; Leipzig: Pfeiffer, 1925], 48–56, here 48–52), *y. Git.* 1:4 (Aqiba); *y. Ber.* 7:1 (Simon ben Gamaliel); *b. Sanh.* 90b; for a differing view, see *m. Qidd.* 4:3.

Finally, *4 Bar.* 9 also picks up on Old Testament traditions. The festival of sacrifices and the prayer of Jeremiah derive from Isa 6 and the tradition of the Day of Atonement found in Lev 16. The prayer of the prophet summarizes the message of *4 Baruch* and stands in place of an actual "sacrifice," an understanding of prayer that reveals links to rabbinic thought.[78] The death of Jeremiah that follows stands in a line of traditions that know of a natural death for the prophet, without suggesting any dependence between them.[79]

The Christian redaction of *4 Baruch* has its own traditional characteristics as well. It consists of the addition of 9:10–32 at the end of the book. Other verses suspected of being (gnostic) Christian additions are actually to be explained with reference to the literary and traditional context of *4 Baruch*.[80] The Christian ending shows awareness of the tradition found in the *Martyrdom and Ascension of Isaiah* concerning Isaiah's death and the tradition of the stoning of Jeremiah that is found in *Liv. Pro.* 2 and that may form the background of Heb 11:37. On the basis of many linguistic clues, one would seek the Christian editor within circles influenced by a Johannine-apocalyptic Christianity.[81]

From a form-critical standpoint, *4 Baruch* is not to be seen as an apocalyptic work,[82] as its literary dependence on *2 Baruch* might suggest. The form-critical question is associated with not merely literary-critical but also historical questions (see below on "Author, Location, and Date"). As will be shown, *4 Baruch* adopts a critical position with regard to the messianic expectations of its day, immediately making the apocalyptic form unsuitable. Rather, *4 Baruch* engages the expectations and discussions of the day in the style of a haggadah:[83] a retell-

---

78. Herzer, *Paralipomena Jeremiae*, 145–46 n. 540.
79. Wolff, *Jeremia im Frühjudentum und Urchristentum*, 89–95; Herzer, *Paralipomena Jeremiae*, 156–58.
80. Herzer, *Paralipomena Jeremiae*, 171–76. M. Philonenko's thesis (Marc Philonenko, "Simples Observations sur les Paralipomènes de Jérémie," RHPR 76 [1996]: 157–77) that *4 Baruch* is a gnostic-Christian work in its entirety, related to Mandaian circles, is unsupported; see Jens Herzer, "Die Paralipomena Jeremiae—Eine christlich-gnostische Schrift? Eine Antwort an Marc Philonenko," *JSJ* 30 (1999): 25–39.
81. Herzer, *Paralipomena Jeremiae*, 160–70.
82. See Harris, *Rest of the Words of Baruch*, passim. Until the beginning of the Christian ending, the typical apocalyptical elements of an apocalypse are missing; see Lars Hartmann, "Survey of the Problem of Apocalyptic Genre," in *Apocalypticism in the Mediterranean World and the Near East: Proceedings of the International Colloquium on Apocalypticism, Uppsala 1979* (ed. David Hellholm; 2nd ed.; Tübingen: Mohr Siebeck, 1989), 329–44; Ed P. Sanders, "The Genre of Palestinian Jewish Apocalypses," in Hellholm, *Apocalypticism in the Mediterranean World*, 447–59.
83. See Kohler, "Pre-Talmudic Haggada," 407–19; Jacob Licht, ספר מעשי ירמיהו מן הספרים התיצונים (*Sefer ma'ase yirmiyahu–Paralipomena Jeremiae*) (Annual of Bar-Ilan University Studies in Judaica and Humanities I; Jerusalem: Kiryath Sepher, 1963), xxi–xxii and 66–80, here 68; Vegas-Montaner, "Paralipomenos de Jeremias," 359; Wolff, "Heilshoffnung," 158.

ing of a chapter of Israel's history involving theological interpretations for the purposes of instruction.[84]

Author, Location, and Date

The interdependencies revealed by tradition criticism between *4 Baruch* and its written precursors indicate that *4 Baruch* could have been produced at any point during a rather lengthy time period. Because of its literary dependence on *2 Baruch*, the work can be no older than the end of the first century C.E. The relationship between the Christian redaction of *4 Baruch* and the *Martyrdom and Ascension of Isaiah* suggests a date no later than the middle of the second century C.E. for the final form of the text.[85] That the Jewish text must be several years older than the Christian one favors a date no later than 140 C.E. On that basis, a period of forty to fifty years emerges in which the Jewish text of *4 Baruch* could have been written.

The most precise date proposed is that of Harris, who based his calculations on the number sixty-six, which occurs several times in the book (*4. Bar.* 5:1, 30; 6:5; 7:24). Adding this number to the year of the destruction of Jerusalem (70 C.E.), Harris concluded that the text was written in 136 C.E. He regarded *4 Baruch* as a Christian text intended to be an *eirenicon* of the church to the synagogue produced by a Jewish Christian.[86] The year 136 fits well with the *eire-*

---

84. Riaud (*Paralipomènes du Prophète Jérémie*, 85 with n. 36) suggests the term "historical haggadah," referring to R. le Déaut, *Introduction à la Littérature Targumique 1* (Rome: Pontifical Biblical Institute, 1966), 14: "(A)ggadah historique ... qui, faisant fi des données réelles de l'histoire, idéalise la tradition, en comblant les lacunes des récits historique, établit des connexions entre épisodes différents, entre divers personnages." Riaud concludes: "Peut-être serait-il préférable de dire, que les Paralipomena Jeremiae sont une haggadah qui, parce qu'elle projette dans l'avenir des leçons du passé, a une 'allure apocalyptique'" (*Paralipomènes du Prophète Jérémie*, 87). Schalom Ben-Chorin (*Narrative Theologie des Judentums anhand der Pessach-Hagadda: Jerusalemer Vorlesungen* [Tübingen: Mohr Siebeck, 1985], 13) names the haggadah as "narrative Theologie des Judentums": "Die Haggada ist wesensverwandt mit dem Midrasch, der homiletischen Auslegung der Heiligen Schrift" (14). This "narrative theology" has a "meditative character" (15). "Durch das immer wiederkehrende Erzählen, das sich nicht auf das Ablesen von Texten beschränken soll, entsteht lebendige Heilsgeschichte" (16). See Schaller, "Paralipomena Jeremiou," 681–82, who on the basis of the title Παραλειπόμενα suggests the description "ergänzende Haggada" (supplementing haggadah).

85. The relation to *Ascension of Isaiah* allowed Dillmann to date *4 Baruch* in the third or even the fourth century C.E. Admittedly, this conclusion only regards the text as we now have it, but even for that such a late date is implausible.

86. Harris, *Rest of the Words of Baruch*, 12–15. See Robinson, "4 Baruch," 414. Dillmann had already put forward the hypothesis of (Jewish-)Christian authorship in Dillmann, *Chrestomathia Aethiopica*, 9–10. Philonenko ("Simples Observations," passim) has recently supported this view. For the problem of interpreting the number sixty-six, see below on 5:1.

nicon view, being the year after the Jews lost Jerusalem to the Romans in 135 C.E., such a document being possible only in such circumstances. However, neither Harris's views on authorship nor those on dating have found much support. Studies in the last two decades make it clear that *4 Baruch* was originally the work of a Jewish author that was given an additional ending by Christian circles.

Nevertheless, still others have also regarded the year 136 as a possible date of composition.[87] Apart from the dubious means of arriving at such a date (adding 70 and 66), one must ask whether a Jewish text such as *4 Baruch* was likely to emerge in a year such as 136. In his early review of Harris's text edition, E. Schürer pointed out that, "were the little book really written in such moving times, one [would] expect stronger traces of that history in it."[88] If that is a valid criticism when one conceives of *4 Baruch* as Christian, as Harris did, it must certainly count if the text is Jewish. It is most unlikely that the book would not deal with the just-finished and, for Israel, catastrophic events of the war against Rome. Consequently, many commentators have dated the work before the outbreak of the Bar Kokhba War, around 130 C.E.[89] Apart from Harris's view, only Riaud has suggested a relatively narrow period for the writing of *4 Baruch*, between 118 and 130 C.E. He even suggests that the Christian reception of the text occurred before 132.[90]

The poor state of the sources makes dating and reconstructing the production of *4 Baruch* difficult. It is unlikely, however, that the work was composed during the Bar Kokhba rebellion (132–135 C.E.), and thus we turn our attention to the period prior to it.

Our first consideration must be that the destruction of Jerusalem and the temple in 70 C.E. had major social, political, and religious consequences. The loss of the temple required a fundamental transformation of religious life in Palestine. The driving force behind the post-70 reorientation and reconsolidation was provided by rabbis from the Pharisaic wing of Judaism. Of particular

---

87. George W. E. Nickelsburg, *Jewish Literature between the Bible and the Mishnah: A Historical and Literary Introduction* (Philadelphia: Fortress, 1981), 315: "between 135 and 136." See also Licht, *Paralipomena Jeremiae*, 70; Saylor, *Have the Promises Failed*, 139.

88. E. Schürer, review of J. R. Harris, *The Rest of the Words of Baruch: A Christian Apocalypse of the Year 136 A.D., TLZ* 15 (1890): 81–83, here 83.

89. George D. Kilpatrick, "Acts VII.52 ΕΛΕΥΣΙΣ," *JTS* 46 (1945): 136–45, here 141: "before 132 C.E."; Albert-Marie Denis, "Les Paralipomènes de Jérémie," in *Introduction aux Pseudépigraphes Grecs d'Ancien Testament* (ed. Albert-Marie Denis; VTSup 1; Leiden: Brill 1970), 75: 70–130 C.E.; Emile Turdéanu, "La Légende du Prophète Jérémie en Roumain," in *Apocryphes Slaves et Roumains de l'Ancien Testament* (SVTP 5; Leiden: Brill, 1981), 307–47, here 307: 70–132 C.E.; Robinson, "4 Baruch," 414: first third of the second century.

90. Riaud, *Paralipomènes du Prophète Jérémie*, 131.

note in this regard is Rabbi Johanan ben Zakkai, a student of the Hillel School[91] and a former member of the Sanhedrin.[92] Within the context of such an enormous political defeat and forcible subjection to Caesar, concentrating on the survival of the spiritual-religious dimension was the only way to save the Jewish people from disappearing. By accepting the Roman government yet preserving Jewish tradition and the law, ben Zakkai and his followers saw a future for the Jewish people.[93] The developments in Judaism since 135 C.E. confirm this interpretation. This view explains ben Zakkai's critical attitude toward messianic movements. For example, *'Abot R. Nat.* B 31 records him saying:

> If there were a plant in your hand and they should say to you: "Look, the messiah is here!" Go and plant your plant and after that go forth to receive him. If the young men say to you: "Let us go and build the temple," do no [sic] listen to them, but if the old men say to you: "Come and let us tear down the temple," do as they say.[94]

The tradition established by ben Zakkai in Yavneh was continued by Gamaliel II, a son of the last leader of the Sanhedrin. Under Gamaliel's leadership the Yavneh school won more influence. Moreover, Shmuel Safrai points out that the wise men of Yavneh were the ones able to maintain Judaism after the destruction of the temple and to restore Jewish life in every respect.[95]

The attempt to concentrate on the spiritual and religious renewal of rabbinic Judaism that began to consolidate itself after 70 C.E. stands in stark contrast to a contemporaneous movement: continued opposition against Roman rule. The latter found its clearest expression in the rebellion of 115–117 C.E. against Trajan (98–117 C.E.) and then in that of Bar Kokhba in 132–135 C.E. against Hadrian (117–138 C.E.). The former was a series of rebellions in the Diaspora during a military action by Trajan in the Orient; the latter was concentrated in the Palestine homeland. The significance of these two movements within Judaism

---

91. *M. 'Abot* 2:8; Adolf Schlatter, *Jochanan Ben Zakkai, der Zeitgenosse der Apostel* (BFCT 3; Gütersloh: Bertelsmann, 1899), 9–10; Jacob Neusner, *Life of Rabban Yohanan ben Zakkai: Ca. 1–80 C.E.* (StPB 6; Leiden: Brill, 1962), 16–27.

92. Whether ben Zakkai was himself a Pharisee is not certain. See Günter Stemberger, *Pharisäer, Sadduzäer, Essener* (SBS 144; Stuttgart: Katholisches Bibelwerk, 1991), 132.

93. Peter Schäfer, "Die Flucht Johanan b. Zakkais aus Jerusalem und die Gründung des 'Lehrhauses' in Jabne," *ANRW* 19.2:43–101, 80–82.

94. Quoted from Antonio J. Saldarini, *The Fathers according to Rabbi Nathan (Aboth de Rabbi Nathan Version B): A Translation and Commentary* (SJLA 11; Leiden: Brill 1975), 182.

95. Shmuel Safrai, *Das jüdische Volk im Zeitalter des Zweiten Tempels* (Neukirchen-Vluyn: Neukirchner Verlag, 1978), 126. See also Peter Schäfer, *The History of the Jews in Antiquity: The Jews of Palestine from Alexander the Great to the Arab Conquest* (Luxembourg: Harwood Academic Publishers, 1995), 139–40.

for the dating of *4 Baruch* lies in their differing attitudes toward Roman government. In the period after ben Zakkai and Gamaliel II, the movement of Rabbi Aqiba, who provided theological support for Bar Kokhba's rise,[96] won increasing influence.[97] A major bone of contention in the run-up to this last Jewish war on Rome was the transformation of Jerusalem into Aelia Capitolina, which Hadrian had commanded during a Palestinian visit in 129–130 C.E. According to the Roman historian Dio Cassius (second half of the second century C.E.), this was the reason for Bar Kokhba's rebellion (*Historia Romanum* 69 12.113.2). The suppression of the 117 C.E. rebellions in the Diaspora had already raised the question of how to cope with Roman authority. The beginning of the building of Aelia Capitolina and the Jupiter/Zeus temple not only intensified this conflict but also changed the cityscape. This otherwise unremarkable point is of particular interest because *4 Bar.* 5:3 reports that Abimelech did not recognize Jerusalem when he returned after his sleep. This failure to recognize the city is not to be explained by the destruction of the city. Although one could see here a purely literary feature of a story about a long sleep, the repetition in 5:12 is particularly noteworthy because in literary terms it is not at all unnecessary: "And he went out of the city and when he looked carefully, he saw the landmarks of the city and said, 'Indeed, this is the city, but I lost my way.'" The discrepancy between the views from inside and outside the city, which is only recognizable from without by its outline, could be an allusion to Hadrian's architectural

---

96. Peter Schäfer, *Studien zur Geschichte und Theologie des rabbinischen Judentums* (AGJU 25; Leiden: Brill, 1978), 64–121, esp. 90–95; see also his *Der Bar Kockba-Aufstand: Studien zum zweiten jüdischen Krieg gegen Rom* (Tübingen: Mohr Siebeck, 1981), 55–57. Cf. *y. Ta'anit* 4:5: "R. Simeon b. Yochai taught, Aqiba, my master, would interpret the following verse: 'A star (kokhab) shall come forth out of Jacob' (Numbers 24:17)—'A disappointment (ko-zeba) shall come forth out of Jacob.' R. Aqiba: When he saw Bar Kozeba, he said, 'This is the King Messiah.' Said to him R. Yohanan ben Toreta, 'Aqiba! Grass will grow on your cheeks, and the Messiah will not yet have come!'" (quoted from Neusner, *Talmud of the Land of Israel*, 18:275). See also Pierre Lenhardt and Peter von der Osten-Sacken, *Rabbi Akiva: Texte und Interpretationen zum rabbinischen Judentum und Neuen Testament* (Berlin: Institut Kirche und Judentum, 1987), 307–17. For a critical perspective on the view that Aqiba supported Bar Kokhba, see Jacob Neusner, "Akiba ben Joseph," *TRE* 2:146–47, here 147: "Die Geschichte über die Beziehung zu Bar Kochba ist jedoch spät und findet in den älteren Überlieferungen keine Bestätigung, jedenfalls nicht vor Abschluß des palästinischen Talmuds, und genügt nicht als Beweis dafür, daß Akiba den Aufstand befürwortet oder gar Bar Kochba zum Messias proklamiert hat." Against Neusner one would ask why such a wrong assessment of Bar Kokhba would be attributed to Aqiba. On ambivalence in the assessing of Bar Kokhba among his contemporaries, see Adele Reinhartz, "Rabbinic Perceptions of Simeon Bar Kosiba," *JSJ* 20 (1989): 171–94, here 191–93: "These positive and negative statements are irrefutable evidence for the messianic identification of Bar Kosiba. Such identification, criticised as it was in the post-revolt period, could only have had its origins during the time of the revolt" (192).

97. Schäfer, *History of the Jews*, 140.

changes. Jerusalem is no longer the Jerusalem that Abimelech had left, although its "marks" (σημεῖα) can still be perceived (see commentary on 5:12). In the view of the changed city and in Abimelech's sadness and confusion, *4 Baruch* picks up on certain feelings that were important among the Jewish people in the period 117–132 C.E. At the same time, the writer is aware of the seething messianic atmosphere in the land that will inevitably lead to new conflict.

Although it is not stated explicitly, this awareness can be seen clearly in the book's eschatological orientation. By emphasizing God's law as the way to the people's salvation, the perspective of eschatological hope in the resurrection, and the expectation of a heavenly Jerusalem, the writer answers the pressing questions of his time, is even ahead of his time: a turning point in the fate of the Jewish people can only be expected from God (*4 Bar.* 6:13–22; 8:1–2), the final end of which will be the gathering of the people in the heavenly Jerusalem. The way the people must follow is to be found in a focus on God's law, which points the way to the heavenly Jerusalem (see 5:34). This double orientation fits well in the period between the rebellions, more precisely in the years leading up to the Bar Kokhba War, around 130 C.E. The writer thinks it necessary to warn against the one-sided hope of political and temple-cultic restoration held by an influential part of the population. History has vindicated him. This view is consistent only if *4 Bar.* 9 relativizes temple worship. Sacrifice is certainly mentioned (9:1–2), but the temple equipment, for which Jeremiah is initially so concerned (*4 Bar.* 3), and the keys to the temple (*4 Bar.* 4) are never returned, and Jeremiah's sacrifice in 9:3–5 consists primarily in the prayer of a righteous man for himself and for the people. Thus the theology of *4 Baruch* seems close to that of ben Zakkai in Yavneh and his successors, as outlined above. On the basis of the author's broad awareness of the Scriptures, perhaps one ought to locate the author either in the ben Zakkai school itself or in the circles around it. This confirms the view, often rightly acknowledged on the basis of the author's knowledge of the places he is discussing, that he is to be located in Palestine, more exactly in the Jerusalem region.[98] Finally, the author's geographical and temporal proximity to early Jewish apocalyptic, which is particularly clear in his dependence on *2 Baruch*, is also shown by his tendency to overcome the feelings of resignation characteristic of apocalyptic thought (e.g., *4 Bar.* 4:9–10) by replacing them with the eschatological hope of salvation.

Dating the Christian redaction of *4 Baruch* is harder than dating and locating the Jewish work. Normally the redaction is dated shortly after the Jewish

---

98. Harris, *Rest of the Words of Baruch*, 12; Robinson, "4 Baruch," 414–15; Turdéanu, "Légende du Prophète Jérémie en Roumain," 306; Denis, "Paralipomènes de Jérémie," 74; Riaud, *Paralipomènes du Prophète Jérémie*, 128.

original, either shortly before the beginning of the Bar Kokhba War[99] or sometime in the middle of the second century.[100] The perspective on the Jewish people found in the Christian conclusion would seem to indicate a date after 135 C.E. Although the people are more negatively portrayed in 9:10–32 than in 1:1–9:9, the Christian redaction is a positive and constructive development of *4 Baruch*'s line of thought after the catastrophe of 135: just as the people had not listened earlier to their prophets, they had not listened to the voice of the author of *4 Baruch* and so had headed to their own destruction. Thinking themselves to be doing right, the people had caused their own fall.

This view in the Christian redaction is not anti-Jewish but rather the redactor's attempt to develop a positive view of Jewish history in light of the failed rebellion. At the same time, a missionary element can also be found, as the very act of developing a Jewish writing suggests: the Jewish people should learn from their past and listen to the voices that the writer of *4 Baruch* let speak loudly, which in the view of the Christian redactor ultimately point to the coming of Christ. The hopes for resurrection and eschatological salvation bind together the Jewish expectation and the Christian hope of salvation. Perhaps this dimension was decisive in the acceptance of this Jewish writing in Christian circles. However, the redaction of this common hope would not be Christian if it did not direct attention to God's Christ, who prepares the way for this eschatological salvation that applies to all the nations of the earth. This Christian perspective is, however, filled with Old Testament traditions. In the light of the failed false messiah Bar Kokhba, this orientation must have been particularly effective. The use of Jeremiah as a Christian witness to the Messiah would have strengthened this orientation, since Jeremiah had already been portrayed as a prophet of eschatological salvation (see especially *4 Bar.* 8:9). The Christian "reminder" of the hope of the eschatological city of God, so important in *4 Baruch*, had new weight in the light of Hadrian's edict against the Jews.[101]

The language used by the Jewish writer of *4 Baruch* to formulate his prophetic haggadah was certainly Greek, as is clear at several points, particularly in references to the Old Testament.[102] The orientation toward Diaspora Jews

---

99. Kilpatrick, "Acts VII.52 ΕΛΕΥΣΙΣ," 141; Riaud, *Paralipomènes du Prophète Jérémie*, 131.
100. Robinson, "4 Baruch," 414.
101. In his "Remarks in the Margin of the Paper 'The Figure of Jeremiah in the Paralipomena Jeremiae,' by J. Riaud," *JSP* 22 (2000): 45–49, Marinus de Jonge raises the question how *4 Baruch* as a Jewish writing could be understood from a Christian point of view at all. This is one of the most difficult chapters in the history of reception, for in the Christian reception it is a difference between the overworking of a Jewish writing known as such and the reception of this Jewish writing already and exclusivly known as a Christian one.
102. See Berndt Schaller, "Is the Greek Version of the Paralipomena Jeremiou Original or a Translation?" *JSP* 22 (2000): 51–89.

must therefore have been a fundamental aspect of the work. The view that the original was in Hebrew or Aramaic has not been sufficiently supported.[103] So-called Hebraisms or Aramaisms alone can no longer be regarded as a sufficient criterion for determining the original language.

The Greek style of *4 Baruch* points more probably toward an author whose mother tongue was probably Hebrew or Aramaic but who was working in a Hellenistic environment in the Diaspora and was shaped by the Greek tradition of the Old Testament.[104]

Text Transmission

The text transmission of the Paraleipomena Jeremiou is well documented in both older and more recent literature.[105] There is as yet no comprehensive modern and stemmatic-focused edition of the text of *4 Baruch* showing the relationship of the different manuscripts. However, the text edition from Harris and that of Kraft and Purintun provide a good basis for reconstructing the Greek text.[106] The basis of the text in this commentary is a critical analysis of these two texts,[107] although the following works were also referenced and compared: Ceriani's edition;[108] a copy of Ceriani's edition by Oskar von Gebhardt with additions of the Codex R (Petropolitanus XCVI, fol. 78b–89, twelfth century);[109] König's translation of the Ethiopic text[110] as well as that of

---

103. Delling, *Paralipomena Jeremiae*, 72; Licht, *Paralipomena Jeremiae*, 71; Robinson, "4 Baruch," 414.

104. Schaller, "Greek Version," 85–89.

105. Dillmann, "Liber Baruch," passim; Antonio Maria Ceriani, *Paraleipomena Jeremiae Prophetae quae in Aethiopica Versione dicuntur Reliqua Verborum Baruchi* (Monumenta Sacra et Profana ex Codicibus praesertim Bibliotheca Ambrosiana 5.1; Milan: Typis et impensis Bibliothecae Ambrosinae, 1868), 9–18; Harris, *Rest of the Words of Baruch*, 26–35; Robert A. Kraft and Ann-Elizabeth Purintun, *Paraleipomena Jeremiou* (SBLTT 1, Pseudepigrapha Series 1; Missoula, Mont.: Society of Biblical Literature, 1972), 3–5; E. Turdéanu, "Légende du Prophète Jérémie en Roumain," 307–47, 364–91. See also M. E. Stone, "Some Observations on the Armenian Version of the Paralipomena of Jeremiah," *CBQ* 35 (1973): 47–59; Riaud, *Paralipomènes du Prophète Jeremie*, 5–15; Schaller, "Paralipomena Jeremiou," 688–92.

106. A new critical text of *4 Baruch* will be edited by Bernhard Heininger (Würzburg, Germany); the project is terminated until 2007. For more information, see http://www.theologie.uni-wuerzburg.de/propaje/php_html/projektbeschreibung.php.

107. Herzer, *Paralipomena Jeremiae*, 9–20.

108. Ceriani, *Paralipomena Jeremiae Prophetae*, which is based on the Milan MS A and from the Menaeum of 1609.

109. Found in the "Nachlass von Oscar von Gebhardt," Karton XXI.2, in the Staatsbibliothek Preußischer Kulturbesitz zu Berlin (No. ZfB, 1907, 15–25). This manuscript ends at 5:34.

110. Eduard König, "Der Rest der Worte Baruchs: Aus dem Aetiopischen übersetzt und mit Anmerkungen versehen," *ThStKr* 50 (1877): 318–38.

Prätorius;[111] Wolff's translation of the Slavic texts;[112] Riaud's translation of the Harris text;[113] and Schaller's critical translation.[114]

Kraft and Purintun's edition makes the problem of the witnesses quite clear. The main problem is the relationship of MS A (Milan Braidensis, AF IX 31, fol. 1–10, fifteenth century) and the closely related MS B (Jerusalem Taphos 34, fol. 251–267b, tenth century), on the one hand, to MS C, on the other hand (Jerusalem Taphos 6, fol. 242^r–247^r, tenth century). These are the main witnesses to the Greek text of *4 Baruch*, more precisely to the so-called "long form" of the book. This designation, however, is only completely valid for A and B, because C leaves the story at 8:5 and concludes with an account of the return from exile that follows the Old Testament accounts.[115] The translations into Ethiopic,[116] Armenian (arm, fifteenth century),[117] and Slavic[118] and MS P (Paris gr. 1534, fol. 159–169, eleventh century)[119] also witness to the longer text. Manuscript C is closely related to the Ethiopic translation.[120] Their text-critical value is normally regarded more highly than that of A and B.[121] However, each case is to be considered on its own merits, not least because of the other existing manuscripts (see table below). It is safest to assume that none of the manuscripts is thoroughly reliable.[122]

---

111. Franz Prätorius, "Das Apokryphische Buch Baruch im Athiopischen," *ZWT* 15 (1872): 230–47.

112. Wolff, *Jeremia im Frühjudentum und Urchristentum*, 196–237.

113. Jean Riaud, "Paralipomènes de Jérémie," in *La Bible: Écrits intertestamentaires* (ed. A. Dupont-Sommer and M. Philonenko; Bibliothèque de la Pléiade 337; Paris: Gallimard, 1987), 1731–63.

114. Schaller, "Paralipomena Jeremiou," 659–777.

115. The wording of the text is to be found in Harris, *Rest of the Words of Baruch*, 60–61 (apparatus).

116. See Dillmann, *Liber Baruch*, passim.

117. Edited by H. Sargis Josepheanz, *Ankanon Girk' Hin Ktakaranac: Uncanonical Books of the Old Testament* (Venice: Lazar, 1896), 349–77; translation by Jaques Issaverdens, *The Uncanonical Writings of the Old Testament Found in the Armenian MSS: Of the Library of St. Lazarus* (Venice: Armenian Monastery of St. Lazarus, 1901), 252–304.

118. For the Slavic versions of the long form, see Turdéanu, "Légende du Prophète Jérémie en Roumain," 307–91. See also Wolff, *Jeremia im Frühjudentum und Urchristentum*, 194–95, and his translations of the texts (196–237). See also Schaller, "Paralipomena Jeremiou," 691–92, and the list below.

119. The readings of MS P as well as the Armenian translation are taken from the apparatus of the edition of Kraft and Purintun as far as it was possible, since the apparatus provides the variant readings only in an English translation and therefore seems not to be precise enough.

120. Harris, *Rest of the Words of Baruch*, 30; Schürer, review of Harris, 81.

121. Harris, *Rest of the Words of Baruch*, 29–30; Schürer, review of Harris, 81. Harris used MS C as the main witness for his critical text. Cf. Harris, *Rest of the Words of Baruch*, 30.

122. Schaller, "Paralipomena Jeremiou," 689 n. 180.

Alongside the older texts of the long form exists a short version of the text, also in two forms. Emil Turdéanu has plausibly demonstrated that the short versions are redactions of the long form,[123] so the priority of the long text can be assumed.

List of Manuscripts[124]

The long form of *4 Baruch* is represented by the manuscripts that have capitals as sigla and the translations eth, arm, slav. The short form is represented by the manuscripts that have small letters as sigla.

MSS representing the long form

A	=	Milan Bibliotheca Regia Braidensis AF IX 31, fol 1–10, 15th century (ed. Ceriani 1868; cf. Harris 1889).
B	=	Jerusalem Taphos (Patriarchal Library, S. Sepulchre) cod. 34, fol 251–267b, 10th century (cf. Harris 1889; Harris has the 11th century).
C	=	Jerusalem Taphos (Patriarchal Library, S. Sepulchre) cod. 6, fol 242^r–247^r, 10th century. In *4 Bar.* 8:5 the text of C leaves *4 Baruch* and continues with a different narrative; cf. Harris 1889.
F	=	Florence Laurentiana plut IV cod. 6, fol 232–249^r, 11th century (character of this MS is uncertain).
G	=	Athens 1027, fol 402–411, 12th century.
H	=	Oxford Bodleian Holkham gr 27, fol 292–303, 15th century.
I	=	Jerusalem Saba Monasteries cod. 373, fol 129–142[?], 16th century.
J	=	Jerusalem Saba Monasteries cod. 281, fol 118–125^r (old fol nos. 134–141), 13th century.
K	=	Athos Lavra 327 (formerly T 87), fol 159–168^r, 13th century.
L	=	Leiden University Library Bibl. Gr 99, fol 119, 14th century (containing *4 Bar.* 5:32b–7:36a; some relations to the C and the eth text).

---

123. Turdéanu, "Légende du Prophète Jérémie en Roumain," 326–28.
124. The following list is based on the lists provided by Harris, *Rest of the Words of Baruch*, 26–29, and Kraft and Purintun, *Paraleipomena Jeremiou*, 3–5. See also Schaller, "Paralipomena Jeremiou," 688–92; Jean-Claude Haelewyck, *Clavis apocryphorum Veteris Testamenti* (Turnhout: Brepols, 1998), 181–85. Schaller ("Paralipomena Jeremiou," 690 n. 186) mentions the fact that there are still manuscripts that have not yet been used for the reconstruction of the text of *4 Baruch*. The sigla used in this edition follow Kraft's edition. See also Riaud, *Paralipomènes du Prophète Jérémie*, 5–15. Schaller ("Paralipomena Jeremiou," 689–90) uses his own system of sigla.

INTRODUCTION

M	=	Venice St. Mark VII.45 (formerly Nanianus 161), fol 254–262, 1616–1618.
N	=	Paris suppl. gr 136, fol 107–134, 16th century.
O	=	Oxford Bodleian Baroc 240.2, fol 1^v–9, 12th century.
P	=	Paris gr 1534.19, fol 159–169, 11th century.
R	=	Leningrad Public Library 96, fol 78^b–89, 12th century.
S	=	Sinai gr 1670, fol 116–130^r, 16th century.
T	=	Cambridge Trinity 191 (formerly B 8.7.58), fol 422–431, 11/12th century.
U	=	Vatican Palatine 27, fol 149–154, 10/11th century.
V	=	Vatican gr 620 (formerly 420), fol 201–206, 16th century.
W	=	Vienna National Library Hist gr 126 (formerly 36,6), fol 39–48^r, 14th century (uncertain).
X	=	Paris gr 760, fol 176^v–181, 14th century.
Y	=	Paris gr 776, fol 9–16, 15th century.
Z	=	Paris gr 1190, fol 186^v–196, 1568.

MSS representing the short form

a	=	Jerusalem Saba Monasteries cod. 226, fol 227.2–230, 15/16th century.
b	=	Jerusalem Saba Monasteries cod. 429.2, item 7, 1619.
c	=	Jerusalem Stauros (Patriarchal Library, S. Crucis) cod. 118, fol 52^v–66^v, 18th century.
d	=	Jerusalem Taphos (Patriarchal Library, S. Sepulchre) cod. 66, fol 208^v–211 (old nos. 212–215), 15/16th century (cf. Harris 1889; probably related to MS A).
e	=	Jerusalem Stauros (Patriarchal Library, S. Crucis) cod. 35, fol 391^v–395, 15th century (cf. Harris 1889).
f	=	Alexandria Patriarchal Library 173, fol 88–113, 16th century.
g	=	Sinai gr 529, fol 214–227 (old nos. 201–214), 1555.
h	=	Sinai gr 531, fol 61–72, 15/16th century.
i	=	Andros 46, fol 203–210, 15th century.
j	=	Athens 346, fol 42–50, 15th century.
jj	=	Athens 838, item 9, 16th century.
k	=	Athens 356, fol unknown, 1634.
kk	=	Athens Amantos A, fol 86–93, date unknown.
l	=	Athens 422, item 39, 1546.

m	=	Athos 2801 (= Dochiariou 127), item 21, 17th century.
mm	=	Athos Lavra Γ 87, fol and date unknown.
n	=	Athos 3695 (= Dionysios 161), item 6, 17th century.
nn	=	Athos Lavra H 206, fol 115–118, 16th century.
o	=	Athos 3766 (= Dionysios 232), fol 530^v–537 (item 16), 17th century.
oo	=	Athos Lavra K 18, fol 157–169, 17th century.
p	=	Athos 3797 [= Dionysios 263], item 23, 17th century.
q	=	Ochrid (Yugoslavia) 29, fol 300–315, 1547.
qq	=	Milan Ambrosian Library A.79 suppl., fol unknown, 15th century (cf. Ceriani 1868).
r	=	Munich 255.1, fol 94–102, 15/16th century.
rr	=	Munich 366, fol and date unknown.
s	=	Vatican gr 1190.114, fol 1044–1049, 16th century.
ss	=	Vatican Palatinae 138, fol 346–353, 14th century.
t	=	Vatican gr 1192.7, fol 79–86, 15th century.
tt	=	Vatican Reginae 49, fol 95^v–102/103, 1574.
u	=	Vatican gr 1700 (= Lollino 16), fol 114ff., date unknown.
v	=	Vatican Barberini 3.3, fol 153–172, 1497 (without *4 Bar.* 8:3b–9:14).
vv	=	Vatican Barberine 284, fol and date unknown.
w	=	Paris gr 947, fol 297^v–298, 1574.
x	=	Paris gr 1313, fol 325–329, 15th century.
y	=	Paris gr 1579, fol 91–96, 15th century.
ww	=	Paris gr 1582, fol 109^v–114, 13/14th century.
xx	=	Paris suppl. gr 54, fol 89–94, 16th century.
yy	=	Paris suppl. gr 1036, fol 12ff., 16th century.
z	=	London British Museum add 10073, fol 271^v–281, 16th century.
zz	=	London British Museum Harley 5782, fol unknown, 14th century.

Translations (long form)

eth	=	Ethiopic translation, ed. A. Dillmann, 1866, based on the following MSS:[125]	
		eth[a]	Paris, National Library, cod. Abbadianus 35, fol 176a–180a, 17th century.
		eth[b]	Paris, National Library, cod. Abbadianus 55, fol 101b–105a, 16th century.
		eth[c]	Frankfurt/M., University Library, Rüppel II.5, fol 61b–67a, 17th century.

arm	=	Armenian translation, based on the following MSS:[126]	
		arm[a]	Venice, S. Lazzaro, cod. 345, 1220.
		arm[b]	Venice, S. Lazzaro, cod. 1447, 16th century.
		arm[c]	Erevan Maténadaran cod. 993 (former Etschmiadzin, cod. 920), 1465.

slav	=	Church Slavic translation, based on the following MSS:[127]	
		slav[A]	private collection, 14th century.
		slav[B]	Moscow Synodal Library, cod. 180, fol 11–17v, 16th century.
		slav[C/S]	Fragment, 12th or 14th century.
		slav[D]	Moscow, Museum of History, 14th century.
		slav[a]	Moscow, Cloister of the Holy Trinity, collection, 15th century.

Manuscripts with Similar Characteristics[128]

Some manuscripts representing the long form and the short form of *4 Baruch* have been divided into certain groups in which the manuscripts show characteristic similarities and therefore a specific relationship.

1. MSS A B H, the Armenian and Slavic versions, and MS F. However, MS F should be given closer examination.

---

125. See Schaller, "Paralipomena Jeremiou," 690–91.
126. See ibid. 691. Cf. Stone, "Observations," passim.
127. See Turdéanu, "Légende," 348–61; Schaller, "Paralipomena Jeremiou," 691–92. For MSS slav[A.B.C/S.a,] see the German translation in Wolff, *Jeremia im Frühjudentum und Urchristentum*, 196–237.
128. Following mostly Kraft and Purintun, *Paraleipomena Jeremiou*, 3–5. Cf. Harris, *Rest of the Words of Baruch*, 29–35; Riaud, *Paralipomènes du Prophète Jérémie*, 5–15.

2. mss P O W S J "exhibit a text form sufficiently different from the other groupings."[129] Kraft and Purintun divide this group further into P O and W S.

3. The third group of manuscripts is represented by C and the Ethiopic versions as well as probably by L I M.

4. A fourth group of manuscripts of the short form of the text is represented by e g a v and probably j l m p.

5. A fifth group of manuscripts is represented by d h and probably o.

The Critical Apparatus

:	indicates the following as variants of a word or phrase that is otherwise found in most of the other manuscripts (e.g., επι τον: A προς τον)
;	separates variants of the same word or phrase. (Within the Greek text, a semicolon indicates a question mark.)
–	between Greek words indicates that the whole phrase between them is the variant in question; for example, "Ιερεμια – ο Βαρουχ A B eth (R om o); C αναστηθη και συ και Βαρουχ" in 1:1 means that the whole phrase Ἰερεμία, ὁ ἐκλεκτός μου, ἀνάστα, ἔξελθε ἐκ τῆς πόλεως ταύτης, σὺ καὶ ὁ Βαρούχ read by A B eth and in which R omits the o before Baruch, is replaced in C by αναστηθη και συ και Βαρουχ
|	separates variants of different words or phrases within the same verse
||	separates verses
mg	marginal note
om	omit(s)
add	add(s)
exponent	indicates the reference to the second or more appearance of a given word within a sentence (e.g., και² refers to the second appearance of και in the verse)
[]	Data in brackets indicate differences in manuscripts within the otherwise same variant. Also placed within brackets are indications of readings by modern translators, if useful.

The specification of one or more manuscripts following a variant with only a space indicates that the manuscripts read this variant.

The English translations of the Ethiopic version of *4 Baruch* are based on the German rendering by Franz Prätorius.

---

129. Kraft and Purintun, *Paraleipomena Jeremiou*, 3.

4 Baruch:
Text and Translation

ΤΑ ΠΑΡΑΛΕΙΠΟΜΕΝΑ ΙΕΡΕΜΙΟΥ ΤΟΥ ΠΡΟΦΗΤΟΥ

I 1 Ἐγένετο, ἡνίκα ἠχμαλωτεύθησαν οἱ υἱοὶ Ἰσραὴλ ἀπὸ τοῦ βασιλέως τῶν Χαλδαίων, ἐλάλησεν ὁ Θεὸς πρὸς Ἰερεμίαν· Ἰερεμία, ὁ ἐκλεκτός μου, ἀνάστα, ἔξελθε ἐκ τῆς πόλεως ταύτης, σὺ καὶ ὁ Βαρούχ· ἐπειδὴ ἀπολῶ αὐτὴν διὰ τὸ πλῆθος τῶν ἁμαρτιῶν τῶν κατοικούντων ἐν αὐτῇ. **2** Αἱ γὰρ προσευχαὶ ὑμῶν ὡς στῦλος ἑδραῖός ἐστιν ἐν μέσῳ αὐτῆς, καὶ ὡς τεῖχος ἀδαμάντινον περικυκλοῦν αὐτήν. **3** Νῦν ἀναστάντες ἐξέλθατε πρὸ τοῦ ἡ δύναμις τῶν Χαλδαίων κυκλώσει αὐτήν. **4** Καὶ ἀπεκρίθη Ἰερεμίας λέγων· Παρακαλῶ σε, Κύριε, ἐπίτρεψόν μοι τῷ δούλῳ σου λαλῆσαι ἐνώπιόν σου. Εἶπεν δὲ ὁ Κύριος· Λάλει, ὁ ἐκλεκτός μου Ἰερεμίας. **5** Καὶ ἐλάλησεν Ἰερεμίας λέγων· Κύριε παντοκράτωρ, παραδίδως τὴν πόλιν τὴν ἐκλεκτὴν εἰς χεῖρας τῶν Χαλδαίων, ἵνα καυχήσηται ὁ βασιλεὺς μετὰ τοῦ πλήθους τοῦ λαοῦ αὐτοῦ, καὶ εἴπῃ ὅτι, Ἴσχυσα ἐπὶ τὴν ἱερὰν πόλιν τοῦ Θεοῦ; **6** Μὴ Κύριέ μου· ἀλλ᾽ εἰ θέλημά σού ἐστιν, ἐκ τῶν χειρῶν σου ἀφανισθήτω. **7** Καὶ εἶπε Κύριος τῷ Ἰερεμίᾳ· Ἐπειδὴ σὺ ἐκλεκτός μου εἶ, ἀνάστα καὶ ἔξελθε ἐκ τῆς πόλεως ταύτης, σὺ καὶ Βαρούχ· ἐπειδὴ ἀπολῶ αὐτὴν διὰ τὸ πλῆθος τῶν ἁμαρτιῶν τῶν κατοικούντων ἐν αὐτῇ. **8** Οὔτε γὰρ ὁ βασιλεύς, οὔτε ἡ δύναμις αὐτοῦ, δυνήσεται εἰσελθεῖν εἰς αὐτήν, εἰ μὴ ἐγὼ πρῶτος ἀνοίξω τὰς πύλας αὐτῆς. **9** Ἀνάστηθι οὖν, καὶ ἄπελθε πρὸς Βαρούχ, καὶ

Title A B C; eth *Rest of the words of Baruch, not the apocryphal, concerning the time when they were in the Babylonian captivity* (cf. W J); R τα περιλιπομενα του αγιου Ιερεμιου του προφητου και περι της αλωσεως της Ιερουσαλημ ‖ **I 1** ηνικα A B; C οτε | οι: C om | απο A B; C υπο | Ιερεμιαν C eth; A B add τον προφητην λεγων (Kraft λεγων) | Ιερεμια – ο Βαρουχ A B eth (R om o); C αναστηθη και συ και Βαρουχ | αναστα: R (Kraft) add και | απολω C; A B απολλω | αυτην A B eth; C την πολιν ταυτην | κατοικουντων A B; C ενοικουντων | εγενετο – λεγων: R εγενετο εν ταις ημεραις εκειναις ηνικα παρωργιζων υιοι Ισμαηλ κυριον τον θεον και εμελλον αιχμαλοτιζεσθαι και η πολις αυτων πορθησθαι υπο του βασιλεως των Χαλδαιων Ναβουχοδονοσωρ ελαλησεν ο θεος προς Ιερεμιαν λεγων ‖ **2** στυλος: R στυλλος | εστιν: C om | περικυκλουν αυτην A; B περικυκλων αυτην; C περι τα τειχη αυτης; R περι κυκλω αυτης ‖ **3** νυν – εξελθατε B; A νυν – εξελθετε (R εξελθεται); C R (Kraft) νυν ουν | η (R α) – αυτην A B C R (A κυκλωση [Ceriani; v.Gebhardt]); d e Menaea (Harris) την δυναμιν των Χαλδαιων κυκλωσαι αυτην; C add αναστάντες εξελθατε ‖ **4** απεκριθη A B; C ελαλησεν | απεκριθη – λεγων: R αποκριθεις ο Ιερεμιας ελαλησεν προς κυριον λεγων | παρακαλω: R παρακαλο | επιτρεψον μοι A B; C κελευσον με | τω δουλω σου A B P eth arm; C om | ενωπιον σου A B; C λογον εναντιον σου | δε: C R eth (Harris Kraft) add αυτω | λαλει: R λαλησον | **5** ελαλησεν A B; C ειπεν | Ιερεμιας: A B ο Ιερεμιας | λεγων A B; C om | παραδιδως A; B παραδιδης; C παραδιδοις; R μη παραδωσεις | πολιν: R (eth) add σου ταυτην | ινα: R add μη | μετα – αυτου A B eth; R om του λαου; P *his multitude;* arm *multitude of his troops;* C om; ‖ **6** μου: R add κυριε | σου¹: B R σον | σου²: C om | εστιν: R add τουτου ‖ **7** κυριος C; A B ο κυριος | τω Ιερεμια A B; C R προς Ιερεμιαν | συ¹: R om | αναστα A B; C αναστηθι | εκ της πολεως ταυτης: eth om | απολω B C R; A om | κατοικουντων A B; C ενοικουντων | αυτη: A add απολλω ‖ **8** εις αυτην A B; C προς αυτην; R εν αυτη | ανοιξω τας πυλας αυτης A B; C ανοιξω αυτοις τας πυλας; R ανυξω αυτης τας πυλας ‖

THE MATTERS OMITTED FROM JEREMIAH THE PROPHET

1:1 It came to pass, when the children of Israel were taken captive by the king of the Chaldeans, (that) God spoke to Jeremiah, "Jeremiah, my chosen one, get up (and) depart from this city, you and Baruch, since I am going to destroy it because of the multitude of the sins of those who dwell in it. **2** For your prayers are like a solid pillar in its midst and like an iron wall surrounding it. **3** Now, then, get up and depart before the host of the Chaldeans surrounds it!" **4** And Jeremiah answered, saying, "I beseech you, O Lord, permit me, your servant, to speak in your presence." And the Lord said to him, "Speak, my chosen one, Jeremiah." **5** And Jeremiah spoke, saying, "O Lord Almighty, would you hand over the chosen city into the hands of the Chaldeans so that the king with the multitude of his people will boast and say, 'I gained power over God's holy city!'? **6** No, my Lord, but if it is your will, let it be done away with by your (own) hands!" **7** And the Lord said to Jeremiah, "Because you are my chosen one: get up and depart from this city, you and Baruch, for I am going to destroy it because of the multitude of the sins of those who dwell in it. **8** For neither the king nor his host will be able to enter it unless I first open its gates. **9** Get up, then, and go to Baruch and

ἀπάγγειλον αὐτῷ τὰ ῥήματα ταῦτα. **10** Καὶ ἀναστάντες ἕκτην ὥραν τῆς νυκτὸς, ἔλθετε ἐπὶ τὰ τείχη τῆς πόλεως, καὶ δείξω ὑμῖν, ὅτι ἐὰν μὴ ἐγὼ πρῶτος ἀφανίσω τὴν πόλιν, οὐ δύνανται εἰσελθεῖν εἰς αὐτήν. **11** Ταῦτα εἰπὼν ὁ Κύριος, ἀπῆλθεν ἀπὸ τοῦ Ἰερεμίου.

II 1 Ἰερεμίας δὲ διέρρηξεν τὰ ἱμάτια αὐτοῦ καὶ ἐπέθηκεν χοῦν ἐπὶ τὴν κεφαλὴν αὐτοῦ· καὶ εἰσῆλθεν εἰς τὸ ἁγιαστήριον τοῦ Θεοῦ. **2** Καὶ ἰδὼν αὐτὸν ὁ Βαροὺχ χοῦν πεπασμένον ἐπὶ τὴν κεφαλὴν αὐτοῦ, καὶ τὰ ἱμάτια αὐτοῦ διερρωγότα, ἔκραξε φωνῇ μεγάλῃ λέγων· Πάτερ Ἰερεμία, τί ἐστι σοι, ἢ ποῖον ἁμάρτημα ἐποίησεν ὁ λαός; **3** Ἐπειδὴ ὅταν ἡμάρτανεν ὁ λαός, χοῦν ἔπασσεν ἐπὶ τὴν κεφαλὴν αὐτοῦ ὁ Ἰερεμίας, καὶ ηὔχετο ὑπὲρ τοῦ λαοῦ, ἕως ἂν ἀφεθῇ αὐτῷ ἡ ἁμαρτία. **4** Ἠρώτησεν δὲ αὐτὸν ὁ Βαροὺχ λέγων· Πάτερ, τί ἐστι τοῦτο; **5** Εἶπε δὲ αὐτῷ Ἰερεμίας· Φύλαξαι τοῦ σχίσαι τὰ ἱμάτιά σου, ἀλλὰ σχίσωμεν τὰς καρδίας ἡμῶν· καὶ μὴ ἀντλήσωμεν ὕδωρ ἐπὶ τὰς ποτίστρας, ἀλλὰ κλαύσωμεν καὶ γεμίσωμεν αὐτὰς δακρύων· ὅτι οὐ μὴ ἐλεήσῃ τὸν λαὸν τοῦτον ὁ Κύριος. **6** Καὶ εἶπε Βαρούχ· Πάτερ Ἰερεμία, τί γέγονε; **7** Καὶ εἶπεν Ἰερεμίας ὅτι, Ὁ Θεὸς παραδίδωσει τὴν πόλιν εἰς χεῖρας βασιλέως τῶν Χαλδαίων, τοῦ αἰχμαλωτεῦσαι τὸν λαὸν εἰς Βαβυλῶνα. **8** Ἀκούσας δὲ ταῦτα Βαρούχ, διέρρηξε καὶ αὐτὸς τὰ ἱμάτια αὐτοῦ, καὶ εἶπεν· Πάτερ Ἰερεμία, τίς σοι

---

10 και αναστάντες: R αναστας δε | ελθετε: R ελθατε | τειχη: R τειχει | δειξω A B; C δικνυω | εαν μη C; A B εαν μητι (Kraft add τι) | αφανισω την πολιν A B P R arm eth; C απολεσω αυτην; A B add και ανοιξω | δυνανται A B; C δυνησονται; R δυνησηται | εις αυτην A B; C R εν αυτη (R add τις) || **11** απηλθεν A B P eth; C ανεχωρησεν | απο του Ιερεμιου: C add εις τον ουρανον; arm *from him* ||

II 1 Ιερεμιας – θεου C eth; A B R (Ceriani v.Gebhardt Kraft) δραμων δε Ιερεμιας (R ο Ιερεμιας) ανηγγειλε ταυτα τω Βαρουχ (A τω Βαρουχ ταυτα) και ελθοντες εις τον ναον του θεου; B R (Kraft) add διερρηξεν τα ιματια αυτου Ιερεμιας (R Ιερεμιας τα ιματια αυτου) και επεθηκεν χουν επι την κεφαλην αυτου και ηρξαντο αμφοτεροι κλεειν (R κλαιειν) εν τω αγιασθηριω (R επι το αγιασθηριον) του θεου (Kraft om και² – θεου) || **2** και ιδων A B; C ειδων δε (R Kraft ιδων δε) | χουν: C om | αυτου¹: C add χουν | φωνη μεγαλη λεγων A; B φωνην μεγαλην λεγων; C om | πατερ A B eth; C om | τι εστι A B eth; C απεστην | εποιησεν A B eth; C ημαρτεν || **3** ημαρτανεν A B eth; C ημαρτεν | εως αν A B; C οπως | αυτω A B eth; R αυτων; C αυτοις | αμαρτια: C add αυτη || **4** ηρωτησεν: A B ερωτησεν; C επερωτησεν (Ceriani v.Gebhardt Harris Kraft ηρωτησε) | αυτον A B R; C αυτω | ο: C om | πατερ – τουτο R P (Kraft); C eth (Harris) πατερ, τι εστι σοι; A B arm (Ceriani) τι εστι τουτο || **5** Ιερεμιας: R add τεκνον | φυλαξαι: R φυλαξον | τα ιματια σου: C om | αλλα¹: A B (Kraft) add μαλλον; R add μαλλον οι αμφοτεροι | και¹: C om | ποτιστρας A C; B ποτιστριας; R ποτηστρας | αλλα²: C add μαλλον | και γεμισωμεν: R εως οτε γεμησωμεν | ελεηση: R ελεησει | τον – Κυριος A B; C R κυριος τον λαον τουτον || **6** πατερ Ιερεμια A B eth; C προς Ιερεμιαν || **7** Ιερεμιας A B R eth; C om | παραδιδωσει A (Ceriani Harris Kraft παραδιδωσι); B παραδιδει; C παραδω; R παραδιδη | πολιν A B eth; C add την εκλεκτην; R add ταυτην | βασιλεως A B eth arm; C R P om | του αιχμαλωτευσαι R; A B και αιχμαλωτευσαι; C και αρουσι || **8** ταυτα A B eth; C om | και αυτος A B eth; C om | και ειπεν A B eth (Ceriani v.Gebhardt Harris Kraft ειπε); C R λεγων |

tell him these words. **10** And when you have arisen at the sixth hour of the night, go onto the city walls and I will show you: unless I first destroy the city, they cannot enter it." **11** When the Lord had said these things, he departed from Jeremiah.

2:1 And Jeremiah tore his garments and put dust on his head and entered the sanctuary of God.[1] **2** Upon seeing him with dust on his head and his garments torn, Baruch cried out in a loud voice, saying, "Father Jeremiah, what (happened) to you or what sort of sin did the people commit?" **3** Because whenever the people sinned, Jeremiah would put dust on his head and pray for the people until their sin was forgiven. **4** And Baruch asked him, saying, "Father, what does this mean?" **5** And Jeremiah told him, "Beware of rending your garments; rather, let us rend our hearts! And let us not draw water for the troughs; rather, let us weep and fill them with tears! For the Lord will not have mercy on this people!" **6** And Baruch said, "Father Jeremiah, what has happened?" **7** And Jeremiah said, "God will hand over the city into the hands of the king of the Chaldeans to take the people captive into Babylon." **8** And when Baruch heard these things, he himself tore his garments and said, "Father Jeremiah, who has

---

1. With the MSS A and B, Kraft/Purintun (cf. Ceriani, v.Gebhardt) read a different text and add a singular reading of B at the beginning of verse 1, which in fact takes up the intention of the reading of C and eth. As the apparatus shows, this construction makes some minor changes necessary, for which there is no textual evidence. In all, the reading of C and eth represents *lectio brevior et difficilior* and is therefore to be preferred here.

ἐδήλωσε τοῦτο; **9** Καὶ εἶπεν αὐτῷ Ἰερεμίας· Ἔκδεξαι μικρὸν μετ' ἐμοῦ ἕως ὥρας ἕκτης τῆς νυκτός, ἵνα γνῷς, ὅτι ἀληθές ἐστι τὸ ῥῆμα. **10** Ἔμειναν οὖν ἐν τῷ θυσιαστηρίῳ κλαίοντες.

III 1 Ὡς δὲ ἐγένετο ἡ ὥρα τῆς νυκτός, καθὼς εἶπεν ὁ Κύριος τῷ Ἰερεμίᾳ, ἦλθον ὁμοῦ ἐπὶ τὰ τείχη τῆς πόλεως Ἰερεμίας καὶ Βαρούχ. **2** Καὶ ἐγένετο φωνὴ σάλπιγγος, καὶ ἐξῆλθον ἄγγελοι ἐκ τοῦ οὐρανοῦ, κατέχοντες λαμπάδας ἐν ταῖς χερσὶν αὐτῶν, καὶ ἔστησαν ἐπὶ τὰ τείχη τῆς πόλεως. **3** Ἰδόντες δὲ αὐτοὺς Ἰερεμίας καὶ Βαρούχ, ἔκλαυσαν λέγοντες· Νῦν ἐγνώκαμεν ὅτι ἀληθές ἐστι τὸ ῥῆμα. **4** Παρεκάλεσε δὲ Ἰερεμίας τοὺς ἀγγέλους λέγων· Παρακαλῶ ὑμᾶς μὴ ἀπολέσθαι τὴν πόλιν ἄρτι, ἕως ἂν λαλήσω πρὸς Κύριον ῥῆμα. Καὶ εἶπεν Κύριος τοῖς ἀγγέλοις· Μὴ ἀπολέσητε τὴν πόλιν ἕως ἂν λαλήσω πρὸς τὸν ἐκλεκτόν μου Ἰερεμίαν. Καὶ εἶπε· Δέομαι, Κύριε, κέλευσόν με λαλῆσαι ἐνώπιόν σου. **5** Καὶ εἶπε Κύριος· Λάλει, ὁ ἐκλεκτός μου Ἰερεμίας. **6** Καὶ εἶπεν Ἰερεμίας· Ἰδοὺ νῦν, Κύριε, ἐγνώκαμεν ὅτι παραδίδως τὴν πόλιν σου εἰς χεῖρας τῶν ἐχθρῶν αὐτῆς, καὶ ἀπαροῦσι τὸν λαὸν εἰς Βαβυλῶνα. **7** Τί ποιήσωμεν τὰ ἅγιά σου ἢ τὰ σκεύη τῆς λειτουργίας σου, τί θέλεις αὐτὰ ποιήσωμεν; **8** Καὶ εἶπεν αὐτῷ ὁ Κύριος· Ἆρον αὐτά, καὶ παράδος αὐτὰ τῇ γῇ καὶ τῷ θυσιαστηρίῳ λέγων, Ἄκουε, γῆ, τῆς φωνῆς τοῦ κτίσαντός σε ἐν τῇ περιουσίᾳ τῶν

---

(8) εδηλωσε A B; C απηγγειλεν; R add το ρημα ‖ **9** ινα γνως: R και γνωσει | το ρημα B C eth; A B R add τουτο ‖ **10** ουν C eth; A B (Ceriani v.Gebhardt Kraft) add αμφοτεροι | κλαιοντες: A B R P arm (Ceriani v.Gebhardt Kraft) add και ησαν διερρωγοτα (R διερρογοτα) τα ιματια αυτων και η γη επι τας κεφαλας (η γη επι τας κεφαλας: R χουν επεθηκαν επι της κεφαλης) αυτων (Kraft om και η γη – αυτων) ‖
III 1 ως A B; C R οτε | η ωρα της νυκτος: R P ημερα; eth *the sixth hour of the night;* arm *the sixth watch* | της νυκτος A B eth; C om | τειχη: R τειχει | Ιερεμιας και Βαρουχ A B P arm; C eth om; eth add *and sat down waiting* ‖ **2** και[1] (eth); A (Ceriani Kraft) και ιδου; C om | εγενετο: C om | σαλπιγγος C eth; A B σαλπιγγων | και[2]: C om | αγγελοι: C οι αγγελοι | κατεχοντες: C εχοντες | εν ταις χερσιν αυτων A B eth; C om | επι A B; C εις | της πολεως A B eth; C om ‖ **3** λεγοντες C eth; A B και ειπαν | εγνωκαμεν A B; C εγνωμεν ‖ **4** μη απολεσθαι – και ειπε: R αγγελοι του θεου εκδεξασθαι μικρον εως αν ερωτησω τον κυριον μου ρημα τοτε Ιερεμιας ελαλησε λεγων | πολιν: C add ταυτην | προς κυριον ρημα C arm; eth *to the Lord God;* A B μετα του θεου του υψιστου | και ειπεν – Ιερεμιαν C eth; A B om | και ειπε: A B add κλαιων; C om; P R arm eth (Kraft) τοτε Ιερεμιας ελαλησεν λεγων | δεομαι – **5** Ιερεμιας A B eth; C om; R add ο εαν βουλει και ειπεν Ιερεμιας | λαλει: R λαλησον ‖ **6** νυν: R om | κυριε: C om | εγνωκαμεν A B; C εγνωμεν | παραδιδως A; B R παραδιδης; C παραδιδοις | σου: C om | των εχθρων αυτης A B eth; C των Χαλδαιων | απαρουσι: C αρουσιν; R επαιρουσιν ‖ **7** C eth; A B R (v.Gebhardt Kraft) τι θελεις ποιησω (R ποιησωμεν; Ceriani v.Gebhardt ποιησαι) τα αγια (Ceriani v.Gebhardt add σου) σκευη (R σκευει) της λειτουργιας ‖ **8** αυτω ο: C om | αρον A B eth; C αρατε | αυτα: R ταυτα | παραδος A B eth; C παραδοτε | και τω θυσιαστηριω C eth; A B (Ceriani v.Gebhardt Kraft) om | λεγων A B eth; C om | ακουε γη: C οτι γη ακουε | της φωνης A B eth; C om | εν τη περιουσια των υδατων A B R P (eth arm); C ο πλασας σε (eth) εν ουσια των κτισματων; Kraft ο πλασας σε |

revealed that to you?" **9** And Jeremiah said to him, "Stay with me a while until the sixth hour of the night, so that you may know that this word is true." **10** So they remained weeping at the altar.

3:1 And when the hour of the night came, as the Lord had told Jeremiah, they came together on the walls of the city, Jeremiah and Baruch. **2** And a trumpet sounded, and angels came out from heaven holding torches in their hands, and they set them on the walls of the city. **3** And when Jeremiah and Baruch saw them, they wept, saying, "Now we know that the word is true." **4** And Jeremiah besought the angels, saying, "I beseech you not to destroy the city just yet, until I speak a word to the Lord." And the Lord said to the angels, "Do not destroy the city, until I speak to my chosen one, Jeremiah." And he said, "I beg you, Lord, command me to speak in your presence." **5** And the Lord said, "Speak, my chosen one, Jeremiah." **6** And Jeremiah said, "Behold, Lord, now we know that you are handing over your city into the hands of its enemies, and they will carry the people off to Babylon. **7** What shall we do (with) your holy (things), (with) the holy vessels of your temple service? What do you want us to do (with) them?" **8** And the Lord said to him, "Take them and consign them to the earth, that is, to the altar, saying, 'Hear, O earth, the voice of him who created you in the abundance of the

ὑδάτων, ὁ σφραγίσας σε ἐν ἑπτὰ σφραγῖσιν, ἐν ἑπτὰ καιροῖς, καὶ μετὰ ταῦτα λήψη τὴν ὡραιότητά σου· φύλαξον τὰ σκεύη τῆς λειτουργίας ἕως τῆς συνελεύσεως τοῦ ἠγαπημένου. **9** Καὶ ἐλάλησε Ἰερεμίας· Παρακαλῶ σε, Κύριε· δεῖξόν μοι, τί ποιήσω Ἀβιμέλεχ τῷ Αἰθίοπι· ὅτι πολλὰς εὐεργεσίας ἐποίησε τῷ λαῷ καὶ τῷ δούλῳ σου Ἱερεμίᾳ· ὅτι αὐτὸς ἀνέσπασέν με ἐκ τοῦ λάκκου τοῦ βορβόρου· καὶ οὐ θέλω αὐτόν, ἵνα ἴδη τὸν ἀφανισμὸν τῆς πόλεως καὶ τὴν ἐρήμωσιν· ἀλλ' ἵνα μὴ λυπηθῆ. **10** Καὶ εἶπε Κύριος τῷ Ἱερεμίᾳ· Ἀπόστειλον αὐτὸν εἰς τὸν ἀμπελῶνα τοῦ Ἀγρίππα διὰ τοῦ ὄρους· καὶ ἐγὼ σκεπάσω αὐτόν, ἕως οὗ ἐπιστρέψω τὸν λαὸν εἰς τὴν πόλιν. **11** Εἶπε δὲ Κύριος τῷ Ἱερεμίᾳ· Ἄπελθε μετὰ τοῦ λαοῦ σου εἰς Βαβυλῶνα, καὶ μεῖνον μετ' αὐτῶν εὐαγγελιζόμενος αὐτοῖς, ἕως οὗ ἐπιστρέψω αὐτοὺς εἰς τὴν πόλιν. **12** Κατάλειψον δὲ τὸν Βαροὺχ ᾧδε, ἕως οὗ λαλήσω αὐτῷ. **13** Ταῦτα εἰπὼν ὁ Κύριος, ἀνέβη ἀπὸ Ἱερεμίου εἰς τὸν οὐρανόν. **14** Ἱερεμίας δὲ καὶ Βαροὺχ εἰσῆλθον εἰς τὸ ἁγιαστήριον, καὶ τὰ σκεύη τῆς λειτουργίας παρέδωκαν τῇ γῇ, καθὼς ἐλάλησεν αὐτοῖς ὁ Κύριος· καὶ αὔθωρον κατέπιεν αὐτὰ ἡ γῆ· ἐκάθισαν δὲ οἱ δύο, καὶ ἔκλαυσαν. **15** Πρωΐας δὲ γενομένης,

(8) ο σφραγισας σε: e Menea του σφραγισαντος σε | εν επτα σφραγισιν A B R P eth; C arm om | (R και) εν επτα καιροις A B R (C καιδροις); eth om | και⁴: C om | ληψη (R ληψει) την ωραιοτητα (R ωραιωτητα) σου A B R P (eth arm); C λημψη την οδον τη ωραιοτητι σου | φυλαξον: C και φυλαξης | φυλαξον – ηγαπημενου d e Menea eth; A B φυλαξον τα σκευη της λειτουργιας του ηγαπημενου; R δεξαι τα σκευει ταυτα και φυλαξον αυτα εως της συντελειας του ηγαπημενου | εως – ηγαπημενου: C εως ερωτησιν ποιηση κυριος περι αυτων οτι ημεις ουκ ευρεθημεν αξιοι φυλαξαι αυτας οτι επιτροποι του ψευδους ευρεθημεν (cf. *4 Bar.* 4:4) || **9** και ελαλησε: A B add κλαιων; C ελαλησε δε; R και παλιν ελαλησε | Ιερεμιας: C P add προς κυριον λεγων; R τω κυριω ο Ιερεμιας λεγων | παρακαλω: A B add και δυσωπω | δειξον: R επιδειξον | Αβιμελεχ τω Αιθιοπι: R Αβιμελεκ τω Αιθιωπι | τω λαω και τω δουλω σου C eth; A B om; R om τω λαω και | Ιερεμια: eth add *far more than all the people of the city* | οτι αυτος ανεσπασεν A B (Harris Kraft ανεσπασε); C αυτος γαρ ανεστησεν | του βορβορου C eth arm; A B P om | αυτον ινα ιδη A B eth; R add την αλωσιν και; C ινα αφης αυτον ιδειν | τον αφανισμον A B eth; C την ερημωσιν | πολεως: A B add ταυτης | και την ερημωσιν: C η τον αφανισμον η την ερημωσιν | αλλ ινα μη λυπηθη eth (Harris); A B R (Ceriani v.Gebhardt) αλλ ινα ελεησης αυτον και (R του) μη λυπηθη (R λυπηθηναι); C ηδη και λυπηθη (Kraft ελεησης αυτον και μη λυπηθη) || **10** τω Ιερεμια: C om | αμπελωνα: C αγρον | δια του ορους και εγω σκεπασω αυτον C eth; A B (Ceriani v.Gebhardt Kraft) και εν τη σκια του ορους σκεπασω αυτον; R καγω αυτον σκεπασω εν τη σκια του ορους | εως ου (R om) επιστρεψω (R add παλιν) A B R; C εως αποσρεψω | εις την πολιν A B eth; R εν τη πολει; C εις Βαβυλωνα || **11** C om | ειπε δε κυριος τω Ιερεμια A B (Ceriani v.Gebhardt Harris); P arm eth (Kraft) συ δε Ιερεμιας; R συ δε | σου: R om | αυτων: R add εκει | αυτοις: R add και παραμυθουμενος | πολιν: R add αυτων || **12** C om | εως ου (R om) λαλησω αυτω: eth om || **13** C λαλησας δε αυτω ο κυριος ανεχωρησεν εις τον ουρανον απο του Ιερεμιου | ανεβη – ουρανον: R εκρυβη απο του Ιερεμιου εις τους ουρανους || **14** αγιαστηριον: C R add του θεου | και²: A B (Kraft) add επαραντες | τα σκευη: A B add τα αγια; R τα σκευει της αγιης | παρεδωκαν: A B (Kraft) add αυτα | γη¹ A B P eth arm; C add και τω θυσιαστηριω | καθως (R καθα) ελαλησεν αυτοις ο κυριος B R eth d e Menea; C καθως ειπεν κυριος; A om | αυθωρον C; A B R (Kraft) ευθεως | και³ – γη²: A B (Ceriani v.Gebhardt) om | οι δυο C R eth; A B om | εκλαυσαν: A B P arm add αμα; R add ομου πικρως ||

waters, who sealed you with seven seals, with seven epochs; and thereafter you will receive your beauty. Guard the vessels of the temple service until the gathering of the beloved one!'" **9** And Jeremiah said, "I beseech you, O Lord, show me what I should do to Abimelech, the Ethiopian, for he has done many good deeds to the people and to your servant Jeremiah. For he pulled me out of the pit of mud. And I do not want him to see the destruction and devastation of the city. He rather should not be grieved." **10** And the Lord said to Jeremiah, "Send him to the vineyard of Agrippa by the mountain (trail). And I will protect him until I return the people to the city." **11** And the Lord said to Jeremiah, "Go with your people to Babylon and stay with them, announcing to them the good news, until I return them to the city! **12** But leave Baruch here until I speak with him!" **13** Having said that, the Lord ascended from Jeremiah into heaven. **14** But Jeremiah and Baruch went into the sanctuary and consigned the vessels of temple service to the earth as the Lord had told them. And immediately the earth swallowed them. And the two of them sat down and wept. **15** And when morning came,

ἀπέστειλεν Ἱερεμίας τὸν Ἀβιμέλεχ λέγων· Ἆρον τὸν κόφινον, καὶ ἄπελθε εἰς τὸ χωρίον τοῦ Ἀγρίππα διὰ τῆς ὁδοῦ τοῦ ὄρους, καὶ ἐνεγκὼν ὀλίγα σῦκα, δίδου τοῖς νοσοῦσι τοῦ λαοῦ· ὅτι ἐπὶ σὲ ἡ εὐφρασία τοῦ Κυρίου, καὶ ἐπὶ τὴν κεφαλήν σου ἡ δόξα. **16** Αὐτὸς δὲ ἀπελήλυθεν καθὼς εἶπεν αὐτῷ.

IV 1 Πρωΐας δὲ γενομένης, ἰδοὺ ἡ δύναμις τῶν Χαλδαίων ἐκύκλωσε τὴν πόλιν· ἐσάλπισεν δὲ ὁ μέγας ἄγγελος λέγων· Εἰσέλθατε εἰς τὴν πόλιν ἡ δύναμις τῶν Χαλδαίων· ἰδοὺ γὰρ ἠνεώχθη ὑμῖν ἡ πύλη. **2** Εἰσῆλθεν οὖν ὁ βασιλεὺς μετὰ τοῦ πλήθους αὐτοῦ, καὶ ᾐχμαλώτευσαν πάντα τὸν λαόν. **3** Ἱερεμίας δὲ ἄρας τὰς κλεῖδας τοῦ ναοῦ, ἐξῆλθεν ἔξω τῆς πόλεως, καὶ ἔρριψεν αὐτὰς ἐνώπιον τοῦ ἡλίου λέγων· Σοὶ λέγω, ἥλιε, λάβε τὰς κλεῖδας τοῦ ναοῦ τοῦ Θεοῦ, καὶ φύλαξον αὐτὰς ἕως ἡμέρας, ἐν ᾗ ἐξετάσει σε Κύριος περὶ αὐτῶν. **4** Διότι ἡμεῖς οὐχ εὑρέθημεν ἄξιοι τοῦ φυλάξαι αὐτάς, ὅτι ἐπίτροποι ψεύδους ἐγενήθημεν. **5** Ἔτι κλαίοντος Ἱερεμίου τὸν λαόν, εἵλκοντο εἰς Βαβυλῶνα. **6** Ὁ δὲ Βαροὺχ ἐπέθηκε χοῦν ἐπὶ τὴν κεφαλὴν αὐτοῦ, καὶ ἐκάθισε, καὶ ἔκλαυσε τὸν θρῆνον τοῦτον, λέγων· Διὰ τί ἠρημώθη Ἱερουσαλήμ; Διὰ τὰς ἁμαρτίας τοῦ ἠγαπημένου λαοῦ παρεδόθη εἰς χεῖρας ἐχθρῶν, διὰ τὰς ἁμαρτίας ἡμῶν καὶ τοῦ λαοῦ. **7** Ἀλλὰ μὴ καυχάσθωσαν οἱ παράνομοι, καὶ εἴπωσιν ὅτι, Ἰσχύσαμεν λαβεῖν τὴν πόλιν τοῦ Θεοῦ

---

15 Αβιμελεχ: R Αβιμελεκ | Αρον τον κοφινον και απελθε: C απελθε; Menea λαβων τον κοφινον τεκνον απελθε | και ενεγκων (R ενεγκαι) ολιγα συκα διδου (R om) τοις νοσουσι του λαου: C om | οτι – η δοξα A B (eth); R add αυτου; C οτι ευφρασια κυριου εις την κεφαλην σου ηξει | ευφρασια: R φρασις || **16** C eth; A B (Ceriani v.Gebhardt Kraft) και ταυτα ειπων Ιερεμιας απελυσεν αυτον Αβιμελεχ δε επορευθη καθα ειπεν αυτω (Ceriani v.Gebhardt add Ιερεμιας) ||
IV 1 ιδου: R add και | την πολιν C eth; A την πολιν Ιερουσαλημ; B R πασαν την πολιν Ιερουσαλημ | εσαλπισε δε ο μεγας αγγελος: R ειτα μετα μικρον εσαλπισεν ο του κυριου αγγελος | η δυναμις: A B πασα η δυναμις | ηνεωχθη: R ηνυχθη | πυλη A B; C θυρα || **2** εισηλθεν C; A B (Ceriani v.Gebhardt Kraft) εισελθετω | του πληθους αυτου A B; C του ιδου πληθους | ηχμαλωτευσαν C; A B (Ceriani v.Gebhardt Kraft) αιχμαλωτευσατω | παντα: C om | λαον: C add εις Βαβυλωνα; R add αυτου || **3** Ιερεμιας δε αρας τας κλειδας: R τοτε αρας ο Ιερεμιας τας σκλεις | κλειδας¹: C κλεις | εξω – λεγων A B eth; C και ειπεν | σοι A eth; B C συ | ηλιε: A B ηλια | λαβε A B; C δεξαι | κλειδας²: C κλεις; R σκλεις ταυτας | του θεου: C om | εως – 4 εγενηθημεν A B eth; C εως ερωτησιν ποιησει κυριος περι αυτων εως της συνελευσεως του ηγαπημενου | εν ῃ: R ενι || **4** ημεις – εγενηθημεν: R επιτροποι του ψευδους εγεννηθημεν και ουχ ευρεθημεν ημεις αξιοι του φυλαξαι αυτας | εγενηθημεν: C add εξενεγκαν ουν αυτον || **5** ετι: R add δε | κλαιοντος: R κλαιοντων και οδυρομενος ο | Ιερεμιου: C αυτου | τον λαον: R ο λαος; C om | ειλκοντο: C ειλκοντες; R ειλκεντο αιχμαλοσια | Βαβυλωνα: A B R add υπο του βασιλεως των χαλδαιων (R also add συνειπετο δε αυτοις και ο μακαριος Ιερεμιας) || **6** ο δε Βαρουχ: C Ιερεμιας δε διερρηξεν τα ιματια αυτου και | εκαθισε: R εκαθησεν | λεγων: R οιμμοι κυριε | Ιερουσαλεμ: R add η παντως | ηγαπημενον: R add τουτου | λαου¹: R add οιμμοι οιμμοι | παρεδοθη: R add η ηγαπημενη πολις | εχθρων: R Χαλδαιων | και του λαου: A B eth; C om; R add οιμμοι οιμμοι πως ενικησαν αι αμαρτιαι ημων την πολλην φιλανθρωπιαν του θεου ει γαρ μη υπερεπλεωνασαν αι αμαρτιαι ημων και του λαου ουκ αν παρεδοθημεν τοις Χαλδαιοις || **7** αλλα μη: R μη ουν | ισχυσαμεν C; ηδυνηθημεν A B eth; (Ceriani v.Gebhardt οτι ηδυνηθημεν) |

Jeremiah sent Abimelech away, saying, "Take the basket and go to the estate of Agrippa by the mountain trail; bring a few figs in it and give (them) to the sick among the people. For the favor of the Lord is on you, and his glory is on your head." **16** And he went away as he told him.

4:1 And when morning came, behold, the host of the Chaldeans surrounded the city. And the great angel trumpeted, saying, "Enter the city, host of the Chaldeans, for behold, the gate has been opened for you."[2] **2** So, the king entered with his multitude and took all the people captive. **3** And Jeremiah took the keys of the temple, went outside the city, and threw them into the presence of the sun, saying, "To you I say, O Sun, take the keys of the temple of God and guard them until the day when the Lord will ask you for them. **4** For we have not been found worthy to guard them, because we became unfaithful trustees." **5** While Jeremiah was still weeping for the people, they were dragged off into Babylon.[3] **6** And Baruch put dust on his head, sat down, and wailed this lament, saying, "Why has Jerusalem been laid waste? Because of the sins of the beloved people it has been surrendered into the hands of enemies, because of our sins and those of the people. **7** But let not the lawless (people) boast and say, 'We were strong (enough) to take the city of God

---

2. In the reading of the mss A and B this sentence still belongs to the speech of the angel and fits the context better. Therefore it probably has to be seen as secondary.

3. The reading of Kraft/Purintun, which is close to eth, seems to be a construction in order to avoid the problems concerning the relationship of Jeremiah and the people while taken captive (cf. Herzer, *Paralipomena Jeremiae*, 12). Eth is more precise at this point because it explicitly mentions the fact that Jeremiah is also taken to Babylon.

ἐν τῇ δυνάμει ἡμῶν. Ἠδυνήθητε ἐπ᾽ αὐτῇ· ἀλλὰ διὰ τὰς ἁμαρτίας ἡμῶν παρεδόθημεν. **8** Ὁ δὲ Θεὸς ἡμῶν οἰκτειρήσει ἡμᾶς, καὶ ἐπιστρέψει ἡμᾶς εἰς τὴν πόλιν ἡμῶν· ὑμεῖς δὲ ζωὴν οὐχ ἕξετε. **9** Μακάριοί εἰσιν οἱ πατέρες ἡμῶν, Ἀβραὰμ, Ἰσαὰκ καὶ Ἰακὼβ, ὅτι ἐξῆλθον ἐκ τοῦ κόσμου τούτου, καὶ οὐκ εἶδον τὸν ἀφανισμὸν τῆς πόλεως ταύτης. **10** Ταῦτα εἰπὼν, ἐξῆλθεν, κλαίων καὶ λέγων ὅτι, [Λυπούμενος] διὰ σὲ, Ἰερουσαλὴμ, ἐξῆλθον ἀπὸ σοῦ. **11** Καὶ ἔμεινεν ἐν μνημείῳ καθεζόμενος, τῶν ἀγγέλων ἐρχομένων, καὶ ἐκδιηγουμένων αὐτῷ περὶ πάντων.

V 1 Ὁ δὲ Ἀβιμέλεχ ἤνεγκε τὰ σῦκα τῷ καύματι, καὶ καταλαβὼν δένδρον, ἐκάθισεν ὑπὸ τὴν σκιὰν αὐτοῦ τοῦ ἀναπαῆναι ὀλίγον, καὶ κλίνας τὴν κεφαλὴν αὐτοῦ ἐπὶ τὸν κόφινον τῶν σύκων ὕπνωσεν, κοιμώμενος ἔτη ἑξηκονταέξ· καὶ οὐκ ἐξυπνίσθη ἐκ τοῦ ὕπνου αὐτοῦ. **2** Καὶ μετὰ ταῦτα ἐγερθεὶς ἀπὸ τοῦ ὕπνου αὐτοῦ, εἶπεν ὅτι, Ἡδέως ἐκοιμήθην ἂν ἄλλο ὀλίγον, καὶ βεβαρημένη ἐστὶν ἡ κεφαλή μου, ὅτι οὐκ ἐκορέσθην τοῦ ὕπνου μου. **3** Καὶ ἀνακαλύψας τὸν κόφινον τῶν σύκων, εὗρεν αὐτὰ στάζοντα γάλα. **4** Καὶ εἶπεν· Ἤθελον κοιμηθῆναι ὀλίγον, ὅτι βεβαρημένη ἐστὶν ἡ κεφαλή μου· **5** ἀλλὰ φοβοῦμαι, μήπως κοιμηθῶ καὶ βραδυνῶ τοῦ ἐξυπνισθῆναι, καὶ ὀλιγωρήσῃ Ἰερεμίας ὁ πατήρ μου· εἰ μὴ γὰρ ἐσπούδαζεν, οὐκ ἂν

---

(7) τη: C om | ηδυνηθητε επ αυτη C eth; A B (Ceriani v.Gebhardt Kraft) om | παρεδοθημεν A B; C om; eth *it has been delivered to you* (Kraft παρεδοθη υμιν) || **8** ημων¹ A B eth; C om | οικτειρησει: C οικτιρησεν; R οικτειρισας | και επιστρεψει (R επιστρεψας) ημας A B R eth; C om | υμεις δε: R add οι αιχμαλωτευσαντες ημας και την πολιν ημων πορθησαντες | ουχ εξετε: R ουκ εξεται || **9** μακαριοι: R add δε | Αβρααμ: R add και | αφανισμον: R add και την ερημωσιν | της πολεως ταυτης A B eth; C Ιερουσαλημ || **10** ειπων: A B (Ceriani v.Gebhardt Kraft) add Βαρουχ | εξηλθεν: A B (Ceriani v.Gebhardt Kraft) add εξω της πολεως | λυπουμενος: C λοιπου; A B P arm eth om | Ιερουσαλημ: C add και | εξηλθον: C εξηλθεν; R εξηλθων | απο σου: C εκ της πολεως; R add κλαιων και οδυρομενος πασας τας ημερας της ζωης μου | και λεγων – σου: eth om || **11** καθεζομενος: C om | ερχομενων: A B (Ceriani v.Gebhardt Kraft) add προς αυτον; R om | και²: R om || παντων: A B R (Ceriani v.Gebhardt Kraft) add ων ο κυριος εμηνυεν (R εμεινυεν) αυτω δι αυτων (R εαυτων) ||

V 1 καυματι: eth add *from where Jeremiah had sent him* | καταλαβων: C κατελαβεν; R add υπο τι | δενδρον: C add και | υπο την σκιαν αυτου: C om | του αναπαηναι C; A του αναπαυσαι; B αναπαηναι; R αναπαυσασθαι | ολιγον: R add τι | κλινας A B; C εκλινεν | αυτου: R om; A B add υπνωσεν | επι C R eth; A B υπο | των συκων: C om; R add παραχρημα αφυπνωσεν και εποιησεν | υπνωσεν: A B om | κοιμωμενος ετη εξηκονταεξ: C και εποιησεν εξηκοντα και εξ ετη εκκοιμωμενος; eth om | εκ: C απο | αυτου³: A B R (Ceriani v.Gebhardt) add κατα προσταξιν (R add του) θεου δια τον λογον ον ειπεν τω Ιερεμια οτι εγω αυτον σκεπασω (R add εν τη σκια του ορους) || **2** και¹: C om | αυτου: R om | εγερθεις: C arm εξυπνησθεις; eth *arose and awoke* | ηδεως: B ιδεως; R ειδεως | αν αλλο ολιγον: A B αλλ ολιγον; C R ολιγον; eth *if only I slept a little* | βεβαρημενη εστιν η κεφαλη μου: R εστιν βεβαρημενη μου η κεφαλη | και βεβαρημενη: C αλλα βαρια | μου²: C R eth om || **3** και: R ειτα | αυτα: R τα συκα | σταζοντα: R add τω || **4** ειπεν: R add ακμην | κοιμηθηναι: R add ετι | ολιγον: d e Menaea αλλο ολιγον | βεβαρημενη: C βαρια | εστιν η κεφαλη μου: R μου εστιν η κεφαλη || **5** ολιγωρηση: R οληγωρισει ο |

by our power.' You did receive power over it, yet we were given up because of our sins. **8** But our God will have mercy on us and will return us to our city. But you will not survive. **9** Blessed are our fathers Abraham, Isaac and Jacob, because they departed from this world and did not see the destruction of this city." **10** Having said this, he (Baruch) left weeping and saying, "[Grieving] because of you, Jerusalem, I went out from you." **11** And he remained sitting in a tomb, while angels came and explained everything to him.

5:1 But Abimelech carried the figs in the heat (of day) and coming upon a tree, he sat down in its shade to rest a while. And leaning his head on the basket of figs, he fell asleep and slept for sixty-six years, and he was not awakened from his sleep. **2** After these things he awoke from his sleep (and) said, "I would gladly have slept a little longer; my head is heavy because I did not get enough sleep." **3** And when he uncovered the basket of figs he found them dripping (with their) milky sap. **4** And he said, "I want to sleep a little because my head is heavy. **5** But I am afraid that I might fall asleep (again) and wake up too late and Jeremiah, my father, would have a low opinion of me. For if he were not in a hurry, he would not

ἀπέστειλέ με ὄρθρου σήμερον. **6** Ἀναστὰς οὖν πορεύσομαι τῷ καύματι, καὶ ἀπέλθω [ὅπου οὐ καῦμα, οὐ κόπος ἔστιν καθ᾽ ἡμέραν]. **7** Ἐγερθεὶς οὖν ἦρε τὸν κόφινον τῶν σύκων, καὶ ἐπέθηκεν ἐπὶ τῶν ὤμων ἑαυτοῦ· καὶ εἰσῆλθεν εἰς Ἰερουσαλὴμ, καὶ οὐκ ἐπέγνω αὐτὴν, οὔτε τὴν οἰκίαν, οὔτε τὸν τόπον, οὔτε τὸ γένος ἑαυτοῦ, καὶ εἶπεν· **8** Εὐλογητὸς Κύριος, ὅτι μεγάλη ἔκστασις ἐπέπεσεν ἐπ᾽ ἐμέ· οὐκ ἔστιν αὕτη ἡ πόλις· **9** Πεπλάνημαι, ὅτι διὰ τῆς ὁδοῦ τοῦ ὄρους ἦλθον, ἐγερθεὶς ἀπὸ τοῦ ὕπνου μου· **10** καὶ βαρείας οὔσης τῆς κεφαλῆς μου διὰ τὸ μὴ κορεσθῆναί με τοῦ ὕπνου μου, πεπλάνημαι τὴν ὁδόν. **11** Θαυμαστὸν εἰπεῖν τοῦτο ἐναντίον Ἰερεμίου, ὅτι πεπλάνημαι. **12** Ἐξῆλθε δὲ ἀπὸ τῆς πόλεως· καὶ κατανοήσας εἶδε τὰ σημεῖα τῆς πόλεως, καί εἶπεν· Αὕτη μὲν ἔστιν ἡ πόλις, πεπλάνημαι δέ. **13** Καὶ πάλιν ὑπέστρεψεν εἰς τὴν πόλιν, καὶ ἐζήτησε, καὶ οὐδένα εὗρε τῶν ἰδίων. **14** Καὶ εἶπεν· Εὐλογητὸς Κύριος, ὅτι μεγάλη ἔκστασις ἐπέπεσεν ἐπ᾽ ἐμέ. **15** Καὶ πάλιν ἐξῆλθεν ἔξω τῆς πόλεως. Καὶ ἔμεινε λυπούμενος, μὴ εἰδὼς ποῦ ἀπέλθῃ. **16** καὶ ἀπέθηκεν τὸν κόφινον λέγων· Καθέζομαι ὧδε, ἕως ὁ Κύριος ἄρῃ τὴν ἔκστασιν ταύτην ἀπ᾽ ἐμοῦ. **17** Καθημένου δὲ αὐτοῦ, εἶδέ τινα γηραιὸν ἐρχόμενον ἐξ ἀγροῦ, καὶ λέγει αὐτῷ Ἀβιμέλεχ· Σοὶ λέγω,

---

(5) ορθρου σημερον C eth; A B P R σημερον; eth *when it became light* || **6** πορευσομαι: R om | τω: R το | και: R om | απελθω: R add προς αυτον εν ταχει | οπου γαρ – ημεραν: Harris; A B (Kraft) ου γαρ καυμα ου κοπος εστιν καθ ημεραν; Ceriani v.Gebhardt και απελθω ου γαρ καυμα ου κοπος εστιν καθ ημεραν; Menea απελθω μαλλον συντομος και θεραπευσο αυτον κακει κοιμωμαι; C R om; eth *because the heat is fierce and never goes away completely* || **7** εγερθεις: C αναστας | των συκων: R om | επεθηκεν: R add αυτον | των ωμων εαυτου A B; R τον ωμον αυτου; C την κεφαλην εαυτου; eth om και επεθηκεν – εαυτου | εισηλθεν: R ελθων | και³: R om | αυτην ουτε την οικιαν ουτε τον τοπον (A B add εαυτου) ουτε το γενος εαυτου (R αυτου) A B R; C om ουτε τον τοπον; eth *neither the city nor his house* | και ειπεν: A B ουτε τινα ευρεν και ειπεν (Kraft ουτε τινα των γνωριμων ευρεν); R ουτε τινα ετερον των γνωριμων αυτου ευρεν εν αυτη και ειπεν || **8** επ εμε: C R (Ceriani v.Gebhardt Kraft) add σημερον | ουκ: C και ουκ; R οντως ουκ; eth *and he said, this is not* | η πολις: P R eth (Kraft) add Ιερουσαλημ || **9** πεπλανημαι: C (Kraft) add γαρ την οδον; R add τοινυν την οδον | ηλθον: C om | μου: R om || **10** και – μου¹: R om | του υπνου: R τον υπνον | μου²: R (v.Gebhardt) om | πεπλανημαι: A B add δε | πεπλανημαι – οδον: R om || **11** θαυμαστον: R add δε | ειπεν: C εστιν | Ιερεμιου: C του Ιερεμιου | οτι πεπλανημαι: C R (Kraft) add την οδον; eth *as the city has changed to me* || **12** εξηλθε δε: C και εξηλθε | κατανοησας (R add ακριβως) ειδε A B R; C ευρεν | της πολεως A B; C αυτης | δε²: R γαρ; C (Kraft) add την οδον || **13** πολιν: C οδον | και εζητησε: R και εισελθων ενδον εζητησεν; C om | ιδιων: R add αυτου η των γνωστων η των φιλων η των γνωριμων η των διαφεροντων εν τω οικω αυτου || **14** και ειπεν: C om | κυριος: A B ο κυριος; C ει κυριε | εμε: C add και ουκ εστιν αυτη η πολις || **15** παλιν: C om | εξω: R εκ | πολεως: A B R add και ελεγεν τα μεν σημεια της πολεως (R μου) εισιν (R add τι δε εχω ειπειν η εννοησασθαι απορω) | λυπουμενος: R add επι ωρας ικανος και λοιπον | ειδως: C ιδων; R add το | απελθη C ; A B απελθειν || **16** και (R om) απεθηκεν A B eth (Harris Kraft και απεθηκε); C αφηκεν δε; R add εν τη γη | κοφινον: C R add των συκων | εως: C add αν || **17** καθημενου: C καθεζομενου | αυτου: R add εξω της πολεως | ειδε: R ιδεν | γηραιον: R γηρειον; C γηραον ανθρωπ | ερχομενον: C om | λεγει: C ειπεν | Αβιμελεχ A B eth; C om | σοι: B συ |

have sent me today at dawn. **6** So I will get up and proceed in the heat and go to where there is neither heat nor toil every day."[4] **7** So he got up, took the basket of figs and placed it on his shoulders. And he entered Jerusalem, but he did not recognize it: neither the house nor the place nor his own family, and he said, **8** "Blessed be the Lord, for a great trance has come upon me: This is not the city. **9** I lost my way because I came by the mountain trail when I awakened from my sleep. **10** And since my head was heavy because I did not get enough sleep, I lost my way. **11** This is an astonishing thing to say to Jeremiah, 'I lost my way.'" **12** And he went out of the city and when he looked carefully, he saw the landmarks of the city and said, "Indeed, this is the city, but I lost my way." **13** And again he went back into the city and searched, but he found no one of his own people. **14** And he said, "Blessed be the Lord, for a great trance has come upon me." **15** And again he went out of the city. And he remained there grieving, for he did not know where to go. **16** And he laid down the basket, saying, "I shall sit here until the Lord lifts this trance from me." **17** And while he was sitting, he saw an old man coming from the field. And Abimelech said to him, "I say to you,

---

4. The text transmission in v. 6 is unclear. The reading of A and B (cf. eth), preferred by Kraft/Purintun (cf. already Ceriani), makes the understanding easier. However, the reading preferred here fits the eschatological context of *4 Baruch,* cf. the commentary on this verse.

πρεσβῦτα, ποία ἐστὶν ἡ πόλις αὕτη; Καὶ εἶπεν αὐτῷ· Ἰερουσαλήμ ἐστι. **18** Καὶ λέγει αὐτῷ Ἀβιμέλεχ· Ποῦ ἔστιν ὁ Ἰερεμίας ὁ ἱερεύς, καὶ Βαροὺχ ὁ ἀναγνώστης, καὶ πᾶς ὁ λαὸς τῆς πόλεως ταύτης, ὅτι οὐχ εὗρον αὐτούς; **19** Καὶ εἶπεν αὐτῷ ὁ πρεσβύτης· Οὐκ εἶ σὺ ἐκ τῆς πόλεως ταύτης, **20** σήμερον μνησθεὶς τοῦ Ἰερεμίου, ὅτι ἐπερωτᾷς περὶ αὐτοῦ μετὰ τοσοῦτον χρόνον; **21** Ἰερεμίας γὰρ ἐν Βαβυλῶνί ἐστι μετὰ τοῦ λαοῦ· ἠχμαλωτεύθησαν γὰρ ὑπὸ Ναβουχοδονόσορ τοῦ βασιλέως, καὶ μετ' αὐτῶν ἐστιν Ἰερεμίας εὐαγγελίσασθαι αὐτοῖς καὶ κατηχῆσαι αὐτοὺς τὸν λόγον. **22** Εὐθὺς δὲ ἀκούσας Ἀβιμέλεχ παρὰ τοῦ γηραιοῦ ἀνθρώπου, εἶπεν· **23** Εἰ μὴ ἦς πρεσβύτης, καὶ ὅτι οὐκ ἐξὸν ἀνθρώπῳ ὑβρίσαι τὸν μείζονα αὐτοῦ, ἐπικατεγέλων ἄν σοι καὶ ἔλεγον, ὅτι μαίνῃ· ὅτι εἶπας, Ἠχμαλωτεύθη ὁ λαὸς εἰς Βαβυλῶνα. **24** Εἰ ἦσαν οἱ καταρράκται τοῦ οὐρανοῦ κατελθόντες ἐπ' αὐτούς; οὔπω ἐστὶ καιρὸς ἀπελθεῖν εἰς Βαβυλῶνα. **25** Πόση γὰρ ὥρα ἐστίν, ἀφ' οὗ ἀπέστειλέ με ὁ πατήρ μου Ἰερεμίας εἰς τὸ χωρίον τοῦ Ἀγρίππα ἐπὶ ὀλίγα σῦκα, ἵνα δίδωμι τοῖς νοσοῦσι τοῦ λαοῦ, **26** καὶ ἀπελθὼν ἤνεγκον αὐτά, καὶ ἐλθὼν ἐπί τι δένδρον τῷ καύματι, ἐκάθισα τοῦ ἀναπαῆναι ὀλίγον, καὶ ἔκλινα τὴν κεφαλήν μου ἐπὶ τὸν κόφινον, καὶ ἐκοιμήθην, καὶ ἐξυπνισθεὶς ἀπεκάλυψα τὸν κόφινον τῶν σύκων, νομίζων ὅτι ἐβράδυνα, καὶ εὗρον τὰ σῦκα στάζοντα γάλα, καθὼς συνέλεξα αὐτά. Σὺ δὲ λέγεις, ὅτι

---

(17) πρεσβῦτα: A B C Menaea πρεσβύτα | αυτω: C om | Ιερουσαλημ: eth *the old Jerusalem* | εστι: R om ‖ **18** λεγει: C R ειπεν | που R: A B και που | ο[1]: R om | ιερευς eth arm; A B ιερευς του θεου; C αρχιερευς; P R αρχιερευς του θεου | ο αναγνωστης: C om; eth *the Levite* | αυτους: R add ενταδε ‖ **19** αυτω ο πρεσβυτης C eth; A B P R arm ο πρεσβυτης τω Αβιμελεχ ‖ **20** μνησθεις: C εμνησθη | επερωτας: R ερωτας | μετα τοσουτον χρονον (R τοσουτους χρονους): eth *although you sat there all the time* ‖ **21** γαρ[2]: R add προ εξικοντα και εξ χρονων | υπο: C υπο του | του (R om) βασιλεως: C add Βαβυλωνος; P R add των Χαλδαιων; eth *from Persia* | εστιν Ιερεμιας: C απηλθεν | ευαγγελισασθαι: R ευαγγελιζομενος | και κατηχησαι αυτους A; B και κατηχησαι αυτοις; R και κατεχων; C eth om | τον λογον A B C; R add του θεου; eth om ‖ **22** ευθυς δε ακουσας: R ακουσας δε ταυτα ‖ **23** ει μη ης: R ει μι οτι εις | πρεσβυτης: R πρεσβυτερος | οτι[1]: C R om | εξον: R εξ ων | ανθρωπω (eth); A B P arm ανθρωπω θεου; C ανθρωπων; R ανθρωπον | αυτου: R εαυτου | επικατεγελων αν: d e Menaea κατεγελων αν; A B R επει καταγελων; C επικατεγελουν | σοι C; A om; d e B Menaea σου | και ελεγον: A om | οτι μαινη A eth; B οτι μενει; C οτι μεν; R σου και ελεγων οτι μενει | οτι ειπας: C om | ηχμαλωτευθη: C ηχμαλωτευσων; R αιχμαλωτησθη ‖ **24** ησαν: R add γαρ | ουπω: C ουπω ουκ | καιρος: C om | απελθειν: C πορευθηναι; R add αυτους ‖ **25** αφ ου: C εξοτου | εις – Αγριππα: C om | επι: C ενεγκαι | συκα: A B add ενεγκα; C R eth om | ινα διδωμι (R διαδωμεν) – λαου: C τοις νοσουσιν ‖ **26** απελθων: C om | ηνεγκον αυτα και ελθων: A B om; eth *I went and reached that place and took what he had ordered me to take, and I turned around and by going* | επι τι – ολιγον: R ηνεγκα αυτα και ως ηλθον επι τι δενδρον δια το καυμα του ηλιου εκαθησα μικρον του αναπαυσασθαι ολιγον | τι: C om | εκαθισα – κοφινον[1]: C om; R add των συκων | εκοιμηθην: A B R add ολιγον | και[5]: R add μετα μικρον | εξυπνισθεις: C αναστας; R add εξ υπνος γενομενος | απεκαλυψα: C ανεκαλυψα | εβραδυνα: C εχρονησα | τα συκα: C αυτα | συνελεξα αυτα: C ανελεξαμην αυτα; R και εξελεξαμην αυτα εκ της συκης |

old man, what city is this?" And he said to him, "It is Jerusalem." **18** And Abimelech said to him, "Where is Jeremiah the priest, and Baruch the reader, and all the people of this city? For I could not find them." **19** And the old man said to him, "You are from this city, aren't you? **20** For today you remembered Jeremiah, seeing that you are asking about him after such a long time. **21** For Jeremiah is in Babylon with the people, for they were taken captive by King Nebuchadnezzar, and Jeremiah is with them to announce to them the good news and to teach them the word." **22** As soon as Abimelech heard (this) from the old man, he said, **23** "If you were not an old man, and if it were not improper for a person to upbraid one older than oneself, I would laugh at you and say that you are crazy because you say, 'The people have been taken captive to Babylon.' **24** Had the heavenly torrents descended on them, there would not yet have been time to go to Babylon. **25** For how long has it been since my father Jeremiah sent me to the estate of Agrippa for a few figs, so that I might give them to the sick among the people? **26** And I went and brought them, and when I came upon a tree in the scorching heat of day, I sat down to rest a little and leaned my head on the basket and fell asleep. And when I awoke I uncovered the basket of figs supposing that I was late, and I found the figs dripping (with their) milky sap, just as I had picked them. And you say that

ἠχμαλωτεύθη ὁ λαὸς εἰς Βαβυλῶνα; **27** Ἵνα δὲ γνῷς, λάβε, ἴδε τὰ σῦκα. **28** Καὶ ἀνεκάλυψε τὸν κόφινον τῶν σύκων τῷ γέροντι. **29** Καὶ εἶδεν αὐτὰ στάζοντα γάλα. **30** Ἰδὼν δὲ αὐτὰ ὁ γηραιὸς ἄνθρωπος, εἶπεν· Ὦ υἱέ μου, δίκαιος ἄνθρωπος εἶ σύ, καὶ οὐκ ἠθέλησεν ὁ Θεὸς δεῖξαί σοι τὴν ἐρήμωσιν τῆς πόλεως. Ἤνεγκε γὰρ ταύτην τὴν ἔκστασιν ἐπὶ σὲ ὁ Θεός. Ἰδοὺ γὰρ ἑξήκοντα καὶ ἓξ ἔτη σήμερόν εἰσιν ἀφ᾽ οὗ ἠχμαλωτεύθη ὁ λαὸς εἰς Βαβυλῶνα. **31** Καὶ ἵνα μάθῃς, τέκνον, ὅτι ἀληθές ἐστιν, ἀνάβλεψον εἰς τὸν ἀγρὸν καὶ ἴδε, ὅτι ἐφάνη ἡ αὔξησις τῶν γενημάτων· ἴδε καὶ τὰ σῦκα, ὅτι καιρὸς αὐτῶν οὐκ ἔστι, καὶ γνῶθι. **32** Τότε ἔκραξε μεγάλῃ φωνῇ Ἀβιμέλεχ λέγων· Εὐλογήσω σε, Κύριε ὁ Θεὸς τοῦ οὐρανοῦ καὶ τῆς γῆς, ἡ ἀνάπαυσις τῶν ψυχῶν τῶν δικαίων ἐν παντὶ τόπῳ. **33** Καὶ λέγει τῷ γηραιῷ ἀνθρώπῳ· Ποῖός ἐστιν ὁ μὴν οὗτος; Ὁ δὲ εἶπε· Νισσάν· καὶ ἔστιν ἡ δωδεκάτη. **34** Καὶ ἐπάρας ἐκ τῶν σύκων, ἔδωκε τῷ γηραιῷ ἀνθρώπῳ, καὶ λέγει αὐτῷ· Ὁ Θεὸς φωταγωγήσει σε εἰς τὴν ἄνω πόλιν Ἱερουσαλήμ.

VI 1 Μετὰ ταῦτα ἐξῆλθεν Ἀβιμέλεχ ἔξω τῆς πόλεως, καὶ προσηύξατο πρὸς Κύριον. Καὶ ἰδοὺ ἄγγελος Κυρίου ἦλθε, καὶ ἀπεκατέστησεν αὐτόν, ὅπου ἦν Βαρούχ· εὗρε δὲ αὐτὸν ἐν μνημείῳ καθεζόμενον. **2** Καὶ ἐν τῷ θεωρῆσαι

---

(26) ηχμαλωτεύθη ο λαος: C ηχμαλωτευθησαν || 27 ινα – 28 και: R δη και συ αυτος γνως το αληθες λαβε δη και συ εκ των συκων και θεωρισον και ευθεως || 28 τον κοφινον – γεροντι: R τα συκα τω γηρεω || 29 ειδεν: R ευρεν | σταζοντα: R add τω | γαλα: R add ωσπερ ηδη σκοπεντα(?) εκ του δενδρου || 30 γηραιος: R γηρεως | δικαιος ανθρωπος ει συ C eth; A B P arm δικαιου ανθρωπου υιος ει συ; R δικαιου ανδρος υιος ει | ουκ ηθελησεν: R μη θελων | δειξαι σοι C eth; A B ιδειν σε (Kraft η ιδειν σε) | πολεως: A B add ταυτης | γαρ¹: C R om | ο θεος²: C P R arm om | σημερον εισιν C P eth; A B arm om | ετη: R χρονοι εισιν | ηχμαλωτευθη ο λαος: C αιχμαλωτευθησαν; R αιχμαλωτισθη ο λαος || 31 τεκνον: C om | αληθες εστιν: A B P arm αληθη εισιν απερ λεγω σοι; R αληθες εστιν απερ σοι λεγω (Kraft αληθες εστιν απερ λεγω σοι) | οτι²: A B add ουκ; R add ακμην ουδαμου | εφανη A B (Kraft ουκ εστι εφανη) | οτι καιρος αυτων ουκ εστι (R add νυν) A B R: C οτι ουκ εστι καιρος των συκων | γνωθι: R add και αυτος τεκνον την μεγαλην του θεου δυναμιν και οικονομιαν την γεναμενην εις σε; eth add *and he realized that it was not the time of all these* || 32 τοτε: C και | μεγαλη φωνη Αβιμελεχ: R Αβιμελεχ φωνη μεγαλη | Αβιμελεχ: C om | ευλογησω: C ευλογω | κυριε ο θεος: A B P R arm (Kraft) ο θεος; C κυριε; eth *O Lord my God, God* | αναπαυσις: R εις τους αιωνας η αναπαυσις και η παραμοιθια | των ψυχων: C om | δικαιων: R add σου | τοπω A B P arm eth; C καιρω || 33 και: R ειτα | και λεγει τω γηραιω ανθρωπω: C το φως το αληθινον η αληθινη ανταποδοσις ο ων μεγας θαυμαστος εις τους αιωνας αμην τοτε λεγει τω γηραιω ανθρωπω; R add ο Αβιμελεχ | Νισσαν και εστιν η δωδεκατη (eth Harris): A B Νισσαν ο εστι δωδεκατος; C Ισαακ εστιν ο μην ουτος; R νισα ος εστιν απριλλιος; eth *the twelfth of the month Nisan, which is Mijazia* || 34 και επαρας: C ουτος αρας ουν | και λεγει: C ειπων | εις: A B R επι ||

VI 1 προσηυξατο: C ηυξατο | ηλθε και: A B P arm (Kraft) add κρατησας αυτου της δεξιας χειρος; Ceriani της δεξιας αυτου | αυτον¹: A B (Ceriani Kraft) add εις τον τοπον | Βαρουχ: A B (Ceriani Kraft) add καθεζομενος | ευρη δε: C και ευρε | καθεζομενον: A B (Ceriani Kraft) om ||

the people have been taken captive to Babylon? **27** But that you might know, take the figs and see!" **28** And he uncovered the basket of figs for the old man. **29** And he saw them dripping (with their) milky sap. **30** And when he saw them, the old man said, "O my son, you are a righteous man and God did not want to show you the desolation of the city, so God brought this trance upon you. Behold, it has been sixty-six years today since the people were taken captive to Babylon. **31** But that you may learn, child, that it is true, look at the field and see that the growth of the crops has (just) begun. Notice also the figs, that their time has not yet come, and understand." **32** Then Abimelech cried out in a loud voice, saying, "I will bless you, O Lord,[5] God of heaven and earth, the Rest of the souls of the righteous in every place." **33** And to the old man he said, "What month is this?" And he said, "Nisan. And it is the twelfth (day)."[6] **34** And taking (a few) of the figs, he gave them to the old man and said to him, "God will lead you (by his) light to the city above, Jerusalem."

6:1 After these things Abimelech went outside the city and prayed to the Lord. And behold, an angel of the Lord came and returned him to where Baruch was. And he found him sitting in a tomb. **2** And when they saw

---

5. Although the address "Lord, God" is a combination of the readings of A, B and C, it fits better in the context of *4 Baruch*, where no address to God stands without the title "Lord."

6. The various readings are confusing, but the eth version has to be preferred here because Nisan is not the twelfth month (so in A and B). Cf. the commentary on this verse.

ἀλλήλους, ἔκλαυσαν ἀμφότεροι καὶ κατεφίλησαν ἀλλήλους. Ἀναβλέψας δὲ Βαροὺχ, εἶδε τὰ σῦκα ἐσκεπασμένα ἐν τῷ κοφίνῳ· καὶ ἄρας τοὺς ὀφθαλμοὺς αὐτοῦ εἰς τὸν οὐρανὸν, προσηύξατο λέγων· Ἔστιν Θεὸς ὁ παρέχων μισθαποδοσίαν τοῖς ἁγίοις αὐτοῦ. 3 Ἑτοίμασον σεαυτὴν, ἡ καρδία μου, καὶ εὐφραίνου, καὶ ἀγάλλου ἐν τῷ σκηνώματί σου, λέγω τῷ σαρκικῷ οἴκῳ σου· τὸ πένθος σου γὰρ μετεστράφη εἰς χαράν. Ἔρχεται γὰρ ὁ ἱκανὸς, καὶ ἀρεῖ σε ἐκ τοῦ σκηνώματός σου. Οὐ γὰρ γέγονέ σοι ἁμαρτία. 4 Ἀνάψυξον ἡ παρθενική μου πίστις, καὶ πίστευσον ὅτι ζήσεις. 5 Ἐπίβλεψον ἐπὶ τὸν κόφινον τοῦτον τῶν σύκων· ἰδοὺ γὰρ ἑξηκονταὲξ ἔτη ἐποίησαν, καὶ οὐκ ἐμαράνθησαν, οὐδὲ ὤζεσαν, ἀλλὰ στάζουσι τοῦ γάλακτος. 6 Οὕτως γίνεταί σοι ἡ σάρξ μου, ἐὰν ποιήσῃς τὰ προσταχθέντα σου ὑπὸ τοῦ ἀγγέλου τῆς δικαιοσύνης. 7 Ὁ φυλάξας τὸν κόφινον τῶν σύκων, αὐτὸς πάλιν φυλάξει σε ἐν τῇ δυνάμει αὐτοῦ. 8 Ταῦτα εἰπὼν ὁ Βαροὺχ, λέγει τῷ Ἀβιμέλεχ· Ἀνάστηθι, καὶ εὐξώμεθα, ἵνα γνωρίσῃ ἡμῖν ὁ Κύριος τὸ πῶς δυνησώμεθα ἀποστεῖλαι τὴν φάσιν τῷ Ἱερεμίᾳ εἰς Βαβυλῶνα διὰ τὴν γενομένην σοι σκέπην. 9 Καὶ ηὔξατο Βαροὺχ λέγων· Ἡ δύναμις ἡμῶν, ὁ Θεὸς ἡμῶν Κύριε, τὸ ἐκλεκτὸν φῶς, τὸ ἐξελθὸν ἐκ στόματος αὐτοῦ, παρακαλῶ καὶ δέομαί σου τῆς ἀγαθότητος· τὸ μέγα ὄνομα, ὃ οὐδεὶς δύναται γνῶναι· 10 ἄκουσον τῆς φωνῆς τοῦ δούλου σου, καὶ γενοῦ γνῶσις ἐν τῇ καρδίᾳ μου. Τί θέλεις ποιήσωμεν; πῶς ἀποστείλω

---

2 εκλαυσαν αμφοτεροι B eth; A om; C εκλαυσαν | αλληλους²: B add εν των θεωρησαι αλληλους | αναβλεψας: eth om | δε: A B om | Βαρουχ: A (Ceriani Kraft) add τοις οφθαλμοις αυτου; B add τους οφθαλμους αυτου | κοφινω: A B P arm (Ceriani Kraft) add του Αβιμελεχ | αρας A B; C eth επηρεν | προσηυξατο λεγων A B eth; C ειπεν | εστιν θεος: A B (Harris εστι θεος); C εις εστιν ο θεος; eth *great is God;* (Kraft συ ο θεος) | αγιοις αυτου C; A B arm (Ceriani Kraft) αγαπωσι σε; arm *those who fear you in truth;* eth *to his righteous* || 3 η: C om | αγαλλου A B; C αγαλλιασον | εν: C ετη λεγων | λεγω: C eth om | οικω σου: C eth τω οικω σου αγιω | μετεστραφη: C μεταστραφητω; eth *they will repent* | γαρ²: C om | αρει: C ερει | εκ του σκηνωματος: C (Ceriani Kraft Schaller) εν τω σκηνωματι; eth *and will let you return into your body* | γεγονε: C εγενετο εν | ου γαρ γεγονε σοι αμαρτια: eth om || 4 αναψυξον η παρθενικη μου πιστις: A B P (Ceriani) αναψυξον εν τω σκηνωματι σου εν τη παρθενικη σου ποιμην; C αναστηθι αναστρεψον εις το ιδιον σου η παρθενικη μου πιστις; eth (arm) *observe your virginity of faith;* (Kraft αναψυξον εν τω σκηνωματι σου εν τη παρθενικη σου πιστει; Bogaert Schaller αναψυξον εν τω σκηνωματι σου η παρθενικη μου πιστις) | οτι: C και || 5 τουτον A B eth; C om || 6 προσταχθεντα σου A B; C προστεταχθεντα σοι; eth *his order* || 8 λεγει τω Αβιμελεχ: C ειπεν ο Αβιμελεχ; eth *answered Abimelech and said to him* | το: C om | δυνησωμεθα A B; C δυναμεθα | φασιν: C add ταυτην | δια – σκεπην (Harris Riaud Schaller): A B (Ceriani Kraft) δια την σκεπην την γενομενην σοι εν τη οδω; C δια την σκεπην σου; eth *the protection with which you covered me* || 9 Βαρουχ: A B P arm add και Αβιμελεχ | λεγων: A B λεγοντες | η δυναμις ημων ο θεος ημων κυριε A B; C ο θεος κυριος η δυναμις μου; eth *my strength is God, the Lord* | εκλεκτον: eth om | εκ: C εκ του | παρακαλω και δεομαι C eth (Schaller); A B (Ceriani Kraft) παρακαλουμεν και δεομεθα | της αγαθοτητος: C την αγαθοτητα | ονομα: A B add σου | γνωναι: C add αυτω || 10 του δουλου C eth; A B (Ceriani Kraft) των δουλων | μου C eth; A B ημων | τι θελεις ποιησωμεν: A B τι ποιησωμεν; C εως αν το θελω ποιησω | πως αποστειλω: A B (Ceriani Kraft) πως αποστειλωμεν; C εως αν αποστειλω; eth *and I send* |

each other, they both wept and kissed each other. But when Baruch looked up, he saw the figs protected in the basket. And he lifted up his eyes to heaven and prayed, saying, "There is a God who provides a reward for his holy ones. **3** Prepare yourself, my heart, and be glad and rejoice in your tent, I mean, in your fleshly house, because your sorrow has been transformed into joy. For the Mighty One is coming and he will take you out of your tent, for you have not sinned. **4** Revive, my virginal faith,[7] and believe that you will live. **5** Look at this basket of figs! For behold, they are sixty-six years old, yet they did not shrivel up or begin to stink, but they are still dripping milky sap. **6** The same thing is going to happen to you, my flesh, if you do what has been commanded you by the angel of righteousness. **7** He who preserved the basket of figs, he it is who will again preserve you by his power." **8** When Baruch had said this, he said to Abimelech; "Get up and let us pray that the Lord might make known to us how we might be able to send the message of your protection to Jeremiah in Babylon." **9** And Baruch prayed, saying, "Our power, O God our Lord, (is) the elect light that proceeded from his mouth;[8] I entreat and beg of your goodness, O Great Name that no one can know, **10** hear the voice of your servant and let there be knowledge in my heart. What do you want us to do? How shall I send

---

7. The text transmission is very uncertain, cf. the commentary on this verse.

8. For the difficulty of the phrase τὸ ἐξελθὸν ἐκ στόματος αὐτοῦ, see the commentary.

πρὸς Ἰερεμίαν εἰς Βαβυλῶνα; 11 Ἔτι δὲ προσευχομένου τοῦ Βαροὺχ, ἰδοὺ ἄγγελος Κυρίου ἦλθε, καὶ λέγει τῷ Βαρούχ· 12 Βαρούχ, ὁ σύμβουλος τοῦ φωτὸς, μὴ μεριμνήσῃς τὸ πῶς ἀποστείλῃς πρὸς Ἰερεμίαν· ἔρχεται γὰρ πρός σε ὥρα τοῦ φωτὸς αὔριον ἀετὸς, καὶ σὺ ἐπισκέψῃ πρὸς Ἰερεμίαν. 13 Γράψον οὖν ἐν τῇ ἐπιστολῇ ὅτι, Λάλησον τοῖς υἱοῖς Ἰσραήλ· Ὁ γενόμενος ἐν ὑμῖν ξένος, ἀφορισθήτω, καὶ ποιήσωσι ιε' ἡμέρας· καὶ μετὰ ταῦτα εἰσάξω ὑμᾶς εἰς τὴν πόλιν ὑμῶν, λέγει Κύριος. 14 Ὁ μὴ ἀφοριζόμενος ἐκ τῆς Βαβυλῶνος, ὦ Ἰερεμία, οὐ μὴ εἰσέλθῃ εἰς τὴν πόλιν· καὶ ἐπιτιμῶ αὐτοῖς, τοῦ μὴ ἀποδεχθῆναι αὐτοὺς αὖθις ὑπὸ τῶν Βαβυλωνιτῶν, λέγει Κύριος. 15 Καὶ ταῦτα εἰπὼν ὁ ἄγγελος, ἀπῆλθεν ἀπὸ τοῦ Βαρούχ. 16 Ὁ δὲ Βαροὺχ ἀποστείλας εἰς τὴν ἀγορὰν τῶν ἐθνῶν, ἤνεγκε χάρτην καὶ μέλανα, καὶ ἔγραψεν ἐπιστολὴν περιέχουσαν οὕτως· 17 Βαροὺχ ὁ δοῦλος τοῦ Θεοῦ γράφει τῷ Ἰερεμίᾳ· Ὁ ἐν τῇ αἰχμαλωσίᾳ τῆς Βαβυλῶνος, χαῖρε καὶ ἀγαλλιῶ, ὅτι ὁ Θεὸς οὐκ ἀφῆκεν ἡμᾶς ἐξελθεῖν ἐκ τοῦ σώματος τούτου λυπουμένους διὰ τὴν πόλιν τὴν ἐρημωθεῖσαν καὶ ὑβρισθεῖσαν. 18 Διὰ τοῦτο ἐσπλαγχνίσθη ὁ Κύριος ἐπὶ τῶν δακρύων ἡμῶν, καὶ ἐμνήσθη τῆς διαθήκης, ἧς ἔστησε μετὰ τῶν πατέρων ἡμῶν Ἀβραάμ, καὶ Ἰσαὰκ, καὶ Ἰακώβ. 19 Ἀπέστειλε γὰρ πρός με τὸν ἄγγελον αὐτοῦ, καὶ εἶπέ μοι τοὺς λόγους τούτους, οὓς ἀπέστειλα πρός σε. 20 Οὗτοι οὖν εἰσὶν οἱ λόγοι, οὓς εἶπε Κύριος ὁ Θεὸς Ἰσραήλ, ὁ ἐξαγαγὼν ἡμᾶς ἐκ γῆς Αἰγύπτου, ἐκ τῆς μεγάλης καμίνου· 21 Ὅτι οὐκ ἐφυλάξατε τὰ δικαιώματά μου, ἀλλὰ ὑψώθη ἡ καρδία ὑμῶν, καὶ ἐτραχηλιάσατε ἐνώπιόν μου, ἐθυμώθην καὶ ἐν ὀργῇ παρέδωκα ὑμᾶς τῇ καμίνῳ εἰς Βαβυλῶνα. 22 Ἐὰν οὖν ἀκούσητε τῆς φωνῆς μου, λέγει Κύριος, ἐκ στόματος Ἰερεμίου τοῦ παιδός μου, ὁ ἀκούων, ἀναφέρω αὐτὸν ἐκ τῆς Βαβυλῶνος, ὁ δὲ μὴ ἀκούων, ξένος γενήσεται τῆς Ἰερουσαλὴμ καὶ τῆς Βαβυλῶνος. 23 Δοκιμάσεις δὲ αὐτοὺς

---

(10) Βαβυλωνα: A B P arm (Ceriani Riaud Kraft) add την φασιν ταυτην || 11 Βαρουχ¹: A B add και του Αβιμελεχ | ηλθε: C om | λεγει: C ειπεν | Βαρουχ²: A B (Ceriani Kraft) add απαντας τους λογους τουτους || 12 Βαρουχ C eth; A B (Ceriani Kraft) om | φωτος¹: A B add λεγει | μεριμνησης C eth; A B μεριμνησητε | αποστειλης C eth; A B αποστειλητε | γαρ: C om | προς³: C τον || 13 λαλησον: C ειπατε | ο: C οτι | ξενος: C εξ ενος || 14 ω Ιερεμια: A B (Ceriani Kraft) om | επιτιμω A; B C επετιμων | αυτους C; A B om | υπο: A B om || 15 και: C om | απηλθεν: C ανεχωρησεν || 16 ο δε Βαρουχ – ουτως (Harris Kraft Schaller); A B P arm (Ceriani) αποστειλας δε εις την διασποραν των εθνων ηνεγκεν χαρτην και μελανα και εγραψεν επιστολην περιεχουσαν ουτως; C ο δε Βαρουχ απεστειλεν εις την αγοραν των εθνων και ηνεγκεν χαρτην και μελαν και εγραψεν επιστολην λεγων οτι; eth *and Baruch accompanied him to the street and got some paper and ink and wrote as follows* || 17 ο²: C om; (eth) τω | αγαλλιω A; B αγαλλιου; C αγαλλιασον || 19 απεστειλα A B eth; C αποστελλω || 20 εκ²: C om || 21 εθυμωθην C; A B eth (Ceriani Kraft) om | εν οργη: A B (Ceriani Kraft) add και θυμω; C eth om || 22 ουν: C om | αναφερω C eth; A B αφορισω | της Βαβυλωνος¹: C του λακκου της Βαβυλωνος | γενησεται: A γενηται; C γινεται | και της Βαβυλωνος: A B P arm om; eth *and they will not be in Babylon as people banned from Jerusalem* || 23 δοκιμασεις: A δοκιμασω; B δοκημασει; C eth δοκιμασης |

to Jeremiah in Babylon?" **11** And while Baruch was still praying, behold, an angel of the Lord came and said to Baruch, **12** "Baruch, counselor of the light! Do not be anxious about how you will send to Jeremiah. For tomorrow at dawn an eagle is coming to you and you will send him to Jeremiah. **13** So write in the letter, 'Tell the children of Israel: Let the stranger who comes among you be separated, and let fifteen days pass; and after this I shall lead you into your city, says the Lord. **14** He who is not separated from Babylon, O Jeremiah, shall not come into the city; and I will censure them so that they are not welcomed again by the Babylonians, says the Lord.'" **15** And when the angel had said this, he departed from Baruch. **16** But Baruch sent to the market of the Gentiles, got papyrus and ink, and wrote a letter reading as follows: **17** "Baruch the servant of God writes to Jeremiah, who is in the captivity of Babylon: rejoice and exult since God did not allow us to depart from this body grieving for the city that has been laid waste and suffered outrage. **18** Therefore the Lord had compassion on our tears and remembered the covenant that he established with our fathers Abraham and Isaac and Jacob. **19** For he sent to me his angel, and he told me these words that I am sending to you. **20** These, then, are the words that the Lord, the God of Israel, who led us out of the land of Egypt, out of the big furnace, has spoken. **21** 'Because you did not keep my ordinances but your heart became haughty and you were stubborn in my presence instead, I became angry and in wrath I surrendered you into the furnace in Babylon. **22** If you, therefore, says the Lord, listen to my voice that comes out of the mouth of Jeremiah, my servant, the one who does heed I will bring back out of Babylon, but the one who does not listen will become a stranger to Jerusalem and to Babylon. **23** But you shall test them

ἐκ τοῦ ὕδατος τοῦ Ἰορδάνου· ὁ μὴ ἀκούων φανερὸς γενήσεται· τοῦτο τὸ σημεῖόν ἐστι τῆς μεγάλης σφραγῖδος.

VII 1 Καὶ ἀνέστη Βαροὺχ, καὶ ἐξῆλθεν ἐκ τοῦ μνημείου. **2** Καὶ ἀποκριθεὶς ἀνθρωπίνῃ φωνῇ ὁ ἀετὸς, εἶπε· Χαῖρε, Βαροὺχ, ὁ οἰκονόμος τῆς πίστεως. **3** Καὶ εἶπεν αὐτῷ Βαροὺχ ὅτι, Ἐκλεκτὸς εἶ σὺ ὁ λαλῶν ἐκ πάντων τῶν πετεινῶν τοῦ οὐρανοῦ· ἐκ τῆς γὰρ αὐγῆς τῶν ὀφθαλμῶν δῆλόν ἐστι. **4** Δεῖξόν μοι οὖν, τί ποιεῖς ἐνταῦθα; **5** Καὶ εἶπεν αὐτῷ ὁ ἀετός· Ἀπεστάλην ὧδε, ὅπως πᾶσαν φάσιν ἣν θέλεις, ἀποστείλῃς δι' ἐμοῦ. **6** Καὶ εἶπεν αὐτῷ Βαρούχ· Εἰ δύνασαι σὺ ἐπᾶραι τὴν φάσιν ταύτην τῷ Ἰερεμίᾳ εἰς Βαβυλῶνα; **7** Καὶ εἶπεν αὐτῷ ὁ ἀετός· Εἰς τοῦτο γὰρ καὶ ἀπεστάλην. **8** Καὶ ἄρας Βαροὺχ τὴν ἐπιστολὴν, καὶ δεκαπέντε σῦκα ἐκ τοῦ κοφίνου τοῦ Ἀβιμέλεχ, ἔδησεν εἰς τὸν τράχηλον τοῦ ἀετοῦ, καὶ εἶπεν αὐτῷ· **9** Σοὶ λέγω, βασιλεῦ τῶν πετεινῶν, ἄπελθε ἐν εἰρήνῃ μεθ' ὑγείας, καὶ τὴν φάσιν ἔνεγκόν μοι. **10** Μὴ ὁμοιωθῇς τῷ κόρακι, ὃν ἐξαπέστειλε Νῶε, καὶ οὐκ ἀπεστράφη ἔτι πρὸς αὐτὸν εἰς τὴν κιβωτόν· ἀλλὰ ὁμοιώθητι τῇ περιστερᾷ, ἥτις ἐκ τρίτου φάσιν ἤνεγκε τῷ δικαίῳ· **11** οὕτω καὶ σὺ, ἆρον τὴν καλὴν φάσιν ταύτην τῷ Ἰερεμίᾳ καὶ τοῖς σὺν αὐτῷ, ἵνα εὖ σοι γένηται, ἆρον τὸν χάρτην τοῦτον τῷ λαῷ τῷ ἐκλεκτῷ τοῦ Θεοῦ. **12** Ἐὰν κυκλώσωσί σε πάντα τὰ πετεινὰ τοῦ οὐρανοῦ, καὶ βουλῶνται πολεμῆσαι μετὰ σοῦ, ἀγώνισαι· ὁ Κύριος δῴη σοι δύναμιν. Καὶ μὴ ἐκκλίνῃς εἰς τὰ δεξιὰ, μήτε εἰς τὰ ἀριστερὰ, ἀλλ' ὡς βέλος ὕπαγον ὀρθῶς, οὕτως ἄπελθε ἐν τῇ δυνάμει τοῦ Θεοῦ. **13** Τότε ὁ ἀετὸς ἐπετάσθη, ἔχων τὴν ἐπιστολήν, καὶ ἀπῆλθεν εἰς Βαβυλῶνα, καὶ ἀνεπαύσατο ἐπί τι ξύλον ἔξω τῆς πόλεως

---

(23) γενησεται: C γινεται | το: A B om ||
VII 2 A B eth (Ceriani); C P (arm) και ευρεν τον αετον καθεζομενον εκτος του μνημειου και ειπεν αυτω ο αετος (Kraft και ευρεν τον αετον καθεζομενον εκτος του μνημειου) | πιστεως A B eth; C πολεως || **3** αυτω: C om | συ ο: C om || **4** ουν: C om || **5** ειπεν αυτω: A B om αυτω | απεσταλην A B eth; P add *by the Lord;* C ο θεος (arm *the Lord*) απεστειλεν με | ωδε: A B add προς σε | πασαν φασιν: C προς πασαν φασιν | δι εμου: C με || **6** ειπεν: C λεγει | δυνασαι συ A; B δυνη συ; C δινηση | επαραι: C αραι || **7** ειπεν (Harris v. 6): C λεγει | εις: A B εγω εις | γαρ και: A B om || **8** αυτω: C om || **9** βασιλευ: C ο βασιλευς | πετεινων: C ορνεων | ενεγκον C; A B ενεγκαι || **10** ετι προς αυτον: A B om || **11** φασιν: Ceriani την φασιν after Ιερεμια; τοις συν αυτω A B (Ceriani): C τοις δεσμιοις αυτου; eth *those who are with him from Israel;* (Kraft τοις συν αυτω δεσμιοις) | τον χαρτην τουτον A B; C ταυτην την χαραν; eth *this good news* | εκλεκτω: C και τω εκλεκτω || **12** κυκλωσωσι: A B κυκλωσουσι | και[1]: C eth (Harris) add παντες οι εχθροι της αληθειας | βουλωνται: C (Harris) βουλομενοι | δωη A B eth; C δωση | εις τα δεξια A C; B δεξια | μητε εις τα: A B η | υπαγον ορθως: A υπαγων ορθως; C υπαγων | ουτως: C eth om | απελθε: C υπαγε | θεου: A B P arm (Ceriani Kraft) add και εσται η δοξα κυριου εν παση τη οδω η πορευση || **13** επιστολην: C P arm (Ceriani Kraft) add εν τω τραχηλω αυτου | ανεπαυσατο C eth; A B (Ceriani Kraft) ελθων ανεπαυσατο | τι ξυλον A B; C στυλου; eth *on a column* |

with the waters of the Jordan; the one who does not listen will be exposed. This is the sign of the great seal.'"

7:1 And Baruch got up and went out of the tomb. **2** And the eagle answered in a human voice (and) said, "Hail, Baruch, steward of the faith!" **3** And Baruch said to him, "You, who speak, are chosen from among all the birds of the sky, for this is clear from the gleam of your eyes. **4** So, show me: What are you doing here?" **5** And the eagle said to him, "I was sent here so that you might send by me whatever message you want." **6** And Baruch said to him, "Can you carry this message to Jeremiah in Babylon?" **7** And the eagle said to him, "Indeed, that is what I was sent for." **8** And Baruch took the letter and fifteen figs out of Abimelech's basket, tied (them) to the eagle's neck, and said to him, **9** "To you, king of the birds, I say: Go in peace and good health and deliver the message for me! **10** Do not be like the raven that Noah sent out and that never came back to him in the ark, but be like the dove that the third time brought a message to the righteous one. **11** So, too, do you: Take this good message to Jeremiah and to those who are with him, so that good things may happen to you. Take this papyrus to the chosen people of God! **12** Even if all the birds of the sky surround you and want to fight with you: struggle! May the Lord give you strength. And turn aside neither to the right nor to the left but fly straight as an arrow, and so go in the power of God! **13** Then the eagle flew away carrying the letter and went away to Babylon, and he rested on a post outside the city

εἰς τόπον ἔρημον· ἐσιώπησε δὲ ἕως οὗ διῆλθεν Ἰερεμίας, αὐτὸς καὶ ἄλλοι τινὲς τοῦ λαοῦ· **14** ἐξήρχοντο γὰρ θάψαι νεκρόν· καὶ γὰρ ᾐτήσατο Ἰερεμίας παρὰ τοῦ Ναβουχοδονόσορ λέγων· Δός μοι τόπον, ποῦ θάψω τοὺς νεκροὺς τοῦ λαοῦ μου. Καὶ ἔδωκεν αὐτῷ. **15** Ἀπερχομένων δὲ αὐτῶν καὶ κλαιόντων μετὰ τοῦ νεκροῦ, ἦλθον κατέναντι τοῦ ἀετοῦ· καὶ ἔκραξεν ὁ ἀετὸς λέγων· Σοὶ λέγω, Ἰερεμία ὁ ἐκλεκτὸς τοῦ Θεοῦ, ἄπελθε, σύναξον τὸν λαὸν, καὶ ἔλθωσιν ὧδε, ἵνα ἀκούσωσι τοῦ καλοῦ κηρύγματος, ὃ ἤνεγκά σοι ἀπὸ τοῦ Βαροὺχ καὶ τοῦ Ἀβιμέλεχ. **16** Ἀκούσας δὲ ὁ Ἰερεμίας, ἐδόξασε τὸν Θεόν· καὶ ἀπελθὼν συνῆξε τὸν λαὸν σὺν γυναιξὶ καὶ τέκνοις, καὶ ἦλθεν ὅπου ὁ ἀετός. **17** Καὶ κατῆλθεν ὁ ἀετὸς ἐπὶ τὸν τεθνηκότα, καὶ ἀνέζησε· γέγονε δὲ τοῦτο, ἵνα πιστεύσωσιν. **18** Ἐθαύμασε δὲ πᾶς ὁ λαὸς ἐπὶ τῷ γεγονότι, λέγοντες ὅτι, Μὴ οὗτος ἔστι ὁ Θεὸς ὁ ὀφθεὶς τοῖς πατράσιν ἡμῶν ἐν τῇ ἐρήμῳ διὰ Μωϋσέως, καὶ νῦν ἐφάνη ἡμῖν διὰ τοῦ ἀετοῦ τούτου; **19** Καὶ εἶπεν ὁ ἀετὸς τῷ Ἰερεμία, Δεῦρο λῦσον τὴν ἐπιστολὴν ταύτην, καὶ ἀνάγνωθι αὐτὴν τῷ λαῷ. Λύσας οὖν τὴν ἐπιστολὴν, ἀνέγνω τῷ λαῷ. **20** Ἀκούσας οὖν ὁ λαὸς, ἔκλαυσαν, καὶ ἐπέθηκαν χοῦν ἐπὶ τὴν κεφαλὴν αὐτῶν· καὶ ἔλεγον τῷ Ἰερεμίᾳ· **21** Σῶσον ἡμᾶς καὶ ἀπάγγειλον ἡμῖν, τί ποιήσωμεν, ἵνα εἰσέλθωμεν πάλιν εἰς τὴν πόλιν ἡμῶν; **22** Ἀποκριθεὶς δὲ Ἰερεμίας εἶπεν αὐτοῖς· Πάντα ὅσα ἐκ τῆς ἐπιστολῆς ἠκούσατε, φυλάξατε· καὶ εἰσάξει ἡμᾶς εἰς τὴν πόλιν ἡμῶν. **23** Ἔγραψε δὲ καὶ ἐπιστολὴν ὁ

---

(13) τοπον ερημον: eth *a piece of untouched land* | ου διηλθεν: C αν παρελθη | αυτος – εξερχοντο (v. 14): A B αυτος γαρ και ο λαος εξηρχοντο; C αυτος γαρ και αλλοι τινες του λαου απηρχοντο γαρ || **14** νεκρον: A B (Ceriani Kraft) add εξω της πολεως | και γαρ ητησατο: C ητησατο γαρ | του Ναβουχοδονοσορ: A B (Ceriani Kraft) του βασιλεως Ναβουχοδονοσορ | που C eth; A B οπως | αυτω: A B P arm (Ceriani Kraft) add ο βασιλευς || **15** κατεναντι: C εναντιον | αετος: arm eth (Kraft) add μεγαλη φωνη; P *in a human voice* | σοι λεγω A B eth; C om | λαον: C eth (Harris) add απαντα | ελθωσιν ωδε: A B (Ceriani Kraft) ελθε ενταυθα | του καλου κηρυγματος (C add του θεου) ο ηνεγκα C eth; A B P arm (Ceriani Kraft) επιστολης ης ηνεγκα; C του καλου κηρυγματος του θεου ο ηνεγκα | του Βαρουχ και του Αβιμελεχ: C Βαρουχ και Αβιμελεχ || **17** και κατηλθεν ο αετος: C om | ανεζησε: A B add και ανεστη | γεγονε δε τουτο A B; C τουτο δε εγενετο; eth *and this he did* || **18** μη ουτος εστι ο θεος C; A B εστιν θεος; eth *perhaps this is the God* | και νυν – τουτου: A B P arm (Kraft); C eth (Harris) και εποιησεν εαυτον εν σχηματι αετου και εφανη ημιν δια του μεγαλου αετου τουτου; Ceriani και εφανη ημιν δια του αετου || **19** τω Ιερεμια: A B σοι λεγω Ιερεμια | αυτην τω λαω C eth; A B εις τα ωτα του λαου | ανεγνω: C add αυτην || **20** ακουσας ουν C; A B ακουσαντες δε πας | εκλαυσαν A B eth; C εκλαυσεν | επεθηκαν A B eth; C επεθηκεν | την κεφαλην αυτων eth; A B (Ceriani Kraft) τας κεφαλας αυτων; C την κεφαλην αυτου || **21** σωσον ημας και C P eth; A B arm om | ινα: C πως | παλιν: C om || **22** αποκριθεις δε Ιερεμιας ειπεν αυτοις C; A B P arm και ειπεν προς αυτους; eth *and Jeremiah rose and said to them* | εκ της επιστολης: A B P arm om | ηκουσατε: C om | ημας: A B (Ceriani Kraft) add κυριος || **23–26** The text of A B arm (Ceriani) varies from C (P) eth (Harris Kraft), which is preferred here. mss A B run as follows: εγραψε δε Ιερεμιας επιστολην εις Ιερουσαλημ προς Βαρουχ και Αβιμελεχ ενωπιον παντος του λαου τας θλιψεις τας (B om) γινομενας εις αυτους το πως παρεληφθησαν υπο του βασιλεως των Χαλδαιων και το πως εκαστος τον πατερα

in a deserted place. And he kept silent until Jeremiah passed through, he himself and some others of the people. **14** For they were coming out to bury a dead person, because Jeremiah had petitioned Nebuchadnezzar, saying, "Grant me a place where I may bury my people's dead!" And he granted (it) to him. **15** And as they were going out with the body and weeping, they came opposite the eagle. And the eagle cried out, saying, "I say to you, Jeremiah, the chosen one of God: go, gather together the people and let them come here to listen to the good message that I have brought to you from Baruch and Abimelech." **16** Upon hearing this, Jeremiah praised God. And he went and gathered the people together with their wives and children, and he came to where the eagle was. **17** And the eagle lit on the deceased and he revived. This happened so that they might believe. **18** All the people were astonished over what had happened, saying: "This is not the God who appeared to our fathers in the desert through Moses, is it, and now has appeared to us by means of this eagle?" **19** And the eagle said to Jeremiah, "Come, untie this letter and read it to the people." So he untied the letter and read it to the people. **20** And when the people heard (it), they wept and put dust on their heads and said to Jeremiah, **21** "Save us and tell us what we have to do in order to enter our city again!" **22** And Jeremiah answered and said to them, "Obey whatever you have heard from this letter, and (the Lord) will lead us into our city." **23** And Jeremiah too wrote a letter

Ἰερεμίας πρὸς Βαροὺχ, οὕτως λέγων· Υἱέ μου ἀγαπητέ, μὴ ἀμελήσῃς ἐν ταῖς προσευχαῖς σου δεόμενος ὑπὲρ ἡμῶν ὅπως κατευοδεύσῃ τὴν ὁδὸν ἡμῶν, ἄχρις ἂν ἐξέλθωμεν ἐκ τῶν προσταγμάτων τοῦ ἀνόμου βασιλέως τούτου· δίκαιος γὰρ εὑρέθης ἐνάντιον αὐτοῦ καὶ οὐκ ἔασέν σε εἰσελθεῖν ἐνταῦθα μεθ' ἡμῶν, ὅπως μὴ ἴδῃς τὴν κάκωσιν τὴν γενομένην τῷ λαῷ ὑπὸ τῶν Βαβυλωνίων· **24** ὥσπερ γὰρ πατὴρ, υἱὸν μονογενῆ ἔχων, τούτου δὲ παραδοθέντος εἰς τιμωρίαν· οἱ οὖν ἰδόντες τὸν πατέρα αὐτοῦ, καὶ παραμυθούμενοι αὐτόν, σκέπουσιν τὸ πρόσωπον αὐτοῦ, ἵνα μὴ ἴδῃ πῶς τιμωρεῖται αὐτὸς ὁ υἱὸς καὶ πλείονα φθαρῇ ἀπὸ τῆς λύπης· οὕτως γάρ σε ἐλέησεν ὁ Θεὸς καὶ οὐκ ἔασέν σε ἐλθεῖν εἰς Βαβυλῶνα· ἵνα μὴ ἴδῃς τὴν κάκωσιν τοῦ λαοῦ· ἀφ' ἧς γὰρ εἰσήλθομεν ἐνταῦθα, οὐκ ἐπαύσατο ἡ λύπη ἀφ' ἡμῶν, ἑξήκοντα καὶ ἓξ ἔτη σήμερον. **25** Πολλάκις γὰρ ἐξερχόμενος ηὕρισκον ἐκ τοῦ λαοῦ κρεμαμένους ὑπὸ Ναβουχοδονόσορ βασιλέως, κλαίοντας καὶ λέγοντας, Ἐλέησον ἡμᾶς, ὁ θεὸς Ζάρ. **26** Ἀκούων ταῦτα, ἐλυπούμην καὶ ἔκλαιον δισσὸν κλαυθμόν· οὐ μόνον ὅτι ἐκρέμαντο, ἀλλ' ὅτι ἐπεκαλοῦντο θεὸν ἀλλότριον· λέγοντες, Ἐλέησον ἡμᾶς. Ἐμνημόνευον δὲ ἡμέρας ἑορτῆς ἃς ἐποιοῦμεν ἐν Ἰερουσαλὴμ πρὸ τοῦ ἡμᾶς αἰχμαλωτευθῆναι. **27** Καὶ μνησκόμενος ἐστέναζον, καὶ ἐπέστρεφον εἰς τὸν οἶκόν μου ὀδυνώμενος καὶ κλαίων. **28** Νῦν οὖν δεήθητι, εἰς τὸν τόπον ὅπου εἶ, σὺ καὶ Ἀβιμέλεχ, ὑπὲρ τοῦ λαοῦ τούτου, ὅπως εἰσακούσωσιν τῆς φωνῆς μου καὶ τῶν κριμάτων τοῦ στόματός μου καὶ ἐξέλθωμεν ἐντεῦθεν. **29** Λέγω γάρ σοι ὅτι, ὅλον τὸν χρόνον ὃν ἐποιήσαμεν ἐνταῦθα, κατέχουσιν ἡμᾶς λέγοντες ὅτι, Εἴπατε ἡμῖν ᾠδὴν ἐκ τῶν ᾠδῶν Σιών, καὶ τὴν ᾠδὴν τοῦ Θεοῦ ὑμῶν. Καὶ ἀντελέγομεν αὐτοῖς, Πῶς ᾄσωμεν ὑμῖν ἐπὶ γῆς ἀλλοτρίας ὄντες; **30** Καὶ μετὰ ταῦτα ἔδησε τὴν ἐπιστολὴν εἰς τὸν τράχηλον τοῦ ἀετοῦ λέγων, Ἄπελθε ἐν εἰρήνῃ, ἐπισκέψηται Κύριος ἀμφοτέρους.

αυτου εθεωρει δεσμευομενον και πατηρ τεκνον παραδοθεν (B παραδοθεντα) εις τιμωριαν οι δε θελοντες παραμυθησασθαι τον πατερα αυτου εσκεπον το προσωπον αυτου ινα μη ιδη τον υιον αυτου τιμωρουμενον και ο θεος εσκεπασεν σε και Αβιμελεχ ινα μη ιδηται ημας τιμωρουμενους || **23** κατευοδευση: C (Kraft) κατευοδοση | δικαιος γαρ ευρεθης: C δικαιοι γαρ ευρεθησαν; eth *but you found justice before God* | μεθ ημων (eth); C (Kraft) om || **24** φθαρη: C φθαρει | ουτως: C ουτος | ενταυθα C (Kraft); eth (Harris Schaller) εις την πολιν ταυτην || **25** κρεμαμενους: C κρεμμαμενους | Ζαρ eth: C L Σαβαωθ; eth[b] *Zör*, eth[b(mg)] *Sorot*, eth[c] *Sarot* || **27** οδυνωμενος eth; A B οδυρομενος || **28** νυν ουν δεηθητι C eth; A B δεηθητι ουν | εις τον τοπον οπου ει C eth arm (*where you are*); A B P (Ceriani) om | εισακουσωσιν – μου[2] C eth; A B P arm (Ceriani) εισακουσθη η δεησις υμων (P arm ημων); arm add *before the Lord* | κριματων: eth *the word* | και εξελθωμεν εντευθεν A B; C εξελθωσιν ενταυθα || **29** ολον: A B om | κατεχουσιν ημας C eth; A B ελεγον | και την: eth *new* (καινην) | υμων: B ημων | αντελεγομεν A B (Ceriani); C λεγωμεν (Kraft λεγομεν) | υμιν C eth; A B την ωδην κυριου || **30** αετου: A B (Ceriani Kraft) add Ιερεμιας | κυριος αμφοτερους A B (Ceriani Harris); C υμας αμφοτερους ο κυριος (Kraft ημας αμφοτερους ο κυριος) ||

to Baruch saying the following, "My beloved son, do not be negligent in your prayers beseeching (God) on our behalf, that he might direct our way until we get out of the jurisdiction of this lawless king. For you have been found righteous before him, and he did not let you come in here with us lest you see the affliction that has fallen upon the people at the hands of the Babylonians. **24** For it is like a father who has (only) one son who is handed over for punishment. Those, then, who see his father and try to console him, cover his face lest he sees how (his) very (own) son is punished and is devastated even more by (his) sorrow. For thus God has had mercy on you and did not let you enter Babylon lest you see the affliction of the people. For grief has not left us since we entered this place sixty-six years ago today. **25** For frequently as I went out (of the city) I found (some) of the people hung up by King Nebuchadnezzar, weeping and crying, 'Have mercy on us, God Zar!' **26** When I heard that I would grieve and cry a twofold lamentation, not only because they were hung up but because they were calling on a foreign god, saying, 'Have mercy on us!' But I remembered the day of the festival that we celebrated in Jerusalem before we were taken captive.[9] **27** And as I remembered, I groaned and returned to my house suffering pains and weeping. **28** Now, then, pray in the place where you are, you and Abimelech, that this people might listen to my voice and to the decrees of my mouth, so that we may get out of here. **29** For I tell you: All the time that we have spent here, they prevented us from leaving, saying: 'Sing for us a song of the songs of Zion, the song of your God!' And we would reply to them, 'How shall we sing for you while we are in a foreign country?'" **30** And after these things he tied the letter to the eagle's neck, saying, "Go in peace and may the Lord watch over both (of you)."

---

9. Manuscripts A and B have a different text in vv. 23–26: "And Jeremiah wrote a letter to Jerusalem to Baruch and Abimelech in the presence of the entire people, concerning the afflictions that had come over them, how they were taken captive by the king of the Chaldeans and how each one saw his father bound, and each father saw his child subjected to punishment. But those who wished to comfort his father covered his face, that he might not see his son punished. And God has covered you and Abimelech, that you might not see us punished." Cf. Herzer, *Paralipomena Jeremiae*, 17 n. 80.

31 Καὶ ἐπετάσθη ὁ ἀετὸς, καὶ ἤνεγκεν τὴν ἐπιστολὴν καὶ ἔδωκε τῷ Βαρούχ. Καὶ λύσας ἀνέγνω, καὶ κατεφίλησεν αὐτήν, καὶ ἔκλαυσε ἀκούσας διὰ τὰς λύπας καὶ τὰς κακώσεις τοῦ λαοῦ. **32** Ἰερεμίας δὲ ἄρας τὰ σῦκα, διέδωκε τοῖς νοσοῦσι τοῦ λαοῦ. Καὶ ἔμεινε διδάσκων αὐτοὺς τοῦ ἀπέχεσθαι ἐκ τῶν ἀλισγημάτων τῶν ἐθνῶν τῆς Βαβυλῶνος.

VIII 1 Ἐγένετο δὲ ἡ ἡμέρα, ἐν ᾗ ἐξέφερε ὁ Θεὸς τὸν λαὸν ἐκ Βαβυλῶνος· **2** Καὶ εἶπεν ὁ Κύριος πρὸς Ἰερεμίαν· Ἀνάστηθι, σὺ καὶ ὁ λαός, καὶ δεῦτε ἐπὶ τὸν Ἰορδάνην, καὶ ἐρεῖς τῷ λαῷ· Ὁ θέλων τὸν Κύριον καταλειψάτω τὰ ἔργα τῆς Βαβυλῶνος, καὶ τοὺς ἄρρενας τοὺς λαβόντας ἐξ αὐτῶν γυναῖκας, καὶ τὰς γυναῖκας τὰς λαβούσας ἐξ αὐτῶν ἄνδρας. **3** Καὶ διαπεράσωσιν οἱ ἀκούοντές σου, καὶ ἆρον αὐτοὺς εἰς Ἰερουσαλήμ· τοὺς δὲ μὴ ἀκούοντάς σου, μὴ εἰσαγάγῃς αὐτοὺς εἰς αὐτήν. **4** Ἰερεμίας δὲ ἐλάλησεν αὐτοῖς τὰ ῥήματα ταῦτα· καὶ ἀναστάντες ἦλθον ἐπὶ τὸν Ἰορδάνην τοῦ περᾶσαι, λέγων αὐτοῖς τὰ ῥήματα, ἃ εἶπε Κύριος πρὸς αὐτόν. Καὶ τὸ ἥμισυ τῶν γαμησάντων ἐξ αὐτῶν οὐκ ἠθέλησαν ἀκοῦσαι τοῦ Ἰερεμίου, ἀλλ᾽ εἶπον

---

31 επετασθη A B eth; C om | αετος: A (Ceriani Kraft) add και ηλθεν εις Ιερουσαλεμ; B add και ηλθεν Ιερουσαλεμ | και ηνεγκεν την επιστολην και εδωκε τω Βαρουχ: A B (Ceriani) και εδωκε την επιστολην Βαρουχ (Kraft και εδωκε την επιστολην τω Βαρουχ); C και ηνεγκεν ο αετος την επιστολην και εδωκε τω Βαρουχ; eth om και εδωκε | εκλαυσε A B eth; C εμεινε κλαιων | του λαου A B eth; C αυτων || **32** διεδωκε A B; C εδωκε | διδασκων: C ενδιδασκων | αλισγηματων B P (arm); A αλγηματων; C πραγματων; eth *the doing and bustling* ||
VIII 1 ο θεος C eth; A B P arm (Ceriani Kraft) κυριος | λαον: A B add αυτου || **2** ο κυριος A B C eth; P arm ο θεος | προς Ιερεμιαν (Harris v. 1) A B; C τω Ιερεμια | Ιερεμιαν: A B add λεγων | επι τον: A προς τον | τα εργα: C eth add των εθνων (cf. 7:32) | λαβοντας A B; C γαμησαντας | λαβουσας A B; C γαμησαντας || **3** διαπερασωσιν A B; C περασωσιν | σου[1]: B σοι | τους δε μη ακουοντας A B; C οι δε μη ακουοντες | εισαγαγης A B; C ενεγκης | εις αυτην C eth; A B (Ceriani Kraft) εκει || **4** αυτοις[1] C eth; A B (Ceriani Kraft) προς τον λαον | αναστατες ηλθον A B; C ηνεγκεν αυτους | κυριος προς αυτον: C αυτω ο κυριος | εξ αυτων: after this point ms C ends as follows: αρω και στησω αυτοις διαθηκην αιωνιον του ειναι με αυτοις εις θεον και αυτοι εσονται μοι εις λαον και ου κινησω τον λαον μου Ισραηλ απο της γης ης εδωκα αυτοις κυριε παντοκρατωρ ο θεος Ισραηλ ψυχη εν στενοις και πνευμα ακηδιον εκεκραγεν προς σε ακουσον κυριε και ελεησον οτι θεος ελεων και ελεησον οτι αμαρτανωμεν εναντιον σου οτι σοι καθημενος τον αιωνα ημεις απολλυμενοι τον αιωνα κυριε παντοκρατωρ ο θεος Ισραηλ ακουσον δη της προσευχης των τεθνηκοτων Ισραηλ και υιων των αμαρτανοντων εναντιον σου οι ουκ ηκουσαν της φωνης θεου αυτων και εκολληθησαν ημιν τα κακα μη μνησθης (μνησθεις) αδικιων πατερων ημων αλλα μνησθητι χειρος σου και ονοματος σου εν τω καιρω τουτω εγενετο δε μετα την συμπληρωσιν των εβδομηκοντα ετων μεχρι του βασιλευσαι Περσας εν τω πρωτω ετει (ετη) Κυρου βασιλεως Περσων του τελεσθηναι λογον κυριου απο στοματος Ιερεμιου εξηγειρεν κυριος το πνευμα Κυρου βασιλεως Περσων και παρηγγειλεν φωνην εν παση τη βασιλεια αυτου και αμα διαγραπτων λεγει ταδε λεγει Κυρος (K.) ο βασιλευς Περσων πασας τας βασιλειας της γης (om) εδωκεν μοι κυριος ο θεος του ουρανου και αυτος επεσκεψατο επ εμε του οικοδομησαι αυτω (αυτον) οικον εν Ιερουσαλημ

31 And the eagle flew away and carried the letter and gave it to Baruch. And having untied it, he read it and kissed it and wept when he heard about the sorrows and afflictions of the people. **32** But Jeremiah took the figs (and) distributed them to the sick among the people. And he continued to teach them to abstain from the defilement of the Gentiles of Babylon.

8:1 And the day came when God brought the people out of Babylon. **2** And the Lord said to Jeremiah, "Get up, you and the people, and come to the Jordan. And you shall say to the people, 'Let everyone who desires the Lord forsake the works of Babylon, as well as the men who took wives from them and the women who took husbands from them as well!' **3** And let those who heed you cross over; bring them to Jerusalem. But as for those who do not heed you, do not lead them into it." **4** And Jeremiah told them these words. And they arose and came to the Jordan to cross over, and he (again) told them the words that the Lord had spoken to him. And half of those who had married[10] from among them did not wish to listen to Jeremiah but said

---

10. For the quite different reading of ms C, see the commentary on chapter 8, note 7.

πρὸς αὐτόν· Οὐ μὴ καταλείψωμεν τὰς γυναῖκας ἡμῶν εἰς τὸν αἰῶνα· ἀλλ' ὑποστρέφωμεν αὐτὰς μεθ' ἡμῶν εἰς τὴν πόλιν ἡμῶν. **5** Ἐπέρασαν οὖν τὸν Ἰορδάνην, καὶ ἦλθον εἰς Ἰερουσαλήμ. Καὶ ἔστη Ἰερεμίας καὶ Βαροὺχ καὶ Ἀβιμέλεχ, λέγοντες ὅτι, Πᾶς ἄνθρωπος κοινῶν Βαβυλωνίταις οὐ μὴ εἰσέλθῃ εἰς τὴν πόλιν ταύτην. **6** Καὶ εἶπον πρὸς αὐτούς· Ἀναστάντες ὑποστρέψωμεν εἰς Βαβυλῶνα εἰς τὸν τόπον ἡμῶν. Καὶ ἐπορεύθησαν. **7** Ἐλθόντων δὲ αὐτῶν εἰς Βαβυλῶνα, ἐξῆλθον οἱ Βαβυλωνῖται εἰς συνάντησιν αὐτῶν λέγωντες· Οὐ μὴ εἰσέλθητε εἰς τὴν πόλιν ἡμῶν, ὅτι ἐμισήσατε ἡμᾶς, καὶ κρυφῇ ἐξήλθετε ἀφ' ἡμῶν· διὰ τοῦτο οὐκ εἰσελεύσεσθε πρὸς ἡμᾶς. Ὅρκῳ γὰρ ὡρκίσαμεν ἀλλήλους κατὰ τοῦ ὀνόματος τοῦ θεοῦ ἡμῶν, μήτε ὑμᾶς μήτε τέκνα ὑμῶν δέξασθαι, ἐπειδὴ κρυφῇ ἐξήλθετε ἀφ' ἡμῶν. **8** Καὶ ἐπιγνόντες ὑπέστρεψαν· καὶ ἦλθον εἰς τόπον ἔρημον μακρόθεν τῆς Ἰερουσαλὴμ, καὶ ᾠκοδόμησαν ἑαυτοῖς πόλιν, καὶ ἐπωνόμασαν τὸ ὄνομα αὐτῆς Σαμάρειαν. **9** Ἀπέστειλε δὲ πρὸς αὐτοὺς Ἰερεμίας λέγων· Μετανοήσατε· ἔρχεται γὰρ ἄγγελος τῆς δικαιοσύνης, καὶ εἰσάξει ὑμᾶς εἰς τὸν τόπον ὑμῶν τὸν ὑψηλόν.

IX 1 Ἔμειναν δὲ οἱ τοῦ Ἰερεμίου, χαίροντες καὶ ἀναφέροντες θυσίαν ὑπὲρ τοῦ λαοῦ ἐννέα ἡμέρας. **2** Τῇ δὲ δεκάτῃ ἀνήνεγκεν Ἰερεμίας μόνος

τη εν τη Ιουδαια ητις ουν εστιν εκ του εθνους αυτου εστω ο κυριος αυτου μετα αυτου και αναβας εις την Ιερουσαλημ την (τηνι) εν τη Ιουδαια οικοδομειτω (οκοδομιτω) τον οικον του θεου Ισραηλ ουτος (ουτως) ο κυριος ο κατασκηνωσας εν Ιερουσαλημ και ο βασιλευς Κυρος εξηνεγκεν τα αγια σκευη (σκευει) του κυριου α μετηγαγεν Ναβουχοδονοσωρ εξ Ιερουσαλημ και ... (απερησατω) αυτα εν τω ειδωλιω αυτου εξηνεγκεν τα παντα Κυρος ο βασιλευς Περσων και παρεδωκεν αυτα Μιθριδατη (Μηθρηδατη) τω εαυτου γαζοφυλακι (γαζοφυλακη) δια τουτου δε παρεδοθησαν Σαραβαρω προστατη της Ιουδαιας αμα Ζοροβαβελ ος (ως) και ητησατο επι Δαριου βασιλεως Περσων την οικοδομην του ναου ην γαρ κωλυσας επι τον Αρταξερξου χρονον ως ιστορησε Εσδρας τω δευτερω ετει (ετη) παραγενομενος εις το ιερον του θεου εις Ιερουσαλημ μηνος δευτερου ηρξατο Ζοροβαβελ ο του Ραθαληλ και Ιησους ο του Ιωσεδεκα και οι αδελφοι αυτων και οι ιερεις και οι Λευιται και παντες οι παραγενομενοι εκ της αιχμαλωσιας εις Ιερουσαλημ και εθεμελιωσαν τον οικον του θεου τη νουμηνια του δευτερου μηνος εν τω ελθειν εις την Ιουδαιαν και Ιερουσαλημ προφητευοντων Αγγεου και Ζαχαριου υιου Αδδων τελευταιων (τελευτων) προφητων ανεβη δε ο Εσδρας εκ Βαβυλωνος ως γραμματευς ευφυης ων εν τω Μωυσεως νομω ος (ως) και επιστημην πολλην ειχεν τω διδασκειν αυτον (αυτω) απαντα τον λαον τα δικαιωματα και τα κριματα επι τον Αρταξερξου χρονον και εποιησαν εγκαινια του οικου του θεου υμνουντες και ευλογουντες τω κυριω επι τη εγερσει του οικου του θεου | εις την πολιν ημων (eth); A B P arm εις Βαβυλωνα || **5** κοινων: B κοινωνων | ταυτην: eth ημων || **6** και ειπον: eth add *who would have married a woman* | αυτούς: Harris αυτούς | εις τον τοπον ημων: eth om | επορευθησαν: eth add *and they turned around* || **7** Ελθοντων δε αυτων εις Βαβυλωνα: eth *when the people of Babylon saw them* | ου μη – ημων[1]: eth om | εμισησατε: eth add *before* | προς ημας: eth *into our city* | υψηλον: P arm add *but they were not willing* (arm *did not listen*) ||
IX 1 οι του Ιερεμιου: eth om | εννεα: eth *seven* (επτα) ||

to him: "We will never ever forsake our wives; rather, let them join us in our return into our city." **5** So they crossed the Jordan and came to Jerusalem. And Jeremiah arose, Baruch and Abimelech as well, saying, "No one married to Babylonian women will enter this city!" **6** And they said to themselves, "Let us arise and return to Babylon, to our place." And they departed. **7** But when they arrived at Babylon, the Babylonians came out to meet them, saying, "You shall not enter our city! For you hated us and went away from us secretly. Therefore you shall not come in to us. For we have sworn an oath to each other by the name of our god to receive neither you nor your children because you went away from us secretly." **8** And upon learning this, they turned back and came to a deserted place far from Jerusalem, and they built a city for themselves and called its name Samaria. **9** But Jeremiah sent to them, saying, "Repent, because the angel of righteousness is coming, and he will lead you to your exalted place."

9:1 Those who were with Jeremiah remained, rejoicing and offering sacrifice for the people for nine days. **2** But on the tenth day Jeremiah alone offered

θυσίαν, καὶ ηὔξατο εὐχὴν λέγων· **3** Ἅγιος, ἅγιος, ἅγιος· τὸ θυμίαμα τῶν δένδρων τῶν ζώντων, τὸ φῶς τὸ ἀληθινὸν τὸ φωτίζον με, ἕως οὗ ἀναληφθῶ πρός σέ. Περὶ τῆς φωνῆς τῆς γλυκείας τῶν δύο Σεραφὶμ **4** παρακαλῶ, ὑπὲρ ἄλλης εὐωδίας θυμιάματος· **5** καὶ ἡ μελέτη μου Μιχαὴλ ὁ ἀρχάγγελος τῆς δικαιοσύνης, ἕως ἂν εἰσενέγκῃ τοὺς δικαίους. **6** Παρακαλῶ σε, Κύριε παντοκράτωρ πάσης κτίσεως, ὁ ἀγέννητος καὶ ἀπερινόητος, ᾧ πᾶσα κτίσις κέκρυπται ἐν αὐτῷ πρὸ τοῦ ταῦτα γενέσθαι. **7** Ταῦτα λέγοντος τοῦ Ἰερεμίου, καὶ ἱσταμένου ἐν τῷ θυσιαστηρίῳ μετὰ Βαροὺχ καὶ Ἀβιμέλεχ, ἐγένετο ὡς εἷς τῶν παραδιδόντων τὴν ψυχὴν αὐτοῦ. **8** Καὶ ἔμειναν Βαροὺχ καὶ Ἀβιμέλεχ κλαίοντες, καὶ κράζοντες μεγάλῃ τῇ φωνῇ ὅτι, Ὁ πατὴρ ἡμῶν Ἰερεμίας κατέλιπεν ἡμᾶς, ὁ ἱερεὺς τοῦ Θεοῦ, καὶ ἀπῆλθεν. **9** Ἤκουσε δὲ πᾶς ὁ λαὸς τοῦ κλαυθμοῦ αὐτῶν, καὶ ἔδραμον ἐπ' αὐτοὺς πάντες, καὶ εἶδον Ἰερεμίαν ἀνακείμενον χαμαὶ τεθνηκότα· καὶ διέρρηξαν τὰ ἱμάτια αὐτῶν, καὶ ἐπέθηκαν χοῦν ἐπὶ τὰς κεφαλὰς αὐτῶν, καὶ ἔκλαυσαν κλαυθμὸν πικρόν. **10** Καὶ μετὰ ταῦτα ἡτοίμασαν ἑαυτοὺς, ἵνα κηδεύσωσιν αὐτόν. **11** Καὶ ἰδοὺ φωνὴ ἦλθε λέγουσα· Μὴ κηδεύετε τὸν ἔτι ζῶντα· ὅτι ἡ ψυχὴ αὐτοῦ εἰσέρχεται εἰς τὸ σῶμα αὐτοῦ πάλιν. **12** Καὶ ἀκούσαντες τῆς φωνῆς, οὐκ ἐκήδευσαν αὐτόν, ἀλλ' ἔμειναν περικύκλῳ τοῦ σκηνώματος αὐτοῦ ἡμέρας τρεῖς, λέγοντες καὶ ἀποροῦντες, ποίᾳ ὥρᾳ μέλλει ἀναστῆναι. **13** Μετὰ δὲ τρεῖς ἡμέρας εἰσῆλθεν ἡ ψυχὴ αὐτοῦ εἰς τὸ σῶμα αὐτοῦ· καὶ ἐπῆρε τὴν φωνὴν αὐτοῦ ἐν μέσῳ πάντων, καὶ εἶπε· Δοξάσατε τὸν Θεόν, πάντες δοξάσατε τὸν Θεόν, καὶ τὸν Υἱὸν τοῦ Θεοῦ ἐξυπνίζοντα ἡμᾶς Ἰησοῦν Χριστόν, τὸ φῶς τῶν αἰώνων πάντων, ὁ ἄσβεστος λύχνος, ἡ ζωὴ τῆς πίστεως. **14** Γίνεται δὲ μετὰ τοὺς καιροὺς τούτους ἄλλα ἔτη τετρακόσια ἑβδομηκονταεπτά, καὶ ἔρχεται εἰς τὴν γῆν· καὶ τὸ δένδρον τῆς ζωῆς τὸ ἐν μέσῳ τοῦ παραδείσου φυτευθὲν ποιήσει πάντα τὰ δένδρα

---

3 το θυμιαμα – ζωντων: eth *a pleasing fragrance for all humans* | προς σε: arm P (Kraft) περι του ελεως σου παρακαλω; eth *I implore you for your people and ask you* || **4** παρακαλω: P arm (eth) *for your mercy* (eth *people*) *I beg you* | παρακαλω υπερ – θυμιαματος: eth *and for the incense of the Cherubim* | δυο: arm *holy*; eth om | υπερ: B περι || **5** eth *I beg you that in any case Michael, who sings well, who is the angel of justice, may keep the doors of justice open until they enter in* | δικαιοσυνης: P (Kraft) add ο ανοιγων τας πυλας τοις δικαιοις || **6** κυριε: B om | κτισις (eth Schaller); A B P arm (Kraft Harris) κρισις | κυριε – γενεσθαι: eth *Lord of all and Lord who holds everything, who created everything, who reveals himself, who was not born, who has completed everything, and in whom the whole creation has been hidden before the things had been made in the hidden* || **7** ταυτα – Ιερεμιου: eth *and this he prayed and as he finished his prayer* || **8** και εμειναν: eth *and Baruch and Abimelech soon fell down* | φωνη: P eth (Kraft) add ουαι ημων || **11** κηδευετε: B κηδευσατε; eth *wrapped him not in linen* || **12** εμειναν – αναστηναι: eth *sat waiting for him three days until his soul returned in his body* || **13** μετα – αυτου³: eth *and his voice sounded* | θεον¹: P eth (Kraft) add εν μια φωνη | θεον²: eth *Christ* (χριστον) | εξυπνιζοντα: eth *awaken and judge* || **14** ετη τετρακοσια εβδομηκονταεπτα A B; P 377 years; eth 303/330/333 *weeks of days*; arm 275/375; slav 307/677/387 | και το δενδρον (eth); A B P arm των δενδρων | φυτευθεν: eth *and was not planted* |

sacrifice and prayed, saying, **3** "Holy, holy, holy, incense of the living trees, true light that enlightens me until I be lifted up to you. For the sweet voice of the two seraphim **4** I beg you, for another fragrance of incense; **5** I meditate on Michael, the archangel of righteousness, until he leads in the righteous. **6** I beg you, Lord Almighty of all creation, unbegotten and incomprehensible, in whom all creation[11] was hidden before these things came into existence." **7** While Jeremiah was saying this and was standing with Baruch and Abimelech at the altar, he became like one of those who had died.[12] **8** And Baruch and Abimelech kept weeping and crying out in a loud voice, "Our father Jeremiah, the priest of God, has left us behind and gone away." **9** And all the people heard their lamentation, and they all ran to them and saw Jeremiah lying dead on the ground. And they tore their garments and put dust on their heads and wept bitterly. **10** And after this they prepared themselves in order to bury him. **11** And, behold, there came a voice, saying, "Do not bury the one who is still alive, for his soul is entering his body again." **12** And when they heard the voice, they did not bury him but stayed around his tent for three days, talking and being at a loss as to when he would arise. **13** And after three days his soul entered his body. And he raised his voice in the midst of them all and said, "Glorify God, all glorify God and the Son of God who awakens us, Jesus Christ, the light of all ages, the inextinguishable lamp, the life of faith. **14** But after these times, 477 years more will elapse, and then (he) will come to the earth. And the tree of life, planted in the midst of paradise, will cause all the fruitless trees

---

11. This reading is highly disputed, cf. the commentary on this verse.
12. Literally and metaphorically: "delivered his soul"; see the commentary on this verse.

τὰ ἄκαρπα ποιῆσαι καρπὸν, καὶ αὐξηθήσονται, καὶ βλαστήσουσι. **15** Καὶ τὰ βεβλαστηκότα, καὶ μεγαλαυχοῦντα, καὶ λέγοντα, Ἐδώκαμεν τὸ τέλος ἡμῶν τῷ ἀέρι· ποιήσει αὐτὰ ξηρανθῆναι μετὰ τοῦ ὕψους τῶν κλάδων αὐτῶν· καὶ ποιήσει αὐτὰ κριθῆναι τὸ δένδρον τὸ στηριχθέν· καὶ ποιήσει τὸ κόκκινον ὡς ἔριον λευκὸν γενέσθαι. **16** Ἡ χιὼν μελανθήσεται, τὰ γλυκέα ὕδατα ἁλμυρὰ γενήσονται ἐν τῷ μεγάλῳ φωτὶ τῆς εὐφροσύνης τοῦ Θεοῦ. **17** Καὶ εὐλογήσει τὰς νήσους τοῦ ποιῆσαι καρπὸν ἐν τῷ λόγῳ τοῦ στόματος τοῦ Χριστοῦ αὐτοῦ. **18** Αὐτὸς γὰρ ἐλεύσεται, καὶ ἐξελεύσεται, καὶ ἐπιλέξεται ἑαυτῷ δώδεκα ἀποστόλους, ἵνα εὐαγγελίζωνται ἐν τοῖς ἔθνεσιν· ὃν ἐγὼ ἑώρακα κεκοσμημένον ὑπὸ τοῦ Πατρὸς αὐτοῦ, καὶ ἐρχόμενον εἰς τὸν κόσμον ἐπὶ τὸ ὄρος τῶν ἐλαιῶν· καὶ ἐμπλήσει τὰς πεινώσας ψυχάς. **19** Ταῦτα λέγοντος τοῦ Ἰερεμίου περὶ τοῦ Υἱοῦ τοῦ Θεοῦ, ὅτι ἔρχεται εἰς τὸν κόσμον, ὠργίσθη ὁ λαός, καὶ εἶπε· **20** Ταῦτα πάλιν ἐστὶ τὰ ῥήματα τὰ ὑπὸ Ἠσαΐου τοῦ υἱοῦ Ἀμὼς εἰρημένα λέγοντος ὅτι, Εἶδον τὸν Θεὸν, καὶ τὸν Υἱὸν τοῦ Θεοῦ. **21** Δεῦτε οὖν, καὶ μὴ ἀποκτείνωμεν αὐτὸν τῷ ἐκείνου θανάτῳ, ἀλλὰ λίθοις λιθοβολήσωμεν αὐτόν. **22** Ἐλυπήθησαν σφόδρα ἐπὶ τῇ ἀπονοίᾳ ταύτῃ Βαροὺχ καὶ Ἀβιμέλεχ, καὶ ὅτι ἤθελον ἀκοῦσαι πλήρης τὰ μυστήρια, ἃ εἶδε. **23** Λέγει δὲ αὐτοῖς Ἱερεμίας· Σιωπήσατε, καὶ μὴ κλαίετε· οὐ μὴ γάρ με ἀποκτείνωσιν, ἕως οὗ πάντα ὅσα εἶδον διηγήσωμαι ὑμῖν. **24** Εἶπε δὲ αὐτοῖς· Ἐνέγκατέ μοι λίθον. **25** Ὁ δὲ ἔστησεν αὐτὸν, καὶ εἶπε· Τὸ φῶς τῶν αἰώνων, ποίησον τὸν λίθον τοῦτον καθ᾽ ὁμοιότητά μου γενέσθαι. **26** Ὁ δὲ λίθος ἀνέλαβεν ὁμοιότητα τοῦ Ἰερεμίου. **27** Καὶ ἐλιθοβόλουν τὸν λίθον, νομίζοντες ὅτι Ἰερεμίας ἐστίν. **28** Ὁ δὲ Ἰερεμίας πάντα παρέδωκε τὰ μυστήρια, ἃ εἶδε, τῷ Βαροὺχ καὶ τῷ Ἀβιμέλεχ. **29** Καὶ εἶθ᾽ οὕτως ἔστη ἐν μέσῳ τοῦ λαοῦ, ἐκτελέσαι βουλόμενος τὴν οἰκονομίαν αὐτοῦ. **30** Ἐβόησε δὲ ὁ λίθος λέγων· Ὦ μωροὶ υἱοὶ Ἰσραὴλ, διὰ

---

(14) βλαστησουσι: eth add *and their fruit will live with the angels;* Harris και ο καρπος αυτων μετα των αγγελων μενει ‖ **15** και¹: (Kraft) add τα δενδρα | βεβλαστηκοτα: A βεβληκοτα | μετα – κριθηναι: A (Ceriani) om | κριθηναι: B (Kraft Schaller); Harris κλιθηναι | the whole verse in eth: *and for the sake of the nursery of the trees we want to give praise to the air, so that they may become green and grow high, and that their roots will not wither like a plant whose roots find no ground* | και ποιησει² (eth); A B (Ceriani Kraft) και | ως (eth); A B και | γενεσθαι: (Kraft) γενησεται ‖ **16** η χιων μελανθησεται: eth om | γενησονται: eth (Kraft) add και τα αλμυρα γλυκεα | εν – θεου: eth *with jubilation and God's delight* ‖ **17** χριστου: P eth *son* ‖ **18** ινα ευαγγελιζωνται – εωρακα: eth *so that they will be shown what I have seen* | κεκοσμημενον A B; eth *sent* | πεινωσας A eth; B ταπεινωσας ‖ **20** και: eth om ‖ **21** μη αποκτεινωμεν – αυτον²: eth *we want to do to him as we did to Isaiah, and some of them said, "No, in truth, we will throw stones at him." And Baruch and Abimelech shouted at them, "Do not kill him that way"* ‖ **22** επι τη απονοια ταυτη A B; P arm eth om | πληρης B; A πληρη ‖ **24** λιθον: eth add *and they brought him a stone* ‖ **25** εστησεν: B ανεστησεν | μου: eth *a man* (ανθρωπου) | γενεσθαι: A B (Ceriani Kraft) add εως ου παντα ορσα ιδον διηγησωμαι τω Βαρουχ και τω Αβιμελεχ ‖ **26** λιθος: A B P arm (Ceriani Kraft) add δια προσταγματος θεου ‖ **28** παντα: P arm om ‖ **29** ειθ ουτως: B ειθ αυτως ‖

to bear fruit, and they will grow and sprout. **15** And those that had sprouted and were haughty and said, 'We have stretched out our top into the air'[13]—he will cause them to wither with the grandeur of their branches. And he will cause the firmly rooted tree to fall.[14] And he will cause the crimson to become like white wool. **16** The snow will turn black, the sweet waters will turn salty by God's great light of joy. **17** And he will bless the islands to bear fruit by the word of the mouth of his Christ. **18** For he himself will come and go out, and he will choose for himself twelve apostles to announce the good news among the nations. He whom I have seen adorned by his Father and coming into the world on the Mount of Olives will satisfy the hungry souls." **19** While Jeremiah was saying this about the Son of God, that he is coming into the world, the people became angry and said, **20** "These again are the words that were spoken by Isaiah, son of Amoz, saying, 'I saw God and the Son of God.' **21** Therefore come and let us kill him, not by the same sort of death as his, but let us stone him with stones." **22** At this frenzy Baruch and Abimelech became very grieved because they wanted to hear in full all the secrets he had seen. **23** But Jeremiah said to them, "Be silent and stop your weeping, for they surely will not kill me until I have told you all I saw." **24** And he said to them, "Bring me a stone!" **25** And he set it up and said, "Light of the ages, cause this stone to take on my appearance!" **26** And the stone took on the appearance of Jeremiah. **27** And they stoned the stone, thinking it to be Jeremiah. **28** But Jeremiah shared with Baruch and Abimelech all the secrets he had seen. **29** And after this he stood in this manner in the midst of the people wanting to fulfill his ministry. **30** But the stone cried out, saying, "O, foolish children of Israel, why

---

13. Literally: "We delivered our end to the air"; see the commentary on this verse.
14. Κριθῆναι here is to be understood metaphorically.

τί λιθοβολεῖτέ με, νομίζοντες ὅτι ἐγὼ Ἰερεμίας; Ἰδοὺ Ἰερεμίας ἐν μέσῳ ὑμῶν ἵσταται. **31** Ὡς δὲ εἶδον αὐτὸν, εὐθέως ἔδραμον πρὸς αὐτὸν μετὰ πολλῶν λίθων. Καὶ ἐπληρώθη αὐτοῦ οἰκονομία. **32** Καὶ ἐλθόντες Βαροὺχ καὶ Ἀβιμέλεχ, ἔθαψαν αὐτὸν, καὶ λαβόντες τὸν λίθον ἔθηκαν ἐπὶ τὸ μνῆμα αὐτοῦ, ἐπιγράψαντες οὕτως· Οὗτός ἐστιν ὁ λίθος ὁ βοητὸς τοῦ Ἰερεμίου.

30 εν μεσω: B εις μεσον || **31** επληρωθη: P add *delivering his worthy and holy soul into the hands of the living God on the first of the month of May* || **32** μνημα: eth add *and set it up as a door* | ουτος: eth *behold this* | ο λιθος: eth om | Ιερεμιου: A B (Ceriani) add και τα λοιπα των λογων Ιερεμιου και πασα η δυναμις ουκ ιδου (A om) ενταυθα εγγεγαπται εν τη επιστολη Βαρουχ || subscription in A B arm: *and the rest of the words of Jeremiah and all his mighty work* (arm *the history of this writing of Paraleipomena*), *are they not written in the letter of Baruch* (arm add *glory be to Christ forever, amen*); P *and all power to Christ Jesus our Lord, to whom be glory and might forever and ever, amen.*

are you stoning me supposing I am Jeremiah? Behold, Jeremiah is standing in your midst." **31** And when they saw him, they immediately ran to him with many stones and (so) his ministry was completed. **32** And Baruch and Abimelech came and buried him, and taking the stone they put it on his tomb and wrote on it the following, "This is the stone, the ally of Jeremiah."

Commentary

Chapter 1

The author of *4 Baruch* assumes considerable knowledge on the part of his readers. Without any introductory explanation of the situation, he directs their attention to a well-known event in Israel's history that had made a deep impact on the nation. The recipients know who the king of the Chaldeans is, even if his name (Nebuchadnezzar) is only mentioned later (5:21; 7:14, 25). The ruler politically responsible for the Babylonian captivity is well-known. Thus one immediately wonders: Why would one retell this story once more?

Interestingly, though, the captivity into which the Chaldean king had taken Israel fades into the background even as it is mentioned, both to give room to the real actor and even now to hint at a dimension of hope. This perspective, although made explicit only at the end of the work, influences it from the beginning: God is the engaged and real actor from the first verse on.[1] Even the "concrete" main characters—Jeremiah, Baruch, and Abimelech—act only in response to God's command. Thus the author already gives a clear indication of the viewpoint to be presented in *4 Baruch*. Just as history is not to be historically but theologically interpreted and described, so the present situation is not to be shaped politically but to be understood and overcome theologically. This giving of a theological dimension to past and present history is an important factor in understanding the entire work appropriately in its context. The work is consciously a historical-theological fiction that seeks to interpret the present situation of the author and his audience theologically by retelling a key event from Israel's history. What makes this fairly common procedure remarkable in this case is that the event chosen from Israel's history had already been interpreted and handed down in its interpreted form. In this process, the present is interpreted through the remembered past and a picture of the future emerges, a picture that both renders the present comprehensible and makes the future the real focus of hope.

---

1. Jens Herzer, "Direction in Difficult Times: How God Is Understood in the Paraleipomena Jeremiou," *JSP* 22 (2000): 9–30.

Alongside this giving of a theological dimension stands a process of authorization. God himself is made author of the story; he himself authorizes and legitimizes the retelling of the remembered history. He takes the initiative, and he is the one through whom the catastrophe brought on Jerusalem by the advancing Chaldeans receives its specific meaning.

The title "king of the Chaldeans" for Nebuchadnezzar is worth noting, being without a textual reference point in our author's sources. The use of the title in the Old Testament is rare and limited to the later traditions: the Septuagint version of Isaiah, 2 Chr 36:17, and Dan 9:1. In *2 Baruch*, assumed as background to *4 Baruch*, the threatening power remains anonymous. An equally obvious background to *4 Baruch* is the book of Jeremiah itself, since it is decisive in the historical understanding of our author. However, this title of Nebuchadnezzar does not appear there, despite Jeremiah's use of "Babylon" and "Chaldea" or "Babylonians" and "Chaldeans" as synonyms. These synonymous expressions match the fact that *4 Baruch* speaks of the Chaldeans and yet names Babylon as their place of origin, whose inhabitants are equally Babylonians (6:14; 7:23; 8:5, 7). The term *Chaldeans* appears in only three phrases: "king of the Chaldeans" (1:1; 2:6), "(military) might of the Chaldeans" (1:3; 4:1), and "hands of the Chaldeans" (1:5). All these references have a political background, whereas the terms *Babylon* and *Babylonians* are used in the context of personal relations. *Chaldean* is thus given a negative overtone. Although Babylon is primarily the location of the exile and hence equally negative in tone, it is also the place of reorientation toward the promises of salvation. Part of this reorientation is a clear separation from the Babylonians. In this context, the political power of "the Chaldeans" no longer plays a role.

Our author appears to use the synonymous references to Babylon and Chaldea or Babylonians and Chaldeans in order to maintain a differentiation within his historical-theological fiction. The term *Chaldeans* remains on the level of remembering, while the terms *Babylon* and *Babylonian* have direct reference to the time of writing and thus unambiguously refer to the Roman Empire and the threat that this hostile power represented to the Jewish people.[2] This impression can be clarified with the observation that the terms *Chaldea* and *Chaldean* are found on the political-historical level of the narrative, while Babylon and Babylonian are used on the theological-eschatological level. From this observation a stunning theological interpretation of history emerges, albeit implicitly: just as the Jewish people had survived the Babylonian exile by conservatively holding

---

2. On the significance of using the name "Babylon" for Rome, see C. H. Hunzinger, "Babylon als Deckname für Rom und die Datierung des 1. Petrusbriefes," in *Gottes Wort und Gottes Land: Festschrift für Joachim Jeremias* (ed. Henning Graf Reventlow; Göttingen: Vandenhoeck & Ruprecht, 1965), 67–77.

on to tradition and constructively developing that tradition, and thus saw judgment turn to salvation, so equally now the Jewish people of the author's day should wait for God's activity in history to turn the Roman threat into blessing.

By using this terminology our author does not merely hold to linguistic conventions[3] but consciously makes a differentiation with which his and his readers' situation is to be outlined. As in Jeremiah's days, the challenge of the author's time was to make a correct assessment of political and religious relationships and to draw the proper conclusions. Included in that was a specific evaluation of both the Roman Empire, which was on the verge of triumphing over Israel and Jerusalem, and of the question of the people's future political and religious survival in such a complex situation. Just as the Chaldean power could not annul God's rule, Roman power could not succeed as long as Israel remained focused on something other than political and military power.

Despite all the political threat, *4 Bar.* 1 makes the undisputed rule of God as clear as possible. The chapter consists of a dialogue between Jeremiah and God that the latter initiates in order to demand that Jeremiah leave the city together with Baruch so that the destruction of the city may proceed. This demand in 1:1 is repeated almost verbatim in 1:7. Thus it is made clear that, although the Chaldeans are in political terms active, ultimately it is God who hands the city over to destruction. At this point one must notice that the city is not actually destroyed in chapter 1. According to 1:10, Jeremiah and Baruch are to scale the city walls so that God might convince them that he is at work. Before reaching that point, however, chapters 2 and 3 introduce scenes that retard the story and make it clear that God is not really interested in destroying the city. Here, even before the judgment, provision is made for overcoming the judgment and for a return into the city. Finally, in chapter 4 the angels open the city gates, and the enemy enters and leads the people into captivity. It is noteworthy that *4 Baruch* does not actually report the destruction of the city; in fact, the only indication of the destruction is offered in the question about the meaning of the event in Baruch's lament (4:6). Moreover, in chapter 5 Abimelech recognizes the city by means of its skyline, but on the inside he finds it dramatically changed. This difference between the outer and inner faces of the city deserves comment. Although the city has remained identifiable, even achieved a new sheen in places, its inner state is and remains so desolate that only lament remains. It is quite possible that Hadrian's planned rebuilding of Jerusalem as Aelia Capitolina is the background here.[4] Such a project is not

---

3. Schaller, "Paralipomena Jeremiou," 711.
4. See Herzer, *Paralipomena Jeremiae*, 177–92, esp. 182–86. See also the discussion of author, location, and date in the introduction above.

destruction in the true sense, though from a particular perspective it can certainly be regarded this way. In order to understand this, one must appreciate the differing evaluations of the inner and outer perspectives.

The reason given for the threatened destruction is clear and simple: the sins of the people (1:1). This sweeping statement is not made more concrete in what follows, which suggests that the author assumes a known understanding of the city's destruction (see, e.g., 2 Kgs 22:16; 23:26–36; 2 Chr 34:28; Jer 13:22; 30:15; Ezek 28:18; 1 Esd 9:2 [LXX]; Bar 4:12; *4 Ezra* 14:31; *2 Bar.* 1:2–4; Josephus, *J.W.* 7.332).[5] According to *4 Bar.* 2:2, Baruch immediately knows what the reader should also know when he recognizes what has caused Jeremiah's lamentations: the people must have committed a terrible sin. The traditional deeds-destiny relation ("Tun-Ergehen-Zusammenhang") is expressly used to explain the incomprehensible. The almost formulaic expression διὰ τὸ πλῆθος τῶν ἁμαρτιῶν τῶν κατοικούντων (1:1) also appears in 1:7 and twice in the remarkable repetition of 4:6–7 (διὰ τὰς ἁμαρτίας τοῦ ἠγαπημένου λαοῦ ... διὰ τὰς ἁμαρτίας ἡμῶν καὶ τοῦ λαοῦ ... διὰ τὰς ἁμαρτίας ἡμῶν), just after the people have been taken into captivity.

The author will allow no doubt that God is at work in this execution of his sentence and that the people brought it about through their own sin. Yet the reader is not told what specific sins the people are guilty of. Baruch's explicit question as to the people's guilt receives no answer. Only in 6:21 during the preparation for the people's return does the author become more concrete: "Because you did not keep my ordinances but your heart became haughty and you were stubborn in my presence instead, I became angry and in wrath surrendered you into the furnace in Babylon." The use of such a well-known understanding of guilt and judgment, together with the fact that the people are not mentioned by name but awkwardly alluded to in 1:1 ("those who dwell in it [the city]") and called, in the context of their sins, "the beloved people" (τοῦ ἠγαπημένου λαοῦ) in 4:6, points out that, despite the primarily negative assessment of the people, they are not rejected but can be assured of God's care.

The prominent role of the prophet Jeremiah finds expression in a special way in his being addressed as God's "chosen one" (ὁ ἐκλεκτός μου, see 1:4; 3:4–5; 7:15). Thus he is placed among the ranks of the great personalities of the

---

5. The book of Jeremiah is particularly more concrete, naming the following as explanation: primarily idolatry (2:5, 8; 3:9, 13; 5:19; 10:2–4 and many others); then despising of the law (2:8; 5:4–5; 6:19 and many others); worship of Baal (2:23); perjury (5:1, 7); adultery (5:8); violence (2:34; 6:7); and foolishness (2:35). These are summarized in the temple speech (7:9). Similarly, *2 Bar.* 1:2–4 also gives a larger list of the sins of the people. On this motif, see Motiv Murphy, "The Temple in the Syriac Apocalypse of Baruch," 671–72.

Old Testament.[6] Yet God's demand to leave the city is addressed to Jeremiah and Baruch, the latter already known from the Old Testament Jeremiah tradition as the prophet's assistant and secretary (Jer 32:12–13; 36:4, 10, 32; 43:3, 6; 45:1). According to Jer 36:6, Jeremiah charged Baruch to read aloud Jeremiah's work, and Baruch is similarly identified in *4 Bar.* 5:18 (Βαροὺχ ὁ ἀναγνώστης). The two must leave the city because[7] their prayers represent a protective wall around the city and prevent God's judgment. Both are intercessors for the people, although it becomes clear in what follows that the intercessory function is particularly Jeremiah's.[8] The prophet played this role in the book of Jeremiah (7:16; 11:14; 14; 15:1, 11; 18:20), and this character trait is found elsewhere in Hellenistic-Jewish literature.[9] This is one of several features that characterize the whole of *4 Baruch* (1:2, 5–6; 2:3; 3:9; 9:4), with further aspects being added to this feature later.[10] A certain tension exists between the demand to leave the city and the note in 1:10 that they should go up on the city walls, because the walls can only be climbed from inside the city.[11] However, this tension is not to be resolved. What matters is that Jeremiah and Baruch become witnesses to God's handing over of the city and later on *as witnesses* come before God in the temple.[12]

The understanding of prayers as a pillar and a wall is unusual. Although the background is Jer 1:18 according to the Masoretic Text ("And I for my part have made you today a fortified city, an iron pillar [missing in the Septuagint!], and a bronze wall, against the whole land—against the kings of Judah, its princes, its priests, and the people of the land"), it immediately becomes clear that the metaphor in *4 Bar.* 1:1 has another intention. It is not the prayers but the prophet himself who becomes the bulwark against the rebellious people and

---

6. See Jean Riaud, "The Figure of Jeremiah in the *Paralipomena Jeremiae Prophetae*: His Originality; His 'Christianization' by the Christian Author of the Conclusion (9:10–32)," *JSP* 22 (2000): 31–44, here 35, who points out the widespread use of this title: Jacob (Isa 45:4), Moses (Ps 106[105]:23), Joshua (Num 11:28), David (Sir 47:22), the Servant (Isa 42:1), and, finally, the whole people (Isa 43:26).

7. Schaller ("Paralipomena Jeremiou," 712) leaves the justifying γάρ untranslated.

8. The Ethiopic translation is therefore true to the content in focusing the prayer function on Jeremiah with the use of the singular.

9. 2 Macc 5:14; *2 Bar.* 2:2; *Liv. Pro.* 2:3; *Apocr. Jer.* 14:2–4; 17:8.

10. See Wolff, *Jeremia im Frühjudentum und Urchristentum,* 83–89; S. E. Balentine, "The Prophet as Intercessor: A Reassessment," *JBL* 103 (1984): 161–73; and esp. Riaud, "La figure de Jérémie," passim. See also his "Figure of Jeremiah," passim; Marinus de Jonge, "Remarks in the Margin of the Paper 'The Figure of Jeremiah in the *Paralipomena Jeremiae*,'" *JSP* 22 (2000): 45–49.

11. See Bogaert, *Apocalypse de Baruch,* 1:200.

12. See Nickelsburg, "Narrative Traditions," 63.

its leadership.[13] Moreover, the reference to Jer 1:18 (cf. 15:20) is only indirect. The direct reference is to the clear parallel in *2 Bar.* 2:1: "For your works are for this city like a firm pillar, and your prayers like a strong wall." Passing over the synonymous *parallelismus membrorum*[14] between prayers and works, *4 Baruch* concentrates again on prayers, the prayers of the righteous in the holy city of Jerusalem playing a special role for the author.[15] It is not only that they hold back God's judgment[16] but also that Jerusalem remains a special place after judgment, and in Jeremiah's letter from Babylon (see 7:23, 28) Baruch is required to intercede *because* he is in Jerusalem. Effective prayer for the people of God is only possible in Jerusalem.[17]

---

13. See the Ethiopic text, which uses the second-person singular possesive adjective ("your prayer"), referring to Jeremiah.

14. See Wolff, *Jeremia im Frühjudentum und Urchristentum*, 148.

15. The metaphorical use of defensive architectural structures was a common motif in Cynic and Stoic popular philosophy and influenced Hellenistic Jewish authors such as Philo of Alexandria (see Abraham J. Malherbe, *Paul and the Popular Philosophers* [Minneapolis: Fortress, 1989], 93–95 [for Philo of Alexandria], 101–3 [for Epictetus and Seneca]). However, in *4 Baruch* it is not a metaphor for self-protection, but the point is that Jeremiah's prayers protect others. This difference between the philosophical motif and *4 Baruch* underlines the priestly function of the prophet. Thus, the idea that the works of the righteous are pillars is unique in early Jewish literature; see M. Görg, "Die 'ehernen Säulen' (1 Kgs 7:15) und die 'eiserne Säule' (Jer 1:18): Ein Beitrag zur Säulenmetaphorik im Alten Testament," in *Prophetie und geschichtliche Wirklichkeit im alten Israel* (ed. by R. Liwak et al.; Stuttgart: Kohlhammer, 1991), 137–54, here 146–48. According to *2 Bar.* 63:3–9, the works of the righteous one (Hezekiah) are the reason for God hearing the prayer and thus also for the rescue of Jerusalem.

16. The idea of the righteous as pillars also appears in rabbinic literature, such as *b. Ber.* 28b concerning Johanan ben Zakkai as well as *Exod. Rab.* 2:6 on Exod 3:3 and Abraham being the pillar of the world. The idea in *Paraleipomena Jeremiou* that the righteous person is a protective force is particularly to be compared with a story told in the context of Johanan ben Zakkai's flight from Jerusalem in *Lam. Rab.* 1:5: "He sent R. Eliezer and R. Joshua to bring out R. Ẓadok. They went and found him in the city gate. When he arrived, R. Joḥanan stood up before him. Vespasian asked, 'You stand up before this emaciated old man?' He answered, 'By your life, if there had been [in Jerusalem] one more like him, though you had double your army, you would have been unable to conquer it'" (translation of J. Rabbinowitz, "Lamentations," in *Midrash Rabbah: Translated into English with Notes, Glossary and Indices* [ed. by H. Freedman and M. Simon; 10 vols.; London: Soncino, 1983], 7:104). See also Görg, "Säulenmetaphorik im Alten Testament," passim. Such metaphorical language also finds reflection in the New Testament (Gal 2:9; also *1 Clem.* 5:2; Eusebius, *Hier.* 5.1.6.17).

17. *4 Bar.* 2:3; see Wolff, *Jeremia im Frühjudentum und Urchristentum*, 85–86; Herzer, *Paralipomena Jeremiae*, 41–42. Wolff (*Jeremia im Frühjudentum und Urchristentum*, 86) notes as a parallel *Midr. Pss.* on Ps 91:11–12: "From the latter words [Gen 18:17] the Rabbis inferred that when a man prays in Jerusalem, it is as though he prays before the throne of glory, for the gate of heaven is in Jerusalem, and a door is always open for the hearing of prayer" (quoted from William G. Braude, *The Midrash on Psalms: Translated from the Hebrew and Aramaic* [Yale Judaica Series 13; 2 vols.; New Haven: Yale University Press, 1959], 2:105). See also Norman Burrows Johnson, *Prayer*

The title κύριε παντοκράτωρ in 1:5 gives particular prominence to God's role in the remembered events. Jeremiah accepts God's decision by pointing to his universal authority. Κύριε is an address to God found in the Septuagint; together with παντοκράτωρ it translates the Hebrew YHWH Sebaoth.[18] God alone, not the enemy, is the almighty ruler deciding the fate of his people.

The expression παραδίδως τὴν πόλιν τὴν ἐκλεκτήν in 1:5 (repeated in 2:7 and 3:6) underlines the all-encompassing nature of God's rule. In this formulation both judgment and salvation come together: the wrath of God against sin leads to the city being handed over yet does not negate the fact that this city is expressly the *chosen* city.[19] Even in the hour of judgment it is confirmed that the city remains the place of salvation, a tension between judgment and salvific significance later resolved in the reorientation toward the eschatological heavenly Jerusalem of the age of salvation. In the same breath in which the enemy's possible victory is mentioned, the city is called the "holy city," although here the difference can be appreciated: the "holy city" is the earthly Jerusalem—to which the enemy has access. Although its holiness is thereby lost, its election is not; rather, the "chosen city" is no longer the earthly but the heavenly city. Election is thus the decisive category by which God's faithfulness to his people is to be understood. This can be seen in the author's use of "chosen" for entities other than Jerusalem: supremely Jeremiah, who guarantees the preservation of the tradition (1:4, 7; 3:4, 5; 7:15);[20] then the people (7:11); and, finally, the eagle through whom the message of salvation comes (return from exile in 7:3).

The reference to God's will in 1:6–7 confirms that the judgment cannot be turned away and simultaneously makes it clear to Jeremiah that the city can be

---

in the Apocrypha and Pseudepigrapha: A Study of the Jewish Concept of God (SBLMS 2; Philadelphia: Society of Biblical Literature, 1948), 44–45, 52.

18. Gerhard Delling, "Zum gottesdienstlichen Stil der Johannes-Apokalypse," in *Studien zum Neuen Testament und zum hellenistischen Judentum: Gesammelte Aufsätze 1950–1968* (ed. Ferdinand Hahn, Traugott Holtz, and Nikolaus Walter; Göttingen: Vandenhoeck & Ruprecht, 1970), 425–50, here 442–46; repr. from *NovT* 3 (1959). Schaller ("Paralipomena Jeremiou," 713) points out the rarity of the expression in postbiblical times, although it is used more often than he presents (Bar 3:1–4; Jdt 4:13; 8:13; 15:10; 16:5; 16:17; Sir 42:17; 50:17; *T. Ab.* A 8:3; 15:12; *Pr. Man.* 1:1; *Odes Sol.* 12:1; 14:12–13; 2 Macc 3:30; 3 Macc 2:2). See further Michael Ehrmann, *Klagephänomene in zwischentestamentlicher Literatur* (BEATAJ 41; Frankfurt am Main: Lang, 1997); Sönke von Stemm, *Der betende Sünder vor Gott: Studien zu Vergebungsvorstellungen in urchristlichen und frühjüdischen Texten* (AGJU 45; Leiden: Brill, 1999). The proximity to the New Testament is remarkable; see 2 Cor 6:18; Rev 1:8; 4:8; 11:17; 15:3; 16:7; 19:6; 19:16; 21:22. The expanded form κύριε ὁ θεὸς ὁ παντοκράτωρ is typical for the Christian Apocalypse of John; see Delling (cited above).

19. On Jerusalem as the chosen city under God's judgment, see Sir 49:6; as the chosen city of salvation, Tob (Symmachus) 13:13.

20. Riaud, "La figure de Jérémie," 373–85. See also idem, "Figure of Jeremiah," 31–44.

handed over only by God himself.[21] The repetition of 1:1b in 1:7 has already been mentioned. The structure of 1:1–3 and 7–9 is also the same: a command to leave the city; an announcement of the city's destruction, with a reason provided; further reason; and a repeated command to leave the city. These similar structures cause the differences to become more apparent: in terms of content, only the first two elements are the same. The reason given in 1:8–9 differs from the earlier reason and picks up on Jeremiah's earlier reference to God's will: the enemy can enter the city only if God wills and enables it to do so.[22] Thus the strange and quite illogical phrase in verse 10—"unless I destroy the city first, they cannot enter it"—should be read in correspondence with 1:8; the opening of the gates by God already implies the destruction, which is merely carried out by the enemies. In this perspective, the Chaldeans once more appear as the instrument used by God in order to execute his judgment. Yet as mentioned above, *4 Baruch* does not in fact report an actual destruction of the city.

In 1:9, Baruch comes to the fore for the first time when God commands Jeremiah to convey this news to him. This transition prepares for chapter 2, where Baruch becomes the second main character alongside Jeremiah.[23]

The reference to "the sixth hour of the night" in 1:10 indicates that the conquest of the city began at midnight. This hour underlines the judgment motif; according to Josephus, the Romans conquered Jerusalem in 70 C.E. at midnight (*Ant.* 10.136).[24]

---

21. *4 Bar.* 1:6 thus demonstrates a certain similarity to *2 Bar.* 4:2, where the topic is the heavenly Jerusalem. A quotation from Isa 49:16 is in play here, which is not taken up as such. See Bogaert, *Apocalypse de Baruch*, 2:14, and the critique in Riaud, "Les Paralipomena Jeremiae dépendent-ils de 2 Baruch?" 110. See also Herzer, *Paralipomena Jeremiae*, 73.

22. *2 Bar.* 1:2–5; 5:3; 77:10; see also *4 Ezra* 13:40–41. Josephus also makes use of this understanding of the conquest of the city (Josephus, *J.W.* 6.110; 7.328, 332; *Ant.* 20.166); on this point, see Delling, *Paralipomena Jeremiae*, 4–5.

23. On the person and traditional understanding of Baruch, see below. According to Robinson ("4 Baruch," 417), *4 Bar.* 1:9 interrupts God's speech to Jeremiah. For Robinson, the problem apparently is Baruch, assuming that he does not belong originally in this context. The occasions of his being mentioned in *4 Bar.* 1 are therefore "editorial additions." However, Robinson fails to offer a reason here, just as he does for his holding that the "subservient character" in *4 Bar.* 2 was originally not Baruch but Abimelech. Robinson also fails to say on which redactional level this change occurred.

24. In contrast to *4 Baruch*, Josephus expressly states it: ἁλούσης δὲ τῆς πόλεως περὶ μέσην νύκτα. On midnight as a certain motif, see also Mark 13:35; Matt 25:6; Acts 16:25; 27:27; in the sixth hour, while Jesus is dying on the cross, it becomes night in the day (Mark 15:33 and parallels); according to John 19:14, the sixth hour of the day is the hour when Jesus is handed over to be crucified (John 19:16). On this see W. Speyer, "Mittag und Mitternacht als heilige Zeiten in Antike und Christentum," in *Frühes Christentum im antiken Strahlungsfeld* (ed. W. Speyer; WUNT 50; Tübingen: Mohr Siebeck, 1989), 340–52.

The dialogue ends with God's departure, again on God's initiative, whereas Jeremiah began the dialogue in 1:4 by responding to God's announcement in 1:1–3.[25] That befits the special role of the prophet, who alone is God's conversation partner; neither Baruch nor Abimelech has this role. The remark concerning God's departure reveals the careful structuring work of the author. The motif is reused and made more precise in 3:13, where God does not simply leave Jeremiah but ascends into heaven. From that moment on, heaven is not simply to be understood locally but receives eschatological significance. The destination of the faithful is, according to 5:34, the heavenly Jerusalem. By ascending to heaven, God goes ahead of his people to the place of their final salvation.

---

25. Schaller ("Paralipomena Jeremiou," 714) rightly points out the parallel in the end of the conversation between God and Abraham in Gen 18:33: ἀπῆλθεν δὲ κύριος ὡς ἐπαύσατο λαλῶν τῷ Αβρααμ.

Chapter 2

Whereas the first chapter began by referring to the time of the events, the second chapter introduces the meeting between Jeremiah and Baruch in terms of its location. God having left him, Jeremiah enters the temple (τὸ ἁγιαστήριον, 2:1), where he meets Baruch (2:2). The dialogue between them is immediately interrupted by an insertion in 2:3 that explains the connection made in 2:2 between the people's sin and Jeremiah's mourning rituals. This makes the repetition of Baruch's question in 2:4 necessary. The main part of the chapter consists of a conversation between Jeremiah and Baruch. It is worth noting that Jeremiah and Baruch do not actually leave the city, as God had required in 1:1, 7, but remain in the sanctuary by the altar (2:10). Like chapter 1, chapter 2 ends with a specific note concluding the scene.

Verse 1 lays the groundwork for Jeremiah's execution of God's command to tell Baruch what God had said, so the narrative here anticipates what will be developed later on in the conversation between Jeremiah and Baruch. However, after 2:2 it is Baruch, not Jeremiah, who begins the conversation with his questions about Jeremiah's mourning.[1] Some translations iron out this tension by setting Baruch next to Jeremiah as a mourner in 2:1b.[2] In this scenario, instead of Jeremiah leaving the city with Baruch, both head into God's holy place, the temple.[3]

The phrase ἁγιαστήριον τοῦ Θεοῦ appears infrequently in the Old Testament, being found only four times (LXX Pss 72:17; 73:7 [τὸ ἁγιαστήριόν σου]; 82:13; Lev 12:4 [without τοῦ Θεοῦ]). Otherwise this expression does not appear in early Jewish tradition. These few references must therefore be of some importance. In tradition criticism, the psalms mentioned seem precisely to be those that provide the motif for *4 Bar.* 2. The reference to the fall of Jerusalem is

---

1. This motif of silent mourning followed by conversation concerning its cause can be found in Job 2:11–13.

2. So the reading in arm^a, arm^b and slav^A ("and they both began to weep at the altar"); MS A does not have this part of the verse.

3. Schaller reads εἰς τὸν ναὸν τοῦ θεοῦ according to A and B ("Paralipomena Jeremiou," 714).

particularly clear in Ps 73:7: ἐνεπύρισαν ἐν πυρὶ τὸ ἁγιαστήριόν σου, εἰς τὴν γῆν ἐβεβήλωσαν τὸ σκήνωμα τοῦ ὀνόματός σου ("they burned your sanctuary with fire; down to the ground they desecrated the tent of your name"). Psalm 82:13 in the LXX also seems to assume this, for the Hebrew version (83:13) speaks of the taking of the land, not of the temple.

The assumed situation—lamentation rites celebrated in the temple itself—seems unusual. The tearing of one's clothes and the sprinkling of ashes on one's head are typical lamentation rites,[4] but the performance of these actions in the temple is particularly worthy of note. Specific parallels in the Old Testament and early Jewish literature are connected with the destruction of the temple. Particularly significant here is, above all, Lam 2:7–10, which, like the entire book of Lamentations, is closely associated with the Jeremiah tradition.

> (7) The Lord has scorned his altar, disowned his sanctuary; he has delivered into the hand of the enemy the walls of her palaces; a clamor was raised in the house of the Lord as on a day of festival. (8) The Lord determined to lay in ruins the wall of daughter Zion; he stretched the line; he did not withhold his hand from destroying; he caused rampart and wall to lament; they languish together. (9) Her gates have sunk into the ground; he has ruined and broken her bars; her king and princes are among the nations; guidance is no more, and her prophets obtain no vision from the Lord. (10) The elders of daughter Zion sit on the ground in silence; they have thrown dust on their heads and put on sackcloth; the young girls of Jerusalem have bowed their heads to the ground. (NRSV)

Another pertinent parallel is found in Jdt 4:11–15:

> (11) And all the Israelite men, women, and children living at Jerusalem prostrated themselves before the temple and put ashes on their heads and spread out their sackcloth before the Lord. (12) They even draped the altar with sackcloth and cried out in unison, praying fervently to the God of Israel not to allow their infants to be carried off and their wives to be taken as booty, and the towns they had inherited to be destroyed, and the sanctuary to be profaned and desecrated to the malicious joy of the Gentiles. (13) The Lord heard their prayers and had regard for their distress; for the people fasted many days throughout Judea and in Jerusalem before the sanctuary of the Lord Almighty. (14) The high priest Joakim and all the priests who stood before the Lord and ministered to the Lord, with sackcloth around their loins, offered the daily burnt offerings, the votive offerings, and freewill offerings of the people. (15)

---

4. Josh 7:6; 2 Sam 13:19; Esth 4:1, 3, 16; Job 2:12; 1 Macc 3:47; *T. Job* 28:3 and many others; see Schaller, "Paralipomena Jeremiou," 714.

> With ashes on their turbans, they cried out to the Lord with all their might to look with favor on the whole house of Israel. (NRSV)

As the people mourned in front of the temple before the impending destruction, the priests did the same in the temple in an attempt to turn aside the judgment.

In *4 Baruch*, however, the point of no return has already been reached, as is made clear by the conversation reflecting on the coming catastrophe (2:2–9). Baruch begins this conversation with two questions that concern Jeremiah and the people and that reflect something characteristic about each. The question concerning the prophet's appearance is immediately combined with the question regarding the people's sin. Consequently, in 2:3 the author inserts a corresponding explanation for the reader, then repeats the questions in abbreviated form in 2:4. Readers need to know as much as Baruch does about Jeremiah's practices in order to understand the conversation correctly.

Alongside this narrative structure, Baruch's reference to Jeremiah as "Father" is also noteworthy. This designation is typical of Baruch's questions to Jeremiah and almost stereotypical (2:4, 6, 8; 5:25; 9:8). The Old Testament Jeremiah tradition does not use this title; of all the prophets, only Elijah is addressed as father (2 Kgs 2:12; 6:21; 13:14). Based on this evidence, Schaller proposed that the conception of the prophet as leader of a school lies in the background, noting also the usual rabbinic addresses used for scribes.[5] This seems reasonable, particularly because *4 Baruch* presents Jeremiah as a teacher, admittedly as teacher of the people in the exile. In the present context, however, the author's explanation in 2:3 should be taken seriously: Jeremiah's characteristic function was as priestly intercessor[6] for the people, one whose stubborn[7] prayers led to forgiveness of sins.[8] Thus "Father" in 2:2 refers not so much to Jeremiah's teaching as to his care for the people, including his intercessory mediation.[9]

Two senses of the title "Father" are suggested at this point: the first in relation to the people, the second in relation to Baruch. The second is expressed most clearly in Jeremiah's reference to Baruch as "my beloved son" in 7:23. But just as Baruch is the beloved son, the people are also "beloved" (3:8; 4:6) and

---

5. Schaller, "Paralipomena Jeremiou," 715.

6. For more, see Riaud, "La figure de Jérémie," passim.

7. He continues to pray (cf. the imperfect ηὔχετο) until (ἕως ἄν) God forgives the sins; see this motif again in Lam 3:49–50.

8. Although sin is referred to in the singular here instead of the plural, as in 1:2, 7, it does not indicate a difference in meaning.

9. A similar structure is found in the parable of 7:24, in which the father suffers at the death of his son and—so it is assumed—would rather die in his place.

compared to an "only son" (μονογενὴς υἱός, 7:24). Jeremiah, Baruch, and the people are thus not simply historical characters in a story being retold but bear significance in the story of God and his people. Their literary interaction has theological relevance for the author and first readers of *4 Baruch* as they seek to understand their own historical situation. One element of this depiction was presumably of great relevance to the original audience. In contrast to the Old Testament book of Jeremiah, *4 Baruch* speaks of the people's sin in traditional, general terms but never concretely names it. Hence from the beginning of the book it is clear that the people are not portrayed negatively but remain, even in the face of the coming judgment, God's own people who will someday turn back to him.[10]

In 2:5 Jeremiah finally answers Baruch's second question about the meaning of his mourning. Instead of tearing his clothes as Jeremiah has done, Baruch is told to tear his heart,[11] "for the Lord will not have mercy on this people." The appropriate response to God's final decision to execute judgment on his beloved people is not an external ritual but an internal rending of the heart. The coming together of love, election, and judgment is heart-breaking.

Joel 2:13 forms the background to this verse. There God himself calls for a tearing of the heart: "Rend your hearts and not your clothing. Return to the Lord, your God, for he is gracious and merciful, slow to anger, and abounding in steadfast love, and relents from punishing" (NRSV). The dependence of *4 Bar.* 2:5 on Joel's text is clear, but one important difference is striking. Joel speaks of the overflowing abundance of God's grace, which can even change his purposes, while in *4 Baruch* the decision for judgment has been made and will not be reversed. This conscious alteration of Joel 2:13, which would have been evident to careful readers, underscores the tragedy of the present situation.

The background to the motif of filling troughs with one's tears is the lament of the prophet in Jer 9:1 (LXX 8:23): "O that my head were a spring of water, and my eyes a fountain of tears, so that I might weep day and night for the slain of my poor people!"[12] (NRSV). The motif appears in *2 Bar.* 35:2 but is taken up and developed differently. Direct dependence on Jer 9:1 cannot be

---

10. See Jens Herzer, "Alttestamentliche Traditionen in den Paralipomena Jeremiae als Beispiel für den Umgang frühjüdischer Schriftsteller mit 'Heiliger Schrift,'" in *Schriftauslegung im antiken Judentum und im Urchristentum* (ed. M. Hengel and H. Löhr; WUNT 73; Tübingen: Mohr Siebeck, 1994), 119–20.

11. This motif goes beyond *2 Bar.* 35:2, which speaks only of tears.

12. See also 9:17 (18).

established; the reference here was probably mediated through *2 Baruch* and combined with the reference to Joel 2:13.[13]

The renewed exchange of question and answer in 2:6–7 appears stereotypical but clearly points to the shattering and incomprehensible depth of the impending events. Only after his third question is Baruch confronted with the reality and inevitability of divine judgment. Initially he asked what sin the people had committed because he understood the prophet's ritual lament in those terms. The prophet's answer to the repeated question of 2:4 pointed Baruch to the consequences of the event without naming them. Thus, the consequences were not yet plausible, so Baruch asked again. However, this time he does not ask about the condition of the prophet's mind but more concretely about what has happened. Only now does Jeremiah speak of God's decision to execute judgment.

This structuring of the dialogue should make it clear how consistent God's judgment is, how incomprehensible it remains, and how serious the people's situation has become. Readers can see their own condition, their own situation and tension, reflected in the text. Baruch's behavior in 2:8 becomes transparent to the author's generation when they take this reader-oriented approach. Baruch responds not as Jeremiah had required but disregards his word and tears his clothes. Reasoned obedience no longer seems possible in the face of the judgment; only lamentation rites remain in the inescapable situation. However, Baruch's acceptance of the situation is hinted at in the fourth question, as he asks about the source of the revelation of the judgment. Jeremiah does not answer but tells him to wait patiently for the sixth hour of the night, midnight,[14] when the truth of the word will be seen. Here too we find a clear hint to the reader.

The scene ends by referring to the altar of the sanctuary, before which Jeremiah and Baruch continue their lament until the hour of judgment. The altar in the forecourt of the sanctuary[15] is introduced into the scene because in the next chapter it will be the place at which the temple vessels will be hidden (3:8[16]).

---

13. Herzer, *Paralipomena Jeremiae*, 46. Note that 2 Bar. 35:2 takes the term "fountain" (*mkwʾ*) from Jer 8:23 (מָקוֹר/πηγή; NRSV 9:1) and is thus closer to the biblical tradition in its terminology.
14. See above on 1:10.
15. The altar is not identical to the sanctuary; θυσιαστήριον is not necessarily identical to ἁγιαστήριον (2:1a.c), as Delling believes (*Paralipomena Jeremiae*, 73 n. 14). See Schaller, "Paralipomena Jeremiou," 716, who however in 2:1a does not read ἁγιαστήριον (see also next note).
16. However, the text is not clear at this point. Among others, Schaller, "Paralipomena Jeremiou," 717 (cf. 720), does not read θυσιαστήριον, in accordance with MSS A and B. A distinction must also be made between 3:8 and 3:14: while θυσιαστήριον probably should be read in 3:8, it is replaced by ἁγιαστήριον in 3:14.

Chapter 3

In chapter 3 Jeremiah again speaks with God, seeking to learn two things with regard to the imminent destruction of the city: the fate of the temple vessels (3:7) and that of Abimelech (3:9). The sin and fate of the people no longer play a major role. By shifting the focus to the fates of the temple vessels and of Abimelech, the writer already looks forward to the promised return of the people from exile, even though judgment has not yet been executed.

The fate of the temple vessels is central in the first part of the dialogue between God and Jeremiah. The discussion regarding them has its immediate climax in God's instruction in 3:8, though the execution of this command is not reported until 3:14. The section concerning Abimelech interrupts this thematic unity, even though 3:14 could immediately follow 3:8 and finish the scene concerning the temple vessels. One might draw literary-critical conclusions from this. It is, to be sure, remarkable that Abimelech, who plays a decisive role in the development and presentation of the overall message of the book (in particular *4 Bar.* 5), first appears here. Because of this, Bogaert sought to demonstrate that 3:9–10 are interpolated, as Jeremiah's question concerning Abimelech in 3:9 is formulated just as that concerning the temple vessels in 3:6. Moreover, in 3:10–11 God offers two separate answers, one after the other, although 3:11 was not motivated by a further question.[1] Bogaert's suggestion is linked to his view that the Abimelech story in chapter 5 is secondary, and to the isolated references to Abimelech outside of chapter 5 as interpolations.[2]

Further to Bogaert's arguments, one should note that Abimelech plays no role in 3:14. As in chapter 2, Jeremiah and Baruch alone bewail the fall of Jerusalem. This could be seen as a literary marker for the end of chapter 3. That 3:15 begins with the same time marker as 4:1 supports such a view.[3] Moreover, the

---

1. Bogaert, *Apocalypse de Baruch*, 1:193–94.
2. See below the introduction to chapter 5.
3. See Bogaert, *Apocalypse de Baruch*, 1:194; Delling, *Paralipomena Jeremiae*, 7 n. 15; and Wolff, *Jeremia im Frühjudentum und Urchristentum*, 46. Bogaert concludes that the whole passage between these two verses is an addition.

sending of Abimelech to "the vineyard of Agrippa" and the surrounding of the city by the Chaldeans happen at the same time. The scene's logic is thus difficult to grasp, as Abimelech would surely have fallen into the hands of the enemy. Finally, since figs are not mentioned in God's instruction to send Abimelech to the vineyard of Agrippa, 3:10 and 3:15 stand in some tension.[4]

These observations do not, however, point to the secondary, interpolated nature of the figure of Abimelech in *4 Baruch* but are rather to be explained from *4 Baruch*'s dependence on *2 Baruch*. The close parallels between *4 Bar.* 3:1–8:14 and *2 Bar.* 6:3–9 lead one to suspect that the author of *4 Baruch* consciously expanded the material in his model and thereby gave his account its own specific profile.[5]

The new scene in chapter 3 begins by referring to the "hour of the night,"[6] making it clear that the event, which Baruch and Jeremiah await, is about to begin. This explains their change of location from the altar (2:10) to the city wall.[7] From there they will witness the promised judgment, which starts with the sound of trumpets and the appearance of angels (*2 Bar.* 6:4). The trumpet is the traditional instrument for announcing God's coming (Exod 19:16, 19; 20:18), particularly for the beginning of his judgment (Jer 6:1, 17; *Pss. Sol.* 8:1; see also Josh 6; the seven trumpets of Rev 8–10). The Septuagint uses the term for the sound of the ram's horn (שׁוֹפָר or קֶרֶן—see, e.g., Exod 19:13; Josh 6:8, 13; Jer 4:5, 19, 21; 6:1, 17; 42:14; 51:27).[8] Torches of fire also symbolize God's appearing (cf. Exod 19:18) and represent the fire of judgment (*2 Bar.* 6:4).

Verse 3 picks up on Jeremiah's words to Baruch in 2:9, as the appearance of angels compels recognition of the terrifying truth. Thus the effect of Jeremiah's renewed objection is all the greater, as he pleads that he might once more speak directly to God. Jeremiah's authority over the angels is accepted,[9] a stay of execution is granted, and God hears the request of his chosen one (3:5). Here, too, an association with *2 Bar.* 6 is clear, the narrative structure being taken from there.[10] As in *2 Bar.* 6:5–7, the reason for delay is a question concerning

---

4. One might also ask why Abimelech was sent to a *vineyard* (ἀμπελών) to collect *figs*. Vineyards and olive tree groves were, however, never monocultural but normally planted with fig trees. The New Testament offers a further example (Luke 13:6; see Claus-Hunno Hunzinger, "συκή κτλ.," *TDNT* 7:753, with further examples).

5. For a comparison of the texts, see Herzer, *Paralipomena Jeremiae*, 47–53.

6. On the witness to the text, see the apparatus to the Greek text above.

7. In *2 Bar.* 6:3, Baruch is at this point lifted above the wall by a spirit or, perhaps, a wind (see the translation of Klijn, "2 Baruch," *OTP* 1:622).

8. I. H. Jones, "Musical Instruments," *ABD* 4:934–39.

9. The phrase παρακαλεῖν τοὺς ἀγγέλους does not mean worship; see Schaller, "Paralipomena Jeremiou," 716.

10. Herzer, *Paralipomena Jeremiae*, 48.

CHAPTER 3

the temple vessels. Jeremiah's formulation of what he has come to recognize sounds almost like an accusation against God (3:6) and introduces a further element that propels the narrative: the deportation. Until this point the sole theme has been the handing over of the city. However, as the readers well knew, the consequence of that was deportation to Babylon. The specific meaning of "Babylon" compared with the term "Chaldea/Chaldeans" has already been discussed.[11]

As though God has seemingly forgotten, Jeremiah reminds him with a question regarding the vessels used in temple service, which should not fall into the hands of the enemy. Although *2 Bar.* 6:7 provides a list of vessels,[12] the author of *4 Baruch* is not interested in recounting the details. As in LXX 1 Chr 9:28, in *4 Baruch* the vessels are called τὰ σκεύη τῆς λειτουργίας and are entrusted to a priestly class. Jeremiah's concern thus underlines his priestly function in *4 Baruch*.

God's answer in 3:8 differs from the biblical tradition, in which the vessels were taken as booty to Babylon and so shared in the fate of the people.[13] According to *4 Baruch*, Jeremiah has to hand them over to the earth.[14] The place

---

11. See the commentary above on 1:1.

12. The following are mentioned: the veil, the holy ephod, the mercy seat, the two tables, the holy raiment of the priests, the altar of incense, the forty-eight precious stones, and the holy vessels of the tabernacle. For the hiding of the vessels, see *2 Bar.* 80:2. An inventory list is also found in 3Q15; see Jósef Tadeusz Milik, "Le Rouleau de Cuivre de Qumrân (3Q15)," *RB* 66 (1959): 321–57.

13. See 2 Kgs 24:13; 25:13–15; Jer 28(35):3, 6; 52:17–19; Bar 1:8; 2 Chr 36:18–19; Dan 1:2; 5:2–4; Ezra 1:7–11; 4Q385^b; *As. Mos.* 3:2; Josephus, *Ant.* 10.145–146. The return of the vessels is recounted in Ezra 1:7–11; 5:14; 6:5; 7:19; 8:26–30. See further Peter R. Ackroyd, "The Temple Vessels—A Continuity Theme," in *Studies in the Religion of Ancien Israel* (ed. Peter R. Ackroyd; VTSup 23; Leiden: Brill, 1972), 166–81; Riaud, *Les Paralipomènes de Jérémie*, 54–55; and Odil Hannes Steck, *Das apokryphe Baruchbuch: Studien zu Rezeption und Konzentration "kanonischer" Überlieferung* (FRLANT 160; Göttingen: Vandenhoeck & Ruprecht, 1993), 34–40. For the understanding of the temple vessels in early Jewish tradition, see Kohler, "The Pre-Talmudic Haggada," 409; Wolff, *Jeremia im Frühjudentum und Urchristentum*, 61–71. The rescue of the temple vessels is already known from traditions found in the books of Maccabees, such as 2 Macc 2:4–8, in which Jeremiah is also responsible for the fate of tent, ark, and vessels, hiding them all in a cave. Other versions are found in Eupolemos 4 (Eusebius, *Praep. ev.* 9.39.5), *Liv. Pro.* 2:9–11; see Anna Maria Schwemer, *Studien zu den frühjüdischen Prophetenlegenden: Vitae Prophetarum I: Die Viten der großen Propheten Jesaja, Jeremia, Ezechiel und Daniel* (TSAJ 49; Tübingen: 1995), 202–4. On the general subject, see Böhl, "Legende," 65–67; R. Bergmeier, "Zur Frühdatierung samaritanischer Theologumena," *JSJ* 5 (1974): 121–53, here 134–35.

14. According to *2 Bar.* 6:6, an angel receives the task. One cannot however conclude that *2 Baruch* eliminates the role of Jeremiah (so Gry, "La Ruine," 220; Böhl, "Legende," 69). If *2 Baruch* is the reference for *4 Baruch*, then Jeremiah is not replaced by an angel in *2 Baruch*, but the angel of *2 Baruch* by Jeremiah in *4 Baruch*, who does not play a major role in *2 Baruch*.

is more precisely defined with a dative τῷ θυσιαστηρίῳ preceded by an explanatory καί.[15] The altar, part of the inventory in *2 Bar.* 6:7 and 2 Macc 2:4–8,[16] becomes the place of protection in *4 Baruch*. The words with which the vessels are to be handed over are structured again with reference to *2 Baruch:* the earth is addressed directly (once in *4 Bar.* 3:8; three times in *2 Bar.* 6:8[17]), commanded to listen (to the voice of the Creator in *4 Bar.* 3:8; to the word of God in *2 Bar.* 6:8), and given the task of guarding the vessels for a particular length of time ("until the gathering of the beloved one" in *4 Bar.* 3:8; until they are once again required from the earth in *2 Bar.* 6:8).

With an imperative echoing the Shema (Deut 6:4), the earth is called upon to obey its Creator. God's creative activity is defined more precisely in terms that span beginning and end: "who created you in the abundance of the waters, who sealed you with seven seals, with seven epochs; and thereafter you will receive your beauty" (*4 Bar.* 3:8). Not only creating but also sealing and perfecting are among those things that make God God. Here is a hint of what shall later become clear: the perfecting of God's people has creation-theological significance.

In the background, once again, is *2 Baruch*. The phrase at the end of *4 Bar.* 3:8 ("until the gathering of the beloved one"; ἕως τῆς συνελεύσεως τοῦ ἠγαπημένου[18]) can be regarded as giving concrete meaning to *2 Bar.* 6:8: "until the last times."[19] The promise in *2 Bar.* 6:9 of the rebuilding of Jerusalem is, however, missing in *4 Baruch* and is not even mentioned in the conclusion in chapter 9 in connection with the sacrifice-festival in Jerusalem. This is probably

---

15. On textual witnesses, see the apparatus to the Greek text above. Schaller does not read the addition as in 3:14 ("Paralipomena Jeremiou," 717).

16. According to 2 Macc 2:7, the place of storage will remain unknown until the renewed gathering of the people of God.

17. The remarkable formulation in *2 Baruch* reminds one of Jer 22:29: "O land, land, land, hear the word of the Lord." The word used in *2 Baruch*, "ר' ("land, earth"; see Brockelmann, *LexSyr* 51), corresponds to the Hebrew ארץ. Although the word in Jer 22 has different content, the reference is not to be explained other than that *2 Baruch* took this text as a model; see Bogaert, *Apocalypse de Baruch*, 1:361–62; Nickelsburg, "Narrative Traditions," 65 n. 26. According to Wolff, *2 Baruch* knew the Hebrew text of Jer 22:29 (*Jeremia im Frühjudentum und Urchristentum*, 148). The motif of speaking to the earth is also found in *4 Ezra* 7:54 but in a different context; see Michael E. Stone, *Fourth Ezra: A Commentary on the Book of Fourth Ezra* (Hermeneia; Minneapolis: Fortress, 1990), 227.

18. See also Delling, *Paralipomena Jeremiae*, 65–67; Bogaert, *Apocalypse de Baruch*, 1:204; Jean Riaud, "Abimélech, Personnage-Clé des Paralipomena Jeremiae?" *DHA* 7 (1981): 163–78; and Kilpatrick, "Acts VII.52 ΕΛΕΥΣΙΣ," 140–42.

19. Wolff, *Jeremia im Frühjudentum und Urchristentum*, 65. The reason for hiding the vessels is explicitly mentioned in *2 Bar.* 6:8: they must not fall into the hands of the enemy. This is, however, implicit in *4 Bar.* 3; see Murphy, "The Temple in the Syriac Apocalypse of Baruch," 679.

because of *4 Baruch*'s eschatological orientation toward the heavenly Jerusalem; the earthly has no eschatological salvific significance.

Kilpatrick has suggested an unusual interpretation of the phrase ἕως τῆς συνελεύσεως τοῦ ἠγαπημένου. He writes, "ἔλευσις ... is a messianic term and nearly always appears in a certain kind of phrase which first occurs in two prophetic pseudepigrapha and probably in others now lost, where it was used to describe the coming of the Messiah."[20] However, in *4 Baruch* the term συνέλευσις refers to the people, not to the Messiah. The suggestion that one read ἔλευσις instead of συνέλευσις[21] is the result of seeking to interpret *4 Bar.* 3:8 messianically. This interpretation does not give due consideration to the context of *4 Baruch*, in which the Messiah plays no role and the return of the people from exile stands at the center of *4 Bar.* 6–9. Thus, the term συνέλευσις is fitting and appropriate in the meaning of "coming together"[22] for the concerns of *4 Baruch*. The term "beloved one" for the people is taken up again in *4 Bar.* 4:6. The understanding that God loves his people is rooted in the Old Testament tradition (particularly in LXX Isa 44:2; Deut 32:15; 33:5, 26; Ps 59[60]:7; 107[108]:7; 126[127]:2; and the already-mentioned 2 Macc 2:7, the context of which is the fate of the temple inventory and the return from exile).[23]

A further difference between *4 Bar.* 3 and *2 Bar.* 6 lies in the former's description of God as the one "who created you in the abundance of the waters, who sealed you with seven seals, with seven epochs." The phrase ἐν ἑπτὰ σφραγῖσιν, ἐν ἑπτὰ καιροῖς is to be understood as a parallel construction: the seven seals are the seven epochs. The Ethiopic translation's omission of ἐν ἑπτὰ καιροῖς might be due to a difficulty in understanding the phrase.[24] One should, however, interpret *4 Bar.* 3:8 within the theological conception of creation and new creation ("until the gathering of the beloved one"): the earth that God created was sealed by him with seven epochs until the eschatological new creation.[25]

---

20. Kilpatrick, "Acts VII.52 ΕΛΕΥΣΙΣ," 144.
21. As Kilpatrick does (ibid., 141). Similarly Delling, *Paralipomena Jeremiae*, 67–68.
22. LSJ, 1707 s.v. 1; Delling, *Paralipomena Jeremiae*, 65–66.
23. See Ginzberg, *Legends*, 6:410; Delling, *Paralipomena Jeremiae*, 65; Wolff, *Jeremia im Frühjudentum und Urchristentum*, 66–67 n. 1; Wolff, "Heilshoffnung," 157; Riaud, *Paralipomènes de Jérémie*, 1744 n. 8; and Koester, *Dwelling*, 54. Marylin F. Collins sees a Christian author behind the phrase "until the coming of the Beloved One" in *4 Bar.* 3:8 introducing an interpolation or at least a change on the basis of 2 Macc 2:7 ("The Hidden Vessels in Samaritan Traditions," *JSJ* 3 [1972]: 97–116, here 103; see also Robinson, "4 Baruch," 419). There too, however, the meaning of συνέλευσις is not taken into account. Moreover, this phrase shows no evidence of being particularly Christian in origin.
24. See Herzer, *Paralipomena Jeremiae*, 162–64.
25. See *T. Levi* 8:15; *Liv. Pro.* 4:13; note also *4 Ezra* 6:20, which speak of the sealing of the passing age; see Stone, *Ezra*, 169–70. Riaud is of the opinion that "the seven seals and the seven

The final phrase—"and thereafter you will receive your beauty"—clearly depicts a horizon that stretches from the old to the new creation. "Beauty" cannot refer to the temple,[26] since that would eliminate the eschatological new-creation perspective and would fit poorly with the preceding description of the old creation.[27] Rather, "beauty" in this context serves as a "poetic" description of the perfection that will characterize the new creation. Delling, for his part, suspects that ἐν ἑπτὰ καιροῖς is a marginal gloss that does not fit the original meaning of the text to which it refers.[28] He argues further that the seven seals refer to the sure foundation of the earth, the completeness and reliability of which is expressed by the number seven. This linking of the seven seals with the founding of the earth at creation is, however, unlikely. Moreover, Delling's appeal to *Jos. Asen.* 12 for textual support is unconvincing, since neither seals (rather, stones) nor the number seven appears there.

Whereas the reference text in *2 Bar.* 6 ends with the swallowing of the vessels by the earth (6:10), this action is delayed in *4 Baruch* by the question concerning Abimelech's fate (3:9–13). By introducing Abimelech for the first time at this point, *4 Baruch* clearly goes beyond *2 Baruch*. The given narrative was consciously interrupted in order to introduce a new character whose important function will be further developed later on. The author then returns to the main thread of the chapter in 3:14, with the temple vessels being consigned to and swallowed by the earth (κατέπιεν αὐτὰ ἡ γῆ), just as in *2 Baruch*. The specific localization of this event at the altar has already been mentioned.

When one considers this chapter's interest in preserving the temple vessels, it is unusual that *4 Baruch* mentions neither the temple vessels nor the temple itself after the people return from exile, only the altar as the place of Jeremiah's death (9:7). This stands in contrast to *2 Bar.* 6:9, in which the temple has a specific significance for the promise of the rebuilding of Jerusalem. Here, too, it

---

moments designate the creation week" (*Paralipomènes de Jérémie*, 1744 n. 8). That is not convincing, since the creation is bound together with the metaphor of the seven seals only when looking forward to the eschatological new creation, not with reference to the first creation. See further the meaning of the number seven in the Apocalypse of John; see also the motif of the seven epochs in John of Damascus, *De fide orthodoxa* 2.1.

26. So Riaud, *Paralipomènes de Jérémie*, 1744 n. 8.

27. Echoes of Jer 31:23 are not to be found, in contrast to Philonenko ("Simples Observations," 162), who must assume an unattested corrupt form of the text; see further Schaller, "Greek Version," passim.

28. Delling, Paralipomena Jeremiae, 41 (see 40–41); so also Philonenko, "Simples Observations," 162 n. 43, although without reason. Philonenko also intends to exclude a creation-theological interpretation by eliminating these words. He argues that the seven seals are of gnostic origin and point to Christian baptism. Such a point of reference is, however, not in the text; see Herzer, "Antwort," 31–32.

is important to notice how our author adds a detail not found in *2 Baruch* (i.e., the mention of the altar in 3:8) that will later become important in his work.²⁹

Before we consider the character of Abimelech, one interesting parallel to 3:8 needs to be mentioned.

> (21) And now show it to them, those who do not know, but who have seen that which has befallen us and our city, up to now, that it is in agreement with the long-suffering of your power, because you called us a beloved people on account of your name. (22) From now, therefore, everything is in a state of dying. (23) Therefore, reprove the angel of death, and let your glory appear, and let the greatness of your beauty be known, and let the realm of death be sealed so that it may not receive the dead from this time, and let the treasuries of the souls restore those who are enclosed in them. (*2 Bar.* 21:21–23)

Despite their significantly different contexts, the two texts share three key words in common: "to be sealed," "beloved (people)" and "beauty." The question naturally arises as to why such an eschatological-apocalyptic vision would be picked up in a narrative text such as *4 Baruch* without any specific need for doing so. If one assumes that *2 Baruch* provided a model for *4 Baruch*, which seems likely on the basis of the links already noted, one may answer this question satisfactorily. The sealing of the realm of death in *2 Bar.* 21:23 becomes the sealing of the created earth in *4 Bar.* 3:8, underlined by the apocalyptic number seven. One might suggest that this is our author's answer to the question posed in *2 Bar.* 21:19: "How long will corruption remain, and until when will the time of mortals be happy?" According to *4 Bar.* 3:8, the corruption, the perishable creation, has been given seven epochs. Likewise, the "beauty" of God from *2 Bar.* 21:23 becomes the "beauty" the earth will receive at the end of the seven epochs by way of new creation. Finally, the giving back of the dead from the graves is transformed into the gathering of the beloved, namely, the people,³⁰ who are called "beloved" by God himself (*2 Bar.* 21:21).³¹ By noting the way in

---

29. A difficult question to answer is why *4 Baruch* does not follow *2 Baruch* in its reference to Jer 22:29 (the triple address to the earth), although major motifs from Jeremiah otherwise play a role in *4 Baruch* (see 3:9 [cf. Jer 38:10–13]; 5:18 [cf. Jer 36:6]). Two possible reasons can be given. First, the context is somewhat different. In *2 Bar.* 6:8 Baruch reports that an angel spoke the words while giving up the vessels; in *4 Bar.* 3:8 God himself gives Jeremiah the words. Second, the emphasis in the expression in *2 Baruch* lies on addressing the earth with the "word of the Mighty God," which gains force with an allusion to Jer 22:29. Because our author places his extended attribution of God in the center, he can leave out the allusion without difficulty.

30. That the motifs of the dead (or their bones) and the re-creation of Israel are connected is known by Ezekiel (Ezek 37).

31. Once again the reader's attention is drawn to 2 Macc 2:7; see above on 3:8.

which our author uses these three terms, one can satisfactorily explain the use of the eschatological-apocalyptic vision of *2 Bar.* 21:21–23 in a nonapocalyptic text such as *4 Baruch*.

As already noted, Abimelech is introduced as a new actor and "key figure"[32] in 3:9–10, which both interrupts the flow from of 3:8 to 3:11 and once again postpones God's judgment after the question about the temple vessels. Here Jeremiah asks about the fate of Abimelech in the light of the imminent destruction of the city. Again the author assumes much of his readers, at minimum that they know of Abimelech from the Jeremiah tradition (Jer 38[45]:7–13) and so understand his background and relationship to the prophet. In *4 Baruch* the people are also named as recipients of Abimelech's good deeds, though this is not immediately apparent in the biblical tradition. In this way the figure and destiny of Abimelech become associated with the destiny of the people.[33]

Jeremiah 38(45):7–13 tells in detail the story of Jeremiah being rescued from the "muddy pit" or cistern[34] by Ebed-melech. By reminding the reader of this text, *4 Bar.* 3:9 identifies the Abimelech of *4 Baruch* with the Ebed-melech of biblical Jeremiah.[35] The author's decision to make Jeremiah instead of Baruch his main character, in contrast to *2 Baruch* before him, and the mention of the link between Jeremiah and Ebed-melech in the biblical tradition create the start-

---

32. On the figure of Abimelech in *4 Baruch*, see Riaud, "Abimélech," passim.

33. Schaller regards the phrase τοῦ λαοῦ καί, found only in C and eth, as secondary ("Paralipomena Jeremiou," 718).

34. The phrase λάκκος τοῦ βορβόρου in *4 Bar.* 3:9 combines terms from LXX Jer 45:7 (λάκκος) and 45:6 (τοῦ βορβόρου); see Riaud, "Abimélech," 174 n. 6. Schaller regards τοῦ βορβόρου (C, eth, arm, slav^A) as secondary ("Paralipomena Jeremiou," 718).

35. On the name Ἀβιμέλεχ in *4 Baruch*, see Delling, *Paralipomena Jeremiae*, 7 n. 16; Bogaert, *Apocalypse de Baruch*, 1:182 n. 4; and Riaud, "Abimélech," 163. Delling, assuming one of the Palestinian languages (72) as the original language of *4 Baruch*, supposes that the name emerged in the translation into Greek, which he would not count as such a Palestinian language (see Schaller, "Greek Version," passim). The Septuagint uses the name Αβδεμελεχ to translate the Hebrew עבד מלך (LXX Jer 45:7, 10–11; 46:16; see Delling, *Paralipomena Jeremiae*, 7 n. 16). Interestingly, as in *4 Baruch*, the LXX translates ὁ Αἰθίοψ where the Hebrew is הכושי. Bogaert notes that in MS 534 of LXX Jer 45:7 and 46:6 the form Ἀβιμέλεχ was used (*Apocalypse de Baruch*, 1:182 n. 4). One can merely see an analogy here, as the name possibly is made to fit the more widely used form. Furthermore "Ebed-melech" is not a proper name, certainly not for an "Ethiopian" (see E. R. Dalgish, "Ebed-Melech," *ABD* 2:259), and so lends itself to being replaced by the known biblical proper name "Abimelech." It is unnecessary to see a hint of the use of the LXX by the writer of the Abimelech story in the LXX variant of fragment 534. The name "Abimelech" is found throughout the Old Testament (Gen 20–21; 26:1, 8–11, 16, 26; Judg 8:31; 9:1–6, 16–56; 10:1; 2 Sam 11:21; 1 Chr 18:16; Ps 34:1; see Delling, *Paralipomena Jeremiae*, 7 n. 16; V. H. Matthews, "Abimelech 1.2," *ABD* 1:20–21; and B. Halpern, "Abimelech 3," *ABD* 1:21–22), whereas "Ebed-Melech" is found only in the book of Jeremiah. The rabbinical tradition also knew the name Abimelech: *Midr. Pss.* 34; *Gen. Rab.* 54:4; and others. See G. B. Levi, "Abimelech," *JE* 1:62.

ing point for developing the narrative. To that we must add, however, a further and more decisive perspective, that of the following promise of salvation in Jer 39(46):16b–18, given by the prophet to Ebed-melech:

> (16b) Thus says the LORD of hosts, the God of Israel: I am going to fulfill my words against this city for evil and not for good, and they shall be accomplished in your presence on that day.[36] (17) But I will save you on that day, says the LORD, and you shall not be handed over to those whom you dread. (18) For I will surely save you, and you shall not fall by the sword; but you shall have your life as a prize of war, because you have trusted in me, says the LORD. (Jer 39[46]:16b–18 NRSV)

This promise of Ebed-melech's preservation, the fulfillment of which is not narrated in Jeremiah, provides the background to the story of Abimelech's preservation in *4 Baruch*.[37] A gap in the tradition is thus picked up on and filled with a new motif that the author uses fruitfully for his particular situation. The account begins with a promise similar to that of Jer 39, likewise passed on by Jeremiah's mediation: "Send him to the vineyard of Agrippa by the mountain (trail). And I will protect him until I will return the people to the city." The similar motifs in the two texts (rescue/preservation of Abimelech in the face of the city's destruction) make it highly likely that the tradition in *4 Baruch* is a development of the biblical motif of Jer 39:15–18. However, the shape of the Abimelech story in *4 Baruch* is unique and not of biblical origin.[38] One nonbiblical element of this story is of particular significance: the temporal reference to the return of the people (3:10) hints at the preservation of Abimelech being a symbol or *typus* of the preservation of the people.[39]

Finally, two realia in the text astound the modern reader because of their concreteness: "the vineyard of Agrippa" and "the mountain (trail)."[40] Neither

---

36. The last sentence in the MT (והיו לפניך ביום ההוא) is not translated in the Septuagint. In addition, *4 Baruch* lays weight on Abimelech not seeing the city's destruction (3:9). This suggests that the author used the Septuagint.

37. See Delling, *Paralipomena Jeremiae*, 7; Heinrich Schützinger, "Die arabische Jeremia-Erzählung und ihre Beziehungen zur jüdischen Überlieferung," *ZRGG* 25 (1973): 10; and Riaud, "Abimélech," 163. On the promise to Ebed-melech in Jer 39(46):16–18, see H. Schulte, "Baruch und Ebedmelech: Persönliche Heilsorakel im Jeremiabuche," *BZ* NS 32 (1988): 257–65, here 259–60.

38. See below the commentary on chapter 5. In this context it is worth noting that Abimelech is mentioned in the title of *3 Baruch*. Even if this is a later addition (Wolfgang Hage, "Die griechische Baruchapokalypse," JSHRZ V.1 [1974]: 15–44, here 18–19), it remains clear that *4 Baruch* can primarily be identified with the Abimelech narrative.

39. The readings of mss A and B and the translations arm^c and slav$^{A.B}$ underline this by adding that God should have mercy on Abimelech and thereby demonstratively on the people.

40. On textual variants, see the apparatus to the Greek text above. Schaller follows mss A and B ("Paralipomena Jeremiou," 718).

can be identified with certainty, but the way in which they are named suggests that both the way and the place were known to both writer and readers.

The repeated mention of εἰς τὸν ἀμπελῶνα (or χωρίον)[41] τοῦ Ἀγρίππα (*4 Bar.* 3:10, 15; 5:25) has suggested to many that the author of *4 Baruch* had a good geographical knowledge of the region in which the story is set and has led to the proposal that *4 Baruch* was written in Jerusalem.[42] While Riaud believes that this place is a literary fiction,[43] many have sought in different ways to establish what is meant by the property of Agrippa or which king of this name—many are mentioned in the Jewish tradition—is meant.[44] Harris argued for the cisterns of Solomon, southeast of Bethlehem.[45] Since this place is relatively far from Jerusalem (some 11 km), this is rather unlikely. Furthermore, there is no evidence that this place was known by the name of Agrippa, such that the readers of *4 Baruch* could have made the identification.

Kohler's suggestion that "vineyard of Agrippa" refers to the parks of Agrippa mentioned by Josephus (*J.W.* 5.172–183) is likewise unlikely,[46] since this park was within the city. Josephus also provides a detailed description of a northern wall begun by Agrippa I[47] and enclosing a considerable area north of Jerusalem (*J.W.* 5.142–183; see also Josephus, *Ant.* 19.326–327).[48] Based on Josephus, this appears to be the only area linked to the name "Agrippa" (Herod Agrippa I), and it was known before Agrippa I as עמק המלך, "the plain of the king" (2 Sam

---

41. On this change of name, see below on 3:15.

42. Harris, *Rest of the Words of Baruch*, 12; Kohler, "The Pre-Talmudic Haggada," 409; and Turdéanu, "Légende," 306.

43. Riaud, "Abimélech," 174 n. 9.

44. For a good overview of the many interpretations, see Riaud, "Abimélech," 174 n. 9. See also Bogaert, *Apocalypse de Baruch*, 1:328–30. On what follows, see Herzer, *Paralipomena Jeremiae*, 100–103.

45. Harris, *Rest of the Words of Baruch*, 12; Mingana and Harris, "Jeremiah Apocryphon," 136.

46. Kohler, "The Pre-Talmudic Haggada," 409. For a description of these parks, see Gustaf Dalman, *Jerusalem und sein Gelände: Mit 50 Abbildungen und einer Karte* (BFCT 2.19; Gütersloh: Bertelsmann, 1930), 94–99.

47. That it is Herod Agrippa I (37–44 C.E.) is clear from Josephus, *J.W.* 5.152, where Josephus mentions the "father of the currently living king, also known as Agrippa." The "currently living king" can only be Herod Agrippa II, who died 93 C.E. See Schäfer, *History of the Jews*, 114. Herbert Donner, *Geschichte des Volkes Israel und seiner Nachbarn in Grundzügen* (2 vols.; Göttingen: Vandenhoeck & Ruprecht, 1987), 2:459, assumes 100 C.E. See further Martin Hengel, *Judentum und Hellenismus: Studien zu ihrer Begegnung unter besonderer Berücksichtigung Palästinas bis zur Mitte des 2. Jahrhunderts v. Chr.* (3rd ed.; WUNT 10; Tübingen: Mohr Siebeck, 1988), 183 n. 323. On the history of the Herodians, see A. Schalit, "Die frühchristliche Überlieferung über die Herkunft der Familie des Herodes: Ein Beitrag zur Geschichte der politischen Invektive in Judaea," *ASTI* 1 (1962): 109–60.

48. Daniel R. Schwartz, *Agrippa I: The Last King of Judaea* (TSAJ 23; Tübingen: Mohr Siebeck, 1990), 140–44.

18:18; Josephus, *Ant.* 7.243). This could suggest that this area north of Jerusalem was the "vineyard/property of Agrippa." However, Josephus describes it as a residential area of Jerusalem, hardly a plausible place for preserving Abimelech at the time of the destruction of the city. Moreover, Titus's main rampart was built against this area during the siege of Jerusalem (Josephus, *J.W.* 5.47–97).[49]

Abel[50] cites Theodosius, *De situ terrae sanctae* 5:6, in which Abimelech's sleep is mentioned: "From the Mount of Olives to the village Hermippo, where Abimelech slept under the fig tree for forty-six years, it is one mile. Abimelech was the disciple of Jeremiah the saint; there also was Baruch the prophet."[51] With reference to this passage, however, one must interpret "Hermippo" as "a deformation of the name Agrippa."[52] According to Bogaert, Theodosius's itinerary took him to the southeast of the "mountain of offense."[53] However, Theodosius's "narrative direction" is west to east: Jerusalem—Mount of Olives—Hermippo.[54] Dalman, again relating to Theodosius, therefore suggested *Hirbet ibk'dan*, a location in the northeast of Jerusalem on an old route to Jericho.[55] Not only is this likely, but it also fits the name of the route taken by Abimelech to the vineyard: διὰ τῆς ὁδοῦ τοῦ ὄρους—through the mountain way (*4 Bar.* 3:15; 5:9), in short form διὰ τοῦ ὄρους (3:10). The threefold repetition and the determining use of the article are noteworthy. One could suspect, applying further the

---

49. See Dalman, *Jerusalem und sein Gelände*, 44. See also *y. Ta'anit* 4:5 on the fall of Bethar (ca. 10 km southwest of Jerusalem) during the Bar Kokhba War: "The evil Hadrian had a large vineyard, eighteen mil by eighteen mil. It was of the dimension of the distance from Tiberias to Sepphoris. They surrounded it by a wall made of [the bones of] those who were slain in Bethar" (quoted from Neusner, *Talmud of the Land of Israel*, 18:278).

50. Félix-Marie Abel, "Deir Senneh ou le domaine d'Agrippa," *RB* 44 (1935): 61–68. See also Bogaert, *Apocalypse de Baruch*, 1:329; Riaud, "Abimélech," 174 n. 9.

51. De monte Oliueti usque in uico Hermippo…, ubi dormuit Abimelech sub arbore ficus annis XLVI…, miliario uno, qui Abimelech discipulus fuit sancti Hieremiae; ibi fuit Baruc propheta (Latin cited according to Bogaert, *Apocalypse de Baruch*, 1:328).

52. Ibid., 1:329. See also Abel, "Deir Senneh," 64 n. 1. Herbert Donner also suggests that "Hermippo" is distorted from the Greek phrase χωρίον τοῦ Ἀγρίππα (*Pilgerfahrt ins Heilige Land: Die ältesten Berichte christlicher Palästinapilger [4.–7. Jahrhundert]* [Stuttgart: Katholisches Bibelwerk, 1979], 206–7 n. 44). Here it becomes clear that "Theodosius" also did not know how to understand "vineyard/property of Agrippa." In "Theodosius" we are dealing with the so-called "Archidiakonus," who wrote in the sixth century C.E.; see W. Enßlin, "Theodosius 70," *PW* 2/10:1951.

53. Bogaert, *Apocalypse de Baruch*, 1:329. See also Abel, "Deir Senneh," 64.

54. Abel's thesis also contains the problematic view that Deir Senneh, his location for the vineyard, was a place of many caves and would thus have provided a place for Baruch (Abel, "Deir Senneh," 65). However, according to *4 Bar.* 4:11, Baruch was sitting in a tomb; *2 Bar.* 21:1 points us to the Kidron Valley! Moreover, contrary to Abel's assumption, *4 Baruch* does not explicitly send Baruch and Abimelech to the same place.

55. Dalman, *Jerusalem und sein Gelände*, 39.

Theodosius citation, that the Mount of Olives is the mountain indicated by the definite article. The place of Abimelech's rest would thus be sufficiently far from the city to remain safe from the destruction. Finally, this west-east direction is of theological significance, being the direction in which God left the temple before its destruction in Ezek 8–11, once again over the Mount of Olives (11:23).[56]

Having dealt with the question of Abimelech's protection, the writer once again takes up the main thread of the narrative in 3:11. Abimelech disappears from view, returning only after further instructions from God and the consigning of the temple vessels to the earth. The conscious weaving of Abimelech into the narrative is thereby highlighted.[57]

In contrast to the biblical tradition, according to which Jeremiah was dragged to Egypt (Jer 43[50]:1–7), *4 Baruch* and *2 Baruch* (10:1–5) portray him as obeying a divine command to accompany the people to Babylon.[58] A similar variation within the tradition is evident in regard to Baruch: *4 Bar.* 3:12 and *2 Bar.* 10:3 state that he remained in Jerusalem, again according to God's word,[59] while Jer 43(50):6–7 has him being taken to Egypt with Jeremiah, and Bar 1:1–2 portrays him as active in Babylon. This latter role is fulfilled in *4 Baruch* by the prophet himself. The reason for Jeremiah's departure with the exiles is given in 3:11: he is to declare to them the good news (εὐαγγελίζεσθαι), which in the context of *4 Baruch* refers to the teaching of the preserving law

---

56. See further 2 Kgs 25:4; Neh 3:15; Jer 39:4; 52:7–8. Zedekiah's flight before Nebuchadnezzar is reported in 2 Kgs 25:4 (see Jer 39:4 and 52:7–8): "Then a breach was made in the city wall; the king with all the soldiers fled by night by the way of the gate between the two walls, by the king's garden, though the Chaldeans were all around the city. They went in the direction of the Arabah" (the Arabah road, דרך הערבה/ὁδὸν τὴν Αραβα; NRSV). It is reckoned that this "garden of the king" (κῆπος τοῦ βασιλέως, 2 Kgs 24:5) was beyond the city limits at the confluence of the Kidron and Hinnom Valleys, as suggested by Martin Rehm, *Das zweite Buch der Könige: Ein Kommentar* (NEchtB; Würzburg: Echter-Verlag, 1982), 241. See Dalman, *Jerusalem und sein Gelände*, 168; Erich W. Cohn, *New Ideas about Jerusalem's Topography* (Jerusalem: Franciscan Print, 1987), 12, 21; and William Lee Holladay, *Jeremiah 1.2: A Commentary on the Book of the Prophet Jeremiah* (Hermeneia; Philadelphia: Fortress, 1986), 292. Although it is unlikely that *4 Baruch* is referring to this place, it is still noteworthy that Zedekiah also fled east from Nebuchadnezzar, probably as this was the only way during a siege (the Arabah road "is the road from Jerusalem down to Jericho," according to T. Raymond Hobbs, *2 Kings* [WBC 13; Waco, Tex.: Word, 1985], 363). See also John Wilkinson, "The Way from Jerusalem to Jericho," *BA* 38 (1975): 10–24. This supports the view that *4 Baruch* also thinks in terms of going east for Abimelech. Perhaps one can go so far as to say that the biblical Arabah road is the "mountain trail" of *4 Baruch*.

57. Against Bogaert, *Apocalypse de Baruch*, 1:193–94.

58. See also 4QapocrJer; *Pesiq. Rab.* 26:18; *S. Olam Rab.* 26:1; *Apocr. Jer.* 30–31, 35–37, 39. The relationship of these traditions is unclear.

59. *2 Baruch*'s unique tradition is adopted in *4 Baruch*.

and to the comforting proclamation of the salvation of return (5:21; 7:32).⁶⁰ God's statement that he has yet more to say to Baruch in 3:12 offers a further signal of the message of return, although judgment has not yet fallen. As earlier in 1:12, the dialogue between God and Jeremiah ends in 3:13 with God's departure. The author is not disturbed by the tension between 3:13 and 3:2, in which angels appeared, not God. This verse is the end of God's direct speech in *4 Baruch*—what remains is left to human actors who should deduce the right actions and beliefs on the basis of these principles. This observation itself could shed light on the author's situation: God has withdrawn himself from the people in judgment on Jerusalem but has left behind a tradition that has power to carry and preserve his people.

Once God departs, the divine instructions are carried out (3:14): in the sanctuary, the temple vessels are handed over to the earth,⁶¹ which swallows them. Jeremiah's and Baruch's lament appears logical and concludes the narrative complex, so the story returns again to Abimelech (3:15). This conscious shaping has already been described and leads here to tensions in the content, which do not, however, require literary-critical resolution. Verse 15 presupposes that Abimelech is with Jeremiah and Baruch: hence Jeremiah can send him away. The details are not significant, but it is noteworthy that the author not only remembers the Abimelech story he has begun (and as with the temple vessels notes the execution of divine command) but that he further develops and extends the story so that it stands in tension with the divine task.

What Jeremiah requires of Abimelech goes beyond the divine command, but this prepares readers for what follows. The places are the same: Abimelech is to go to the property of Agrippa by way of the mountain trail. Instead of

---

60. κατηχῆσαι ... τὸν λόγον in 5:21 has the primary meaning "to teach the law"; see Delling, *Paralipomena Jeremiae*, 21–22, 25; Riaud, "La figure de Jérémie," 381–82. This expression does not appear in the Septuagint (see Hermann Wolfgang Beyer, "κατηχέω," *TDNT* 3:638); it does, however, appear in many Targumim; see Peter Stuhlmacher, *Das paulinische Evangelium I* (FRLANT 95; Göttingen: Vandenhoeck & Ruprecht, 1968), 178 n. 2. In *4 Bar.* 5:21 one needs to note not just κατηχῆσαι but also the term εὐαγγελίσασθαι. The καί is not purely explicative in this context (contra Stuhlmacher). On the link between law and having a share in salvation in apocalyptic literature, see, e.g., Dietrich Rössler, *Gesetz und Geschichte: Untersuchungen zur Theologie der jüdischen Apokalyptik und der Pharisäischen Orthodoxie* (WMANT 3; Neukirchen: Neukirchner Verlag, 1960), 101. Kraft and Purintun characterize Jeremiah's activity in general as "preaching" (*Paraleipomena Jeremiou*, 19; so also Delling, *Paralipomena Jeremiae*, 21; Schaller, "Paralipomena Jeremiou," 719). According to *2 Bar.* 10:2, Jeremiah should "stand by" the people and "uphold" them (see 33:2); there is no concrete reference here. Therefore, *4 Baruch* gives more precision to Jeremiah's standing by the people in *2 Baruch*, which is exercised in teaching the law and promising the salvation of return.

61. The explication "and the altar" is here—in contrast to 3:8—probably secondary. However, the locating of the action in the sanctuary associates the verse with 3:8.

"vineyard" (ἀμπελών), the more neutral word "piece of land" or "property" (χωρίον) is used and maintained (see 5:25). This probably is intended to address the question as to how Abimelech is to gather figs in a vineyard. The more neutral word fits better at this point. It is, however, to be noted that vineyards and olive groves were punctuated with a number of fig trees (see Luke 13:6).[62] More important than this detail is an intertextual association of particular importance for understanding what follows. The key words "basket" and "figs" point readers to the vision of the baskets of figs in Jer 24:1–10.[63] Our author does not restrict himself to the Jeremiah text, however, but takes up a known fact reflected in several texts and applies it spiritually: figs were used to strengthen and to heal the sick.[64] In *4 Baruch* they thus become symbols of the salvation of the people as a whole, both of their strengthening in exile and of their coming healing. Provision for that comes, as is repeatedly emphasized, before the execution of God's judgment. This salvation promise is further highlighted by the prophet's words to Abimelech: "the favor of the Lord is on you, and his glory is on your head." The expression ἡ εὐφρασία τοῦ Κυρίου is singular and therein remarkable.[65] The same root is used in 6:3 to denote a prevailing joyful mood in the light of the coming salvation that Baruch sees in Abimelech's figs. Thus, the joy of God[66] that is on Abimelech becomes the joy of the faithful through the figs. It is in this context that the term δόξα must be interpreted. The absolute usage (literally, "the glory") is surprising but is an abbreviation that, in parallelism with εὐφρασία, should be understood as referring to God. The absolute usage here underlines the fact that God stands by the people, as δόξα may also refer to God himself (Jer 2:11).[67] If the latter is in view, a special divine blessing for Abimelech is being expressed, a blessing that is passed on to the people through the gathering of the figs, a blessing that has a salvific effect for them as well. Verse 16 briefly notes the execution of the task. The brevity of the concluding scene reflects the fact that the author will provide more extensive details concerning Abimelech later in the book.

---

62. Hunzinger, "συκή κτλ.," 7:753.

63. Herzer, *Paralipomena Jeremiae*, 104. See below. That the term κόφινος is not found in Jer 24:1 (LXX; there κάλαθος) but in the Symmachus translation was seen by Marc Philonenko ("Les Paralipomènes de Jérémie et la Traduction de Symmaque," *RHPR* 64 [1984]: 143–45) as an indication that *4 Baruch* used the Symmachus text; see further, Schaller, "Greek Version," passim.

64. For the strengthening and healing properties of figs, see Isa 38:21 and 2 Kgs 20:7; see also Victor Reichmann, "Feigen I," *RAC* 7: 647–648.

65. Schaller, "Paralipomena Jeremiou," 720.

66. *Genitivus subjectivus.*

67. Philonenko, "Simples Observations," 165.

CHAPTER 4

On the morning of the following day, the strategically best moment, the Chaldeans surround Jerusalem (4:1). The time marker is the same as in 3:15, so the two events—the sending away of Abimelech and the occupation of the city—are portrayed as occurring simultaneously. No literary-critical conclusions are to be drawn from that. The time in 4:1 is determined by *2 Bar.* 6:1, and the earlier mention of the same time in *4 Bar.* 3:15 is the result of the way in which the author has worked the Abimelech story into his text.

The reference to "the great angel" in 4:1 reminds the reader that the angels who in chapter 3 were held back are still present in the background. Now it is "the great angel" who blows the trumpet. Thus far we have not met such an angel, but the definite article suggests that a specific angel is meant, although no name is given. The attribute μέγας suggests Michael on the basis of Dan 12:1; statements in *4 Bar.* 8:9 and 9:5 will confirm this identification later on, but chapter 4 merely hints at such an association.[1] Michael's name is only mentioned at the end, once the people's salvation has been completed; in this judgment context he remains unnamed.

The trumpet is the traditional signal for divine intervention in creation and history; particularly in view here is its appearance at judgment (see Jer 6:1, 17; *Pss. Sol.* 8:1). With the trumpet blast the angel signals to the enemy that the city has been handed over to them.[2] The passive ἠνεῴχθη allows no doubt that it is

---

1. The phrase "the great angel" in *4 Bar.* 4:1 picks up and defines the term "another angel" from *2 Bar.* 6:5. This definition makes identification with the archangel possible.

2. In *2 Bar.* 8:1 a "voice from the midst of the temple" calls on the enemy to enter. Nickelsburg (*Jewish Literature,* 282) points out a similar phenomenon reported in Josephus, *J.W.* 6.299–301. See also Albertus F. J. Klijn, "The Sources and the Redaction of the Syria Apocalypse of Baruch," *JSJ* 1 (1970): 64–76. Murphy ("The Temple in the Syriac Apocalypse of Baruch," 679) mentions a comparable passage in Tacitus, *Hist.* 5.13. One must, however, be aware that, although the motif of voices from the temple or the "inner court" (as in Josephus) are similar, Josephus speaks of the call of many voices (φωνὴ ἀθρόας), and the content of the call is different; see Otto Michel and Otto Bauernfeind, eds., *Josephus Flavius, De Bello Judaico—Der jüdische Krieg: Zweisprachige Ausgabe der sieben Bücher* (3 vols.; Darmstadt: Wissenschaftliche Buchgesellschaft, 1959–69), 2.2:185 n. 142;

God himself who hands the city over (*passivum divinum*).³ Verse 2 confirms the capture of the city and of the people. The author probably consciously omits the narration of the destruction named in Baruch's lament in 4:6, although the lament presupposes it.⁴

The temple once again comes into view in a particular way in 4:3. The temple-keys episode has been taken from *2 Bar.* 10:18 but has been given its own profile. The text in *2 Baruch* reads: "You priests, take the keys of the sanctuary, and cast them to the highest heaven, and give them back to the Lord and say, 'Guard your house yourself, because, behold, we have been found to be false stewards.' "⁵ Jeremiah's giving over of the temple keys⁶ to the sun (*4 Bar.* 4:3–4) is formulated in *2 Bar.* 10:18 as a request to the priests by Baruch in his lament over the fall of the city.⁷ By doing in *4 Bar.* 4:3⁸ what the priests of *2 Baruch* are to do, Jeremiah takes on the priestly function. This is a further hint at his priestly office (already noted at 2:3; see further 5:18; 7:14, 32; and particularly 9:2, 8, in which Jeremiah as high priest brings the sacrifice of the Day of Atonement).⁹ This priestly function emerges from Jer 1:1, which reports that Jeremiah was of priestly lineage, as does Josephus (*Ant.* 10.80), alongside Ezekiel.¹⁰

---

see also Ezek 10:5: "The sound of the wings of the cherubim was heard as far as the outer court, like the voice of God Almighty when he speaks" (NRSV).

3. The parallel in *2 Bar.* 6:1, 5; 8:1–5—a parallel that goes to the level of the wording—describes this in more detail and names both Baruch and King Zedekiah as prisoners deported to Babylon with the people. While the surrounding of the city and the command to take it follow immediately one after the other in *4 Bar.* 4:1, they are interrupted between *2 Bar.* 6:1 and 8:1–5 by the story of the temple vessels and the angel's destruction of the city walls (7:1–3). In *4 Baruch*, however, 4:1a could not come before 3:1, since the time references at these points would contradict.

4. By contrast, the angel's destruction of the city is described in *2 Bar.* 7:1–8:1a; see Herzer, *Paralipomena Jeremiae*, 56.

5. Quoted from Klijn, "2 Baruch," *OTP* 1:624.

6. On this view, see *y. Šeqal.* 7:2; *b. Ta'anit.* 29a; *Lev. Rab.* 19:6; *Pesiq. Rab.* 26:16. See also Martin Hengel, *Die Zeloten: Untersuchungen zur jüdischen Freiheitsbewegung in der Zeit von Herodes I. bis 70 n.Chr.* (2nd ed.; AGSU 1; Leiden: Brill, 1976), 228; Wolff, *Jeremia im Frühjudentum und Urchristentum*, 76–79; Riaud, "Abimélech," 174 n. 1; Riaud, *Les Paralipomènes du Prophète Jérémie*, 54–55; and Herzer, *Paralipomena Jeremiae*, 56–58, 83–84.

7. Bogaert, *Apocalypse de Baruch*, 1:236; Murphy, "The Temple in the Syriac Apocalypse of Baruch," 681.

8. Harris (*Rest of the Words of Baruch*, 23) suspects the influence of Maccabean tradition (see 2 Macc 2:5).

9. On Jeremiah the priest, see Wolff, *Jeremia im Frühjudentum und Urchristentum*, 48; Riaud, "La figure de Jérémie," 378–79.

10. That Ezekiel was a priest is clear from Ezek 1:3, his interest in the temple, and his knowledge of the temple facilities, such as in 1:4–28; 8:1–18; 10:1–22, to mention but a few; see further Walther Zimmerli, *Ezekiel: A Commentary on the Book of the Prophet Ezekiel* (2 vols.; Hermeneia; Philadelphia: Fortress, 1979–83), 1:16–21. On Jeremiah in the Old Testament, see Jack R.

The "highest heaven" in 2 Bar. 10:18 is described more concretely in *4 Bar.* 4:3 as the sun (ὁ ἥλιος), and the time during which the keys should be guarded ("until the day when the Lord will ask you for them") is missing in *2 Baruch*. More important, the wording of the statement has a different intention: in *2 Bar.* 10:18 the priests are to throw the keys "to the highest heaven," but it is the Lord himself who is to guard the keys; in *4 Bar.* 4:3 Jeremiah takes on the priests' function, and it is not God but the sun that is required to guard the keys. The reason for mentioning the sun is not clear, though it leaves the impression that *4 Baruch* clarifies the reference to God implicit in the phrase "highest heaven" (note the rest of *2 Bar.* 10:18: "give them back to the Lord ... guard your house yourself"). The Old Testament provides the only clear example of this sun symbolism for God in Ps 84:12.[11] Rabbinical literature, however, saw the sun as serving creation, as a gift to it.[12] The service of the sun is central here in *4 Baruch*, as it is called upon to guard the keys "until the day when the Lord will ask you for them" (4:3). A direct identification of God and the sun is thus avoided. It is noteworthy that the expectation, raised by specifying the time when the keys will be returned, is not met within *4 Baruch*. Neither are the temple keys returned, nor are the temple articles given up by the earth. This unfulfilled expectation plays an important role in the overall concept of *4 Baruch*.

As in *2 Bar.* 10:18, the reason for handing over the keys is that those previously responsible have proven to be "unfaithful trustees" (ἐπίτροποι ψεύδους,[13] *4 Bar.* 4:4). This statement reveals a tension in the narrative: thus far Jeremiah and Baruch have not been included among the guilty; rather, the assignment

---

Lundbom, "Jeremiah," *ABD* 3:686–87; Rüdiger Liwak, Der Prophet und die Geschichte: Eine literarhistorische Untersuchung zum Jeremiabuch (BWANT 7; Stuttgart: Kohlhammer, 1987), 58–78, esp. 74–75. Although Jer 1:1 notes Jeremiah's priestly decent, Wilhelm Rudolph states that the Old Testament tradition neither mentions nor denies the priestly service of the prophet (*Jeremia* [2nd ed.; HAT 12; Tübingen: Mohr Siebeck, 1958], 3). For precisely this reason, it was later possible to characterize Jeremiah as a priest.

11. On this text, see Hans-Peter Stähli, *Solare Elemente im Jahweglauben des Alten Testaments* (OBO 66; Göttingen: Vandenhoeck & Ruprecht, 1985), 41–43; Birgit Langer, *Gott als "Licht" in Israel und Mesopotamien: Eine Studie zu Jes 60,1–3.19–20* (ÖSB 7; Klosterneuburg: Österreichisches Katholisches Bibelwerk, 1989), 34–36, 144–46. Further application of sun motifs to God are found in Isa 60:1–3; Mal 3:20; Sir 42:16; 50:7; see Johann Maier, "Die Sonne im religiösen Denken des antiken Judentums," *ANRW* 19.1:346–412, here 354; M. S. Smith, "The Near Eastern Background of Solar Language for Yahweh," *JBL* 109 (1990): 29–39, here 30–34.

12. *Lev. Rab.* 35:8; Maier, "Die Sonne im religiösen Denken," 352, 406 (further references there); see also P. Maser, "Sonne und Mond: Exegetische Erwägungen zum Fortleben der spätantikjüdischen in der frühchristlichen Kultur," *Kairós* 25 (1983): 41–67.

13. The genitive marks the adjective; Schaller rightly suspects a Hebraicism ("Paralipomena Jeremiou," 721). The reference to a similar construction in *4 Bar.* 7:2 is, however, not helpful, as there the accentuation given by the genitive is of meaning (see below).

of guilt has been limited to the people (1:1, 7; 2:2, 3). One can resolve this tension by assuming that Jeremiah and Baruch take responsibility for what has happened. In his priestly function, Jeremiah, together with Baruch, becomes accountable for the deterioration of the situation among the people. The author's indirect criticism against those responsible for the religion of his times is clearly to be seen in this tension as well. The end of the matter is reported in the briefest of terms: the people are deported while Jeremiah weeps for them (4:5).

The new scene beginning in 4:6 redirects the reader's attention from Jeremiah and the people to Baruch, who remains mourning in the occupied city, singing a lament that is marked as such with the term θρῆνος, which in the Septuagint is typical in prophetic literature for a lament over Israel or Jerusalem.[14] The lament is thematically structured in four verses.

1   Lament over the destruction; reason for the destruction (4:6)
2   Statement against the lawless (4:7)
3   Certainty of salvation for the people; judgment for the enemy (4:8)
4   Blessing of the fathers (4:9)

"Why has Jerusalem been devastated?"—Baruch's lament begins with a brief recapitulation of what has just happened (the destruction of the city) and a rhetorical shift to his primary concern: the reason for the devastation. Like Jeremiah before him, Baruch attributes the destruction to the people's sin. However, here for the first time the sinful people are explicitly and simultaneously referred to as the *beloved* people. The reference in 3:8 to the "beloved" looked forward to the return from exile. Based on this clarification in 4:6, one can assume that the people were also in view in 3:8.[15] Interestingly, Baruch concludes 4:6 by naming his own personal sin: "because of *our* sins and those of the people." In light of the reference to the "unfaithful trustees" in 4:4, "our" refers to Jeremiah and Baruch. As elsewhere, the sin is not described concretely. Given the sheer magnitude of the events, concrete description would not be fitting.

Despite this sin, 4:7 makes it clear that the law remains, which distinguishes Israel from the nations. The enemies are described with the term παράνομοι, as those who live without or beyond the law and worship other gods.[16] They will

---

14. See, for example, Amos 5:1; Lam 1:1; Ezek 19:1; and, of course, Jer 7:29; 9:9, 17, 19. On the ritual of the dust-covered head, see above on 2:1.

15. See the commentary on 3:8 above.

16. Those falling away in Israel could also be described as παράνομοι, for which see Deut 13:14; 1 Macc 1:11; 10:61; 11:21; Ps 119(118):85; 86(85):14, among others; the nations are probably meant in 3 Macc 2:17.

not be able to boast that they have overcome the beloved people by their own strength. Lamenting the boasting of the enemy is a motif firmly anchored in Israel's psalms of lament,[17] and boasting in self is rejected in many places, including Jer 9:23 [22 LXX].[18] God's handing over of the people,[19] not the strength of the enemies, is the cause of the people's fate. Consequently, the enemies' capture of the city is but a superficial reality that offers no basis for boasting.[20]

Turning from the enemies back to the people, 4:8 expresses certainty concerning salvation and return, resulting from trust in God's mercy toward his beloved people. The word οἰκτειρεῖν often refers to sympathy for one already punished,[21] so the result of this mercy is the reversal of the judgment: God will bring the deported people back to the city. For the enemy, this means judgment: they will have no life, a formulation with Johannine overtones.[22] The Christian conclusion to *4 Baruch* also has reminders of Johannine formulations, but the phrase here is not specific enough that one should consider it to be a Christian interpolation.[23]

The lament concludes in 4:9 with Baruch's blessing of the patriarchs Abraham, Isaac, and Jacob. The parallel in *2 Bar.* 11:4–6 refers generally to the patriarchs and the righteous; *4 Bar.* 4:9 names them.[24] The blessing form is

---

17. Ps 14(13):5; 38(37):17 (NRSV 38:16); 94(93):3–4; see also 1 Sam 2:3.

18. See also Judg 7:2; 1 Sam 2:10 (LXX); *Odes Sol.* 3:10; Ps 12(11):4–5 (NRSV 12:3–4); *2 Bar.* 5:1; 7:2; 67:2; 80:3; *T. Jud.* 13:2; *L.A.B.* 31:1; *Pesiq. Rab.* 26:16. For a discussion of praise and self-praise in the Greco-Roman world, see John T. Fitzgerald, *Cracks in an Earthen Vessel: An Examination of the Catalogues of Hardships in the Corinthian Correspondence* (SBLDS 99; Atlanta: Scholars Press, 1988), 107–14, which appears to be more differentiated than in Old Testament and early Jewish traditions: "Precisely because of its frequency and the odium attached to it, rhetoricians and ethicists gave particular attention to the situations in which it was permissible to praise oneself and the methods for doing so inoffensively" (109). Referring particularly to Plutarch, *De laude ipsius*, Fitzgerald points out: "Whatever the situation, it is as appropriate as it is modest to credit one's success either to luck or to God (542E–543A; 543C), giving the glory to the divine (541C...)" (110).

19. As in *4 Bar.* 4:6, παρεδόθημεν is a *passivum divinum*.

20. The Greek form ἠδυνήθητε in 4:7c has been variously identified and translated. Kraft and Purintun (*Paraleipomena Jeremiou*, 21: "you were not able to prevail against it") and Riaud (*Les Paralipomènes du Prophète Jérémie*, 143: "vous étiez impuissants contre elle"—you had no power against it) both derive it from the rare verb ἀδύναμαι. Schaller rightly sees an Attic aorist of δύναμαι and refers to Josephus, *Ant.* 12.278 ("Paralipomena Jeremiou," 722).

21. Ps 60(59):3 (NRSV 60:1); Mic 7:19; Lam 3:32; 2 Macc 8:2; 3 Macc 5:51, and others; the term is used negatively in Jer 13:14; 21:7. In Exod 33:19, it is synonymous with ἐλεεῖν.

22. John 3:15–16; 5:24, 26, 39–40; 6:40, 47, 53–54; 10:10; 20:31; 1 John 3:15; 5:12–13.

23. On the question of Christian interpolations in *4 Baruch*, see Herzer, *Paralipomena Jeremiae*, 171–76.

24. Ibid., 60.

supremely shaped by the language of the Psalms.[25] The reference to the dead patriarchs[26] is easily understood: long gone is the "golden age" of Abraham, Isaac, and Jacob, when judgment against Jerusalem was unthinkable and the history of salvation and election was beginning.[27] This is the sense with which the author will mention the patriarchs again later in the book, speaking concretely of the covenant God established with them that marked the beginning of salvation. In those days, Baruch would not have had to witness the city's destruction—but witness it he did. He describes the destruction itself with the term ἀφανισμός, which carries the sense of disappearing.[28] From this point on the city is no longer recognizable.

After finishing his lament, Baruch follows Abimelech and Jeremiah in leaving the city (4:10). That each one heads in a different direction and that they thus end up spatially separated is now for the first time clear to the reader. The scattering of the people is therefore portrayed through the scattering of the main characters. This spatial problem will be taken up again later and used positively (5:38; 7:28). The motif of space is, however, now metaphorically underscored. It is not just that Baruch leaves the city, but that he sits down in a grave. The imagery is here far more significant than any attempt to identify the grave.[29] It symbolizes the state of the people, whose life with God is at an end with the fall

---

25. Pss 1:1; 2:12; 32(31):1–2; 34(33):9 (NRSV 34:8); see also Gen 30:13; 1 Kgs 10:8; Job 5:17; Sir 34:15; in the New Testament, see Matt 5:3–11; Luke 1:45; John 20:29; Jas 1:12; 1 Pet 4:14; Rev 1:3; 14:13.

26. Expressed here with ἐξῆλθον ἐκ τοῦ κόσμου τούτου.

27. A similar reference to the patriarchs is to be found in *2 Bar.* 21:24, in which the first creation was on behalf of the patriarchs. Hence *4 Baruch* seems to interpret *2 Bar.* 11:4 in the light of *2 Bar.* 21:24, formulating the new text on the basis of an exegesis of the old.

28. LSJ, 286, s.v. ἀφάνει II.

29. Wolff, "Heilshoffnung," 155; Schaller, "Paralipomena Jeremiou," 723. According to Herbert Schmid, the grave in *4 Bar.* 4:11 should be located in the Kidron Valley ("Baruch und die ihm zugeschriebene apokryphe und pseudepigraphe Literatur," *Jud* 30 [1974]: 54–70, here 64; so also Schaller, "Paralipomena Jeremiou," 723). Kohler wishes to find it "in the neighbourhood of Hebron" ("The Pre-Talmudic Haggada," 410; so also Bogaert, *Apocalypse de Baruch*, 1:328–30). None of this can be verified; local Christian traditions (Theodosius [*De situ terrae sanctae* 5:6] establishes a connection between the place of Abimelech and that of Baruch; so also Schaller, "Paralipomena Jeremiou," 723) are fictional. It must be taken into account that one is primarily faced with the use of a motif from *2 Bar.* 21:1. The reference there is to a cave (*m'rt' d"r'*). Gry (quote from Bogaert, *Apocalypse de Baruch*, 2:48) suggested changing the expression, which he regarded as a pleonasm, to "cave of silence," assuming that the Greek text read ἡ ὀπὴ σιγῆς instead of ἡ ὀπὴ τῆς γῆς. The use of μνημεῖον in *4 Bar.* 4:11 is easier to explain on the basis of this conjecture, for the "cave of silence" is made tangible with the word "grave." There are, however, insufficient grounds for this conjecture, and the pleonasm can be alternatively explained; see Bogaert, *Apocalypse de Baruch*, 2:49.

of Jerusalem, lying in a grave in Babylon.[30] Looking ahead to the Abimelech story, one could almost speak of a death-sleep, from which the people will be awakened. One might even go one step further. With Baruch's entrance into the grave, the narrative now enters a phase that will not be completed until Abimelech awakens and is reunited with Baruch (6:2). Abimelech's sleep will be narrated between the end of chapter 4 and the beginning of chapter 6, a sleep that is similarly symbolic of the Babylon exile.

If one sees this structure as consciously shaped, then the note concerning the angels in 4:11 makes sense: the angels give Baruch—and the readers—necessary information. The content of this information is the story of Abimelech's sleep, and 4:11 forms its introduction. This observation finds support in a compositional comparison with *2 Baruch*, as there too Baruch sets himself down in a cave (21:1). However, instead of the Abimelech story, *2 Baruch* records a prayer at this point. The interruption of the narrative flow of the model at exactly this point makes clearer the authorial intention described above: to introduce Abimelech as a *typus* of the beloved people and to tell his story as an anticipation of the people's story, which becomes transparent to the readers' situation.

---

30. Cf. the symbolism of graves in Ezek 37:12–13.

Chapter 5

Chapter 5 is not just the compositional center of *4 Baruch* but is also its center in terms of content. The author uses the story of the Ethiopian Abimelech to give a specific accent to his work over against the text he has taken for his model. Simultaneously, however, he uses traditional material as well.[1]

The story of Abimelech's sixty-six-year sleep and the build-up to it in chapter 3 lead to literary-critical problems that gave Bogaert cause to remove this material from *4 Baruch*.[2] The following texts come into question: 5:1–6:7 as the main narrative; 3:9–10, 15–16; 7:8, 15, 28, 32; 8:5; and references to Abimelech in 9:7–32. Although even Bogaert recognized that the narration of Abimelech's sleep represents the central part of the work,[3] he concluded that the main story as well as its connections to earlier and later chapters were added by a later hand.[4] It is correct to conclude that, if *4 Baruch* is dependent on *2 Baruch* and Abimelech does not appear in *2 Baruch,* then redactional work has brought the two together. The question is, however, on which redactional level this fusion took place. As has already been established, the Abimelech story is the literary center of *4 Baruch*. It stands in place of the report concerning the people's time in exile,[5] which would have been expected after chapter 4, since the deportation is reported in 4:5. If one recognizes that *4 Baruch* uses *2 Baruch* and that *2 Baruch* ends with Baruch's letter to the exiled people but says nothing about the exile and its end, one must also acknowledge that the story of Abimelech in *4 Baruch* picks up the narrative exactly where it ends in *2 Baruch*. One must further conclude that the continuation of the narrative frame taken

---

1. For tradition criticism of the Abimelech story, see Herzer, *Paralipomena Jeremiae*, 89–116.
2. Bogaert, *Apocalypse de Baruch,* 1:192–195; see also Herzer, *Paralipomena Jeremiae,* 23, 25–26.
3. Bogaert, *Apocalypse de Baruch,* 1:192. On the meaning of this episode in *4 Baruch*, see particularly Riaud, "Abimélech," passim. Riaud calls Abimelech a "personnage-clé" (key character) in *4 Baruch*.
4. Bogaert, *Apocalypse de Baruch,* 1:194–96.
5. Riaud, "Abimélech," 168–69.

from *2 Baruch* with the Abimelech story is a conscious compositional decision on the part of the writer of *4 Baruch*, not a later redactor.

Verse 1 refers back to the task given to Abimelech by Jeremiah (3:15). Until this point the Ethiopian has only played a small role; now he becomes the focus of events. The term καῦμα might initially imply that Abimelech picked the figs after the cool of the morning (3:15). However, the term has a metaphorical dimension, the midday heat being associated with the "heat" of judgment, which on a narrative level has taken place since Abimelech was last on the scene. This motif appears again in 5:6. The transparency of the Abimelech account with regard to the story and fate of the people determines the following presentation to a great extent. Although the figs gathered by Abimelech are not expressly made symbolic of anything, one hardly goes too far in seeing deeper significance in Abimelech's resting under a tree with his head on the basket of figs.[6] He sleeps thus for sixty-six years, and the author notes explicitly that he does so without any interruption. Here already the figs are associated with lengthy preservation. Later they will explicitly be interpreted in the same way (6:7).

The specification of exactly sixty-six years has led to a number of assumptions and explanations. Obviously, the repetition of this number (5:30; 6:5; 7:24) emphasizes its importance. According to the biblical tradition, the exile lasted seventy years,[7] and many attempts have been made to explain *4 Baruch*'s variation from this tradition. Harris's suggestion, already presented in the introduction above, was that we find here an indication of the dating of the work.[8] Delling understands sixty-six as a "round number," like the seventy-seven years found in *As. Mos.* 3:14.[9] He also refers to the number 666 in 1 Kgs 10:14, also supposedly a round number used to indicate a large sum. However, seventy seems far more obviously a "round number,"[10] precisely because it is part of the

---

6. Kohler's conjecture ("The Pre-Talmudic Haggada," 409) that δένδρον should be read as ἄντρον (cave) cannot be supported, supremely because of the parallels with *2 Bar.* 6:1; 77:18.

7. Jer 25:11; 29(36):10; Zech 1:12; 7:5; Dan 9:2; 2 Chr 36:21; Josephus, *Ant.* 10.184; 11.2; 20.233; *J.W.* 5.389; *b. Ta'anit* 23a; *y. Ta'anit* 3:9; *Midr. Pss.* on Ps 126:1, and others. See Wolff, *Jeremia im Frühjudentum und Urchristentum*, 113–16; Schaller, "Paralipomena Jeremiou," 724. Accordingly, some manuscripts have changed "sixty-six" to "seventy" (v, slav[A]); in arm[b] one finds "sixty-eight" years; see Schaller, "Paralipomena Jeremiou," 724.

8. Harris's suggestion (*Rest of the Words of Baruch*, 13–15) that sixty-six is the author's reference to the date (66 [Abimelech's sleep] + 70 [year of Jerusalem's fall] = 136 [year of the writing of *4 Baruch*]) is problematic. See Wolff, *Jeremia im Frühjudentum und Urchristentum*, 115; Herzer, *Paralipomena Jeremiae*, 177–78; and the introduction above. To understand the number sixty-six (ξς) as a gematric play on numbers and words is equally unconvincing, since there is neither a word or name of significance in the context of *4 Baruch* that has the numerical value sixty-six.

9. Delling, *Paralipomena Jeremiae*, 9; Riaud, "Abimélech," 177 n. 32.

10. See Wolff, *Jeremia im Frühjudentum und Urchristentum*, 115.

exile tradition.[11] Moreover, the seventy-seven in *As. Mos.* 3:14 is best understood as emphasizing the exile tradition rather than rounding the number. Wolff, who assumes a model that had the number seventy,[12] regards the sixty-six as a conscious change in the tradition by the author, since according to *4 Baruch* a certain length of time still must expire before the people finally return home.[13]

Even given the justified assumption of a conscious change from seventy to sixty-six, the interpretation of this sixty-six remains problematic. A definitive explanation of the problem must remain an open question, but at least some texts allow a satisfactory understanding. Most interesting concerning the interpretation of this number is a text in Pseudo-Hecataeus (fragment found in Josephus, *Ag. Ap.* 1.187), in which the age of a high priest named Ezekias is given as *approximately* sixty-six years (ὡς ἑξήκοντα ἓξ ἐτῶν).[14] This is surprising, because sixty-six is not at all an approximate number. Yet the fact that sixty-six can stand for an approximate age supports Wolff's suggestion concerning the understanding of this number in *4 Baruch*.[15]

Not only the number of years but also the motif of a long sleep has a storied history. Indeed, Abimelech's sleep, which takes the place of a description of the exile and so presents it as a time that passes as if one were asleep, reminds one of Ps 126(125):1, which reads: "When the Lord restored the fortunes of Zion, we were like those who dream"[16] (NRSV). This association is clear, particularly since both *4 Bar.* 3:10 and Ps 125:1 (LXX) describe the people's return with the word ἐπιστρέφω. The ones who, on returning from the exile, are "like those who dream" correspond to Abimelech, who after sleeping beneath the tree has a

---

11. Similarly, Riaud, "La figure de Jérémie," 383 n. 1.
12. Wolff, *Jeremia im Frühjudentum und Urchristentum*, 116.
13. Ibid., 115–16.
14. See Robert Doran, "Pseudo-Hecataeus," *OTP* 1:905–18, esp. 917. On Ezekias, see Nikolaus Walter, "Fragmente jüdisch-hellenistischer Historiker," *JSHRZ* 1.2 (1976): 89–163, here 146–47 n. 15. See further Nikolaus Walter, *Der Thoraausleger Aristobulos: Untersuchungen zu seinen Fragmenten und zu pseudepigraphischen Resten der jüdisch-hellenistischen Literatur* (TU 86; Berlin: Akademie-Verlag, 1964), 187–94; Carl R. Holladay, *Historians* (vol. 1 of *Fragments from Hellenistic Jewish Authors;* SBLTT 20, Pseudepigrapha Series 10; Chico, Calif.: Scholars Press, 1983), 325–26 nn. 11 and 12.
15. Alongside *4 Bar.* 5 and *As. Mos.* 3:14; Ep Jer 2 is a further interesting reference in terms of changing the seventy years of the exile: "Therefore when you have come to Babylon you will remain there for many years, for a long time, up to seven generations; after that I will bring you away from there in peace"; on this, see Weigand Naumann, *Untersuchungen über den apokryphen Jeremiasbrief* (BZAW 25; Gießen: Töpelmann, 1913), 53; Wolff, *Jeremia im Frühjudentum und Urchristentum*, 113; Antonius H. J. Gunneweg, "Der Brief des Jeremias," *JSHRZ* 3.2 (1975): 186; and Taatz, *Frühjüdische Briefe*, 58.
16. Wolff, *Jeremia im Frühjudentum und Urchristentum*, 52. See also Wolff, "Heilshoffnung," 148; Riaud, "Abimélech," 177–78 n. 35; and Herzer, "Alttestamentliche Traditionen," 125–26.

"heavy" head, as is repeatedly mentioned (5:2, 4, 10).[17] This state is described as ἔκστασις in the sense of deep sleep (5:8, 14, 16, 30).[18] Aside from the association with Ps 126(125), other sleep narratives also come into view.

Excursus on 4 Baruch in the Context of Ancient Sleep Narratives[19]

b. Ta'anit 23a and y. Ta'anit 3:9

The first narratives to mention are the legends concerning Honi the Circle Drawer[20] in *b. Ta'anit* 23a and *y. Ta'anit* 3:9. These rabbinic traditions clearly demonstrate that Ps 126(125):1 was interpreted as referring to the exile.[21] For example, *b. Ta'anit* 23a (see also *Midr. Pss.* on Ps 126:1[22]) states:

---

17. Remarkably, the tree in *4 Bar.* 5:1 is not described as a fig tree. This conclusion is, however, likely, as Abimelech has picked figs. Furthermore, the fig tree provides excellent shade and is a motif of protection, as in 1 Kgs 4:25: "During Solomon's lifetime Judah and Israel lived in safety, from Dan even to Beersheba, all of them under their vines and fig trees" (NRSV). See further Mic 4:4; Zech 3:10; 1 Macc 14:12. J. A. Steiger draws out the prophetic-eschatological expressiveness of the phrase "under the fig tree" as follows: "The OT never speaks of sitting under the fig tree without adding 'and under the vine'" (see "Nathanael—Ein Israelit, an dem kein Falsch ist: Das hermeneutische Phänomen der Intertestamentarizität aufgezeigt an Joh 1:45–51," *BThZ* 9 [1992]: 50–61, here 56, my trans.). The previously mentioned problematic of fig tree and vine together thereby gains a new accent that fits well in the eschatological orientation of *4 Baruch*.

18. Schaller, "Paralipomena Jeremiou," 725, referring to Gen 2:21; 15:12; Philo, *Her.* 249; 257; *T. Reu.* 3:1.

19. See Herzer, *Paralipomena Jeremiae*, 91–103.

20. Died ca. 65 B.C.E.; see Adolph Büchler, *Types of Jewish-Palestinian Piety from 70 B.C.E. to 70 C.E.: The Ancient Pious Men* (JCP 8; London: Gregg, 1922), 196; Otto Betz, "Der Tod des Choni-Onias im Licht der Tempelrolle von Qumran: Bemerkungen zu Josephus, Antiquitates 14,22–24," in *Jesus: Der Messias Israels. Aufsätze zur Biblischen Theologie I* (ed. Otto Betz; WUNT 42; Tübingen: Mohr Siebeck, 1987), 62. The importance of this date is that a connection between *4 Bar.* 5 and the Honi legend is only possible when there is a certain period of time for the development of a legend. When the legend emerged is, however, unknown. Should the Onias mentioned by Josephus, *Ant.* 14.22ff., be the Honi of the talmudic tradition (see Betz, "Tod des Choni," 61), then it is probable that Josephus assumed the tradition in the Talmudim, as he describes the death of Honi/Onias as martyrdom (Betz, "Tod des Choni," 65). Nothing is reported on Honi's death in *y. Ta'anit* 3, and in *b. Ta'anit* 23a Honi's death by grieving is an earlier tradition. One can thus assume that the Honi legends emerged by the middle of the first century, probably, however, sooner after his death. That Honi did not count as a rabbi also supports this view (see Betz, "Tod des Choni," 61; "Charismatic"), and therefore a later development of the legend after *4 Baruch* is unlikely.

21. Bogaert, *Apocalypse de Baruch*, 1:197; Wolff, *Jeremia im Frühjudentum und Urchristentum*, 52 n. 9; Wolff, "Heilshoffnung," 148 n. 5; and Herzer, *Paralipomena Jeremiae*, 92–96. Riaud calls the Abimelech story in *4 Baruch* a "midrash" on Ps 126 ("Abimélech," 177–78 n. 35, with reference to Jacob Licht).

22. *Midr. Pss.* is, however, later (Strack and Stemberger, *Introduction*, 350–51) and as such of most interest as a parallel of Ps 126 in terms of tradition criticism.

R. Johanan said: This righteous man [Honi] was throughout the whole of his life troubled about the meaning of the verse, *Song of Ascents, When the Lord brought back those that returned to Zion, we were like unto them that dream.* Is it possible for a man to dream continuously for seventy years? One day he was journeying on the road and he saw a man planting a carob tree; he asked him, How long does it take [for this tree] to bear fruit? The man replied: Seventy years. He then further asked him: Are you certain that you will live another seventy years? The man replied: I found [ready grown] carob trees in the world; as my forefathers planted these for me so I too plant these for my children. Honi sat down to have a meal and sleep overcame him. As he slept a rocky formation enclosed upon him which hid him from sight and he continued to sleep for seventy years. When he awoke he saw a man gathering the fruit of the carob tree and he asked him, Are you the man who planted the tree? The man replied: I am his grandson. Thereupon he exclaimed: It is clear that I slept for seventy years. He then caught sight of his ass who had given birth to several generations of mules; and he returned home. He there enquired, Is the son of Honi the Circle-Drawer still alive? The people answered him, His son is no more, but his grandson is still living. Thereupon he said to them: I am Honi the Circle-Drawer, but no one would believe him. He then repaired to the Beth Hamidrasch and there he overheard the scholars say, The law is as clear to us as in the days of Honi the Circle-Drawer, for whenever he came to the Beth Hamidrasch he would settle for the scholars any difficulty that they had. Whereupon he called out, I am he; but the scholars would not believe him nor did they give him the honour due to him. This hurt him greatly and he prayed [for death] and he died. Raba said: Hence the saying, Either companionship or death.[23]

The proximity of this talmudic tradition to *4 Bar.* 5 has often been established,[24] but the parallel text *y. Ta'anit* 3:9 IV regarding the grandson of the Circle Drawer should also be taken into account:

(IV.A) Said R. Yudan Giria, This is Honi the circle drawer, the grandson of Honi the circle drawer. Near the time of the destruction of the Temple, he

---

23. Quoted from J. Rabbinowitz, *Ta'anith: Translated into English with Notes, Glossary and Indices*, in *The Babylonian Talmud: Seder Mo'ed* (ed. Isidore Epstein; 35 vols.; London: Soncino, 1938), 9:117–18.

24. Bogaert, *Apocalypse de Baruch*, 1:197–98; Moses Gaster, "Beiträge zur vergleichenden Sagen- und Märchenkunde XI: Choni hamagel," *MGWJ* 30 NS 13 (1881): 137. Gaster uses the text of *4 Bar.* 5 from the Σύνοψις τῶν Ἱστοριῶν, the chronicle of Bishop Dorotheus of Monembasia (Venedig, 1684), which at some points is more extensive than the text edited by Harris, yet in the main a summary. See further Bernard Heller, "Éléments, Parallèles et Origine de la Légende des Sept Dormants," *REJ* 49 (1904): 204 n. 2. See also Michael Huber, *Die Wanderlegende von den Siebenschläfern: Eine literargeschichtliche Untersuchung* (Leipzig: Hinrichs, 1910), 409–10.

went out to a mountain to his workers. Before he got there, it rained. He went into a cave. Once he sat down there, he became tired and fell asleep. (B) He remained sound asleep for seventy years, until the Temple was destroyed and it was rebuilt a second time. (C) At the end of the seventy years he awoke from his sleep. He went out of the cave, and he saw a world completely changed. An area that had been planted with vineyards now produced olives, and an area planted in olives now produced grain. (D) He asked the people of the district, "What do you hear in the world?" (E) They said to him, "And don't you know what the news is?" (F) He said to them, "No." (G) They said to him, "Who are you?" (H) He said to them, "Honi, the circle drawer." (I) They said to him, "We heard that when he would go into the Temple courtyard, it would be illuminated." (J) He went in and illuminated the place and recited concerning himself the following verse of Scripture: "When the Lord restored the fortune of Zion, we were like those who dream." (Ps 126:1)[25]

Comparing the two passages, one notes two commonalities: the seventy-year sleep and the reference to Ps 126:1. The differences, however, are striking. In *y. Ta'anit* 3:9 reference is expressly made to the time of the destruction of the temple, which in *b. Ta'anit* 23a plays no role. Likewise, the reconstruction of the temple is mentioned in *y. Ta'anit* 3:9 but not in *b. Ta'anit* 23a. Further, the mountain to which Honi heads in *y. Ta'anit* 3:9 is missing in *b. Ta'anit* 23a, thought the motif is hinted at by the rock that miraculously surrounds Honi. The role of Ps 126:1 also differs: in *b. Ta'anit* 23a it is the point of departure for a question of exposition, in *y. Ta'anit* 3:9 the punch line at the end. In *b. Ta'anit* 23a Honi sleeps under the open skies, if surrounded by the previously mentioned rock, whereas in *y. Ta'anit* 3:9 he sleeps in a cave into which he has withdrawn for protection from the rain. Like *4 Baruch*, *y. Ta'anit* 3:9 highlights the way in which the world has totally changed, a question not discussed in *b. Ta'anit* 23a. Finally, though not less significantly, in *b. Ta'anit* 23a Honi dies of grief at the failure of his disciples to recognize him, whereas in *y. Ta'anit* 3:9 he is able to prove his identity and hence his miraculous seventy-year preservation. These differences clearly indicate the existence of two significantly different traditions concerning Honi the Circle Drawer (or the grandson of the same name).[26] That both accounts are found in *Midr. Pss.* on Ps 126:1, one after the other, supports this view. Although scholars have previously noted the com-

---

25. Quotation and numbering according to the edition in Neusner, *Besah and Taanit*, 226.
26. They are probably two legends concerning the same person; see *b. Ta'anit* 23a, in which the grandson of Honi the Circle Drawer is one "Abba-Hilqija"; see Dietrich Correns, *Seder 2 Moed, Traktat 9 Taanijot Fastentage: Text, Übersetzung und Erklärung nebst einem textkritischen Anhang* (vol. 2 of *Die Mischna: Text, Übersetzung und ausführliche Erklärung;* ed. Karl Heinrich Rengstorf and Siegfried Herrmann; Berlin: de Gruyter, 1989), 84–85 app.

parable seventy-year sleeps,[27] they have not adequately taken into account the differences between the two talmudic traditions.

Significantly, *4 Bar.* 5 shares only two elements with *b. Ta'anit* 23a: the long-sleep motif and the connection of the overall intention of the story back to Ps 126:1. The differences between the two passages are, however, noteworthy: *b. Ta'anit* 23a seeks neither to comfort nor to promise salvation, as is the case in *4 Bar.* 5:1–6:7, especially at the end of chapter 5 and in 6:1–7. Rather, it deals with the question raised by Ps 126:1 as to how one can sleep seventy years: the story of Honi seeks to demonstrate that it is possible. The sleep, moreover, is not meant to serve a salvific function (i.e., to preserve life), as in *4 Baruch,* but ends negatively with Honi's death.

In contrast, the similarities between *4 Bar.* 5 and *y. Ta'anit* 3:9 are far greater:[28] (1) the reference to the time of the temple's fall (*4 Bar.* 4:4; 5:30); (2) the mention of a mountain (*4 Bar.* 3:1; 5:9); (3) the emphasis on the changing of the world (*4 Bar.* 5:7, 12); (4) the seventy-year sleep (*4 Bar.* 5:1, 30); reference to vineyards (*4 Bar.* 3:10, 15); (6) a conversation concerning the changes in the world (*4 Bar.* 5:17–34); and (7) the motif of illumination (*y. Ta'anit* 3:9 IV.I, J), which is similar to Abimelech's wish for the old man: "May God lead you (by his) light to the city above, Jerusalem" (*4 Bar.* 5:34).[29] The illumination scene in *y. Ta'anit* explicitly localizes the events of the story in Jerusalem, as in *4 Baruch* and in contrast to *b. Ta'anit* 23a. In all probability, *4 Baruch* takes up this rabbinic tradition,[30] and the author's milieu, as described in the introduction, supports this assumption. However, no literary dependence should be supposed here.

The Legend of Epimenides' Sleep

These rabbinic traditions are not the only ones that take up the motif of a long sleep. A "close connection" between the Abimelech story and a sleep legend concerning Epimenides[31] has already been discussed by Gaster.[32] This legend is passed on by Diogenes Laertius 1.10.109–110:

---

27. Bogaert, *Apocalypse de Baruch,* 1:197; Delling, *Paralipomena Jeremiae,* 54 n. 2.
28. Schaller, "Paralipomena Jeremiou," 723, who however only cites 3:9 (alternative numbering in Schaller: 3:10).
29. See the commentary below on 5:34.
30. Herzer, *Paralipomena Jeremiae,* 96.
31. The dating of the philosopher's life is uncertain. According to O. Kern ("Epimenides," *RAC* 6:174), Epimenides lived in the period shortly after the Persian wars around 500 B.C.E., whereas Huber (*Wanderlegende,* 378–90) dates him between 660 and 510 B.C.E. On the sleep motif in classical literature, see Huber, *Wanderlegende,* 378–90; on the Epimenides legend in particular, 387–90.
32. Gaster, "Beiträge," 368.

Epimenides, according to Theopompus and many other writers, was the son of Phaestius; some, however, make him the son of Dosiadas, others of Agesarchus. He was a native of Cnossos in Crete, though from wearing his hair long he did not look like a Cretan. One day he was sent into the country [εἰς ἀγρόν] by his father to look for a stray sheep, and at noon he turned aside out of the way, and went to sleep in a cave [ὑπ' ἄντρῳ], where he slept for fifty-seven years. After this he got up and went in search of the sheep, thinking he had been asleep only a short time [νομίζων ἐπ' ὀλίγον κεκοιμῆσθαι]. And when he could not find it, he came to the farm, and found everything changed and another owner in possession. Then he went back to the town in utter perplexity; and there, on entering his own house, he fell in with people who wanted to know who he was. At length he found his younger brother, now an old man [ἤδη γέροντα ὄντα], and learnt the truth from him. So he became famous throughout Greece, and he was believed to be a special favourite of heaven.[33]

This narrative's parallels to *4 Bar.* 5 are not as clear as its links to the tradition about Honi the Circle Drawer in *y. Ta'anit* 3:9. Both Honi and Epimenides seek shelter in a cave, though in Epimenides' case not in order to be sheltered from the rain (*y. Ta'anit* 3:9 IV.A). The motif of the changed area and the question of his identity are in both accounts. The closer relationship between *y. Ta'anit* 3:9 and *4 Baruch* makes a direct connection between *4 Baruch* and the Epimenides tradition unlikely. If this is correct, then *y. Ta'anit* 3:9 should be regarded as an intermediary step linking the two traditions. By comparing the three versions of the motif, it is possible to identify the process by which the narrative was revised to conform to the individual interests of the authors of *y. Ta'anit* 3:9 and *4 Baruch*. In the Yerushalmi version of the tradition, for example, Epimenides' fifty-seven years is lengthened to the seventy years of the exile, a length again changed by the writer of *4 Baruch* to sixty-six years. Further, *y. Ta'anit* adds a description of events during the sleep (3:9 IV.B), and re-forms the identity question with reference to Ps 126:1. Thus one can follow an interesting process of reworking a tradition that also provides evidence for knowledge of Greek classical traditions and their reuse in Jewish circles.[34]

---

33. Diogenes Laertius, *Lives of Eminent Philosophers* 1.10.109–110 (Hicks, LCL). Diogenes Laertius wrote the *Vitae Philosophorum* toward the end of the third century C.E. (see H. Dörrie, "Diogenes 12," *KlPauly* 2:45–46), at which time he most probably reworked ancient traditions, since Pliny the Elder (*Nat.* 7:53 [175]) knew this Epimenides legend in the middle of the first century C.E. See K. Sallmann, "Plinius 1," *KlPauly* 4:928–36, who dates Pliny the Elder's *Natural History* to 77 C.E. (932). Gaster ("Beiträge," 368) has a varying text on Epimenides, the origin of which is unclear; see Herzer, *Paralipomena Jeremiae*, 97 n. 280.

34. This is to differentiate from the thesis of a Jeremiah legend being the link between the Epimenides legend and the *Jeremiah Apocryphon* (see Riaud, *Les Paralipomènes du Prophète Jérémie*, 58–63, esp. 61 for reference of J.-M. Rosenstiehl). See also Herzer, *Paralipomena Jeremiae*, 98. The

CHAPTER 5

The Legend of the Seven Sleepers

A further tradition that belongs in this context is the legend of the Seven Sleepers.[35] Of Christian origin, the story is situated in the time of Caesar Decius (249–251 C.E.).[36] Seven young men, seeking to escape persecution and fleeing into a cave, fall into a deep sleep there. The length of the sleep is not stated, but it is noted that they slept until the reign of Theodosius the Younger (probably Theodosius II, 408–450 C.E.).[37] There are, in fact, points of contact between this Seven Sleepers Legend and *4 Bar.* 5: (1) just as Abimelech is preserved from experiencing the destruction of Jerusalem, so also the seven sleepers are preserved from Decius's persecution by their sleep; (2) like Abimelech, the seven leave the city for a mountain (*4 Bar.* 3:15–16); (3) when the seven awake, they are convinced they have slept only a short time (see 5:2, 4, 10, 26); (4) the seven are amazed by the different appearance of the city (5:7–16); (5) just as Abimelech asks the old man, the seven ask a passing man the name of the city (5:17); and (6) finally, as in *4 Bar.* 5:28–34, the miraculous preservation is revealed.

On the basis of these remarkable similarities on several levels, it is easy to suppose a literary connection between the Abimelech narrative in *4 Baruch* and the Seven Sleepers legend. Because other suggestions cannot sufficiently explain

---

quotations in Titus 1:12 and perhaps also in Acts 17:28a indicate that early Christians were also interested in the Cretan philosopher Epimenides, though with different intentions.

35. According to Huber (*Wanderlegende*, 553), Jacob of Sarug was the first to write about the seven men, around 520 C.E., in Syriac.

36. On this legend, see John Koch, *Die Siebenschläferlegende, ihr Ursprung und ihre Verbreitung* (Leipzig: Reissner 1883); Heller, "Légende," passim; and Huber, *Wanderlegende,* 552–67. For text editions, see Heller, "Légende," 190–91 n. 1.

37. Donner, *Pilgerfahrt,* 220 n. 96. See also Heller, "Légende," 215. This legend has also been passed on in the Islamic tradition: Qur'an, Sure 18:8–25. According to Sure 18:24 they sleep three hundred years. The Qur'an has a further noteworthy tradition in Sure 2:259: "Or like the man who passed by a town whose roofs had caved in. He said: 'How will God revive this following its death?' God let him die for a hundred years; then raised him up again. He said: 'How long have you been waiting here?' He said: 'I've been waiting a day or a part of a day.' He said: 'Rather you have stayed here a hundred years. Yet look at your food and drink: they have not yet even become stale! And look at your donkey. We will grant you it as a sign for mankind. Look how we set its bones together, then clothe them with flesh!' When it was explained to him, he said: 'I know that God is capable of everything!'" (quoted from Thomas Ballantine Irving, *The Qur'an: The First American Version, Translation and Commentary* [Brattleboro: Amana Books, 1985], 22). Cf. Denise Masson, *Le Coran et la Révélation Judéo-Chrétienne* (Paris: Adrien-Maisonneuve, 1958), 442–43; Schützinger, "Jeremia-Erzählung," passim; and Huber, *Wanderlegende,* 335–54. The identity of the person in question is not clear. Abel identifies him as Ezra ("Deir Senneh," 67). Knowledge of and reworking of the Abimelech narrative in the Islamic tradition is likely here (see Harris, *Rest of the Words of Baruch,* 39–42). The donkey motif is found, for example, in *b. Ta'anit* 23a. It is furthermore clear that elements of Ezek 37 are relevant.

the similarities noted,[38] one can conclude that the story of Abimelech's sleep probably served as a significant model for the legend. As *4 Bar.* 9 makes clear, the book of *4 Baruch* was received within Christian circles,[39] and the Seven Sleepers legend is but one example of this reception. The Abimelech narrative of the *4 Baruch* can thus be seen as a link between the rabbinical Honi tradition and the Christian Seven Sleepers legend.

As early as the second verse in chapter 5, the reader is told of Abimelech's waking. In narrative terms, time passes so quickly that none of the events of the intervening time is narrated. The waking is described with the relatively unusual phrase ἐγερθεὶς ἀπὸ τοῦ ὕπνου αὐτοῦ (see LXX Gen 28:16; Prov 6:9; Jer 28[51]:39; Zech 4:1; Sir 22:7). Despite his long sleep, Abimelech does not feel rested. This sensation of having slept but a short time paves the way for the next motif. It is thereby hinted that the people's exile, although of significant duration, also passed as quickly as Abimelech's impression of his sleep. That Abimelech finds still-fresh figs in his basket underlines this perception.[40] The use of Jer 24:1–10, the vision of good and bad figs, has already been noted in *4 Bar.* 3:15. Here the reference to figs that have remained fresh over a long period brings the reader to reflect again on our author's exposition of this text. It is striking that the focus now falls on the good figs.[41] That the bad are left out is not only obvious but also clearly intentional, a way of beginning to make it plain that only salvation remains. With Abimelech's awakening, God once again turns to his people to bring them out of their exile. There is thus no place for rotten figs as a symbol of rejection and expulsion.

After discovering the figs, Abimelech begins a monologue in which he attempts to understand his situation (5:4–6). This gives readers the impression that Abimelech has no knowledge of anything that has happened. They thus know more than he does and can think further ahead than the figure in the text. It is in this sense that the key word καῦμα is used, which already appeared in 5:1. The textual tradition is not clear at this point,[42] so the interpreter should be

---

38. Gaster, "Beiträge," 368–69; Heller, "Légende," 214; and Huber, *Wanderlegende,* 422.

39. Herzer, *Paralipomena Jeremiae,* 159–76; see also below the commentary on 9:11–32. The book of *4 Baruch* was known also in the Christian tradition in the Middle Ages, as an eleventh-century Psalter that uses motifs from *4 Baruch* to illustrate Ps 33 demonstrates; on this, see first Riaud, "Abimélech," 171–72. Theodosius also knew the story in the sixth century (*De situ terrae sanctae* 5:6; text in Donner, *Pilgerfahrt,* 205–6).

40. The phrase στάζοντα γάλα hints at the characteristic giving off of a sticky, milky liquid of a ripe fig. Hence the figs' freshness is made realistically visible.

41. Wolff, "Heilshoffnung," 148.

42. See above and Herzer, *Paralipomena Jeremiae,* 13.

cautious. If one does not merely see daily struggle here[43] but follows the reading in MS C, the eschatological dimension is already hinted at. This dimension will be expanded later on in the reference to the place where there is neither heat nor struggle, the "(heavenly) Jerusalem above" (5:34), and will be of decisive significance for what follows.

This orientation is also found in 5:7, which reports Abimelech's return to Jerusalem and his failure to recognize the city or to find his family and friends. Already the "Jerusalem above" is being presented more clearly as the true home of God's people. Likewise, the terms "house" (οἰκία) and "place" (τόπος) are both markers of the place to come in the future, as is evident by the repetition of the term "place" in 5:32: God will become the "rest" for the righteous no longer only in this one earthly place but in every place.[44]

The words of praise following in 5:8 therefore foreshadow the more fulsome praise of 5:32. Even the term ἔκστασις thereby gains a specific meaning,[45] and one must choose between the possible senses of the word—ecstasy, fright, or deep sleep[46]—within this larger context. Abimelech has already awakened from his sleep (5:5, 10)[47] and found himself in a situation that he cannot explain. "Confused fright" would seem the most appropriate translation,[48] as this "confused fright" is described stereotypically—so as to underline the point—in 5:9–16. Since it is a confusion, Abimelech can praise God for it because what he sees does not reflect reality.[49] This confusion concerning the state of the earthly Jerusalem will lead Abimelech finally to understand his situation in a conversation with an old man, a situation that becomes transparent on his way to recognizing the centrality of the Jerusalem above.[50]

The phrase τὰ σημεῖα τῆς πόλεως (5:12) in the description of Abimelech's confusion is both remarkable and difficult to interpret. The "signs of the

---

43. As Kraft and Purintun (*Paraleipomena Jeremiou*, 23), Riaud (*Paralipomènes*, 1748), and Schaller ("Paralipomena Jeremiou," 725) do in their translations.

44. A reference to the temple is not necessarily meant; see Schaller, "Paralipomena Jeremiou," 725, as opposed to Bogaert, *Apocalypse de Baruch*, 1:183 n. 5. However, the primary reference to the "property [Grundstück]" (Schaller) is transcended by the intratextual referents.

45. Riaud, "Abimélech," 176 n. 28.

46. Schaller, "Paralipomena Jeremiou," 725.

47. Schaller's reference (ibid.) to Gen 2:21 and 15:12 in order to explain the meaning of ἔκστασις would seem in the light of even these references to be unlikely.

48. See Dan 10:7 (Q): ἢ ἔκστασις μεγάλη ἐπέπεσεν ἐπ' αὐτούς καὶ ἔφυγον ἐν φόβῳ, also Gen 27:33; Zech 14:13; Pss 30:23 (LXX); 115:2 (LXX); Dan 7:28; and Isa 29:9.

49. See *m. Ber.* 3:5, according to which one should praise God for the bad as well as the good.

50. On the motif of conversation as an aid to understanding, see Diogenes Laertius 1.10.109–110; *y. Ta'anit* 3:9.

city" enable Abimelech to identify Jerusalem in spite of his confusion, so one might assume that the city's outline, landmarks,[51] or milestones[52] are the signs in question. The latter is unlikely, since Abimelech only recognizes the signs of the city on observing it more closely rather than by searching for such stones. Still, Abimelech remains uncertain about the identification and later must confirm it with the old man (5:17). This seems, therefore, to be a reference to a notable change to the city that still leaves intact the outline of its landmarks. Such a reconstruction of the city was demonstrably undertaken by Hadrian and fits with the suspected date of the writing of *4 Baruch*.[53]

In 5:17 a long conversation begins between Abimelech and an old man (γηραιός) who has just come "from the field" (ἐξ ἀγροῦ). The purpose of reference to the field is unclear. The parallel to the passion narrative, in which Simon of Cyrene comes in from the field and must carry Jesus' cross (Mark 15:21), is interesting. This short note has frequently been seen as an indication that Jesus' crucifixion could not have taken place on a holy day, since work in the fields was not allowed on such days. In *4 Bar.* 5:17, however, this expression need not necessarily refer to work in the fields.[54]

Once the old man confirms the identity of the city (5:17–18), the question concerning Jeremiah, Baruch, and the people brings the reader back to the theme of exile (5:18), and for the first time exile and Abimelech's sleep are brought together. The problem of the exile comes once again to the fore. Simultaneously, both Jeremiah and Baruch receive new titles corresponding to the people's situation. Although Jeremiah's priestly function was earlier alluded to through the motifs of intercession and concern for the temple vessels (*4 Bar.* 2–4), the prophet is now explicitly called a priest. Thus, one does not overinterpret the term ὁ ἱερεύς in 9:2 to see there a high-priestly function for the prophet.[55] Baruch, for his part, is identified as "the reader," a specification of his role within the book of Jeremiah as one whose ability to read and write enabled him to record Jeremiah's words and to read them to various audiences (see LXX Jer 43[36]:4–18). Placing these titles for Jeremiah and Baruch here at this turning point witnesses to the author's conscious shaping of the story.

According to 5:19–22, the old man is initially astounded by Abimelech's questions but explains the situation fully. He proves to be well informed, knowing not only the name of the Chaldean king Nebuchadnezzar (Ναβουχοδονόσορ),

---

51. Delling, *Paralipomena Jeremiae*, 46 n. 22.
52. Schaller, "Paralipomena Jeremiou," 725: "boundary- and milestones of the city."
53. Herzer, *Paralipomena Jeremiae*, 186; see also the introduction above.
54. Differently in Judg 19:16, which expressly adds: ἐξ ἔργων αὐτοῦ. See Christian Wolff, "Die *Paralipomena Jeremiae* und das Neue Testament," *NTS* 51 (2005): 126–28.
55. MS C thus reads ἀρχιερεύς in 5:18.

a form that conforms to the Greek tradition,[56] but also that Jeremiah is with the people in Babylon in order to preach the good news to them. This previously used phrase (3:11) is expanded and explained by the addition καὶ κατηχῆσαι αὐτοὺς τὸν λόγον. This prepares the way for the greater significance that the teaching of the law or the commands of God will assume in the expansion of the good news.[57] The absolute use of the term λόγος referring to the content of teaching is, however, unusual in a Jewish document.[58]

Abimelech's objection in 5:23 grants the conversation greater impact and by way of a negative statement turns it to the essential issue, which remains unbelievable. Respect for the age of the man keeps Abimelech from stating directly what he thinks (that the old man is crazy), but he makes the same point indirectly. The captivity of the people remains incomprehensible to Abimelech, in large part because the passage of time he has experienced does not coincide with actual time (see 5:24). Even the slowest reader by now understands that his or her own situation is being reflected here, the situation of a captive people that must keep hope alive in order to survive. It is this process of surviving in the light of the certain hope of liberation that will later be described.

In the meantime, the conversation continues with Abimelech once again repeating what has happened from his perspective. As the figs once again become the topic of conversation (5:25–26), it becomes clear how different perspectives on one and the same thing are possible. Abimelech sees in the figs evidence that the old man cannot possibly be right (5:27); the old man, however, sees much more than fresh figs; he sees symbols of salvation (5:28–31). In contrast to Abimelech, the old man recognizes what has *really* happened: Abimelech has been miraculously protected since the deportation of the people. In order to open Abimelech's eyes, he refers to the young growth on the vegetation, evidence that there cannot yet be ripe figs. With the words "the growth of the crops has (just) begun" (5:31), the old man proves that it is indeed the season before the early spring harvest, specifically the month of Nisan (see 5:33).[59] Abimelech can draw

---

56. Schaller, "Paralipomena Jeremiou," 726.

57. See Herzer, *Paralipomena Jeremiae*, 61–62. The term νόμος is missing in *4 Baruch*, which speaks rather of "holding to the commands" and "hearing the voice" of God (6:21–22; 8:3). The term κατηχῆσαι in 5:21 means the same as διδάσκειν in 7:32.

58. Otherwise only found in Christian literature, where it is not common and is normally found related to Jewish ideas; see Delling, *Paralipomena Jeremiae*, 22; Schaller, "Paralipomena Jeremiou," 726; Gal 6:6; Luke 1:4. Delling further notes the wide use of κατηχεῖν und κατήχησις in extrabiblical literature. See also Wolff, "Die *Paralipomena Jeremiae* und das Neue Testament," 124–26, who emphasizes that the Christian "teaching of the word" is not focused on the law.

59. The period of the spring harvest usually lasts from mid-March to mid-April (see Oded Borowski, "Harvests, Harvesting," *ABD* 3:63). The firstfruits of this harvest served as the offering for the Feast of Unleavened Bread.

only one conclusion: the people have indeed been in Babylon for sixty-six years (5:30).[60]

The specification of the twelfth of Nisan presents several problems. First, the varying readings of 5:33 in the manuscripts[61] demand a judgment concerning which to follow. Harris's reading is preferred here: Νισσάν καὶ ἔστιν ἡ δωδεκάτη. This follows the Ethiopic tradition—"the twelfth of the month Nisan, which is the Mijazia" (similarly *Apocr. Jer.* 39:13)—although the naming of the day is probably secondary. Manuscripts A and B and slav[B] misunderstand Nisan as the twelfth month; arm[c] sets this right: "Nisan, the *first* month." The text of slav[A] changes the name of the month in order to count it as the twelfth: "Sarew, that is the twelfth."[62] All these variants make it likely that both the name of the month as Nisan and the number 12 are original, since there is no plausible combination of the two and this is thus the most difficult reading. Therefore, the name of the month and the specific date must be bound to one another in the way they are in the Ethiopic tradition.

It is only by retaining this reading that one comes closer to the tradition-historical references and the meaning of this unusual combination. On the level of the narrative, the month Nisan confirms that the season for figs has not arrived. Linking verses 32 and 34, however, this short observation takes on particular meaning, as it associates important intertexts. Nisan immediately brings to mind Passover, being the month of Passover; this association would have been unavoidable for the original readers. Passover is the festival of the exodus, when the Israelites left their slavery in Egypt. Therefore, the naming of Nisan arouses certain expectations given by the exodus association that the author will fulfill in the course of the narrative: the theme is the people's departure from Babylon, the "second exodus" that becomes the basis of hope for liberation and new orientation in the author's time. Old Testament texts reveal a similar association with Nisan. For example, Nehemiah received the Persian king's permission to return to Jerusalem to ensure the rebuilding of the temple and city in the month of Nisan (Neh 2:1). Likewise, in *4 Baruch* Nisan becomes the month in which the signs of the return and departure of the people occur. In this context, the number twelve may be explained as well. According to Ezra 8:31, the deported people left for Jerusalem "on the twelfth day of the first month." The short note in *4 Bar.* 5:33 thus reminds readers of both the first exodus and the second exodus, both of which should form the frame of reference, or even paradigm, for the present situation. The readers' recollection of these past events is the necessary

---

60. For the interpretation of the number sixty-six, see above on 5:1.
61. See Herzer, *Paralipomena Jeremiae*, 111 n. 357; Schaller, "Paralipomena Jeremiou," 728.
62. According to Schaller, all additions to Nisan are secondary ("Paralipomena Jeremiou," 728).

condition for correctly understanding what follows: God will once again redeem his people, as he had done before.

At the same time, the different goal of this new hope is made yet clearer, especially in 5:34, where Abimelech expresses a wish for the old man: "May God lead you (by his) light to the city above, Jerusalem." The goal of the faithful is no longer the earthly city—as with the Babylonian exile—but the heavenly city. Hence the author subtly involves himself in the debates of his day concerning the relevance of Jerusalem and the temple for the future of Israel.[63]

Within this broader context, the meaning ascribed above to the number sixty-six, which has been in the reader's mind since the beginning of the chapter (5:1) and must have seemed unusual, is confirmed.[64] That it had significance for the author is underlined by its renewed mention at the end of the chapter (5:30). As the many corrections of this unusual number in the manuscript tradition indicate, readers often saw a contradiction, since the people spent seventy years in captivity, not sixty-six. If sixty-six is correct, however, the exile is not yet over, and the people must still prepare for their return.

Granted, one should guard against reading too much into this. Still, on a deeper level the reader realizes that the current exile story will not simply follow the traditional pattern and, therefore, that the goal of this return will differ likewise from that of the earlier one. This goal has not yet been reached, and it will not be reached even by the end of *4 Baruch* and the return of the people in view there (*4 Bar.* 9). Rather, it will be reached only in the heavenly Jerusalem, where the exile of the Jewish people will come to an end.

This is the very perspective introduced in 5:34. Together with 5:32, 5:34 frames the statement concerning Nisan 12 in 5:33. Whereas 5:33 awakens the memory of God's intervention in the history of his people (the Passover-exodus allusion), 5:32 and 34 point to a change of perspective, as indicated by the terms ἀνάπαυσις (5:32) and ἄνω πόλις Ἰερουσαλήμ (5:34). The statement concerning God as the "rest [ἀνάπαυσις] of the souls of the righteous" is introduced with a word of praise like those often found in the Psalms (Pss 63[62]:5; 145[144]:2; see also 1 Kgs 8:56) and also in the Qumran *Hodayot*.[65] The word of praise continues with two designations for God. The first is common in both the Old Testament and early Judaism: "God of heaven and earth."[66] God is the God of heaven and

---

63. See the introduction above.
64. See above on 5:1; see also Schaller, "Paralipomena Jeremiou," 724.
65. See particularly Günter Morawe, *Aufbau und Abgrenzung der Loblieder von Qumrân: Studien zur gattungsgeschichtlichen Einordnung der Hodajôth* (ThA 16; Berlin: Evangelische Verlagsanstalt, 1960), 29–30; Bilhah Nitzan, *Qumran Prayer and Religious Poetry* (trans. Jonathan Chipman; STDJ 12; Leiden: Brill, 1994).
66. Gen 24:3; 2 Chr 36:23; Ezra 5:11; Neh 1:4–5; Ps 136(135):26; Dan 2:18–19; Jdt 5:7; 9:12; Tob 12:7.

earth, for he created both (see Gen 1:1; Ps 115:15 [LXX 113:23]; 121[120]:2). God, who "lives in heaven" (Deut 26:15; 1 Kgs 8:30; Isa 63:15; 2 Chr 30:27), shows himself to be the Mighty One vis-à-vis humans, even concerning personal faith.[67] Given this biblical background, it is unlikely that Abimelech uses this form of address for God merely by chance. He thanks the God of heaven and earth, who is therefore mighty enough to grant such protection.[68]

By contrast, the attribution "rest [ἀνάπαυσις] of the souls of the righteous in every place" is unique in this form.[69] Contrary to the arguments of some, an interpretation assuming a gnostic background is inappropriate.[70] In the given context, the designation is initially tied to God's protection of Abimelech during and through his sleep.[71] The addition of the phrase "in every place," however,

---

67. Ps 113(112):5–7: "Who is like the LORD our God, who is seated on high, who looks far down on the heavens and the earth? He raises the poor from the dust, and lifts the needy from the ash heap" (NRSV). See further Gerhard von Rad, "οὐρανός," *TDNT* 5:497–509, esp. 504–7. See also *4 Bar.* 9:6!

68. See esp. Ps 121(120); 1 Sam 2:8b–9; Pss 108(107); 146(145):5–9.

69. Delling, *Paralipomena Jeremiae*, 31; Otfried Hofius, *Katapausis: Die Vorstellung vom endzeitlichen Ruheort im Hebräerbrief* (WUNT 11; Tübingen: Mohr Siebeck, 1970), 73; and Wolff, "Heilshoffnung," 149.

70. The divine name ἀνάπαυσις is also found in gnostic texts such as *Ps.-Clem. Homilies* 17.10.1: αὐτὸς γάρ ἐστιν ἡ τῶν ὅλων ἀνάπαυσις. See also *Ps.-Clem. Homilies* 3.72.1–2: δέσποτα καὶ κύριε τῶν ὅλων ὁ πατὴρ καὶ θεός … σὺ ἡ πρόφασις … ἡ ἀνάπαυσις. In the gnostic Thomas documents it is often a predicate for Christ and is often seen as a "particularly Gnostic term"; see Philipp Vielhauer, "ΑΝΑΠΑΥΣΙΣ: Zum gnostischen Hintergrund des Thomasevangeliums," in *Aufsätze zum Neuen Testament* (ed. P. Vielhauer; TB 31; Munich: Kaiser, 1965), 215–34; similarly Georg Strecker, "Judenchristentum und Gnosis," in *Altes Testament, Frühjudentum, Gnosis* (ed. Karl-Wolfgang Tröger; Gütersloh: Gütersloher Verlagshaus, 1980), 278; Victoria Arnold-Döben, *Die Bildersprache der Gnosis* (Arbeitsmaterialien zur Religionsgeschichte 13; Köln: Brill, 1986), 80. See in particular Jan Helderman, *Die Anapausis im Evangelium Veritatis: Eine vergleichende Untersuchung des valentinianisch-gnostischen Heilsgutes der Ruhe im Evangelium Veritatis und in anderen Schriften der Nag Hammadi-Bibliothek* (NHS 18; Leiden: Brill, 1984), 337, who finally reaches the same conclusion. Helderman thoroughly researched the gnostic idea of ἀνάπαυσις (Coptic ⲘⲦⲞⲚ/ⲀⲚⲀⲠⲀⲨⲤⲒⲤ; see Helderman, *Anapausis*, 16–17 and 39 n. 137). In his interesting presentation, Helderman, however, consciously left out of consideration the tradition history of the idea of rest. For discussion of the problem, see Herzer, *Paralipomena Jeremiae*, 107–8 n. 337. Gnostic ideas of "rest" do not contribute greatly to the interpretation of rest in *4 Baruch*, partly due to their late dating, mainly due to differences of content. Here note only what Hans Martin Schenke called the "best and safest criterion" for identifying a text to be gnostic, namely, the presentation of a certain "cosmogony" or a "topography of the world above" (Schenke, "Das Evangelium nach Philippus: Ein Evangelium aus dem Funde von Nag-Hamadi," in *Koptisch-Gnostische Schriften aus dem Papyrus-Codices von Nag-Hamadi* [ed. Johannes Leipoldt and Hans Martin Schenke; TF 20; Hamburg-Bergstedt: Reich, 1960], 34). Such is not found in *4 Baruch*, a fact that also differentiates *4 Baruch* from apocalyptic literature.

71. Wolff, "Heilshoffnung," 149.

universalizes the statement. This is of particular significance in the broader context of *4 Baruch*, since "the righteous" are truly scattered around the world: Jeremiah and the people in Babylon, Baruch in the cave, Abimelech in Jerusalem.[72] The saving presence of God as ἀνάπαυσις counts only for the Holy Land but also in every place in the Diaspora.

The term ἀνάπαυσις in *4 Bar.* 5 adds yet another dimension to the developing picture. Delling suggests Wis 3:1 and 4:7 as the background here,[73] according to which one may reckon with a state of rest after death.[74] The notion of a state of rest after death is plausible here due to the correspondence with the "heavenly Jerusalem" in 5:34. One should not, however, confuse the *idea* of rest in 5:32 with a *place* of rest.[75] In fact, *4 Bar.* 5:32 does not speak of a heavenly *place*, as is usually the case, when referring to the eschatological residence of the righteous.[76] The idea of "soul chambers" as places where the pious would reside until judgment was popular[77] but not always linked to the

---

72. See *4 Bar.* 7:28, where Jeremiah asks Baruch and Abimelech in his letter to pray for the people, εἰς τὸν τόπον ὅπου εἶ.

73. Delling, *Paralipomena Jeremiae*, 30–31. One must consider, however, that both Wis 3:1 and 4:7 talk about the dead: "But the souls of the righteous are in the hand of God, and no torment will ever touch them. In the eyes of the foolish they seemed to have died, and their departure was thought to be a disaster, and their going from us to be their destruction; but they are at peace" (3:1–3 NRSV); "But the righteous, though they die early, will be at rest." (4:7 NRSV). In *4 Bar.* 5:32, however, the context is that Abimelech has been protected by God in a miraculous way and kept alive.

74. Hofius, *Katapausis*, 73 with 188 n. 439; Wolff, "Heilshoffnung," 149.

75. Ulrich Fischer, *Eschatologie und Jenseitserwartung im hellenistischen Diasporajudentum* (BZNW 44; Berlin: de Gruyter, 1978), 120–21, apparently relying on Hofius, *Katapausis*, 73. See Riaud, *Les Paralipomènes du Prophète Jérémie*, 102 with n. 61. Ernst Käsemann says: "The 'rest' is a purely spatial entity, the name for a heavenly place" (*The Wandering People of God: An Investigation of the Letter to the Hebrews* [trans. Roy A. Harrisville and Irving L. Sandberg: Minneapolis: Augsburg, 1984], 68). So also on Heb 3, Hans-Friedrich Weiß, *Der Brief an die Hebräer* (15th ed.; KEK NT 13; Göttingen: Vandenhoeck & Ruprecht, 1991), 268–69.

76. *4 Ezra* 7:36, 121; see Michael E. Stone, *Features of Eschatology of IV Ezra* (HSS 35; Atlanta: Scholars Press, 1989), 101–2; Stone, *Ezra*, 221–22; and Sverre Aalen, *Heilsverlangen und Heilsverwirklichung: Studien zur Erwartung des Heils in der apokalyptischen Literatur des antiken Judentums und im ältesten Christentum* (ed. K. H. Rengstorf; ALGHJ 21; Leiden: Brill, 1990), 45. See further *Jos. Asen.* 8:10; 15:7; 22:13 (numbering according to Christoph Burchard, "Joseph und Aseneth," JSHRZ 2.4 [1983]: 577–735); *1 En.* 22:1–3; see also *Gos. Truth* 36:35–39, and on that see Helderman, *Anapausis*, 145–55.

77. *2 Bar.* 30:2; *1 En.* 22; *4 Ezra* 4:35–37; 7:32, 80, 95, 101. See Paul Volz, *Die Eschatologie der jüdischen Gemeinde im neutestamentlichen Zeitalter nach den Quellen der rabbinischen, apokalyptischen und apokryphischen Literatur* (2d ed.; Tübingen: Mohr Siebeck, 1934), 248; Hans C. C. Cavallin, *Life after Death: Paul's Argument for Resurrection of the Dead in 1 Cor 15: Part 1, An Enquiry into the Jewish Background* (Lund: Gleerup, 1974), 264. On the rabbinic understanding of the heavenly world, see Ego, *Himmel*, passim.

notion of rest.[78] One should thus think initially of an after-death *state* of rest in *4 Baruch,* not a concrete *place.* Such is most easily harmonized with the context of Abimelech's sleep. His sleep also spanned a "between-time," at the end of which final salvation for the individual and the people, from the perspective of the eschatological Jerusalem, is still to come.

Although it is inappropriate to regard the concept of rest in *4 Bar.* 5:32 as identical to that of the heavenly Jerusalem in 5:34, their obvious association requires explanation. One should first note Abimelech's wish for the old man in 5:34: "May God lead you (by his) light[79] to the city above, Jerusalem." The motif of God illuminating the way of the pious with his light is expressed in many ways in the Old Testament: God's lighting of the way with the pillar of fire during the exodus (Exod 13:21; Ps 105[104]:39); the word of God as the light that illumines the way of the pious (Ps 119[118]:105; Prov 6:23); or God himself as the light who accompanies the pious (2 Sam 22:29 = Ps 18[17]:29 [NRSV 18:28]; Pss 4:7 [NRSV 4:6]; 27[26]:1; 89[88]:16 [NRSV 89:15]; Isa 2:5; 60:19–20; Mic 7:8; Sir 50:31; Bar 5:9). This last reference, Bar 5:9, provides an interesting parallel to *4 Bar.* 5:34: after announcing the return of those led into exile (Bar 5:6–8), the text promises that God will "lead [ἡγήσεται] Israel with joy by the light [φῶς] of his glory with mercy and justice, which are with him." Comparing Ps 119[118]:105 ("Your word is a lamp to my feet and a light to my path") or Prov 6:23 ("For the commandment is a lamp and the leading of light, and the reproofs of discipline are the ways of life"; see Wis 18:4), *4 Bar.* 5:34 must also refer back to the law, by which God lights the way of the pious to heaven.[80] Second, once again the figs play an important role, as Abimelech gives the old man some as healthy provisions for the way to the heavenly Jerusalem. For the faithful, the way to the heavenly Jerusalem is lit by God through his law, and the figs symbolize this salvation.

---

78. It is remarkable, for example, that in *2 Baruch* there is no clear mention of an eschatological place of rest. Thus *2 Bar.* 85:11 speaks of the after-death rest of the souls but without mentioning a place.

79. Whether the term φωταγωγεῖν used here was borrowed from the language of the mystery cults, as Jean Riaud claims, is not certain (" 'Le Puissant t'emportera dans ta Tente': La Destinée ultime du Juste selon les Paralipomena Jeremiae Prophetae," in *Hellenica et Judaica: Hommage à V. Nikiprowetzky* [ed. A. Caquot, M. Hadas-Lebel, and J. Riaud; Leuven: Peeters, 1986], 261 n. 26). He points to 4 Macc 17:5 and *T. Abr.* 2:7, but God is not the subject of φωταγωγεῖν in either text.

80. Delling, *Paralipomena Jeremiae,* 59; Riaud, "'Le Puissant t'emportera dans ta Tente,'" 261 n. 26; and Wolff, "Heilshoffnung," 156. This text thereby fits well into the narrative development of *4 Baruch,* for holding to the law concerning the cleansing of the people will play a decisive role in the return of the people (7:22, 32; see also 3:11; 5:22). On the significance of the law in setting apart the people, see Gerhard Delling, *Die Bewältigung der Diasporasituation durch das hellenistische Judentum* (Berlin: Evangelische Verlagsanstalt, 1987), 19–26.

The heavenly Jerusalem was not seen as a *temporary* place for the pious dead in early Judaism but as an eschatological place of salvation for the resurrected.[81] Therefore, an identification of the rest in 5:32 with the heavenly Jerusalem is unlikely. Rather, the relationship of the two ideas must be described as a certainty of postmortem security in God's rest. The goal of this is participation in God's final salvation in the heavenly Jerusalem, where the righteous will be gathered together (see *4 Bar.* 3:8).[82] The tradition of the heavenly Jerusalem as the goal of resurrection and the tradition of the intermediate state of rest are thus linked by the narration of Abimelech's sleep. It is noteworthy in this context that the intermediate state is described as a short dream despite its long duration.[83]

---

81. Wolff, "Heilshoffnung," 149 (references: *2 Bar.* 4:1–6; *4 Ezra* 7:26; 8:52; 9:38–10:54; 13:36; *1 En.* 90:28–36; *T. Dan* 5:12; *Jos. Asen.* 8:9–10; 15:7; 17:6; 22:13 [numbering according to Batiffol]; Rev 21:2–4). See also Nikolaus Walter, "Hellenistische Eschatologie im Neuen Testament," in *Glaube und Eschatologie* (ed. Erich Gräßer and Otto Merk; Tübingen: Mohr Siebeck, 1985), 335–56, esp. 340–41. Bogaert sees in *4 Bar.* 5:34 a Christian expression (*Apocalypse de Baruch*, 1:211–12, building on Kohler, "The Pre-Talmudic Haggada," 408). The main argument for this assumption is the linking of the verb φωταγωγεῖν with the expression "city of Jerusalem above"; see, however, above. Concerning *2 Bar.* 4:3, Murphy writes: "In expecting God's protection for the earthly sanctuary, Baruch confuses the earthly city with the heavenly" ("The Temple in the Syriac Apocalypse of Baruch," 675). But this is not the case. The context of *2 Bar.* 4:3 makes quite clear the difference between the heavenly and the earthly Jerusalem; see also Ego, *Himmel*, 146–47.

82. Despite the text-critical problems, from this final perspective the sentence of Abimelech in *4 Bar.* 5:6 reaches also eschatological dimensions, and this strengthens the text-critical decision in favor of the reading of ms C (= Harris).

83. For the difference between this concept and gnostic ideas, see Herzer, *Paralipomena Jeremiae*, 111 n. 356.

Chapter 6

As previously observed, *4 Bar.* 5 presents a perspective that transcends earthly contingencies; this perspective is developed in 6:1–7 by adding a further aspect to the individual hope of salvation, again related to the figs.[1] After meeting the old man, Abimelech is transferred by an angel to the tomb (6:1) where Baruch has been since the deportation of the people (4:11). The reference to the angel of righteousness, meaning the archangel Michael (see 9:5), prepares the reader for the meeting in 6:11.[2] The mutual kiss of greeting is a well-known symbol of companionship.[3] When he sees the fresh figs in Abimelech's basket, Baruch, like the old man before him, recognizes their salvific symbolism (6:2–7). In a prayer addressed to heaven,[4] Baruch understands the fresh figs from Abimelech's basket as a symbol of the reward (μισθαποδοσία)[5] of the pious, or the "holy ones,"[6] in the time of salvation, specifically the hope of resurrection: the righteous person has even in the face of his or her own death reason to hope in the life-creating power of God (ὁ ἱκανός[7]), for it is God who brings the

---

1. Delling, *Paralipomena Jeremiae*, 55–58; Riaud, "Le Puissant t'emportera dans ta Tente," 238–60; and Wolff, "Heilshoffnung," 150–53.
2. According to *Apoc. Mos.*, introduction, and *Pesiq. Rab.* 21:5, 9, 11, Michael is the "mediator of divine instructions" (Schaller, "Paralipomena Jeremiou," 731).
3. Gen 27:27; 29:11, 13; 33:4; Exod 4:27; 18:7; 2 Sam 14:33; 15:5.
4. See Ps 123(122):1.
5. The LXX does not use the term μισθαποδοσία but rather the synonymous μισθός: compensation, reward from God for the righteous (see Deut 24:15; Wis 5:15; Jer 22:13; 38:16; Sir 2:8; Prov 11:21). On its connection to the time of salvation, see Jer 31(38):13–16; see also Delling, *Paralipomena Jeremiae*, 56–57.
6. As God is the Holy One (see esp. Isa 5:16, 19; 12:6; 30:12, 15; 47:4; 57:15), so are his own "the holy people" (Isa 62:12) or the "the holy ones" (Ps 34[33]:10 [NRSV 34:9]; Dan 7:21, 27; Wis 18:1–2, 5, 9 [holy children]; Tob 8:15; 14:7; see further *Pss. Sol.* 4:25; 6:6; 10:3; 14:1; 1QS 11:7–8; 1QSIsa^b 1:5).
7. This is the Septuagint translation of שַׁדַּי; see G. Bertram, " ΙΚΑΝΟΣ in den griechischen Übersetzungen des Alten Testaments als Wiedergabe von schaddaj," *ZAW* 70 (1958): 20–31; Bogaert, *Apocalypse de Baruch*, 1:208–9; and Schaller, "Paralipomena Jeremiou," 730.

righteous from his or her "tent,"[8] and thus it is also he who preserves the righteous one until the resurrection.

Excursus on *4 Baruch* 6:3

The varying manuscript traditions in *4 Bar.* 6:3 have led to various interpretations. Instead of ἐκ τοῦ σκηνώματός σου, MS C reads the variant ἐν τῷ σκηνώματί σου.[9] The variant's intention is reminiscent of *2 Baruch:* Baruch will not see death but will be kept until the "last times" (13:3; 76:2). This does not mean that Baruch will be translated into heaven, since *2 Baruch* assumes that Baruch will die (78:5; 84:1). In addition, when 46:7 and 48:30 speak of Baruch "being taken away," one need not think of a translation, since the form used in both places may have the sense of "dying,"[10] which fits the context of *2 Baruch*.[11] Nevertheless, although the textual variant of MS C in *4 Bar.* 6:3 fits the perspective of *2 Baruch*, *4 Baruch*'s model text, it cannot be sustained for reasons internal to *4 Baruch* itself.[12] Most important is the end of *4 Baruch*, in which Jeremiah really dies (9:7–9). Consequently, the figs are no symbol of immortality for him (also 6:17), as Riaud argues.[13] Riaud interprets 9:3–7 as a story of the translation of the righteous[14] because the verb ἀναλαμβάνεσθαι is used (9:3). However, Jeremiah's death in 9:10 makes it clear that this is not the point and that ἀναλαμβάνεσθαι has a different sense in 9:3.[15] Riaud, for his

---

8. On the terms "tent" and "fleshly house" for physicality, see Wolff, "Heilshoffnung," 150, who makes clear the parallels with 2 Cor 5:1; see also Wis 9:15; 2 Pet 1:13–14; and *T. Job* 43:7. The latter says of Elihu: "His kingdom is gone, his throne is rotted. And the honour of his tent lies in Hades" (quoted from R. P. Spittler, "Testament of Job," *OTP* 1:862). Berndt Schaller understands the word "tent" as the "royal splendor tent" on the basis of Josephus, *Ant.* 11.187 ("Das Testament Hiob," *JSHRZ* 3.3 [1979]: 363). See, however, Marc Philonenko, "La Littérature Intertestamentaire et le Nouveau Testament," *RST* 47 (1973): 273–74. Josephus cannot support the view, however, as in the context a kingly tent is being described. That such might be found in Hades, as Schaller reads *T. Job* 43:7, makes no sense, since Hades is the place (of punishment) for the souls and not the place for earthly treasures; see Schaller himself, "Testament Hiob," 363 n. 7e.

9. Read by Riaud, "Le Puissant t'emportera dans ta Tente," 259–60; Kraft and Purintun, *Paraleipomena Jeremiou*, 28–29; and Schaller, "Paralipomena Jeremiou," 730.

10. Herzer, *Paralipomena Jeremiae*, 63; Bogaert, *Apocalypse de Baruch*, 2:84.

11. On the problem of the death of the righteous in *2 Baruch*, see Wolfgang Harnisch, *Verhängnis und Verheißung der Geschichte: Untersuchungen zum Zeit- und Geschichtsverständnis im 4. Buch Esra und in der syrischen Baruchapokalypse* (FRLANT 97; Göttingen: Vandenhoeck & Ruprecht, 1969), 80–87.

12. Delling, *Paralipomena Jeremiae*, 55–56; and particularly Wolff, "Heilshoffnung," 150–53.

13. Riaud, "Le Puissant t'emportera dans ta Tente," 260.

14. Ibid., 263, 265. See also Herzer, *Paralipomena Jeremiae*, 151 n. 575.

15. Delling, *Paralipomena Jeremiae*, 57–58.

part, suggests that one should remove this ending of *4 Baruch* for literary-critical reasons.[16]

Of further significance in the present context is the word αἴρω in 6:3. Just as ἀναλαμβάνεσθαι in 9:3 should not be understood as referring to translation because of the broader context of *4 Baruch*, so also with αἴρω in 6:3. The word αἴρω has far more the sense of "to take away" with regard to death,[17] so that 6:3 speaks not of translation but reckons with death. It is noteworthy that God is expressly named as the subject of the keeping in 6:7, while the corresponding references in *2 Baruch* are passive, even if they are to be understood as *passivum divinum*. In this way *4 Bar.* 6:7 makes the sense of its template more concrete: God himself will preserve the faithful by raising them from the dead.

Of interest here is a reference in *Derek Eretz Rabbah* in which Abimelech is named as one of many translated to paradise during their lifetimes: "Nine entered paradise during their lives; Enoch, Elijah, the Messiah, Eliezer the servant of Abraham, Ebed-Melech the Ethiopian King, Hiram the King of Tyre, Jabez the grandson of Judah ha-Nasi, Serah the daughter of Asher, and Bithiah the daughter of Pharaoh" (*Der. Er. Rab.* 1:18).[18] Assuming that the tradition about Ebed-Melech reflected in *Derek Eretz Rabbah* was known to the author of *4 Baruch*, one must also suppose that he intentionally contradicted this tradition, given his arguments against the idea of translation. If one can speak of some relationship between the two texts, then *Derek Eretz Rabbah* as well as the Second Alphabet of Ben Sira 28b were influenced by an Ebed-Melech tradition that had its origins in the same circle as that which produced the interpretation leading to the MS C variant of *4 Bar.* 6:3. One should also make reference to *L.A.E.* 37, which states that the archangel Michael will lift the dead Adam to paradise (37:31–32), where he will be kept until judgment. Using the word αἴρω, 37:5 makes Adam's death paradigmatic for the fate of all humans: ἆρον αὐτὸν εἰς τὸν παράδεισον (see also 37:6).[19]

---

16. Riaud, "Le Puissant t'emportera dans ta Tente," 264. On that, see Herzer, *Paralipomena Jeremiae*, 29–30.

17. See Joachim Jeremias, "αἴρω," *TDNT* 1:185–86: "death rather than snatching away or rapture." That the sense in *4 Baruch* is not translation is also of significance for the intention of the author; see Herzer, *Paralipomena Jeremiae*, 157–58; against Riaud, "Le Puissant t'emportera dans ta Tente," 265.

18. Quoted from Michael Higger, *The Treatises Derek Erez: Masseket Derek Erez—Pirke Ben Azzai—Tosefta Derek Erez. Edited from Manuscripts with an Introduction, Notes, Variants and Translation* (New York: The Rabanan, 1935), 36. See the Second Alphabet of Ben Sira 28b and, on that, Ginzberg, *Legends*, 5:95–96. For the idea of translation into heaven, see *b. Ḥag.* 14b; 2 Cor 12:4; see on that Lenhardt and von der Osten-Sacken, *Rabbi Akiva*, 124–37.

19. Quoted from Albert Marie Denis, *Concordance Greque des Pseudepigraphes d'Ancien Testament: Concordance, Corpus des Textes Indices* (Leiden: Brill, 1987), 817. See further Thomas Knittel,

In light of this discussion, the reading that speaks of Baruch's *death* is to be preferred. This is of great importance for understanding the following statements, as the shape of the hope of resurrection gains clear contours only by this reading.

The aspect of preservation (φυλάσσειν) until the resurrection forms a link to chapter 5, this being found in the hope of the intertemporal rest (5:32) that leads to the consummation of the hope in the heavenly Jerusalem (5:34). Hence chapter 6 answers the question concerning the possibility of a physical resurrection by referring to God's power to preserve even beyond death.[20] Abimelech's preservation and the fresh figs represent this. One among many early Jewish references to such an idea of resurrection[21] can be found in 2 Bar. 50:1–4.[22] The relationship between the texts becomes clear in the light of certain notable similarities.

> (1) And he answered and said to me: Listen, Baruch, to this word and write down in the memory of your heart all that you shall learn. (2) For the earth will surely give back the dead at that time; it receives them now in order to keep them, not changing anything in their form. But as it has received them so it will give them back. And as I have delivered them to it so it will raise them. (3) For then it will be necessary to show those who live that the dead are living again, and that those who went away have come back. (4) And it will be that when they have recognized each other, those who know each other at this moment, then my judgment will be strong, and those things which have been spoken of before will come. (*2 Bar.* 50:1–4)[23]

Most noticeably, both *4 Bar.* 6:7 and *2 Bar.* 50:2 speak of the preservation of the righteous until the resurrection, using the same motif of the intertemporal state.[24] While *2 Baruch* emphasizes that they do not change in their appearance

---

Das griechische "Leben Adams und Evas": Studien zu einer narrativen Anthropologie im frühen Judentum (Tübingen: Mohr Siebeck, 2002), 288.

20. Wolff, "Heilshoffnung," 153.

21. Primarily 2 Macc 7:11; *Sib. Or.* 4:178–180; *4 Ezra* 7:32; see Stone, *Features,* 141–43; Günter Stemberger, *Der Leib der Auferstehung: Studien zur Anthropologie und Eschatologie des palästinischen Judentums im neutestamentlichen Zeitalter (ca. 170 v. Chr.–100 n. Chr.)* (AnBib 56; Rome: Biblical Institute Press, 1972), 82, 116–17; Cavallin, Life after Death; and Wolff, "Heilshoffnung," 153.

22. Stemberger, *Der Leib der Auferstehung,* 86–88; Wolff, "Heilshoffnung," 153.

23. Quoted from Klijn, "2 Baruch," *OTP* 1:637–38.

24. In contrast to *4 Baruch,* the preservation of *all* dead, not just the righteous, is explicitly indicated in *2 Bar.* 50:4 by the reference to the final judgment (see also 51:1).

until the time of resurrection, in *4 Baruch* this motif is linked with the fresh figs that did not change during the sixty-six years, neither drying out nor rotting (*4 Bar.* 6:5),[25] which serves symbolically to support faith in God's ability to preserve the righteous even in death.[26] Just as God is the subject of the death of the righteous and the guarantee of their preservation until the resurrection in *4 Bar.* 6:3, so also is God the one who gives the righteous over to the preservation of the earth until they emerge again in the resurrection.[27] The death of the righteous is once again expressly in view. A second similarity is the motif of resuscitation referred to in *2 Bar.* 50:3. A similar idea is found in *4 Bar.* 6:4: "Revive, my virginal faith, and believe that you will live."[28] Of further interest is the broader context in *2 Bar.* 51:1–4, which identifies obedience to the law as the measure for participating in the glorious transformation of the righteous, a connection that is also taken up in *4 Bar.* 6:6, yet here focusing on resurrection.

The expression ἡ παρθενική μου πίστις (6:4) is surprising in this context.[29] Delling's appeal to Rev 14:4[30] is of no help, since this text does not refer to faith.[31] In the context of *4 Baruch*, the content of the attribute παρθενικός is a description of the faith that Baruch must preserve in the grave despite his lament (see 7:2, where Baruch is referred to as a "steward [οἰκονόμος] of faith"). "Faith" should here be understood as trust in God that he will turn the people's fate around. The call to revive (ἀνάψυξον), directed at the faith, underlines this understanding: this trust in God, lost in lament after the destruction of Jerusalem (4:6–11), can only be discovered once again when Baruch understands the meaning of Abimelech's preservation by way of the figs.[32] In particular, *4 Bar.*

---

25. The expression ὄζειν is also used to describe the smell of decay (see John 11:39); see LSJ, 1200 s.v. II.

26. On the expression in 6:3: "prepare yourself, my heart, and be glad and rejoice" see Pss 56:8 (LXX); 108(107):2 (NRSV 108:1), in which God is called upon to prepare the heart of the one praying; see also *Ps. Sol.* 6:1: μακάριος ἀνὴρ οὗ ἡ καρδία αὐτοῦ ἑτοίμη ἐπικαλέσασθαι τὸ ὄνομα κυρίου.

27. See *1 En.* 51:1: "In those days, Sheol will return all the deposits which she had received and hell will give back all that which it owes" (quoted from E. Isaac, "1 [Ethiopic Apocalypse of] Enoch," *OTP* 1:36).

28. See Herzer, *Paralipomena Jeremiae*, 172–73.

29. The manuscript tradition (see above) is not clear at this point; a conjecture seems unavoidable; see Schaller, "Paralipomena Jeremiou," 730–31: "All are expedients" (731). The text suggested by Harris and used here seems, after consideration of the variants, plausible. Schaller follows Bogaert's conjecture (Bogaert, Apocalypse de Baruch, 1:210–11).

30. Delling, *Paralipomena Jeremiae*, 9; Riaud, *Les Paralipomènes du Prophète Jérémie*, 189.

31. See Schaller, "Paralipomena Jeremiou," 731.

32. Schaller (ibid.) refers to *L.A.E.* 19:3; 20:4 concerning the symbolic power of the figs. However, 19:3 does not speak of figs but of the poisonous fruit of the serpent; 20:4 concerns the leaves of the fig tree, from which Eve makes her covering. The reference is therefore unclear.

4:8 demonstrates that Baruch's trust or faith in God's restoration of the people is present in the lament, even when overshadowed by it. Hence this "virginal faith," this reawakened faith, may be adequately understood in the context of *4 Baruch* and need not be credited to a (gnostic-) Christian editor.[33]

Having recognized the symbolic significance of Abimelech's preservation, Baruch determines to send this message of salvation to Babylon and asks God to show him a way to do so (6:8–10). By contrast, *2 Bar.* 77:12 reports that the people called on Baruch to write a letter to the Babylonian exiles.[34] In addition, in *2 Baruch* the addressee is assumed to be the entire people, but *4 Bar.* 6:8, 10, 12, 14 expressly state that Jeremiah is to receive the letter. The people will hear its salvific message only through him (6:13). In contrast to *2 Baruch*, *4 Baruch* cannot ignore Jeremiah's significance at this stage, so he becomes the transmitter of the letter. Still other differences are also worth noting. In *2 Bar.* 77 Baruch responds to the people's request but wants to write two letters, one to be brought over by three men, the other by a bird to the "nine and a half tribes." The bird is then identified as an eagle. This motif—an eagle bringing a letter—is taken up in *4 Bar.* 6:12. However, the letter that the eagle is to take in *2 Baruch* is the only one that Baruch actually writes, according to *4 Baruch*.[35] In *4 Baruch*, moreover, the eagle takes the letter to Babylon (7:18), whereas in *2 Baruch* the three men convey it to Babylon.[36] Furthermore, the light motif from *2 Bar.* 77:13 appears in the name of God in *4 Bar.* 6:9. This light holds no promise of future hope within the context of *2 Baruch*, because the "shepherds" of the people have darkened it, but in *4 Baruch* it represents the real hope of salvation that continues to exist and thus refers to God.

Once again, as often before, our author's reworking of material from *2 Baruch* enables us to see his theological perspective: two letters reduced to one,[37] carried not by the men but by the eagle, and God's detailed involvement

---

33. Bogaert, Apocalypse de Baruch, 1:210: "It has primarily a gnostic flavor." However, there is no evidence, that this phrase was ever a gnostic terminus. See Herzer, *Paralipomena Jeremiae*, 172–73; Schaller, "Paralipomena Jeremiou," 731.

34. On Baruch's letter, see J. Ramsey Michaels, "Jewish and Christian Apocalyptic Letters: 1 Peter, Revelation, and 2 Baruch 78–87" (*SBLSP* 26; Atlanta: Scholars Press, 1987), 269–70. For greater detail, particularly concerning form criticism, see Taatz, *Frühjüdische Briefe*, 64–76.

35. Michaels, "Jewish and Christian Apocalyptic Letters," 270.

36. Taatz (*Frühjüdische Briefe*, 63 n. 259) sees a parallel with Jer 29:3, which speaks of Zedekiah's emissaries who brought over Jeremiah's letter. However, there were only two emissaries. Bogaert was the first to point not to biblical traditions but to LXX Baruch (*Apocalypse de Baruch*, 1:80).

37. Whereas *2 Bar.* 77:19 states, "And I wrote two letters. One I sent by means of an eagle to the nine and a half tribes, and the other I sent by means of three men to those who were in Babylon" (quoted from Klijn, "2 Baruch," *OTP* 1:647), in 78:1 only the one to the nine and a half tribes sent out by the eagle is explicitly mentioned as being written (see 77:20–26; 87:1). Although

in the writing of the letter. This theologizing represents a clear reinterpretation of the source material in order to develop a different and more hopeful perspective than that found in *2 Baruch*.

The names with which Baruch addresses God in 6:9 further reveal this perspective: "Our power, O God our Lord, (is) the elect light that proceeded from his mouth ... O Great Name that no one can know."[38] Meeting Abimelech and realizing the imminence of salvation changes Baruch's understanding of God. From this point on God's effective power for his people comes to the fore. Thus God is "our power," a name for God taken from the Old Testament.[39] That God is the Almighty was already clear in his judgment on Jerusalem and the people; now God uses his strength to save the people.[40]

Reference to God as "light" reminds the reader of Abimelech's wish for the old man (5:34). There, too, the association with the law was clear; this is now expressly picked up with the explanatory "that proceeded from his mouth."[41] God's law, which comes from his mouth, is the light that strengthens the faithful and shows them the right way out of captivity.[42] It will later become clear that it is through Jeremiah's teaching that the law reveals its light; his teaching thus plays a decisive role in the return of the people (6:22; 7:22, 32; 8:3, 4).[43]

The designation "great name that no one can know" should also be read in the light of Old Testament and Jewish understandings.[44] The expression "great

---

one could assume two copies of the same letter in *2 Baruch*, this differentiation seems, however, to be significant for the reduction to only one letter in *4 Baruch*; see Herzer, *Paralipomena Jeremiae*, 67–68. On the problem of the "lost letter," see Bogaert, *Apocalypse de Baruch*, 1:78–80.

38. For the understanding of God in *4 Baruch*, see Herzer, "Direction in Difficult Times," passim.

39. Ps 46(45):2, and in the singular Ps 18(17):2; Jer 16:19; see Delling, *Paralipomena Jeremiae*, 31–32. Schaller follows MS C and the Ethiopic translation ("Paralipomena Jeremiou," 732).

40. Philonenko's observation ("Simples Observations," 165) that Mandaic texts also regularly use the name "power" for God is not of use in this context; see Herzer, "Antwort," 34.

41. There is, of course, a difficulty with the phrase τὸ ἐξελθὸν ἐκ στόματος αὐτοῦ ("that proceeded from his mouth") because of the change from the vocative to the third-person singular. According to Schaller, "Paralipomena Jeremiou," 732 n. e, the phrase should be seen as a secondary insertion. Kraft and Purintun, *Paraleipomena Jeremiou*, 28–29, read "from your mouth," which better fits the context but has only one witness in the manuscripts (arm[c]; cf. Schaller, "Paraleipomena Jeremiou," 732 n. e).

42. Contra Philonenko, "Simples Observations," 164, who thinks of light in a mythical-gnostic sense, referring among others to *Odes Sol.* 12:3. But the motif is known in contexts concerning the return from exile in the Old Testament (Isa 52:7–12!) and not from a gnostic tradition; see the commentary above on *4 Bar.* 5:34 and Herzer, "Antwort," 33–34.

43. According to Philonenko, the light is Jeremiah ("Simples Observations," 165). However, Jeremiah nowhere else bears this title in *4 Baruch*; see further Riaud, "La figure de Jérémie," passim.

44. Delling, *Paralipomena Jeremiae*, 32.

name" is found often in the Old Testament (Josh 7:9; 1 Kgs 8:42; 2 Chr 6:32; Pss 76[75]:2 [NRSV 76:1]; 99[98]:3; Jer 44[51]:26; Ezek 36:23),[45] but the most significant reference in this context is probably *2 Bar.* 5:1, in which Baruch asks God concerning the destruction of Jerusalem: "what have you done to your great name?"[46]

According to *4 Bar.* 6:9, no one can know God's name. For this idea, Delling makes reference to Philo's *Mos.* 2.114: "A piece of gold plate, too, was wrought into the form of a crown with four incisions, showing a name which only those whose ears and tongues are purified may hear or speak in the holy place, and no other person, nor in any other place at all."[47] However, Philo's reference here is to the prohibition against speaking God's name aloud, a widespread convention,[48] not the inability to know God's name.[49] A further reference would be Jer 44:26: "Lo, I swear by my great name, says the Lord, that my name shall no longer be pronounced on the lips of any of the people of Judah in all the land of Egypt, saying, 'As the LORD God lives'" (NRSV). Both the motif of the great name and a prohibition against speaking it are found, yet this and the Philo reference assume that God's name is known. By contrast, *4 Bar.* 6:9 speaks of no one being able to know God's name, which goes much further. Once again we may refer to Philo, who approaches this view in his exegesis of Exod 3:13–15.

Moses knew well that his own nation and all the others would disbelieve his words, and said: "If they ask the name of him who sent me, and I cannot

---

45. See also Mal 1:11; Prov 18:10; Sir 39:15; 46:1; 3 Macc 2:9; see Delling, *Paralipomena Jeremiae*, 32.

46. Quoted from Klijn, "2 Baruch," *OTP* 1:622. Bogaert translates "illustre Nom [illustrious name]" but adds "littéralement: *grand* Nom [literally: great name]" (*Apocalypse de Baruch*, 2:18). See also *4 Ezra* 4:25; 10:22 (Stone, *Ezra*, 89). For the rabbinic tradition, see Clemens Thoma, "Gott III," *TRE* 13:629–30.

47. See Delling, *Paralipomena Jeremiae*, 32; translation from Colson and Whitaker, LCL.

48. See *m. Tamid* 7:2; *y. Yoma* 3:7; 6:2; *b. Qidd.* 71; *Sipre Num.* 39; *Sipre Zuta* 15–16, 39. Particularly clear is *m. Sanh.* 10:1C–G: "And these are the ones who have no portion in the world to come: (1) He who says, the resurrection of the dead is a teaching which does not derive from the Torah, (2) and the Torah does not come from Heaven; and (3) an Epicurean. R. Aqiba says, 'Also: He who reads in heretical book …' Abba Saul says, 'Also: he who pronounces the divine Name as it is spelled out'" (quoted from Neusner, *Mishnah*, 604). According to *b. Yoma* 39b and *t. Sotah* 138, the death of the high priest Simon the Just (ca. 200 B.C.E.) seven days after the Day of Atonement was caused by his speaking out God's name.

49. Philo is working with the philosophical notion of God as ἄρρητος (inexpressible), which was sometimes conceptually related to the idea of God as ἄγνωστος (unknown [cf. Acts 17:23] or unknowable as to essence [cf. Josephus, *Ag. Ap.* 2.167]). In this passage, however, Philo's understanding is that God's name is ἄρρητος in the sense that it is too sacred to pronounce (cf. 2 Cor 12:4).

myself tell them, will they not think me a deceiver?" God replied: "First tell them that I am He who is, that they may learn the difference between what is and what is not, and also the further lesson that no name at all can properly be used of Me [ὡς οὐδὲν ὄνομα τὸ παράπαν ἐπ' ἐμοῦ κυριολογεῖται], to whom alone existence belongs." (Philo, *Mos.* 1.74–75)[50]

Here it is assumed that no one can know God's name, since it was not given to Moses. This unusual interpretation caused Gese to remark that Philo had not done justice to the original sense of Exod 3:13–15.[51] One can offer two rebuttals to his claim: (1) Philo is not concerned with exegetical "correctness" in the historical-critical sense; (2) *4 Baruch* represents a second witness to this interpretation. Moreover, *4 Bar.* 6:9 cannot be seen as a Christian interpolation, as some have argued. Gese rightly showed the continuity between Exod 3:13–15 and John 17:6 ("I have made your name known to those whom you gave me from the world" [NRSV]),[52] but it is precisely the key difference between the Christian understanding in John 17:6 and the viewpoint of *4 Bar.* 6:9 that one must note: God's name has been revealed in the former text but cannot be known in the latter. The gnostic origin suggested by Philonenko is also groundless,[53] though he offers several texts as "gnostic" references: Irenaeus, *Haer.* 1.21.3; *Ginza* 98:9–10; and *1 En.* 69:14. The last is most revealing, since this part of *1 Enoch* dates most likely to the first or second century B.C.E. and thus cannot be gnostic.[54] Furthermore, this reference does not concern the name of God but the hidden name of the Son of Man (69:26). Even the clearly (and also later and Christian) gnostic reference from *Ginza* does not speak of the name of God but of the

---

50. Translation Colson and Whitaker, LCL. See Hartmut Gese, "Der Name Gottes im Alten Testament," in *Der Name Gottes* (ed. H. von Stietencron; Düsseldorf: Patmos, 1975), 76; Thoma, *TRE* 13:628–29. See further Isa 52:6, where knowing or the knowledge of God's name has an *eschatological* meaning: "Therefore my people shall know my name; therefore in that day they shall know that it is I who speak; here am I." Finally, *Exod. Rab.* 3:6 on Exod 3:14 reads: "R. Abba b. Mammel said: God said to Moses: 'Thou wishest to know My name. Well, I am called according to My work; sometimes I am called 'Almighty God,' 'Lord of the Hosts,' 'God,' 'Lord.' When I am judging created beings, I am called 'God,' and when I am waging war against the wicked, I am called 'Lord of the Hosts.' When I suspend judgment for a man's sin, I am called '*El Shadday*' (Almighty God), and when I am merciful towards My world, I am called '*Adonai*,' for '*Adonai*' refers to the Attribute of Mercy, as it is said: *The Lord, the Lord* (Adonai, Adonai), *God, merciful and gracious* … Hence I AM THAT I AM in virtue of My deeds'" (quoted from S. M. Lehrman, *Exodus* [vol. 3 of *Midrash Rabbah*; ed. H. Freedman and M. Simon 3rd ed.; 10 vols.; London: Soncino, 1983], 64). Cf. *Mek. de Rabbi Ishmael* on Exod 20:2; *b. Ber.* 9b.
51. Gese, "Der Name Gottes im Alten Testament," 76.
52. Cf. ibid.
53. Philonenko, "Simples Observations," 165.
54. See Isaac, "1 Enoch," *OTP* 1:7 ("late pre-Maccabean").

hidden name of the archangel Gabriel.⁵⁵ In sum, then, one should understand the phrase "great name that no one can know" in terms of its Old Testament and Hellenistic-Jewish background, not as a Christian or gnostic intrusion into the text. The striking frequency of divine predicates in Baruch's prayer appears to be a reference to God as the moving power of history in general and to the fate of his people in particular. The sapiential understanding of the law as the light from God's mouth refers to the principle of wisdom lying behind everything that happens in the history of the people of Israel. This corresponds to the idea that it is the power of this light that strengthens the people so that they will be able to handle their future. It also corresponds to the idea that God's name is unknown, which might refer again to a sapiential idea of the seclusion of God's nature, which of course is primarily characterized by his willingness to save and free his people. Accordingly, the following content of Baruch's prayer takes up this concern.

Baruch's prayer ends with a request for knowledge (6:10). The term γνῶσις does not allude to a particular spiritual movement but rather refers concretely to the next steps in the preparation for the people's return (6:8). The mention of Baruch's "heart" is likewise related to the return, the announcement of which was already declared reason for joy in the heart in 6:3.⁵⁶ God does not answer Baruch's prayer directly but by means of an angel sent by him (ἄγγελος κυρίου, 6:11), since direct communication with God is the unique privilege of the priest-prophet Jeremiah. The angel addresses Baruch as σύμβουλος τοῦ φωτός (6:12), playing on Baruch's role in the Old Testament Jeremiah tradition as Jeremiah's helper, though the term σύμβουλος does not appear there (Jer 36:6–18; see also Bar 1:3–4). In *4 Bar.* 5:18 Baruch is called the "reader," and in 7:2 he is designated οἰκονόμος τῆς πίστεως.⁵⁷ In the light of Baruch's role as reader, the expression in *4 Bar.* 6:12 becomes clear. The specific term ἀναγνώστης is used in the Old Testament only for Ezra as the "reader of the law" (Ezra 8:19: Εσδρας ὁ ἱερεὺς καὶ ἀναγνώστης τοῦ νόμου τοῦ θεοῦ τοῦ ὑψίστου—see also 8:8, 9; 9:39, 42, 49). As already noted, the term "light" is a metaphor for the law in *4 Baruch,* so the title σύμβουλος τοῦ φωτός can be explained as follows: like Ezra, Baruch is a reader, a "counselor," of the law. It is in this role that Baruch calls Jeremiah to establish the law in the exilic community as the condition for the return.⁵⁸

---

55. See Herzer, "Antwort," 35.
56. Herzer, *Paralipomena Jeremiae,* 175.
57. See Delling, *Paralipomena Jeremiae,* 26–27.
58. See ibid., 25–26: "Ratgeber (zum Tun) des Lichts = des Guten, des Gotteswillens [adviser (of doing) the light, i.e., the good, the will of God]" (with reference to 4 Macc 9:3; 2 Chr 22:3; similarly Riaud, *Les Paralipomènes du Prophète Jérémie,* 35; Philonenko, "Simples Observations,"

Indeed, this is the message that the angel instructs Baruch to include in his letter to Jeremiah (6:12–14).[59] The instruction in the letter is that the people are to separate themselves from the Babylonians, which Jeremiah should accomplish on the basis of the divine law. That the final content of Baruch's letter goes beyond this instruction (6:17–23) demonstrates once again that Baruch is the "advisor" or "counselor" as regards the law, since he clarifies and interprets the angel's instructions.[60]

The motif of a letter to the exilic community is borrowed from the story in Jer 29:1–23, in which Jeremiah sends a letter to the exiles. Although the story here is developed differently, a structural parallel can be observed. The content is, however, borrowed from 2 Bar. 77:11–19, which also mentions a letter that Baruch sent to Babylon.[61] The "epistolographically unusual" shape of the letter makes it clear that it is a literary work with a particular function in the book of 4 Baruch.[62] For this reason the author chooses not to name the writer and addressee. The addressee is only initially Jeremiah, as 6:21–22 indicates that through him all the exiles are being addressed.

That the letter does not refer to Abimelech and the figs is remarkable, considering that they have provided the reason for writing. However, the eagle is given fifteen figs (7:8) for the sick among the people (7:32). Moreover, when the eagle arrives in Babylon it raises a dead person (7:17), creating an obvious link back to the salvation and resurrection symbolism of the figs in chapter 6.[63] Finally, the first sentence of Baruch's letter has clear echoes of 6:3 by way of the themes of joy and celebration and not least in the motif of leaving the body, which parallels God's preservation of Abimelech.

As earlier in the Abimelech story, Baruch's letter seems not to refer explicitly to the divine word (6:13–14), which it was supposed to transmit, although Baruch claims to quote it (6:19–20). The separation of the people as the condition for return from exile (6:13) plays no role in the letter. Conversely, the waters of the Jordan as a means of testing (6:23) are not mentioned in the divine word. Only the double alienation from both Jerusalem and Babylon for all those who will not set themselves apart (6:14) or hear Jeremiah's word (6:22) is

---

164–65: "un conseiller dont les avis sont 'lumineux' [an adviser whose words of advice are enlightening]."

59. The instruction to write is typically apocalyptic (Rev 2:1; Herm. Vis. 5:5); the introduction "speak to the children of Israel" gives it, however, prophetic character (Exod 14:2, 15; Lev 1:2; 18:2; Ezek 3:1; Amos 7:15).

60. On the eagle motif, see below on 7:2.

61. See Herzer, Paralipomena Jeremiae, 64–72.

62. So Taatz, Frühjüdische Briefe, 79–80, here 79.

63. Wolff, "Heilshoffnung," 154–55.

mentioned in both texts. Thus does the author prepare for chapter 8, in which aspects of the divine word in 6:13–14 and of Baruch's letter in 6:17–23 are taken up and in which the common motif of double alienation plays the major role (8:5b–7).[64] The traditional intention of the command regarding separation was cultic cleanness, and *4 Baruch* reaches its climax in a cultic context as well: the celebration of Yom Kippur under the high priesthood of Jeremiah.[65]

Given the literary function of 6:13–23 for the development of *4 Baruch*, one cannot divide the angel's speech and Baruch's letter from one another despite the tensions mentioned above. They are better understood as complementary.[66] As he set the stage for chapter 8, the author saw no need to reproduce the divine word literally in Baruch's letter. The literary intention is more important here than the narrative consequence. The decisive moment is that of double alienation, as 8:5–9 reveals. One may thus understand the interruption in 6:15–16 as little more than a literary device[67] to make the background of the situation more realistic.

The unusual description ἀγορὰ τῶν ἐθνῶν (market of the Gentiles) is seen by Riaud[68] to refer to Mamre, which may have been, at least from Hadrian's time, an important marketplace.[69] The relatively great distance between Mamre and Jerusalem (ca. 30 km) could be problematic, but it becomes irrelevant once one understands the reference to the market of the Gentiles as a narrative device[70] that

---

64. Jean Riaud, "Les Samaritains dans les 'Paralipomena Jeremiae,'" in *La Littérature Intertestamentaire: Colloque de Strasbourg 1983* (ed. André Caquot; Paris: Presses Universitaires de France, 1985), 141; Herzer, *Paralipomena Jeremiae*, 131. See below.

65. Schaller ("Paralipomena Jeremiou," 733, referring to Delling, *Paralipomena Jeremiae*, 44 n. 13) sees cultic connotations in the number fifteen as well, understanding the fifteen days as two weeks, which actually means fourteen days, which represents a doubling of the normal cleansing time of seven days.

66. Bogaert, *Apocalypse de Baruch*, 1:206: "Cette lettre précise certaines données du message de l'ange. Elle ajoute surtout la mention du Jourdain et du sceau [This letter makes more precise certain aspects of the angel's message. Above all, it adds the mention of Jordan and the seal]."

67. Taatz, *Frühjüdische Briefe*, 80.

68. Riaud, *Les Paralipomènes du Prophète Jérémie*, 130 with 133 n. 29. See already Harris, *Rest of the Words of Baruch*, 32.

69. Peter Welten, "Mamre," *TRE* 12:12.

70. Bogaert notes the mention of an "oak" in *2 Bar.* 77:18, which he also identifies with Mamre. This must be the reference in *4 Baruch*, because it borrows this place from *2 Baruch* (*Apocalypse de Baruch*, 1:324–27). Bogaert's most important text reference is found in Jerome, *In Hieremiam Prophetam* 6:1064–1065 on Jer 31(38):15 (cf. PL 24:877), where Jerome explains the name of Bethlehem-Ephrata and why it is linked with the lament of Rachel by mentioning an important marketplace: "Some of the Jews explain this location in a way that—when Jerusalem was taken captive by Vespasian—over this place thousands of captured people were brought to Gaza, Alexandria, and Rome. Others, however, think that at the time of the last conquest under Hadrian, countless people of different ages and of both genders were sold on the Terebinth market. And

presumably uses an authentic motif to develop the scene.[71] There is no deeper meaning to this detail.

Because of its compositionally important function, one must see the hand of the author of *4 Baruch* at work consciously shaping the letter of 6:17–23. As elsewhere, *2 Baruch* provided the point of departure for the motifs of the narrative frame, but so far as the letter's content is concerned, there are no commonalities that would point to a direct borrowing from *2 Baruch*. The argument of the letter, "fall—punishment—obedience—salvation,"[72] is comparable to the structure of the letter in *2 Baruch*[73] but is already present in the Old Testament.[74]

A further question concerns the relationship between Baruch's letter and that which Jeremiah sent to the exiles in Jer 29:1–23.[75] There are no direct points of contact, as Jeremiah's letter points in a completely different direction: the exiled are to build houses, plant gardens (29:5), and marry (29:6). The lack of an explicit prohibition against intermarrying with foreigners in 29:6 might be regarded as inconsistent with *4 Bar.* 6:13–14. However, the note in Jer 29:6c ("multiply there, and do not decrease") could be interpreted to mean that they should keep themselves separate, for the concern is the preservation of the people of Israel.[76] One must consider in this context that, although the end of the exile

---

therefore for Jews it is impossible to visit this well-known market." After 135 C.E., paganization was so far advanced that the Jews avoided the place, for which reason according to Bogaert Baruch did not go himself but sent the proselyte Abimelech. That would, however, assume that the *4 Baruch* was written after 135 C.E.; see, however, the introduction above.

71. Schaller counts it as a further indication of the author's knowledge of the area ("Paralipomena Jeremiou," 734).

72. Taatz, *Frühjüdische Briefe*, 80.

73. Fall (*2 Bar.* 79:2; 84:2, 5)—punishment (78:5; 80:1–6)—obedience (84:6–85:4)—salvation (82:2–83:8; 85:9–11). Donald E. Gowan speaks of the "pattern 'Sin-Exile-Restoration' which ... typically describes the pre-exilic period by a series of general references to sin without mentioning any specific historical details" ("The Exile in Jewish Apocalyptic," in *Scripture in History and Theology: Essays in Honor of J. Coert Rylaarsdam* [ed. Arthur L. Merrill and Thomas W. Overholt; PTMS 17; Pittsburgh: Pickwick, 1977], 215).

74. See the so-called Deuteronomistic scheme of the time of the judges, esp. Judg 2:11–18: fall (11–13)—punishment (14–15)—salvation (16, 18); see also Judg 3:7–9. In the prophetic preaching, see esp. Joel: fall and punishment (1:1–2:11)—repentance (2:12–17)—salvation (2:18–4:21). The structure of Jeremiah is also worthy of note here: fall and judgment (1–30)—promises of salvation (30–33); see Christopher R. Seitz, "The Prophet Moses and the Canonical Shape of Jeremiah," *ZAW* 101 (1989): 3–27. According to Hans Walter Wolff, the call to repentance in exile is the central message of the Deuteronomistic History ("Das Kerygma des deuteronomistischen Geschichtswerks," *ZAW* 32 [1961]: 180). Likewise in *4 Baruch* the call to repentance as condition for the return from exile is decisive (6:14, 22; 7:32; 8:2–3; see also 8:9).

75. For the motif in 4Q389 of Jeremiah writing a letter to the exiles, see n. 73 of the introduction.

76. Taatz, *Frühjüdische Briefe*, 51.

is promised in Jer 29:10, 14, it is not imminent, as is assumed in *4 Bar.* 6: the more imminent the return, the more important the command to separate. In addition, the problem of mixed marriages has not yet been explicitly mentioned in *4 Baruch*. Initially the text gives only a general command to remain separate,[77] presumably from the foreign idol cults (see Lev 19:4; 26:1; Deut 27:15; Pss 96:4–5; 97:7; Isa 42:8, 17; Jer 2:4–13; 4:1–2). The same concern with worship of foreign gods is also central in Jeremiah's reply (*4 Bar.* 7:25–26). Thus, although mixed marriages often led to religious syncretism and participation in foreign idol cults (Deut 7:3–4; Judg 3:6; 1 Kgs 1–11), there is no clear and direct relationship between *4 Bar.* 6 and Jeremiah's letter.[78]

Before Baruch writes down the final wording of the letter he has been commissioned to write (6:21–23), he gives it a lengthy introduction (6:17–20) that conveys to the exilic audience the previously noted theme of joy. Of significance for our reading of 6:3 is the statement that God has not allowed the death of the righteous (6:17). Death is here described with the same words as before—(ἐξελθεῖν) ἐκ τοῦ σώματος (τούτου)—and the turn in the people's fate is expressly credited to God's mercy (6:18). As before, both judgment and salvation are fully in God's hands. The reference to God's covenant with the patriarchs is decisive in this regard. When God remembers his covenant, his faithfulness to it means salvation for his people. The use of Old Testament ideas and language is particularly noticeable here.[79] The naming of Abraham, Isaac, and Jacob brings one specific covenant to mind: not that of Sinai, but that which was first established with Abraham (see esp. Exod 2:24). This covenant is linked explicitly to the promise of the land in the later tradition (Exod 6:4; Ps 105:8–11). One reference in particular sheds light on the themes of Baruch's letter here: Bar 2:29–35:

> (29) If you will not obey my voice, this very great multitude will surely turn into a small number among the nations, where I will scatter them. (30) For I know that they will not obey me, for they are a stiff-necked people. But in the land of their exile they will come to themselves (31) and know that I am the Lord their God. I will give them a heart that obeys and ears that hear; (32) they will praise me in the land of their exile, and will remember my name (33) and turn from their stubbornness and their wicked deeds; for they will remember the ways of their ancestors, who sinned before the Lord. (34) I will bring

---

77. Bogaert, *Apocalypse de Baruch*, 1:206.

78. Similar reasons exclude a link between *4 Baruch* and the Epistle of Jeremiah, which is concerned primarily with the warning against worshiping foreign idols.

79. The motif of remembering the covenant is widespread in the Old Testament; see Gen 9:15; Exod 2:24; 6:5; Lev 26:42–45; Pss 105:8; 106:45; for further examples, see Schaller, "Paralipomena Jeremiou," 735.

them again into the land that I swore to give to their ancestors, to Abraham, Isaac, and Jacob, and they will rule over it; and I will increase them, and they will not be diminished. (35) I will make an everlasting covenant with them to be their God and they shall be my people; and I will never again remove my people Israel from the land that I have given them. (NRSV)

As in Bar 2, but in contrast to what the angel instructed him to write in *4 Bar.* 6:13–14, Baruch draws attention to the past situation in 6:21 and uses the reference to the disregard for God's δικαιώματα to make clear the significance of the law in judgment. The Babylonian captivity is described with the term κάμινος (6:20), which Jer 11:4 uses with reference to the Egyptian repression.[80] This term makes the hardness of the judgment tangible, yet the parallel to the exodus from Egypt also hints at the coming salvation. This salvation depends, however, on obedience, which the people did not demonstrate earlier, thus bringing God's wrath on themselves. The specific sins listed in 6:21 represent the standard behavior of the disobedient: disregard of God's ordinances,[81] haughtiness of the heart,[82] and stubbornness.[83] Still, even now the people can experience salvation, but only if they listen to God's voice[84] by way of Jeremiah as the teacher of the law (6:22). This association between salvation and Jeremiah's teaching represents for the original readers a clear reference to their own times, in which they also should link their salvation to the tradition, not to an overplayed messianic ideology.[85]

The mention of the "waters of the Jordan," which functions as a test of the people's obedience, has often be seen as a Christian reference to baptism,[86] particularly because of the term σφραγίς.[87] In New Testament times as well as in the apostolic fathers and the apologists, however, the waters of the Jordan were not seen as a type of baptismal water.[88] Similarly, σφραγίς is not specifi-

---

80. See also Jer 21:10; 32(39):36; 37(44):17.
81. See Exod 15:26; Deut 4:40; 6:2; 7:11–12.
82. Deut 17:20; Jer 48(31):29; Ezek 28:2, 5, 17.
83. Job 15:25; in other terms, Ps 81(80):13 (NRSV 81:12).
84. See esp. Exod 19:5 (in a covenant context); Deut 13:19; 15:5; 28:1, 2, 9, 13; 30:8; Jer 7:23; 11:4, 7; 26(33):13; Bar 2:29.
85. See the introduction above.
86. Harris, *Rest of the Words of Baruch*, 14; Bogaert, *Apocalypse de Baruch*, 1:206–7; Robinson, "4 Baruch," 415; and Philonenko, "Simples Observations," 160.
87. Bogaert, *Apocalypse de Baruch*, 1:207. Bogaert claims support from Herm. *Sim.* 9:16.3–7: ἡ σφραγὶς οὖν τὸ ὕδωρ ἐστίν, cf. 9:17.4; 8:2.3–4; 8:6.3; see below.
88. See Wolff, *Jeremia im Frühjudentum und Urchristentum*, 45 n. 1. Even Bogaert's reference from Shepherd of Hermas (see previous note) does not mention the water of the Jordan.

cally used for baptism[89] (see 1 Cor 9:2[90]). In *4 Baruch* the term has already appeared in 3:8,[91] where the text spoke apocalyptically of the seven seals and seven epochs. If one sees an eschatological meaning there,[92] then the sense in 6:23 becomes clear. The time of the people's salvation begins with the crossing of the Jordan, the last of the "seven seals" and thus the "great seal." The "seal" of the first time of creation corresponds to the "great seal" of the time of salvation (6:23). The water of the test is thus as τὸ σημεῖον τῆς μεγάλης σφραγῖδος also the sign for the beginning of the time of salvation.[93] The end of Baruch's letter actually fits the eschatological context of *4 Baruch* well and need not be seen as a Christian interpolation.[94]

Philonenko has argued most clearly for a Christian-gnostic interpretation of *4 Bar.* 6:22–23.[95] According to him, 6:22–23 forms the real center of the document.[96] The term "great seal," therefore, is to be located in the Mandaean baptismal tradition. Admittedly, he can identify but one text in the tradition that names a great seal: "Reprimand your friends sincerely and lead your friendship rightly. Do not flatter one another and speak no talk of lie and deceit. Whoever flatters, he will be dragged away in the judgment to the blazing fire. *Put the great seal* on your whole body and do not remove it from your body until the day, on which you will leave your body, that day of redemption" (*Ginza* 39:23).[97] How-

---

89. So even Bogaert, *Apocalypse de Baruch*, 1:207 n. 1. Contra Harris, *Rest of the Words of Baruch*, 14, who without offering any references states that "sign of the great seal" was "the conventional patristic term for baptism."

90. See Delling, *Paralipomena Jeremiae*, 46 n. 23; Wolff, *Jeremia im Frühjudentum und Urchristentum*, 45 n. 1; Herzer, *Paralipomena Jeremiae*, 120 with n. 407; and Schaller, "Paralipomena Jeremiou," 736–37.

91. Bogaert regards *4 Bar.* 3:8 and 6:23 as incomparable (*Apocalypse de Baruch*, 1:207 n. 1).

92. Herzer, *Paralipomena Jeremiae*, 50 and n. 72.

93. See *4 Ezra* 6:20: "and when the seal is placed upon the age which is about to pass away, then I will show these signs" (quote from Bruce M. Metzger, "The Fourth Book of Ezra," *OTP* 1:535).

94. Riaud (*Les Paralipomènes du Prophète Jérémie*, 30 and 64–65 n. 18; see also Riaud, "Les Samaritains," 139–40 with n. 3) sees in σφραγίς reference to circumcision, building on Nickelsburg, *Jewish Literature*, 316. See also Michael E. Stone, "Baruch, Rest of the Words of," *EncJud* 4:276. Judaism certainly saw circumcision as a seal; see G. Fitzer, "σφραγίς κτλ.," *TDNT* 7:947 (references there); for a more skeptical perspective, see Schaller, "Paralipomena Jeremiou," 736, However, circumcision is no method of testing. Moreover, one would have to assume a different sense of the word σφραγίς in *4 Bar.* 6:23 than in 3:8, which is not likely.

95. Philonenko, "Simples Observations," passim. See Herzer, "Antwort," 28–31, for greater detail.

96. Philonenko, "Simples Observations," 160.

97. Translated according to the German text in Marc Lidzbarski, *Ginza: Der Schatz oder das große Buch der Mandäer* (Quellen der Religionsgeschichte 13; Göttingen: Vandenhoeck & Ruprecht, 1925), 39. Numbering according to this edition. The reference from *Ginza* 39:23 contains a common motif of

ever, this text does not refer to baptism,[98] and there is no mention of a seal in the many references to baptism in the *Ginza*.[99] Philonenko's further appeal to the Jewish *hekalot* literature also offers no substantial contribution,[100] not only because this literature is much later (tenth century C.E.; *Merkabah Rabbah* perhaps fifth or sixth century C.E.[101]) but also because in those rare cases where a great seal is mentioned, baptism would have been the last thing in mind: "R. Yishma'el said: One question I asked R. Nehunya b. Haqana, my master, concerning the name of the great seal [and the name of the terrible crown. The name of the great seal.] Thus I learned it from R. Nehunya b. Haqana, my master: ... This is *the great seal with which heaven and earth were sealed.*"[102] The "great seal" or "great secret," is, of course, the Torah. Thus, this is no gnostic baptismal speculation but praise of the creation and of the Torah.[103] As this text is certainly Jewish, the creation-theological use of the term "seal" is far more revealing, as *4 Baruch* also interprets this term in terms of *creation theology*.[104]

The Jordan as the place of testing points, rather, initially to the conquest of the land under Joshua (Josh 3).[105] Before the fulfillment of God's promise to grant the land (Josh 1:13), the people had to make themselves holy (3:5). The context of the letter in *4 Bar.* 6 permits further references to Josh 3. Just as the

---

Greco-Roman ethics by linking friendship and frank speech, contrasting it with flattery. See esp. the collection of essays in John T. Fitzgerald, ed., *Friendship, Flattery, and Frankness of Speech: Studies on Friendship in the New Testament World* (NovTSup 82; Leiden: Brill, 1996).

98. See Lidzbarski, *Ginza*, 39 n. 3, without reason in the text or otherwise in the term's semantic meaning: "Mit 'Siegel' ist sonst die Ölung gemeint ... Hier bezeichnet es die Taufe mit ihrem ganzen Beiwerk [In the *Ginza*, 'seal' usually means the unction ... Here it refers to baptism with all of its accessories]."

99. See *Ginza* 19:24–25; 48:20; 51:1–3; 58:3; 184–186; 190–193*; 283–284; 310:15; 326:3; 360:35.

100. Philonenko, "Simples Observations," 160.

101. Peter Schäfer suggests this dating in "Prolegomena zu einer kritischen Edition und Analyse der Merkhava Rabba in Hekaloth-Studien," in *Hekhalot-Studien* (ed. Peter Schäfer; TSAJ 19; Tübingen: Mohr Siebeck, 1988), 29–30; building on Gershom Scholem, *Die jüdische Mystik in ihren Hauptströmungen* (Frankfurt am Main: Metzner, 1957), 47–48; on dating and origin, see also Peter Schäfer and Klaus Herrmann, eds., *Übersetzung der Hekhalot-Literatur* (TSAJ 17/2; Tübingen: Mohr Siebeck, 1987), xx–xxii; they throw doubt on the sometimes suggested dating of the oldest tradition as early as the third or fourth century C.E. (xxii).

102. Translated after Schäfer, "Prolegomena zu einer kritischen Edition," 39.

103. See ibid., 40–41.

104. Philonenko ("Simples Observations," 161) refers to other texts that seem haphazardly to have been brought together and contribute nothing to the interpretation of *4 Baruch*, among others Hippolytus, *Haer.* 5.7.41; 10.11.6; *Ps.-Clem.* 16.19.2; 17.7.4; Herm. *Sim.* 93:4; *Odes Sol.* 29:7; 39:7; see also Herzer, "Antwort," 30–31.

105. See Wolff, *Jeremia im Frühjudentum und Urchristentum*, 50. Differently Delling, *Paralipomena Jeremiae*, 48.

first exodus ended after the wanderings in the desert with the march through the Jordan, so again the Babylonian exile ends with the test at the Jordan.[106] Also significant in this regard may be Ezek 36:24–25: "I will take you from the nations, and gather you from all the countries, and bring you into your own land. I will sprinkle clean water upon you, and you shall be clean from all your uncleannesses, and from all your idols I will cleanse you" (NRSV). The decisive elements in *4 Bar.* 6—return, water of cleansing,[107] and separation from foreign gods—are all mentioned here. Reading Ezek 36:24–25 from the perspective of exiles coming from the east, the Jordan is the first water one must cross before entering the land. Therefore, *4 Bar.* 6:23 can be seen as an exposition of this Old Testament idea from Ezek 36.[108]

---

106. See also Nickelsburg, *Jewish Literature*, 316, who in interpreting σφραγίς refers to Josh 5:2–9 but with reference to circumcision.

107. See 1QS 4:21.

108. Schaller ("Paralipomena Jeremiou," 736–37) suspects that it is not the Jordan itself that is the method of testing but that the text names the place from which point on the testing of the returnees should proceed (737). The phrase ἐκ τοῦ ὕδατος would, therefore, be locally or temporally understood (736). But this does not at all fit, as Schaller suggests, the flow of 8:3–5, as here it is assumed that the testing occurs *before* the crossing of the Jordan, as per even Schaller's translation (744–46).

Chapter 7

Chapter 7 begins with Baruch leaving the tomb to meet the eagle (7:1–2). The terms used to present the scene in 7:1 (ἀνέστη and ἐξῆλθεν ἐκ τοῦ μνημείου) clearly pick up the resurrection theme from chapter 6.[1] Abimelech has gone off the stage and no longer plays a role; only his figs retain their significance for the narrative. Baruch ties the letter to the eagle's neck in 7:8, along with fifteen figs, but no reference is made to them in the letter. One might suspect that the figs are part of the "good news," but 7:13 states only that the eagle flies off with the letter. Amazingly, even in the scene legitimating the eagle, in which it raises someone from the dead (7:15–18), the figs play no role, although they were decisive in revealing the coming salvation, and the hope of resurrection was expressly linked to them earlier (6:3–7). In 7:32, where Jeremiah finally refers to the figs as he hands them to the sick among the people (see also 3:15), there is again no reference to their healing effect or symbolic power. Of far greater significance is Jeremiah's teaching of the law.

In Jeremiah's reply to Baruch's letter, the text of 7:23–26 in MSS A and B varies greatly from the other witnesses. In A and B the letter is addressed not simply to Baruch but to both Baruch and Abimelech. How this text emerged remains unclear. The transition from a narrative style to an addressing style at the end of the section leads to the assumption that originally a narrative summary of the letter was intended. This style was, however, impossible to maintain, as soon as the concern was the reference to Baruch *and* Abimelech. Moreover, the situation of the exile is made to appear worse. Whereas in C and eth the word concerning the father and his exiled son is a parable applied to the people, A and B present this as having really happened to every father and his child.

Mentioning Abimelech is also problematic within Jeremiah's letter, since the verbs in 7:28 assume that only one person is being addressed, which suggests that a secondary revision has occurred.[2] The context also fits better with one addressee. The phrase "you and Abimelech" thus seems to be an addition, as

---

1. Wolff, "Heilshoffnung," 156.
2. So eth puts all the verbs into the plural.

does the mention of Abimelech in 7:15. The deletion of Abimelech in these cases would fit Jeremiah's reference to Baruch's preservation in 7:23–24 and his failure to mention Abimelech's preservation, which according to 6:8 was so important to Baruch (cf. also Jeremiah's worries concerning Abimelech in 3:9). Yet all these tensions hint again at the author's intention to integrate the Abimelech material into the older story motif of *2 Baruch*.

The function of 7:29 also poses problems, as the quotation from Ps 137(136):3–4 ends the letter in a highly unusual way. Jeremiah's request for Baruch's (and Abimelech's?) intercession in 7:28 offers a more fitting end to the letter. If one prefers not to regard this as a later addition,[3] one must assume a structure that pays little attention to formal criteria.[4]

The motif of an exchange of letters between Baruch and Jeremiah is provided by *2 Baruch*, although *4 Baruch* shapes its version quite differently.[5] Whereas the narrative construction of the exchange of letters is problematic in *2 Baruch*, that in *4 Baruch* is tightly structured: Baruch decides to write (6:8–12), and God provides the letter's content (6:13–15). Having been brought paper and ink (6:16), Baruch writes the letter (6:17–23). The eagle then arrives and conveys the letter to Jeremiah (7:1–12). This chronological order stands in stark contrast to the more complex events of *2 Baruch:* Baruch is encouraged by the people to write a letter (77:12–14) and decides to do so (77:15–18). In fact, Baruch writes two letters (77:19), one of which he sends by way of the eagle (77:20–26). Only then is the content of the letter actually presented, in the form of an addition (78:1–86:1). This requires a second report of the sending of the eagle (87:1), which creates a certain doubling. The most sensible way to explain the differences between the two versions is to conclude that *4 Baruch* simplified and ordered the complex and literarily difficult presentation of *2 Baruch*. The fact that *4 Baruch* mentions but one letter should be understood in this light, especially since *2 Baruch* actually presents only one letter even though two are mentioned.

As Baruch emerges from the tomb (7:1), he encounters the eagle promised by the angel (7:2; cf. 6:12). The following conversation, initiated by the eagle, begins with the eagle greeting Baruch as the οἰκονόμος τῆς πίστεως. The word πίστις picks up a motif from 6:4,[6] but the title οἰκονόμος is unusual.

---

3. For a critique of this solution, see Herzer, *Paralipomena Jeremiae*, 29, 124, 127; contra Schaller, "Paralipomena Jeremiou," 743.

4. Schaller suspects that the dialogue was shaped along the lines of Ps 137(136):3–4 ("Paralipomena Jeremiou," 743); see also Schaller, "Greek Version," 84–85; Marc Philonenko, "Les Paralipomènes de Jérémie et la Traduction de Symmaque," *RHPR* 64 (1984): 144.

5. Herzer, *Paralipomena Jeremiae*, 122–28, 167–72.

6. The variant in MS C (οἰκονόμος τῆς πόλεως) simplifies the content problem, but Baruch has not been presented as steward of Jerusalem either.

Schaller understands the construction as a *genitivus qualitatis* and thus translates the phrase "faithful steward."[7] This is possible on a grammatical level, but it obscures the significance of 6:4 for understanding the *content* of the title. Because Baruch's faith has been brought back to life in the light of the saving news, and so has not disappeared, the title more likely is characterizing Baruch as one who keeps faith despite the crisis, who is responsible in faith. As a good steward of faith, he seeks to make a great "profit" that will benefit the people.[8]

During the ensuing conversation, the author introduces an exposition about messenger birds that highlights the eagle's distinctive qualifications for the task at hand. It is particularly significant that the bird is an eagle, a motif adopted from *2 Baruch*.[9] Granted, the eagle of *2 Baruch*, unlike its compatriot here, is unable to speak, but this only shows that *4 Baruch* is using the *2 Baruch* material in a fable-like way. In spite of this difference, the intention of Baruch's greeting to the eagle in each passage is the same: the eagle has been chosen by God (*4 Bar.* 7:3 = *passivum divinum*) or created by God to fly higher than other birds (*2 Bar.* 77:21a), which makes it superior to other birds.[10] The positive symbolism of the eagle as a royal bird (7:9: "the king of the birds") enhances this characterization (see Exod 19:4; Deut 32:11; Ps 103[102]:5; Isa 40:31; Ezek 17:3, 7),[11] as does the clear correspondence between the election of the eagle and that of the people (*4 Bar.* 7:11).

In addition to attributing positive characteristics to the eagle, our author also depicts its supremacy by comparing the eagle to earlier messenger birds. As in *2 Baruch*, the first bird mentioned is one sent by Noah to discover if the catastrophe was over (*2 Bar.* 77:23; *4 Bar.* 7:10).[12] However, the similarities between *2 Baruch* and *4 Baruch* end here. Three positive examples of serving birds are recounted in *2 Baruch*: the dove that brought the olive branch to Noah (77:23; see Gen 8:10–11); the crows that supplied Elijah with food (*2 Bar.* 77:24; see 1 Kgs 17:4–6); and Solomon's messenger birds (*2 Bar.* 77:25; no biblical reference). Clearly, the role of the birds in *2 Baruch* is not limited to announc-

---

7. Schaller, "Paralipomena Jeremiou," 737: "treuer Haushalter."

8. See Bogaert, *Apocalypse de Baruch*, 1:216, referring to Gal 6:10; 1 Cor 4:1; 1 Pet 4:10. Schaller offers as evidence for a *genitivus qualitatis* text *4 Bar.* 4:4a (as a linguistic parallel) and Luke 12:42 and 1 Cor 4:2 (as content parallels; see "Paralipomena Jeremiou," 737). However, the definite article is missing in 4:4a (ἐπίτροποι ψεύδους), and Luke 12:42 and 1 Cor 4:2 are constructed with the adjective πιστός. If one reads *4 Bar.* 7:2 in this sense, the intention is deflated. For a discussion of the motif, see also Wolff, "Die *Paralipomena Jeremiae* und das Neue Testament," 131–33.

9. Herzer, *Paralipomena Jeremiae*, 68–71.

10. On the connection between creation and election in the prophetic tradition, see above all Isa 43:1–7; 44:24; Jer 10:16; 51(28):19 (cf. Karl-Heinz Bernhardt, "ברא," *TDOT* 2:247–48).

11. Further references, see Schaller, "Paralipomena Jeremiou," 738.

12. Bogaert, *Apocalypse de Baruch*, 1:190–92.

ing the end of the catastrophe. In contrast, *4 Baruch* focuses on the birds in the Noah account: the raven that never returned as a negative example and the dove that brought the good news of the flood's end as a positive one. The dove, not the raven, is the example the eagle should follow, since the eagle likewise has a good message to bring (7:11: καλὴ φάσις): the end of the catastrophe and the promise of return.[13] Perhaps this focus is the reason why our author reduced the many examples in *2 Baruch* to these two birds.[14] The term καλὴ φάσις corresponds not to εὐαγγελίζεσται (3:11; 5:21),[15] as this term is directed to the teaching of the law,[16] but is limited to the announcement of the end of the exile and the imminent return. The importance of this task is emphasized in Baruch's final call to the eagle in *4 Bar.* 7:12 as well as in its parallel, *2 Bar.* 77:26: "And do not be reluctant and do not deviate to the right nor to the left, but fly and go straight away that you may preserve the command of the Mighty One as I said to you."[17]

In light of the preceding discussion, Philonenko's interpretation of the eagle as a divine being must be rejected.[18] Appealing to *4 Bar.* 6:12, he speaks of

---

13. On Old Testament bird symbolism, see Othmar Keel, *Vögel als Boten: Studien zu Ps 68:12–14; Gen 8:6–12; Koh 10:20 und dem Aussenden von Botenvögeln in Ägypten: Mit einem Beitrag von Urs Winter zu Ps 56:1 und zur Ikonographie der Göttin mit der Taube* (OBO 14; Fribourg: Universitätsverlag, 1977). On the ancient Near East background of the dove as bird of the gods, specifically of the goddess Astarte bringing good news, see Winter in Keel, *Vögel als Boten*, 38–78.

14. Bogaert, *Apocalypse de Baruch*, 1:191–92. According to Bogaert (1:191), *2 Baruch* does not use the negative example of the raven from Gen 8 because there is no assumption of enemies there as in *4 Bar.* 7:12. This opposition of dove and crow in *4 Bar.* 7 is, for Bogaert, a confirmation of the dualist outlook of *4 Baruch*, emerging from a reflection on Gen 8:7–11. However, the crow in *4 Baruch* is no enemy, neither of the dove nor of the eagle, as would be expected from Bogaert's perspective. The decisive point, which speaks for *2 Baruch*'s priority, is the reduction of three examples to one in *4 Baruch*, in the light of Gen 8:7–11. Bogaert rightly draws attention to this but misconstrues it. This is not the result of dualism but is an example of the previously mentioned approach used by the author of *4 Baruch*, who is often concerned to concentrate a statement. If one assumes this tendency toward concentration, then the reference to Noah's raven, which is not mentioned in *2 Baruch*, reflects the mention of Elijah's ravens in *2 Bar.* 77:24. Further, the negative portrayal of the raven in the Noah story is used by our author to present the positive task of the eagle more clearly than in *2 Baruch*, by comparing the eagle with Noah's dove. On the specific relation of the dove and the raven and its imagery in ancient iconography, see Keel, *Vögel als Boten*, 90–91.

15. Against Bernhardt Heininger, who wishes "unintentionally" to associate the term with εὐαγγέλιον ("Totenerweckung oder Weckruf [ParJer 7,12-20]? Gnostische Spurensuche in den Paralipomena Jeremiae," *SNTU.A* 23 [1998]: 96]). The proclaiming of the good news, expressed by εὐαγγελίζομαι in *4 Baruch*, is exclusivly linked with the teaching of Jeremiah.

16. See above on 3:11 and 5:21.

17. Translation of Klijn, "2 Baruch," *OTP* 1:647. See Herzer, *Paralipomena Jeremiae*, 70–71. The motif of not turning to the left or the right is widespread in the tradition, the exact parallel to *4 Bar.* 7:12 being Prov 4:27 (LXX); see also Deut 2:27; 5:32; 17:11.

18. Philonenko, "Simples Observations," 169–70. On this, see Herzer, "Antwort," 35–36.

the "*great* eagle," even though the adjective "great" is not used (see, however, Ezek 17:3: great eagle). Of greater significance for Philonenko's interpretation is the resurrection caused by the eagle (7:17). Philonenko sees the background for this scene in Egyptian Isis mythology, where Isis occasionally appears as a falcon.[19] However, *4 Baruch* speaks not of a falcon but of an eagle.[20] Moreover, in Egyptian mythology the falcon generally represents Horus, the sky-god with sometimes warlike characteristics, an association that clearly does not fit this context.[21] In fact, the eagle in *4 Baruch* has no divine quality but is merely sent in the power of God (7:4, 12, 18).[22] In terms of the background of the idea, one would rather think of the eagle as a divine messenger in Greco-Roman mythology, for example, as a messenger of Zeus and a herald.[23]

After using motifs from *2 Baruch* in *4. Bar.* 7:2–12, the author begins a new section in 7:13 that has no parallel in his source text: 7:13–22 narrates the meeting between Jeremiah and the people; and 7:23–29 quotes Jeremiah's reply to Baruch. Curiously, the eagle does not fly directly to Jeremiah in Babylon but waits outside the city for the prophet (7:13: ἔξω τῆς πόλεως εἰς τόπον ἔρημον). This already hints at the message Jeremiah is proclaiming from Baruch's letter, that the people are to separate themselves from the Gentiles (7:32).

The mention of the "desert" as the eagle's location is also significant. The desert is not only a life-threatening and lonely place but also and for this reason the traditional place where God meets his chosen people.[24] God led the people out of Egypt and into the desert to establish his covenant with them (Exod 19:1–24:8)[25] and promised eschatological renewal of that covenant in the desert (Hos 2:16–25 [NRSV 2:14–23]). The desert is thus the place of refuge (Ps 55[54]:8) through which God leads his people in safety (Ps 78[77]:52; 136[135]:16). It is, to be sure, the place of judgment (Ps 107[106]; Ezek 20:13, 21), but it is also the place where God's grace is received (esp. Jer 31[38]:1–4[26]). Finally, according

---

19. Philonenko, "Simples Observations," 170. The reference is of significance above all for the Armenian version of *4 Bar.* 7:14; see Issaverdens, *Uncanonical Writings of the Old Testament*, 108.

20. According to Plutarch, *Mor.* 357C and *Is. Os.* 16, Isis has the form of a swallow; see Schaller, "Paralipomena Jeremiou," 739.

21. See H. Felber, "Horus," *Der Neue Pauly* 5:743; M. Heerma van Voss, "Horus," *DDD*, 808–9.

22. See further Herzer, "Antwort," 36. On Philonenko's thesis, see also Schaller, "Paralipomena Jeremiou," 739: "reines Konstrukt." Explicitly against Philonenko, Heininger understands the eagle as close to a Mandaic gnostic idea, where the eagle represents a messianic figure ("Totenerweckung," 97–103, esp. 100).

23. See C. Hünemörder, "Adler," *Der Neue Pauly* 1:116.

24. Exod 3:18; 5:1, 3; 7:16; 16:10.

25. See Lev 7:38; Num 1:1; Deut 1:1.

26. Jer 31:1–4: "At that time, says the Lord, I will be the God of all the families of Israel, and they shall be my people. Thus says the Lord: The people who survived the sword found grace in the

to Ezek 20:10–20 it is in the desert that God encourages his people to obey his commands—a matter of significance for the context of *4 Baruch*.

> (10) So I led them out of the land of Egypt and brought them into the wilderness. (11) I gave them my statutes and showed them my ordinances, by whose observance everyone shall live. (12) Moreover I gave them my sabbaths, as a sign between me and them, so that they might know that I the Lord sanctify them. (13) But the house of Israel rebelled against me in the wilderness; they did not observe my statutes but rejected my ordinances, by whose observance everyone shall live; and my sabbaths they greatly profaned. Then I thought I would pour out my wrath upon them in the wilderness, to make an end of them. (14) But I acted for the sake of my name, so that it should not be profaned in the sight of the nations, in whose sight I had brought them out. (15) Moreover I swore to them in the wilderness that I would not bring them into the land that I had given them, a land flowing with milk and honey, the most glorious of all lands, (16) because they rejected my ordinances and did not observe my statutes, and profaned my sabbaths; for their heart went after their idols. (17) Nevertheless my eye spared them, and I did not destroy them or make an end of them in the wilderness. (18) I said to their children in the wilderness, Do not follow the statutes of your parents, nor observe their ordinances, nor defile yourselves with their idols. (19) I the Lord am your God; follow my statutes, and be careful to observe my ordinances, (20) and hallow my sabbaths that they may be a sign between me and you, so that you may know that I the Lord am your God. (Ezek 20:10–20 NRSV)

This many-faceted background of the desert motif adds color to the desert events described in *4 Bar.* 7. The rather unusual element of the eagle waiting in the desert, which slows down the narrative pace, calls this tradition to mind and provides part of the text's hopeful tenor. The further description of the reason that Jeremiah and the people were leaving the city underlines this narrative intent. Negotiations with the Babylonian king[27] had secured land for burying the dead among the people (7:14), which by Jewish custom would have been outside the city.[28]

In their exact moment of mourning, the funeral party meets the eagle, upon whose instructions Jeremiah gathers the whole people (7:15–16). The symbolic meaning of the contrast between the situation of the people (mourning in captivity) and the eagle's resurrection miracle could not be more clearly drawn

---

wilderness; when Israel sought for rest, the Lord appeared to him from far away. I have loved you with an everlasting love; therefore I have continued my faithfulness to you. Again I will build you, and you shall be built, O virgin Israel! Again you shall take your tambourines, and go forth in the dance of the merrymakers" (NRSV).

27. This reminds the reader of Moses' negotiations with Pharaoh (see Exod 5).

28. See *m. B. Bat.* 2:9; *t. Neg.* 6:2.

(7:17). Not only is the eagle legitimated as a divine messenger,[29] but the miracle gives notice of the salvific content of the eagle's message and seeks to awake the same faith in the coming salvation that Baruch had demonstrated earlier. The eagle shows itself through the resurrection miracle to be a symbol of self-renewing life.[30] The traditional associations of the eagle with renewed strength (Isa 40:31) and youthful joy (Ps 103[102]:5) are thereby programmatically placed before the return of the people.[31]

Plausibly, the people interpret the eagle as an appearance of God (7:18), to be compared with his appearance to Moses in the desert.[32] As before with 6:20–21, in 7:18 there is a parallel to the exodus: God revealed himself to Moses in the desert, and now he reveals himself in the form of the eagle, already a symbol for God's preservation in the exodus from Egypt (Exod 19:4; Deut 32:11).[33]

---

29. See Riaud, *Les Paralipomènes du Prophète Jérémie*, 112–13; Delling, *Paralipomena Jeremiae*, 11–12; Bogaert, *Apocalypse de Baruch*, 2:135–36; and now in particular Heininger, "Totenerweckung." Although it is neither possible nor necessary to present all the details of Heininger's hypothesis, the main point should be mentioned. According to Heininger, *4 Bar.* 7:12–20 has been worked over by a Christian gnostic author close to dissenting Johannine circles (109–10). Interpreting the original eagle motif in gnostic manner, the eagle becomes a gnostic *salvator*, and the resurrection of the dead symbolizes the gnostic process of salvation (105). This interpretation remains unconvincing, not only because of methodological questions concerning the way in which *4 Baruch* is compared to New Testament and gnostic texts (among others, Heininger refers in particular to *Right Ginza* I 5:15–16; 6:3–5; II,3 58:23–28; *Ap. John* 53:11–17 [NHC II 23:27–31]; 61:1–5 [BG 8502,2/NHC III 30:17–20]; *Acts Thom.* 91; 111:49–54), but also because there are so many characteristic differences suggesting that some specific traditional material could have been used in different ways by different authors in different times. Thus, one could probably follow Heininger in assuming that the author of *4 Baruch* adopted a traditional motif of the eagle as a symbol of God's life-giving and protecting power (Exod 19:4; Deut 32:11) into the story he wrote anew according to *2 Baruch*. Yet the conclusions Heininger draws from some texts in which a similar motif appears go to far. The resurrection terminology in *4 Baruch* certainly does not point to a gnostic salvation process but to the "coming together of the beloved one" (*4 Bar.* 3:8) in the heavenly Jerusalem (5:32) linked with the individual hope for the resurrection of the body (6:3–7).

30. See Wolff, "Heilshoffnung," 155. See also Ginzberg, *Legends*, 5:187: "In 2 Alphabet of Ben Sira 29b and 35b–36a it is the eagle and the raven who, after leaving the ark, set an example of immortality and murder."

31. See Jacob Neusner, *Early Rabbinic Judaism: Historical Studies in Religion, Literature and Art* (SJLA 13; Leiden: Brill, 1975), 176, who presents the changes in the reception of the eagle motif: "For example, in first-century Jerusalem, Jews allegedly so hated the pagan eagle that they rioted when Roman troops carried the symbol with them into the city. Yet a century later it was common place to put eagles over synagogue doorways." On the meaning of the eagle, see also Erwin R. Goodenough, *Jewish Symbols in the Greco-Roman Period* (Princeton: Princeton University Press, 1992), 137–42.

32. For the term ὤφθη as a term for revelation, see Exod 3:2; 16:10; see also Gen 12:7; 17:1; Lev 9:23; Num 14:10.

33. See Riaud, "Abimélech," 176 n. 22; Wolff, "Heilshoffnung," 155; Schaller, "Paralipomena Jeremiou," 740; and Heininger, "Totenerweckung," 90.

The reading of the letter is presented, in contrast, rather unspectacularly, its content already known to the readers. The brevity of the reported reading highlights the immediate reaction of the people, which includes both recognized rites of sorrow and repentance (7:20)[34] as well as an appeal to Jeremiah for guidance (7:21). The prophet states that obedience to the letter's instructions is the precondition for their return to Jerusalem (7:22), but the term φυλάσσειν is taken from the Old Testament's language of law-giving,[35] so once again the implicit reference is to the law of God as the content of the letter.

After reading the letter, Jeremiah writes one of his own to Baruch (7:23–29).[36] The structuring and content of the letter are noteworthy in several respects. Instead of offering the usual form of prescript (Baruch's name and greetings), the letter begins with only a personal address: "my beloved son." Although unusual, this fits the title often used in *4 Baruch* for Jeremiah, namely, "father" (see 2:2, 4, 6, 8; 5:25; 9:8).[37]

Further links to the context in *4 Baruch* can be found in Jeremiah's letter, such as Baruch not seeing the devastation of Jerusalem (7:23c and 3:9–10; 5:30); the sixty-six years of exile (7:24 and 5:1, 30; 6:5); and the phrase εἰς τὸν τόπον ὅπου εἶ (7:28 and 5:32). Jeremiah's reply does not refer directly to the promise of the end of exile announced in Baruch's letter,[38] which is characterized by deep mourning for the people who have suffered in exile and have not stood firm under testing, but one can implicitly find the hope of return in Jeremiah's urgent requests for intercession (7:23–29). Baruch should pray that the people hear Jeremiah's voice and heed the decrees of his mouth (7:28).[39] This obedience is, of course, the condition for the return that Baruch laid out in his letter (6:22).

---

34. See above on 2:1.
35. See Exod 12:17, 24, 25; 13:10; 23:13; Lev 8:35; Num 18:5; Deut 8:1.
36. See Herzer, *Paralipomena Jeremiae*, 122–28. In 7:23-26 mss A and B vary greatly again, reading: "And Jeremiah wrote a letter to Jerusalem to Baruch and Abimelech in the presence of the entire people, concerning the afflictions that had come over them, how they were taken captive by the king of the Chaldeans and how each one saw his father bound, and each father saw his child subjected to punishment. But those who wished to comfort his father covered his face, that he might not see his son punished. And God has covered you and Abimelech, that you might not see us punished" (translated after the text provided by Harris, *Rest of the Words of Baruch*, 59).
37. See Delling, *Paralipomena Jeremiae*, 20; Riaud, "La figure de Jérémie," 376–77; and Riaud, "The Figure of Jeremiah," 36–37.
38. Taatz, *Frühjüdische Briefe*, 81.
39. See 4Q266 (D^a)VIII:18c–20: "And like this judgment will be that of all who reject God's precepts and forsake them and move aside in the stubbornness of their heart. This is the word which Jeremiah spoke to Baruch, son of Neriah" (quoted from Florentino García Martínez and Eibert J. C. Tigchelaar, eds., *The Dead Sea Scrolls Study Edition* [2 vols.; Leiden: Brill, 1997–1998], 1:563).

In addition to such intratextual links, Jeremiah's letter contains motifs in 7:24–26 that have no direct connection to other parts of *4 Baruch*. Delling, for example, sees a typical Jewish parable in 7:24.[40] One can certainly agree as regards form, but with respect to its content the expression μονογενὴς υἱός is particularly noteworthy, being an important christological term in the Christian tradition.[41] Yet even the Christian use of the term has its background in the language of the Septuagint,[42] where μονογενής can translate the Hebrew יָחִיד (= unique, incomparable). This Hebrew word also appears in, among other verses, Gen 22:2, 12, 16; Jer 6:26; Amos 8:10; and Zech 12:10,[43] though the Septuagint translates it with ἀγαπητός in these cases.[44] Genesis 22 is particularly interesting for our purposes, since Josephus, in contrast to the Septuagint, uses μονογενής in his recounting of Abraham's near-sacrifice of Isaac (*Ant.* 1.222). The synonymity of the adjectives μονογενής and ἀγαπητός can be seen precisely in this equation: the only son is at the same time the beloved son. Although μονογενής/יָחִיד derives from the personal or family context, it is applied to the people of Israel in its relationship to God. In Jer 6:26, for example, lament for the people is called for as one would lament for an only son (אֵבֶל יָחִיד; see also Amos 8:10; Zech 12:10). The people are compared with an "only son" in a special way in *Pss. Sol.* 18:4: "Your discipline for us (is) as (for) a firstborn son, an only child" (υἱὸν πρωτότοκον μονογενῆν).[45] Similarly, *4 Ezra* 6:58 states, "But we your people, whom you have called your first-born [*primogenitum*], only begotten [*unigenitum*], zealous for you [*aemulatorem*], and most dear [*carissimum*], have been given into their hands."[46] It should be clear that *4 Bar.* 7:24 belongs to this group of texts.[47] Thus, as Delling suggested, this verse

---

40. Delling, *Paralipomena Jeremiae*, 10–11 (references there); on the meaning of ὡς as an introduction of the *rhema*, see, e.g., *y. Ber.* 2:5c. See Peter Dschulnigg, *Rabbinische Gleichnisse und das Neue Testament: Die Gleichnisse der PesK im Vergleich mit den Gleichnissen Jesu und dem Neuen Testament* (Judaica et Christiana 12; Bern: Lang, 1988), 8, 31, 563–64.

41. See John 1:14; 3:16, 18; 1 John 4:9.

42. See Judg 11:34; Tob 3:15; 6:11, 15; 8:17; Ps 21:21; 34:17 (LXX); *Pss. Sol.* 18:4; *4 Ezra* 6:58; see also Josephus, *Ant.* 1.222; 20.20.

43. The Greek translation of Gen 22:2; Ps 67:7 (Aquila) and 22:12 (Symmachus); and Jer 6:26 (Aquila and Symmachus) show Christian influence.

44. On the translation of יָחִיד in the LXX, see H.-J. Fabry, "יָחִיד," *TDOT* 6:43–44.

45. Quoted from R. B. Wright, "Psalms of Solomon," *OTP* 2:669. See also *Pss. Sol.* 13:9: "For he will admonish the righteous as a beloved son [υἱὸν ἀγαπήσεως], and his discipline is as for a firstborn." See Fabry, "יָחִיד," 6:46: "'Mourning for an only son' ... is almost proverbial as a metaphor for the situation at the eschatological judgment (Jer. 6:26; Am. 8:10; Zec. 12:10)."

46. Quoted from Bruce M. Metzger, "The Fourth Book of Ezra," *OTP* 1:536. Latin according to Klijn, *Esra-Apokalypse*, 43. See also Stone, *Ezra*, 189: "This collection of titles for Israel is notable."

47. Delling, *Paralipomena Jeremiae*, 10; Wolff, *Jeremia im Frühjudentum und Urchristentum*, 46 n. 5.

conforms in both form and content to the Old Testament-Jewish tradition. In fact, a comparison of the people to the "only son" has particular significance here precisely because of the affinity of μονογενής and ἀγαπητός, since the people have already been referred to as ἠγαπημένος (see 3:8).[48]

Certain details in 7:25 and 26 are likewise without parallel. Bogaert claimed to find evidence of Marcionite teaching in 7:25 and used this to date the composition of the book,[49] but this hypothesis is hardly sustainable.[50] Alternatively, the term κρεμαμένους might cause one to recall Lam 5:12,[51] but by the time of *4 Baruch* it was a standard term for crucifixion.[52] The apparent problem here is not the method of execution but the people's apostasy from the God of Israel and worship of the "god Zar" (7:25–26). König, observing that "Zar" is the last syllable of the name "Nebuchadnezzar,"[53] suggested that this is a reference to the worship of Caesar in the Roman Empire. However, this thesis cannot be proved and remains speculative.[54] There is no evidence that Nebuchadnezzar was worshiped as God or functioned as a picture of the Roman worship of Caesar in Judaism.[55] Although Nebuchadnezzar certainly plays the role of the Roman emperor who destroyed Jerusalem within our narrative, *4 Baruch* uses the Greek name Ναβουχοδονόσορ, which undermines any attempt to associate the name of the god Ζαρ with the name of this king.

In fact, the explanation of "god Zar" is much simpler. One must first note that the Hebrew word זָר, when transliterated into Greek, has the character of a proper name, which may be misleading.[56] In fact, זָר is a common word in the

---

48. See above on 3:8. Philonenko noted in a short article (Marc Philonenko, "Un titre messianique de Bar Kokheba," *TZ* 17 [1961]: 434–35) that the leader of the second Jewish war, Bar Kokhba or Ben Kosiba, was called the ὁ μονογενής as a messianic title, even if only in a Byzantine text. Given the contemporary context assumed here for *4 Baruch* (see the introduction above), one might see here in *4 Baruch* a clear contrast to messianic hopes presumably tied to Bar Kokhba. Not the Messiah but the entire people are God's beloved, which he himself will lead into salvation.

49. Bogaert, *Apocalypse de Baruch*, 1:219–20.

50. See Wolff, *Jeremia im Frühjudentum und Urchristentum*, 45 n. 1; Schaller, "Paralipomena Jeremiou," 742.

51. Schaller, "Paralipomena Jeremiou," 741.

52. See Herodotus, *Hist.* 7.194.1–2; 9.120; Plutarch, *Caes.* 2.2; Josephus, *J.W.* 7.202; on this, see Heinz-Wolfgang Kuhn, "Die Kreuzesstrafe während der frühen Kaiserzeit: Ihre Wirklichkeit und Wertung in der Umwelt des Urchristentums," *ANRW* 25.1:648–793, esp. 680–82.

53. König, "Rest der Worte Baruchs," 332 n. 2 (following Dillmann). See also Licht, *Paralipomena Jeremiae*, 71.

54. So at least Bogaert, *Apocalypse de Baruch*, 1:219 n. 2; and Riaud, *Les Paralipomènes du Prophète Jérémie*, 112.

55. On Nebuchadnezzar's significance in the Jeremiah tradition, see T. W. Overholt, "King Nebuchadnezzar in the Jeremiah Tradition," *CBQ* 30 (1968): 39–48.

56. See Delling, *Paralipomena Jeremiae*, 53; Herzer, *Paralipomena Jeremiae*, 126–27. Delling sees here the work of the translator of *4 Baruch*, who at this point leaves the original Hebrew word

Old Testament that the Septuagint translates as ἀλλότριος.⁵⁷ Further, in this context the word "Zar" in Hebrew has the same meaning as the following word ἀλλότριος (7:26) and is translated by it.⁵⁸ The term "god Zar" means, therefore, nothing more than "foreign god" (7:26: θεὸν ἀλλότριον).⁵⁹ This worship of a "foreign god" in Babylon reminds one further of Jer 16:13: "Therefore I will hurl you out of this land into a land that neither you nor your ancestors have known, and there you shall serve other gods day and night, for I will show you no favor" (NRSV). Although both the Greek and Hebrew texts of Jer 16:13 use other words than those in *4 Bar.* 7:25, the negative intentions of both are the same: the threat of Jer 16:13 has become reality in exile. Jeremiah's memory of the "holy day" in Jerusalem (*4 Bar.* 7:26) underlines this lamentable situation, as it had been the true God who had been praised in Jerusalem. In this light, one can see the link between 7:25–26 and the rest of the book. God's people have become contaminated through their worship of a foreign god. Thus, the precondition for their return to Jerusalem (7:28) and their celebration of a holy day there (9:1) is separation from the Gentiles and purification from idol worship (7:32; see also 6:13–14).

In view of this dramatic situation, Baruch and Abimelech are called on to pray that the people will keep Jeremiah's commands and will thus make themselves worthy to be led out of exile. The power of these prayers is doubtless linked by their being prayed in Jerusalem, which is implicit in the phrase "where you are" (7:28). This indirect reference calls Jerusalem to mind for the readers and helps them once again to see the coming salvation.

This could suffice as an end to Jeremiah's letter. The tension that emerges in the unexpected continuation in 7:29 has already been noted.⁶⁰ Both formally and in terms of content the following quotation is insufficiently tied to the context. It is an almost literal citation of Ps 137(136):3–4: "For there our captors asked us for songs, and our tormentors asked for mirth, saying, 'Sing us one of the songs of Zion!' How could we sing the LORD's song in a foreign land?" (NRSV). Literal citations are otherwise absent in *4 Baruch*,⁶¹ but the previous use

---

transliterated. That raises the question whether the word זָר could also be seen as a proper name in the Hebrew original that Delling assumes.

57. See Delling, *Paralipomena Jeremiae*, 53; L. A. Snijders, "זוּר/זָר," *TDOT* 4:52–58. See also Deut 32:16; Ps 44(43):21 (NRSV 44:20); Jer 3:13.

58. See further Bogaert, *Apocalypse de Baruch*, 1:219 n. 2. See also Delling, *Paralipomena Jeremiae*, 53.

59. Schaller, "Paralipomena Jeremiou," 742.

60. See above.

61. On the avoidance of word-for-word quotations in early Jewish literature, see Schwemer, "Septuaginta," 85–86, 90.

of Psalm texts in this chapter (cf. Ps 44:21 with *4 Bar.* 7:26) may have prompted this addition.[62] That the context of the entire psalm is thus brought to the reader's mind is obvious, as the circumstances of the exile are particularly clear in this psalm.

The verses that end this chapter (7:30–32) also bring the exchange of letters between Baruch and Jeremiah to an end. The eagle is sent back with Jeremiah's reply, accompanied by a peace greeting similar to the one Baruch used earlier (7:9). For the last time before the return of the people, the figs are mentioned (7:32), which were intended for the sick among the people (3:15). In this way the composition of the Abimelech story is brought to a close.

The final reference to Jeremiah's teaching prepares the way for the next chapter concerning the people's return to Jerusalem, for which keeping distance from the pollution of the Gentiles will become an essential condition. The cultic dimension is drawn out with the unusual term ἀλίσγημα.[63] Because of its singular form and its otherwise unique appearance in Acts 15:20, Bogaert again sees here a Christian interpolation,[64] but this cannot be sufficiently supported.[65] The root of the word is used exclusively in Jewish texts.[66] The ongoing narrative assumes a separation, and this means that the defilement here is the coming from contact with the Babylonians. Thus the author prepares for the topic of the next chapter: separation from the Babylonians.

---

62. See also the root κρεμ- (*4 Bar.* 7:25), which is found also in Ps 136:2 (LXX). The connection seen by Murphy between *2 Bar.* 3:6 and Ps 137:4 is, however, not convincing ("The Temple in the Syriac Apocalypse of Baruch," 673–74); see Herzer, *Paralipomena Jeremiae*, 124 n. 424.

63. See Schaller, "Paralipomena Jeremiou," 743.

64. Bogaert, *Apocalypse de Baruch*, 1:204.

65. See Herzer, *Paralipomena Jeremiae*, 130 with n. 456; Schaller, "Paralipomena Jeremiou," 666 with n. 15.

66. Mal 1:7, 12; Dan 1:8; Sir 40:29; Aris. Ex. 142; in Eusebius, *Praep. ev.* 8.9.13; see Herzer, *Paralipomena Jeremiae*, 130 with n. 456; Schaller, "Paralipomena Jeremiou," 743. Concerning the use in Acts 15:20, one must consider that the word is put into the mouth of a Jewish Christian to regulate the tense relationship between Jewish and Gentile Christians in the early days of the Christian fellowship; see Traugott Holtz, "Die Bedeutung des Apostelkonzils für Paulus," in *Geschichte und Theologie des Urchristentums: Gesammelte Aufsätze* (ed. Eckhart Reimuth and Christian Wolff; WUNT 57; Tübingen: Mohr Siebeck, 1991), 152. The change in the so-called Western text of Acts at this point shows further that the cultic significance was later reduced to an ethical one; see Y. Tissot, "Les Prescriptions des Presbytres (Actes XV,41,D): Exégèse et Origine du Décret dans le Texte syro-occidental des Actes," *RB* 77 (1970): 327–28. The variant in MS C of *4 Bar.* 7:32 changes ἀλισγημάτων to πραγμάτων in a similar vein; see also eth and the quite different wording of the Slavic tradition T1 (see Wolff, *Jeremia im Frühjudentum und Urchristentum*, 234). The alternative texts for Acts 15:28–29 and 21:25 hint to the problem of the *hapax legomenon* in 15:20 from a Christian perspective.

Chapter 8

After a long preparation, the people's return from Babylon is finally narrated in chapter 8. The separation from Babylon (6:14) or the "defilement of the Gentiles of Babylon" (7:32), the precondition of return, is now particularized in terms of the issue of mixed marriages (8:2, 4–5). The author combines with this topic a presentation of the emergence of Samaria and the Samaritans. Furthermore, Jeremiah's preaching of the law, to this point general, now focuses on the matter of mixed marriages. These specific concerns lead one to suspect that some significant traditional material has been introduced into the plot of the story.

Without reflecting on the time between the note in 7:32 about Jeremiah's continued teaching (ἔμεινε διδάσκων) and the day of the final return in 8:1, chapter 8 binds itself to chapters 6 and 7 by means of the divine instructions in 8:2. Jeremiah is to lead the people to the Jordan (8:2a; see 6:23) and challenge them to leave the "works of Babylon" (8:2), just as he has been doing previously (7:32).[1] Now, however, the deeds of Babylon are specified. At issue is the mixture between Jews and Gentiles.[2] The problem of mixed marriages, which concerns Jewish men and women alike, is thereby brought to the fore (8:2b). From a social-historical perspective, one suspects that a strongly Jewish-Hellenistic setting in which women, like men, could divorce lies in the background.[3] That mixed marriages could be viewed as the concrete nature of the "defilement" (7:32) is a motif already provided in the biblical traditions of the return from exile (Ezra 9–10; Neh 13:23–31). On this basis one can safely assume that the ban on mixed marriages was widespread.[4] To what extent *4 Baruch* consciously

---

1. On this, see the commentary above on 7:32.
2. See Vegas-Montaner, "Paralipomenos de Jeremias," 356, who speaks in this context of the writer's "judaismo ... manifesta" (manifest Judaism), although he assumes Christian interpolations outside the Christian ending (357).
3. See Zeev W. Falk, "Ehe/Eherecht/Ehescheidung IV," *TRE* 9:313–18. See also 1 Cor 7:10–11, although it is not clear whether the woman here is Jewish; the advice, however, comes from the Jewish Christian Paul.
4. *T. Job* 45:3; Tob 4:12; 1 Macc 1:15; *T. Jud.* 14:6; *T. Levi* 9:10; 14:6; *Jub.* 20:4; 22:20; 25:1–10; 30:1–3; *Jos. Asen.* 7:5; 8:5, 7; Theodotus, frg. 4 (= Eusebius, *Praep. ev.* 9.22.6; on this,

makes use of the biblical tradition will be addressed later,[5] where, remarkably, the problem of mixed marriages is linked to the founding of Samaria (8:8). This is, at this point, an anti-Samaritan polemic from an exclusivist Jewish perspective, grounded in traditional ideas of the relationship between these two Jewish groups, though at the end of the argument in chapter 8 conciliatory ideas come to the fore. The Samaritans as a Torah-observant group would of course have rejected mixed marriages, too.[6] For now we need only to note that obedience becomes the condition for crossing the Jordan (8:3). This is once again a clear indication that the testing does not take place when the people enter Jerusalem. Rather, the identification of the disobedient on the banks of the Jordan has a purifying and cleansing effect on the people as a whole, and it forms the basis for the later dismissal of all who will not obey.[7]

The following verses demonstrate this.[8] Verses 4 and 5 assume that Jere-

---

see Reinhard Pummer, "Antisamaritanische Polemik in jüdischen Schriften aus der intertestamentarischen Zeit," *BZ* 26 [1982]: 234–37), Josephus, *Ant.* 8.191; 18.340–342; Philo, *Spec. Laws* 3.29; *L.A.B.* 9:5; 18:13–14; 21:1; 43:5. On the problem in general, see Delling, *Die Bewältigung der Diasporasituation*, 14–15.

5. See the commentary on 8:6–8 below.

6. See also below the "Excursus on the Story of the Samaritans according to *4 Baruch* 8."

7. See the commentary on 6:22–23 above.

8. MS C leaves the tradition as of 8:4b and offers a short conclusion based on the Septuagint, particularly the Ezra tradition and the books of Baruch, Jeremiah, and Ezekiel; see the overview in Schaller, "Paralipomena Jeremiou," 745. The text of MS C reads: "(And half of those married of them) I will take, and I will establish with them an eternal covenant, to be their God and they will be my people, and I will not remove my people Israel from the land that I gave them. O Lord Almighty, God of Israel, a soul in anguish and a wearied spirit has cried out to you. Hear, O Lord, and have mercy, for (you are) a God of mercy, and have mercy, for we (continually) sin before you, for you are the one enthroned forever and we are perishing forever. O Lord Almighty, God of Israel, hear the prayer of the dead of Israel and the sons of those who sin before you, who did not listen to the voice of their God and evils clung to us. Do not remember the injustices of our fathers; rather, remember your hand and your name at this time. And it came to pass after the completion of the seventy years, when the Persians ruled, in the first year of Cyrus, the king of the Persians, that the word of the Lord from the mouth of Jeremiah was accomplished: the Lord stirred up the spirit of Cyrus, king of the Persians, and he ordered a proclamation in his entire kingdom and at the same time this decree: 'Thus says Cyrus, the king of the Persians: the Lord, the God of heaven, has given me all kingdoms of the earth and has selected me, that I might build him a house in Jerusalem in Judea. Whoever, therefore, is from his people, let his Lord be with him, and let him go up to Jerusalem, which is in Judea, and let him build the house of the God of Israel.' This is the Lord who established his tent in Jerusalem. And Cyrus the king brought out the holy vessels of the Lord that Nebuchadnezzar had brought from Jerusalem and … put them in his idol temple. Cyrus the king of the Persians brought them all out and gave them to Mithridates, his treasurer. They were given by him to Sarabaros, the administrator of Judea, together with Zerubbabel, who also asked Darius, the king of the Persians, for the rebuilding of the sanctuary. For there was one who hindered the work in the time of Artaxerxes, as Ezra reports. Having arrived at the temple of God in Jerusalem,

miah's admonitions continue until he reaches the Jordan with the people. Unfortunately, half of those in mixed marriages refuse to obey (8:4).[9] Jeremiah cannot prevent them from continuing to Jerusalem, which is surprising, considering the significance of the Jordan. However, what became clear at the Jordan is confirmed before the gates of the city. Together with Baruch and Abimelech, Jeremiah turns the disobedient away.[10]

The story of Samaria and the Samaritans begins in 8:6 with the dismissal of the disobedient. Although they speak of Jerusalem as "our city" in 8:4b, they change their minds quickly after being turned away and decide to return to Babylon, which they similarly call "our place." The expressions ἡ πόλις ἡμῶν (8:4) and τὸ τόπος ἡμῶν (8:6)[11] are particularly interesting, insofar as the inhabitants of Samaria are promised that, should they repent, they will be brought to their "exalted place" (εἰς τὸν τόπον ὑμῶν τὸν ὑψηλόν) by "the angel of righteousness" (8:9). Thus, the phrase τόπος ὑψηλός bears a twofold meaning within the story by referring to the earthly Jerusalem as an exalted place on Mount Zion to which the people are headed, but this meaning is transparent for the perspective of the heavenly Jerusalem, which already has been part of the promise of the return (5:34).[12]

Initially Babylon becomes the "place" (8:6) for those dismissed, yet in Babylon they are also turned away. Thus God executes the judgment threatened in 6:22. The reason for their being turned away, that they left "secretly" (κρυφῇ,

---

in the second year, in the second month, Zerubbabel (the son) of Rathalael and Joshua (the son) of Jehozadak, and their brothers and the priests and the Levites and all who had come from captivity to Jerusalem—and they founded the house of God at New Moon in the second month of their arrival in Judea and Jerusalem, when Haggai and Zechariah, the son of Iddo, as the last of the prophets, prophesied. And Ezra went up out of Babylon, as a scribe well-versed in the law of Moses. He had great knowledge, so that he was able to teach all the people the ordinances and laws, in the time of Artaxerxes. And they consecrated the house of God by singing and praising the Lord for the rebuilding of the house of God."

9. Riaud suspects here a play on Neh 13:24 ("Les Samaritains," 137 n. 1). This is, however, hardly likely, since the issue is not that half the people have mixed marriages; rather, it is all about half the children, who cannot speak like the Israelites. The issue in *4 Baruch* is how many have not obeyed, namely, half the people!

10. The waters of the Jordan as a means of testing (6:23) do not play a role here. This circumstance once again demonstrates that 6:23 does not refer to Christian baptism, as one would expect a further reference to baptism in chapter 8, where it would be more fitting; see Herzer, *Paralipomena Jeremiae*, 120–21. In the absence of such a reference, if 6:23 were a Christian reference, it would be so unclear as to be meaningless.

11. See Delling, *Paralipomena Jeremiae*, 48 n. 32.

12. According to Kohler, the phrase τόπος ὑψηλός is "the Septuagint translation of the name Moriah" ("The Pre-Talmudic Haggada," 414). This, however, cannot be verified. In 2 Chr 3:1 (see also Isa 29:1), however, Moriah is identified with the Temple Mount.

8:7),[13] reminds one of the story of the Israelite flight during the exodus from Egypt (Exod 14:5). Our author thus reinforces his understanding that the return from the exile was a "new exodus."[14] In the light of these allusions, we should not regard this event as a historical explanation[15] but as the narrative consequence of the unusual combination of the story of the exile and the founding of Samaria. The double turning away from both Jerusalem and Babylon is thus the narrative reason for settling down "in a lonely place, far from Jerusalem," and for founding the city of Samaria (8:8).

However unusual and anachronistic this etiology of Samaria's founding might appear, the chapter's narrative could have ended here. Nonetheless, the final sentence in 8:9 indicates that the issue and concern is, in fact, not the etiology but the people who have settled there, "far from Jerusalem."[16] Despite the clear division between the groups, Jeremiah leaves a door to return open and states the condition for the Samaritans' return, namely, repentance. The term μετανοεῖν is known in Jewish contexts, but as an admonition of a Jewish prophet to the Samaritans, given the normal tensions between Jews and Samaritans,[17] Jeremiah's

---

13. See Wolff, *Jeremia im Frühjudentum und Urchristentum*, 58 with n. 1, noting the difference to the *Jeremiah Apocryphon*, where the Babylonians let the Jews leave with valuable gifts.

14. Wolff, *Jeremia im Frühjudentum und Urchristentum*, 50, 80; Riaud, *Les Paralipomènes du Prophète Jérémie*, 106; and Herzer, *Paralipomena Jeremiae*, 121–24.

15. See in this sense Delling, *Paralipomena Jeremiae*, 48 n. 32.

16. Riaud's negative assessment of this expression as a value judgment ("Les Samaritains," 141) is therefore wide of the mark and does not correspond to the narrative.

17. See James Alan Montgomery, *The Samaritans, the Earliest Jewish Sect: Their History, Theology, and Literature* (New York: Ktav, 1968), passim; Richard James Coggins, *Samaritans and Jews: The Origins of Samaritanism Reconsidered* (Atlanta: John Knox, 1975), passim; and Martina Böhm, *Samarien und die Samaritai bei Lukas: Eine Studie zum religionshistorischen und traditionsgeschichtlichen Hintergrund der lukanischen Samarientexte und zu deren topographischer Verhaftung* (WUNT 2.111; Tübingen: Mohr Siebeck, 1999), esp. 151–202. Josephus often confirms the Samaritan enmity toward the Jews (*Ant.* 11.84; see also 11.114–116); see Pummer, "Antisamaritanische Polemik," 236; Rita Egger, *Josephus Flavius und die Samaritaner: Eine terminologische Untersuchung zur Identitätsklärung der Samaritaner* (NTOA 4; Fribourg: Universitätsverlag, 1986), 54–55. However, although Josephus follows the tradition of 2 Kgs 17, in which the Samaritans are of Gentile origin, he does portray the Roman destruction of the Samaritans as a type of martyr story and calls them "struck by misfortune" (*J.W.* 3.307–315). On that, see Egger, *Josephus Flavius und die Samaritaner*, 310. According to Egger, Josephus could differentiate between Samaritans of Jewish descent and Persian and Mede settlers (312). On Jewish-Samaritan enmity, see also Sir 50:25–26; *Jub.* 30:5, 7; 49:16–21; *T. Levi* 5:3–4; 6:8–10; 7:2; John 4:9. See further Hans G. Kippenberg, *Garizim und Synagoge: Traditionsgeschichtliche Untersuchungen zur samaritanischen Religion der aramaeischen Periode* (Religionsgeschichtliche Versuche und Vorarbeiten 30; Berlin: de Gruyter, 1971), 88–90; Reinhard Pummer, "The Book of Jubilees and the Samaritans," *EgT* 10 (1979): 164–78; Pummer, "Antisamaritanische Polemik," 225–29 (on *Jub.* 30 and 49); contra Coggins, *Samaritans and Jews*, 92. However, Jdt 9:2–4 is no anti-Samaritan polemic; against Kippenberg, *Garizim und*

call for repentance is unprecedented.[18] Moreover, Jeremiah mentions the angel of righteousness, who has earlier been associated with the salvation, the return, of the people (6:6). Should the angel also lead the Samaritans to "your exalted place," meaning Jerusalem, then it is clear that our author has a deep interest in this people. Although the Samaritans can be called ἀλλογενής from even a Christian perspective (Luke 17:18),[19] it is clear from the etiology here that this is exactly what the Samaritans are not, since they have the same origins as the Jews[20] and are "only" separate because of their disobedience. Furthermore, inasmuch as the Samaritans' disobedience and separation are exclusively the result of their origin in Babylonian mixed marriages, the author here is presumably referring to 2 Kgs 17:24–41.[21] The possibility of repentance, however, remains. Thus *4 Bar.* 8 effectively narrates the depths of the tension of the problem, making a solution possible.

Excursus on the Story of the Samaritans according to *4 Baruch* 8[22]

A few observations are required to set the historical aspects in relation to the shaping of the narrative. First, *4 Baruch* avoids giving the separated people a particular or distinct name; only the mention of the city of Samaria permits identification. Second, the constitutive element of the people's prehistory is marriage with foreign partners; the people are therefore of "mixed population," and their children are, from both an Israelite and a Gentile perspective, without identity (8:7). The author of *4 Baruch,* therefore, views this people as a Jewish-Gentile mixed population, rejected by both Jews and Gentiles but for different reasons.

The oldest tradition concerning the emergence of the Samaritans is that of the Old Testament in 2 Kgs 17:24–41. According to 1 Kgs 16:24, Samaria was

---

Synagoge, 88, n. 159; Coggins, *Samaritans and Jews,* 89. See on that, however, Pummer, "The Book of Jubilees and the Samaritans," 170–71; Pummer, "Antisamaritanische Polemik," 229–31. See further Gedalia Alon, "The Origin of the Samaritans in the Halakhic Tradition," in *Jews, Judaism and the Classical World* (ed. G. Alon; Jerusalem: Magnes, 1977), 360–361, who sees in the phrase ἡ Σύκημα λεγομένη πόλις ἀσυνέτων in *T. Levi* 7:2 (see Sir 50:26: ὁ λαὸς μωρὸς ὁ κατοικῶν ἐν Σικίμοις—on that, see Böhm, *Samarien und die Samaritai,* 155–59) a typical name for the Samaritans in the Hasmonean era.

18. Schaller, "Paralipomena Jeremiou," 747.
19. See Böhm, *Samarien und die Samaritai,* 194–203, 274–77.
20. A similar tendency can also be found in the New Testament; see Böhm, *Samarien und die Samaritai,* 194 (on Luke).
21. See the "Excursus on the Story of the Samaritans according to *4 Baruch* 8."
22. See also Riaud, "Les Samaritains," passim; Herzer, *Paralipomena Jeremiae,* 132–43.

built by the Israelite king Omri (881–870),[23] whom the biblical text regards as an unfaithful king who led the people into idolatry (1 Kgs 16:25–26).[24] Omri, the text reports, bought the mountain from a man named "Shemer," from which the city was to have received its name. The etiological intention makes this presentation difficult to accept.[25] Centuries later, during the Assyrian conquest, a great portion of the population was deported under Sargon and replaced by foreign settlers (2 Kgs 17:24).[26] This repopulation is linked to the emergence of the Samaritans in 2 Kgs 17:24–41, so that the question of mixing comes to the fore, though the concern is religious, not political. The settlers do not worship "the god of the land" (17:26), so a priest is brought back from the deported population to teach them the worship of YHWH (17:28).[27] This attempt fails (17:29–32), and a syncretistic cult emerges instead (17:33),[28] a cult that does not adhere to YHWH's law (17:34–41).[29] According to 2 Kgs 17, then, the reason for the division between Jews and Samaritans is religious: "They would not listen, however, but they continued to practice their former custom" (2 Kgs 17:40 NRSV).

Comparing the traditions of 2 Kings (and Josephus) and *4 Bar.* 8, it appears that the author of *4 Baruch* had the biblical tradition in mind but used it freely to fit his own situation.[30] Differing from the biblical tradition, our author moves the founding of Samaria to the time after the return from the exile. Rather than the resettled ethnic groups of 2 Kgs 17, which are expressly Gentile, *4 Baruch*

---

23. Stefan Timm, *Die Dynastie Omri: Quellen und Untersuchungen zur Geschichte Israels im 9. Jahrhundert vor Christus* (FRLANT 124; Göttingen: Vandenhoeck & Ruprecht, 1982), 22–23, 142–44.

24. Cf. Josephus, *Ant.* 8.312; see also Timm, *Dynastie Omri*, 30–32, 40; Antonius H. J. Gunneweg, *Geschichte Israels bis Bar Kochba* (Stuttgart: Kohlhammer, 1972), 95–97.

25. Cf. Josephus, *Ant.* 8.312. On the problem of this etiology, see Timm, *Dynastie Omri*, 43–45, 142–44.

26. Cf. Josephus, *Ant.* 9.278–279; see also Gunneweg, *Geschichte Israels*, 104; Kippenberg, *Garizim und Synagoge*, 35; Nathan Schur, *History of the Samaritans* (BEATAJ 18; Frankfurt am Main: Lang, 1989), 20–21; and Bob Becking, *The Fall of Samaria: An Historical and Archeological Study* (SHANE 2; Leiden: Brill, 1992), 47–56, 95–104. According to Josephus, they were primarily "Chuthaeans" from Persia, a group consisting of five ethnic groups (*Ant.* 9.288). Josephus explains that "Chuthaeans" (Χουθαῖοι) was the Hebrew and "Samaritans" (Σαμαρεῖται) the Greek name of the same group of people; see Becking, *Fall of Samaria*, 95–104; Egger, *Josephus Flavius und die Samaritaner*, 176–79.

27. Cf. Josephus, *Ant.* 9.289–290.

28. See Kippenberg, *Garizim und Synagoge*, 80–82.

29. See Josephus, *Ant.* 9.289–290. Josephus does not overlook the worship of foreign gods; see Egger, *Josephus Flavius und die Samaritaner*, 178.

30. Riaud speaks of "inspiration" from the biblical text ("Les Samaritains," 136).

assumes a Jewish-Gentile mixed group of people.³¹ The essential problem in *4 Baruch,* mixed marriages, is not an issue in either 2 Kgs 17 or Josephus but does appear in the Ezra-Nehemiah tradition's account of this postexilic dilemma (Ezra 9–10; Neh 13:23–31). Because the issue in *4 Baruch* is the situation of the return from exile, the author combines these two independent traditions, even though the Samaritans play no role in Ezra-Nehemiah. However, this combination of the traditions allows him to present his perspective concerning the relationship of Israel to the Samaritans.

In order to understand the background of *4 Bar.* 8, one needs to refer to Josephus. Whereas Neh 13:28 mentions an unnamed grandson of the high priest who was chased from Jerusalem due to his marriage to the daughter of Sanballat,³² Josephus links this inner-Jewish division to the founding of the Samaritan temple on Mount Gerizim (*Ant.* 11.321–328).³³ Nehemiah ends by noting that the disobedient were driven out. Hence *4 Baruch* and Josephus have common elements that go beyond the Old Testament tradition: (1) Jewish mixed marriages lead to the division; (2) the division occurs only when those in mixed marriages do not obey the call to obedience and to the dissolving of these marriages; (3) those driven out head for Samaria; and (4) a new entity is then founded in Samaria, either the Gerizim temple (Josephus) or the city of Samaria (*4 Bar.* 8).

However, the tradition-critical links between Josephus, *Ant.* 11.321–328, and *4 Bar.* 8 remain unclear. Direct reference to Josephus in *4 Baruch* is unlikely, if not impossible. Assuming that Josephus did not depend uniquely on Nehemiah but used other traditions about the founding of the Gerizim temple, the similarities between his work and *4 Baruch* allow one to assume that a similar process lies behind *4 Bar.* 8.

Our author's particular concern for the Samaritans was determinative for his composition of *4 Bar.* 8. Only thus can his joining of such diverse aspects be explained. It was important to our author to maintain the original relationship between the Samaritans and the Jews—in spite of the biblical tradition. The

---

31. See ibid., 136–37. Josephus likewise assumes the Gentile origins of the Samaritans (see *Ant.* 9.278–279, 288), but he also refers to the indifferent attitude of the Samaritans. As regards the rabbinic tradition, Alon states: "Rabbinic tradition in its entirety negates the Israelite origin of the Samaritans" ("The Origin of the Samaritans," 354); yet see below n. 38.

32. See Herzer, *Paralipomena Jeremiae,* 138–40.

33. See Kippenberg, *Garizim und Synagoge,* 56–57, who states that the Gerizim cult is not the result of a political act but the result of the superseding of priests associated with north-Israelite traditions. See also Alon, "Origin of the Samaritans," 358–59.

resettlement theory of 2 Kgs 17 was insufficient for that purpose, but Ezra-Nehemiah's depiction of postexilic mixed marriages worked well.[34] Thus, although *4 Bar.* 8's portrayal of Samaria's foundation is anachronistic and mixes separate traditions, it is logical given the author's literary concerns. He consciously contradicts the given traditions by portraying the Samaritans as still bound to Israel by a common history in spite of their past and current disobedience.[35]

The Samaritan narrative is, therefore, not anti-Samaritan.[36] Granted, the narrative confirms the status quo, but it also provides a way for moving beyond the status quo: trust in God's promise. The unity of God's people is of greater import than the divisive disobedience, which can be overcome by the prophetic promise. To be sure, reunification requires repentance, but in 8:9 this is not expressed grammatically as a condition but commanded in the light of the imminent coming of the angel of righteousness. It seems that the author of *4 Baruch* believed that the Samaritans would repent,[37] since there is no further announcement of judgment against them.[38]

---

34. According to Ezra 9:1–4, the question is not just mixed marriages in the Babylonian Golah but in the whole Diaspora. Marrying foreigners was understood to be disloyalty to God (9:2, 4, 11–12; see Neh 13:27). Hence the dissolving of mixed marriages was needed to restore the relationship with God (see Ezra 9:9–15; 10:3, see J. Blenkinsopp, *Ezra-Nehemiah: A Commentary* [Philadelphia: Westminster, 1988], 174–95; Hugh G. M. Williamson, *Ezra, Nehemiah* [WBC 16; Waco, Tex.: Word, 1985], 159–61).

35. Riaud, "Les Samaritains," 138; Delling, *Paralipomena Jeremiae*, 52; Kippenberg, *Garizim und Synagoge*, 139; and Egger, *Josephus Flavius und die Samaritaner*, 310.

36. Against Kohler, "The Pre-Talmudic Haggada," 408, 414; R. Meyer, "Paralipomena Jeremiae," *RGG* 3d. 5:103. Delling emphasizes the negative attitude of *4 Baruch* toward the Samaritans, although he concedes that it is not as sharp as in Josephus and some rabbis (*Paralipomena Jeremiae*, 52). Cf. Riaud, "Les Samaritains," 141.

37. εἰσάξει is future *indicative*.

38. 2 Macc 5:22–23 and 6:1–3 seem also to assume that the Jews and Samaritans belong to one people (for the time under Antiochus IV Epiphanes [175–164 B.C.E.]; on the dating of 2 Maccabees between 124 B.C.E. and 70 C.E., see C. Habicht, "2. Makkabäerbuch," *JSHRZ* 1.13 [1976]: 176); see on that Alon, "Origin of the Samaritans," 355; Egger, *Josephus Flavius und die Samaritaner*, 108–13; and M. Mor, "The Persian, Hellenistic and Hasmonean Period," in *The Samaritans* (ed. Alan D. Crown. Tübingen: Mohr Siebeck, 1989), 13–15. For a different view, see Coggins, *Samaritans and Jews*, 90. Particularly clear is 2 Macc 5:22–23: "He [i.e., Antiochus IV] left governors to oppress the people: at Jerusalem, Philip, by birth a Phrygian and in character more barbarous than the man who appointed him; and at Gerizim, Andronicus; and besides these Menelaus, who lorded it over his compatriots worse than the others did. In his malice toward the Jewish citizens" (NRSV). The inhabitants of Jerusalem and Gerizim are both called "Jewish citizens" (πολῖται Ἰουδαῖοι). Positive views concerning the Samaritans were also found among many rabbis in the second century C.E. So, e.g., R. Aqiba (died 135 C.E.) saw the Samaritans as "wholly proselytes" or "true proselytes" (*y. Git.* 1:4). Handed down from R. Simeon ben Gamaliel (about 140) is the following text: "R. Simeon b. Gamaliel says: A Samaritan has the status of a Jew in every respect" (*y.*

The question of the relation between the Jews and the Samaritans must have been a pressing issue when *4 Baruch* was composed.[39] The author advocates a Samaritan-friendly position, seen above all in his emphasis on their relationship with the Jews, their common history, and the concluding promise (8:9). The uncertainty at that time about the origins of the Samaritans, evident in Josephus and some rabbinic sources,[40] possibly contributed to our author's decision to take a stand on this important problem and contemporary issue.

Ber. 7:1, quoted from Jacob Neusner, *The Talmud of the Land of Israel: A Preliminary Translation and Explanation*, vol. 1: *Berakhot* [CSJH; Chicago: University of Chicago Press, 1993], 260). See Herzer, *Paralipomena Jeremiae*, 141–42 n. 524, on *Kutim* 2:28. See also F. Dexinger, "Samaritan Eschatology," in Crown, *The Samaritans*, 266–92.

39. Contra Delling, *Paralipomena Jeremiae*, 52.

40. See esp. *m. Qidd.* 4:3, *y. Qidd.* 4:3: "And who are those who are of doubtful status? The 'silenced one,' the foundling, and the Samaritan" (quoted from Jacob Neusner, *The Talmud of the Land of Israel: A Preliminary Translation and Explanation*, vol. 26: Qiddushin [CSJH; Chicago: University of Chicago Press, 1984], 229).

Chapter 9

Having portrayed the fate of the disobedient among the people, the author turns in 9:1 to those who return to Jerusalem with Jeremiah. Immediately on arriving in Jerusalem, they celebrate a festival of sacrifice. Both the place and the nature of the festival are unnamed, and there is no mention of the rebuilding of the temple. Only the altar plays a role in what follows as the place where Jeremiah dies (9:7). After those "with Jeremiah" sacrifice for nine days, Jeremiah alone offers a sacrifice (9:2), though Baruch and Abimelech are witnesses of his death (9:7).

Verse 5 makes direct reference to 5:1–6:8. The "angel of righteousness" of 6:6 is identified in 9:5 as "Michael, the archangel of righteousness." The motif of leading the righteous into the city has likewise been alluded to earlier (5:34). Curiously, Jeremiah's prayer does not thank God for the return from exile. Noteworthy also is that the temple vessels, which were objects of Jeremiah's special care in 3:7, the temple keys (4:3), and the temple itself are no longer of importance.

The precise demarcation between the original Jewish conclusion to the book and the later Christian addition is a point of dispute.[1] The first report concerning Jeremiah's death, up to 9:9, is generally regarded as the original conclusion.[2] Riaud, however, considers 9:7 to be the beginning of the Christian ending,[3] the Jewish original closing with Jeremiah's prayer. Finishing such a work with κλαυθμὸς πικρός (9:9) is, of course, remarkable, since this does not cohere comfortably with the many hope-filled aspects of *4 Baruch*. The problem would

---

1. See Bogaert, *Apocalypse de Baruch*, 1:212; Delling, *Paralipomena Jeremiae*, 2; Wolff, *Jeremia im Frühjudentum und Urchristentum*, 51; Jean Riaud, "Jérémie, martyr chrétien. Paralipomènes de Jérémie 9:7–32," in *ΚΕΧΑΡΙΤΩΜΕΝΗ Mélanges R. Laurentin* (Paris: Desclée, 1990), 231–35; and Herzer, *Paralipomena Jeremiae*, 30–32.

2. So Delling, *Paralipomena Jeremiae*, 2, 58; Wolff, *Jeremia im Frühjudentum und Urchristentum*, 51.

3. Riaud, "Le Puissant t'emportera dans ta Tente," 263–64. So also Riaud, *Les Paralipomènes du Prophète Jérémie*, 57. Riaud makes 9:10 the end of the Jewish conclusion in "Paralipomena Jeremiou," 216.

thus be solved by seeing the end in 9:6. That raises, however, a question as to what Jeremiah actually prays for. Moreover, the Christian conclusion would also have two different accounts of Jeremiah's death: 9:7–9 and 19–32. It is difficult to imagine that the original Jewish work ended later than 9:9, since 9:10 clearly begins a new section. The fact that 9:11 picks up on the key word from 9:10 supports this assumption (9:10: κηδεύσωσιν; 9:11: μὴ κηδεύετε).[4]

Robinson, on the other hand, claims that the Christian conclusion begins earlier, in 8:9 (his numbering 8:12).[5] He writes, "The Christian redactor has changed the original Jewish polemic against the Samaritans into a promise of exaltation by adding this verse."[6] However, 8:9 is in no sense a specifically Christian statement[7] (see also 6:6), nor must one presume a Christian background to μετανοήσατε, as Robinson admittedly does not say but seems to assume.[8] The eschatological work of salvation is performed by the Son of God in the Christian redaction, as proclaimed through the apostles to the Gentiles (9:13–18), not by the angel of righteousness. Finally, the festival of sacrifice in 9:1–7 does not fit a Christian intention. If, therefore, the first tradition regarding Jeremiah's death belongs to the Jewish text, one could assume on the basis of the difficulties of 9:9 that the original Jewish text had a different conclusion that was replaced by the Christian editor.[9]

Remarkably, the reader is not told where the festival of sacrifice takes place. The temple vessels (3:7–8), altar (3:8), and keys (4:3–4) were mentioned at the beginning of *4 Baruch*, but the destruction of the temple was not.[10] The temple as such seems to have no special significance and is overshadowed by the city of Jerusalem, which as a whole has national and eschatological significance.

After the people offer sacrifices for nine days, Jeremiah alone brings a sacrifice on the tenth day (9:1–2). This is clearly a reference to Yom Kippur, which was observed on the tenth day of Tishri. Traditionally, the people would offer sacrifices the first nine days of the month, and the high priest would bring the atoning sacrifice for the people on the tenth day.[11] Therefore, Jeremiah's priestly

---

4. Bogaert also accredits 9:10 to the Christian ending (*Apocalypse de Baruch*, 1:212); see Vegas-Montaner, "Paralipomenos de Jeremias," 356.
5. Robinson, "4 Baruch," 415. On that, see Herzer, *Paralipomena Jeremiae*, 175–76.
6. Robinson, "4 Baruch," 423 n. 8b.
7. See the commentary above on 8:9.
8. See Delling, *Paralipomena Jeremiae*, 52. On μετανοεῖν, see, e.g., Sir 17:24; 48:15; *Jos. Asen.* 15:7; *T. Reu.* 1:9; 4:4; *T. Sim.* 2:13; *T. Gad* 6:6.
9. Herzer, *Paralipomena Jeremiae*, 32.
10. Wolff, *Jeremia im Frühjudentum und Urchristentum*, 51 n. 2. Riaud regards the mention of the altar as a reference to the destruction of the temple (*Les Paralipomènes du Prophète Jérémie*, 199).
11. Lev 16:29; see also 23:27; Num 29:7. See Bogaert, *Apocalypse de Baruch*, 1:212; Riaud, "La figure de Jérémie," 378. On the dating of Yom Kippur, see J. Morgenstern, "Two Prophecies

function culminates in the task of the high priest (see 5:18).[12] However, in this context Jeremiah's prayer comes to the forefront,[13] nearly replacing the sacrifice.[14] The description of the sacrifice reminds one once again of the Ezra and Nehemiah tradition (Ezra 3:4; Neh 8:13–18).[15]

---

from the Fourth Century B.C. and the Evolution of Yom Kippur," *HUCA* 24 (1952/53): 1–74, esp. 39–41. The ten days from New Year on the first of Tishri and Yom Kippur were considered ten days for penitence and repentance; see *Midr. Pss.* on Pss 17 and 102; *y. Roš Haš.* 1:3, 15. See Shmuel Safrai, "Der Versöhnungstag in Tempel und Synagoge," in *Versöhnung in der jüdischen und christlichen Liturgie* (ed. Hanspeter Heinz; QD 124; Freiburg: Herder, 1990), 54; and, in the same volume, J. Magonet, "Der Versöhnungstag in der jüdischen und christlichen Liturgie," 138. See further Theodor H. Gaster, *Festivals of the Jewish Year: A Modern Interpretation and Guide* (New York: Sloame, 1978), 147–48; Jacob Milgrom, *Leviticus 1–16* (AB 3; New York: Doubleday, 1991), 1070–71.

12. See Schaller, "Paralipomena Jeremiou," 748.

13. There are different kinds of prayers at Yom Kippur; see, e.g., *m. Yoma* 5:1; *y. Yoma* 5:2; *b. Yoma* 53b; *Lev. Rab.* 20:3–4; *Pesiq. Rab Kah.* 26; *Tanḥ.* B §4. See Safrai, "Versöhnungstag," 38.

14. In the rituals of Yom Kippur prayer took on a central role in the time after the Second Temple, as there was no longer any sacrifice; see Safrai, "Versöhnungstag," 48–51. See also H. Kosmala, "Jom Kippur," *Jud* 6 (1950): 12; Hans Joachim Schoeps, *Die Tempelzerstörung des Jahres 70 in der jüdischen Religionsgeschichte: Agadisches zur Auserwählung Israels* (Uppsala: Seminarium neotestamenticum Upsaliense, 1942), 169. In *b. Sukkah* 55b, a quotation from R. Johanan b. Zakkai is handed down: "Woe to the idolators, for they had a loss and do not know what they have lost. When the temple was in existence the altar atoned for them, but now who shall atone for them?" (quoted from Israel W. Slotki, *Sukkah: Translated into English with Notes, Glossary and Indices*, in *The Babylonian Talmud: Seder Mo'ed* [ed. Isidore Epstein; 35 vols.; London: Soncino, 1935–52], 8:269). *Midr. Haseroth we Yeteroth* reads: "Israel speaks to God, Lord of the World, when the Temple was still in existence, we offered our sacrifices in order to atone for our sins, but now, for the Temple has been destroyed—would he be rebuilt again in our days—we do not have offerings for the forgiveness of our sins. We only have the prayer" (translated after Schoeps, *Tempelzerstörung*, 174; further references there). Thus Yom Kippur achieves atonement without sacrifice; see *y. Yoma* 8:7 (cf. 8:9): "A strict rule applies to the goat which does not apply to the Day of Atonement, and to the Day of Atonement which does not apply to the goat. The Day of Atonement effects atonement without a goat, but the goat does not effect atonement without the Day of Atonement" (quoted from Jacob Neusner, *The Talmud of the Land of Israel: A Preliminary Translation and Explanation*, vol. 14: *Yoma* [CSHJ; Chicago: University of Chicago Press, 1990], 231–32). According to Hans-Jürgen Hermisson, *Sprache und Ritus im altisraelitischen Kult: Zur Spiritualisierung der Kultbegriffe im Alten Testament* (WMANT 19; Neukirchen-Vluyn: Neukirchner Verlag, 1965), 29–64, esp. 37–39, 60–62, the idea of prayer as a substitute for sacrifice emerged after the exile. See further Othmar Keel, *Jahwe-Visionen und Siegelkunst: Eine neue Deutung der Majestätsschilderungen in Jes 6, Ez 1 und 10 und Sach 4: Mit einem Beitrag von A. Gutbub über die vier Winde Ägyptens* (SBS 84, 85; Stuttgart: Verlag Katholisches Bibelwerk, 1977), 122 n. 271; Ego, *Himmel*, 24, 161.

15. See Ezra 8:35: "At that time those who had come from captivity, the returned exiles, offered burnt offerings to the God of Israel, twelve bulls for all Israel, ninety-six rams, seventy-seven lambs, and as a sin offering twelve male goats; all this was a burnt offering to the LORD" (NRSV). Cf. Neh 8–9. See Gaster, *Festivals of the Jewish Year*, 184–85.

The missing references to the temple and its accoutrements at the end of *4 Baruch* must be understood in relation to the concern for the temple vessels and particularly the keys in *4 Bar.* 3 and 4. Thus the disinterest here is only pretended, since readers will be prompted to think about them. That nothing is said explicitly calls readers to interpret the silence in the light of the message of salvation that has preceded. Just as this was focused on the Jerusalem above, so also the silence concerning vessels and keys seems to point in this direction.[16] They were preserved not for another earthly temple but for an eschatological, heavenly temple. This is, of course, left for readers to identify on their own, but Jeremiah's final prayer gives them help as well as hope for their journey.[17] Jeremiah's prayer seems in this context his real legacy.

The prayer begins with the Trishagion of Isa 6:3[18] and a variety of divine names.[19] Although the focus of these names is clearly on God, his relation to the pious is not lost from view, as is evident in Jeremiah's praise of God as the "incense of *the living trees*" (θυμίαμα τῶν δένδρων τῶν ζώντων, *4 Bar.* 9:3).[20] The use of θυμίαμα underlines the link with Yom Kippur (Lev 16:12–13 LXX),[21] the background to which should inform our reading of the present text. According to Lev 16:2 and 13, the cloud of smoke resulting from the burning of the incense is the place of God's presence.[22] At the same time, the cloud protects the priest from dying in his encounter with God. Thus, calling God the "incense of (or "for") the living trees"[23] can be understood as an exegesis of the description

---

16. In contrast, the *Jeremiah Apocryphon* does report the return of the keys (188:12–14; see 189:3–5; cf. also Ezra 1:7–11).

17. On the author's editorial work here, see Herzer, *Paralipomena Jeremiae*, 147–48.

18. See *1 En.* 39:12; *T. Ab.* A 3:3; Rev 4:8; see also Harris, *Rest of the Words of Baruch*, 22; Delling, *Paralipomena Jeremiae*, 33, 62–63.

19. See Herzer, "Direction in Difficult Times," 22–28.

20. On translating θυμίαμα "incense," see LSJ, 801 s.v. 1. See also Schaller, "Paralipomena Jeremiou," 748. On "living trees" as a designation for the pious, see n. 23 below.

21. See Bogaert, *Apocalypse de Baruch*, 1:213; Riaud, *Les Paralipomènes du Prophète Jérémie*, 56; and Schaller, "Paralipomena Jeremiou," 748. See *1 En.* 24:3–25:6, esp. 25:6: "Then they shall be glad and rejoice in gladness, and they shall enter into the holy (place); its fragrance shall (penetrate) their bones, long life will they live on earth" (quoted from Isaac, "1 Enoch," *OTP* 1:26).

22. See, e.g., Exod 13:21; 16:10; 33:9–10; Num 11:25; 12:5; 1 Kgs 8:10–11 = 2 Chr 5:13–14; see also *Sipra* 16:12–13 (third century C.E.; see Strack and Stemberger, *Introduction*, 287). "Thus 'cloud' and 'fire' symbolize God's being and presence, while at the same time concealing God's nature" (David N. Freedman and B. E. Willoughby, "ענן," *TDOT* 11:255). Lev 16:2 makes it clear that the cloud of incense in 16:13 is the place of God's presence; on this, see Herzer, *Paralipomena Jeremiae*, 150.

23. The phrase τῶν δένδρων τῶν ζώντων is an adnominal objective genitive; see Friedrich Blaß, Albert Debrunner, and Friedrich Rehkopf, eds., *Grammatik des neutestamentlichen Griechisch* (15th ed.; Göttingen: Vandenhoeck & Ruprecht 1979), 134–35, §163. See Herzer, *Paralipomena*

of the incense offering in Lev 16.[24] The God met in the incense can symbolically be identified with the incense, as it is here. This is consistent with the prior reference to the three "holies" of Isa 6:3, since there too the house is full of smoke (Isa 6:4). In the context of Isa 6, the smoke (i.e., God's presence) is all that Isaiah's vision can refer to. Thus the picture is similar to that found here in *4 Baruch* with reference to Lev 16:12–13.[25]

The title "true light" for God, the light that enlightens the righteous, reminds one of 5:34. Although "light" in 6:9 stands for the law coming from God's mouth that accompanies the righteous on his or her way,[26] the light motif in 9:3 refers to the direct enlightenment of the righteous. These two uses of this motif do not contradict, however, since the context here also concerns the way of the righteous to God (ἕως οὗ ἀναληφθῶ πρός σε).[27] The switch from plural to first-person singular is, nonetheless, worthy of note: "true light that enlightens *me*[28] until *I* be lifted up to you." Here already Jeremiah's death is in view, though the final goal is, in the end, the leading of the righteous into the heavenly Jerusalem (9:4–5) by Michael.[29]

Jeremiae, 150; Schaller, "Paralipomena Jeremiou," 749. To read it as a subjective genitive, in which case it would concern incense won from living trees (such as from resin or the like; see Milgrom, *Leviticus*, 1026–28), is possible but makes no sense in *4 Bar.* 9. On calling the pious δένδρα τὰ ζῶντα, see esp. *Pss. Sol.* 14:3 (ὁ παράδεισος τοῦ κυρίου τὰ ξύλα τῆς ζωῆς ὅσιοι αὐτοῦ); see further Ps 92(91):13–15 (NRSV 92:12–14).

24. Herzer, "Direction in Difficult Times," 24.

25. Philonenko, "Simples Observations," 172, again refers to Mandaic liturgies (see Mark Lidzbarski, *Mandäische Liturgien* [Hildesheim: Olms, 1962], 165:11–12). This is, however, unlikely in the light of the Old Testament background; cf. Herzer, "Antwort," 37.

26. Herzer, "Direction in Difficult Times," 25. See *T. Ab.* B 7:6; *T. Levi* 14:4; 19:1; *T. Zeb.* 9:8–9; *T. Ash.* 5:3; *1 En.* 1:8 and esp. 5:8; 1QS 2:3; 4:2; 1QH^a 4:5. This is therefore no Christian statement (so Harris, *Rest of the Words of Baruch*, 26, referring to John 1:9); see Delling, *Paralipomena Jeremiae*, 35 n. 25; Herzer, *Paralipomena Jeremiae*, 151 n. 574.

27. Riaud regards ἀναλαμβάνεσθαι as hinting at the translation of the prophet (referring to 6:3–6; see "Le Puissant t'emportera dans ta Tente," 263). That was unlikely for 6:3–6 (see above on 6:3–6) and is defined in 9:3 by Jeremiah's imminent death; see also *Pss. Sol.* 4:18; *T. Ab.* B 7; see further Wis 4:10–11, where ἡρπάγη, a term for translation, is used for death (see Ezek 18:7, 12; Acts 8:39; 2 Cor 12:2, 4).

28. Schaller cross-references to *Corpus Hermeticum* XIII:19 and John 1:9 ("Paralipomena Jeremiou," 749). It thereby becomes clear that such views made *4 Baruch* acceptable for certain Christian circles.

29. Wolff, "Heilshoffnung," 156–57. See also *L.A.E.* 37:5, where God hands the dead Adam to the archangel Michael with the words: "ἆρον εἰς τὸν παράδεισον" (text according to Knittel, *Das griechische "Leben Adams und Evas,"* 128; see Herzer, *Paralipomena Jeremiae*, 136; Knittel, *Das griechische "Leben Adams und Evas,"* 141, 143–44). See further *Apoc. Paul* 14; 22; 27. Being a work of a later time, the *Apocalypse of Paul* shows the continuing importance of Michael in Christian apocalyptic eschatology, particularly as a leader of the righteous into the heavenly "city of Christ."

The object of the prophet's meditation or concern (μελέτη) is, therefore, also the archangel Michael.[30] As the other "fragrance" associated with the "incense"[31] (i.e., God), Michael is qualified to be God's messenger, to lead the righteous into the heavenly Jerusalem (see the earlier reference concerning the Samaritans in 8:9). Thus is the word ἄλλη to be understood. Although our author does not state explicitly what the other εὐωδία is, the explanation lies in the imbalance between the singular and plural in 9:3. Just as the prophet is differentiated from the righteous (= the people), so the "incense" must have two "fragrances." God thereby becomes active in two ways, first for Jeremiah, until God takes Jeremiah to himself (after death); then for the righteous, whom Michael, the "other fragrance," will lead into the heavenly Jerusalem. In short, the prophet's concern is for Michael because Jeremiah must pass on responsibility for the people to Michael before his death.

The theme of the seraphim in 9:3 is directly related to Isa 6, since the alternating voices of the seraphim in Isa 6:3a lead to the conclusion that there are two of them.[32] The characterization of their voices[33] as sweet is a reference to what they proclaim: praise of God.[34] By basing his request on the content of their praise, Jeremiah is implicitly appealing to God's holiness, which forms the basis of his hope that God will fulfill his prayer. That national and eschatological-individual hopes of salvation are intertwined is again clear: now back in Jerusalem, Jeremiah prays to God hoping and expecting that all the righteous will be taken into the heavenly Jerusalem.

The end of the prayer in 9:6 is characterized by further titles for God, as Jeremiah entrusts his request to the "Lord Almighty of all creation ... in whom all creation was hidden before these things [i.e., the eschatological completion of God's people] came into existence." The address Κύριε παντοκράτωρ was

---

30. The καί in *4 Bar.* 9:5 is explanatory. On the basis of Kraft-Purintun's conjecture, Schaller ("Paralipomena Jeremiou," 749) emends the text: "Und es möge für mich sorgen, Michael, bis er die Gerechten hineinführt [And Michael may take care of me until he leads in the righteous]" (cf. Kraft and Purintun, *Paraleipomena Jeremiou*, 45: "and may Michael ... be my guardian"). Neither his formal reason, that nominal sentences are rare in *4 Baruch*, nor the unnamed reasons of content can justify this conjecture, as the text fits the context as it is reconstructed here.

31. Contra Delling, *Paralipomena Jeremiae*, 62 n. 44. θυμίαμα in both cases refers to God. On εὐωδία as a reference to a fragrance pleasing to God, see Gen 8:21; Lev 1:9, 13, 17; 2:2, 9, 12; 3:5; Num 15:3, 5, 7. See also *L.A.E.* 29:4–5; Knittel, *Das griechische "Leben Adams und Evas,"* 133.

32. See Keel, *Jahwe-Visionen*, 70–79, 114–15. See also *Pirqe R. El.* 4, which speaks of two seraphim in a creation-theological context (see Friedlander, *Eliezer*, 24). The additional περὶ τοῦ ἐλέως σου παρακαλῶ in the Armenian translation and the Codex P in *4 Bar.* 9:4 (included by Kraft and Purintun, *Paraleipomena Jeremiou*, 44–45) is most likely secondary; see Herzer, *Paralipomena Jeremiae*, 18.

33. Schaller translates "singing" ("Paralipomena Jeremiou," 749).

34. See Song 2:14; Sir 6:5.

already used in 1:5.[35] As the Almighty, God is responsible for judgment (1:5) and for final salvation (9:6). As early as 3:8, God's creative power is said to span beginning and end. Although MSS A and B read κρίσις instead of κτίσις (eth) in 9:6b,[36] there is no convincing argument in favor of κρίσις. The Ethiopic text κτίσις must be preferred,[37] since God's eschatological activity as Creator is in view here as well: God not only created at the beginning but will reveal the nature of his creation in the eschatological redemption.[38] Moreover, *4 Baruch* never speaks of κρίσις, not even as a "hidden judgment." God is rather the Almighty Ruler of the whole creation (9:6) who made and sealed the earth as his creation (3:8). According to 9:6 he is the one who hid the work of his creation in himself before all things.[39] There is, therefore, no reference to judgment as an element of eschatological fulfillment here.[40] Furthermore, the motif of judgment is traditionally bound up with Rosh Hashanah, not Yom Kippur, which lies in the background here.[41]

Unusual for an early Jewish text is the attribution ἀγέννητος καὶ ἀπερινόητος with respect to God.[42] Philo occasionally uses ἀγένητος ("uncreated, unoriginated"),[43] but Delling's suspicion that the more common ἀγένητος was the original reading in *4 Bar.* 9:6 remains speculative.[44] One must assume that the original text read ἀγέννητος, a form found almost exclusively[45] in Christian literature beginning in the second century C.E.[46] Because a similar

---

35. Herzer, "Direction in Difficult Times," 26. See esp. Amos 4:13; 5:27; 9:6: "Almighty is his Name" (κύριος [ὁ θεὸς] παντοκράτωρ ὄνομα αὐτῷ); see further Jer 50(27):34; 51(28):57; 31(38):35(36); *T. Ab.* A 8:3; 15:12; 16:2; *3 Bar.* 1:3; Aris. Ex. 185:2; *2 Bar.* 6:8; 7:1; 13:2, 4; Jdt 9:12; 3 Macc 2:2, 7; cf. Delling, *Paralipomena Jeremiae*, 36; Bogaert, *Apocalypse de Baruch*, 1:392–93.

36. So also Harris, *Rest of the Words of Baruch*, 62; Kraft and Purintun, *Paraleipomena Jeremiou*, 44–45; and Riaud, *Les Paralipomènes du Prophète Jérémie*, 157. For this reading, see Delling, *Paralipomena Jeremiae*, 38–39.

37. See also Schaller, "Paralipomena Jeremiou," 750–51.

38. Wolff, "Heilshoffnung," 157.

39. See Herzer, *Paralipomena Jeremiae*, 50 n. 72.

40. So Delling, *Paralipomena Jeremiae*, 39. See further on this Herzer, *Paralipomena Jeremiae*, 153–54.

41. See *b. Roš Haš.* 32b.

42. Herzer, "Direction in Difficult Times," 27–28. It does not appear in the Septuagint.

43. LSJ, 8 s.v. I. See, e.g., Philo, *Sacr.* 57, 60, 66; *Det.* 124, 158; see also Josephus, *Ag. Ap.* 2.167.

44. Delling, *Paralipomena Jeremiae*, 37; Schaller, "Paralipomena Jeremiou," 750. Justin, *1 Apol.* 14:2, uses the attribute ἀγέννητος for God but can switch in *1 Apol.* 25:2 to ἀγένητος (see Justin, *Dial.* 5:1). As a Christian example, this sheds some light on the linguistic problem.

45. See also Schaller, "Paralipomena Jeremiou," 750. Delling mentions a sentence ascribed to Thales of Miletus in which God is called ἀγέννητος (*Paralipomena Jeremiae*, 37).

46. See Justin, *1 Apol.* 14:1–2; 25:2; 49:5; 53:2; *2 Apol.* 6:1; 12:4; 13:4; *Dial.* 5:1, 4–6; 114:3; 126:2; 127:1; Clement of Alexandria, *Ecl.* 25:3; *Exc.* 45:1; *Strom.* 2:5.4; 2:51.5; 5:82.3; 6:58.1; 6:165.5; see further the α-*privativum* forms in *Pre. Pet.* frg. 2.

pattern of usage emerges for ἀπερινόητος,⁴⁷ it *seems* plausible to suspect that the entire title is a later Christian addition.⁴⁸ However, Christian redactional work in *4 Baruch* is limited to the addition of the ending from 9:10 on.⁴⁹ The references from Philo, moreover, demonstrate the possibility of applying such α-*privativum* words to God in Greek-speaking Judaism.⁵⁰ Furthermore, Philo can describe God's creative work as γεννᾶν (*Alleg. Interp.* 3.219; see also Pss 2; 109 [LXX]; Prov 8:25; Josephus, *Ant.* 4.319).⁵¹ In consideration of this evidence, it is plausible to assume that *4 Baruch* speaks of God not only as "not being born," as often in the tradition, but makes that more precisely by speaking of his being "unbegotten." In the context of the references to creation in *4 Bar.* 9:6, it is most likely that these words originated from a Jewish author. The term ἀπερινόητος also fits well with the language of "the hiddenness of the creation."⁵² The statement concerning the hiddenness of the creation refers to the coming salvation that is to be revealed,⁵³ which is best understood in this context as a new creation or a new begetting.⁵⁴

The short description of Jeremiah's death, witnessed by Baruch and Abimelech, begins in 9:7. The phrase παραδιδόναι τὴν ψυχήν is an unusual expression for death (see esp. Isa 53:12; cf. *L.A.E.* 31:4; 42:8) but is particularly mean-

---

47. Philo, *Fug.* 141; *Mut.* 15; Clement of Alexandria, *Ecl.* 21; see Delling, *Paralipomena Jeremiae*, 38 (further references there).

48. Bogaert sees in the prayer a Christian or gnostic speculation concerning the ritual of Jewish liturgy (*Apocalypse de Baruch*, 1:212–13).

49. See the introduction above.

50. See also α-*privativum* words in *Apoc. Ab.* 17:8–10, a text probably written in Greek and not of Christian origin; see B. Philonenko-Sayar and Marc Philonenko, "Die Apokalypse Abrahams," *JSHRZ* 5.5 (1982): 417. For a different opinion concerning the original language, see R. Rubinkiewicz, "Apocalypse of Abraham (First to Second Century A.D.): A New Translation and Introduction," *OTP* 1:682.

51. See esp. Philo, *Mos.* 2.171 (see on that Leopold Cohn and Paul Wendland, *Philonis Alexandrini Opera quae supersunt* [7 vols.; Berlin: Typis et impensis Georgii Reimerii, 1896–1926], 4:240 apparatus on the text), see also the variants in the manuscripts V O K in this text (see the introduction in Cohn and Wendland, *Philonis Alexandrini Opera*, 4:i–xix).

52. See Isa 40:13 (LXX); Jer 23:18; Job 5:9; 9:10; 15:8; Ps 147(146):5; *Pr. Man.* 6; Philo, *Fug.* 165. See also Rom 11:34 and 1 Cor 2:16, where Paul quotes Isa 40:13. Thus the Christian language of God's incomprehensibility is to be understood in the light of the Old Testament.

53. Schaller's translation—"ehe die Dinge wurden [before things came into being]" ("Paralipomena Jeremiou," 750) with a "freien Wiedergabe des ταῦτα [free translation of ταῦτα]" (751)—attempts to smooth the content but does not fit the future perspective held to in the text, opened up by the events of the present.

54. The author's use here of ἀγέννητος and ἀπερινόητος thus represent a Hellenistic-Jewish version of the philosophical penchant for using alpha-privatives in discourse about God. Christian patristic writers also did the same, completely independent of *4 Baruch*. See n. 49 of the commentary on chapter 6.

ingful in the light of the resurrection hope repeatedly expressed since *4 Bar.* 5. The allusion to the vicarious death of the Suffering Servant of Isa 53:12 may be seen as intentional and raises new associations in the minds of readers about the priest and prophet Jeremiah. Presumably this perspective prompted the Christian redactor's development of the brief death report into a martyr story.

Baruch and Abimelech's lament expresses the people's feelings of abandonment: the priest who prays for the people lives no more (9:8). The lament draws in the entire people, who immediately join the lament (9:9). The rituals portrayed are those that Jeremiah and Baruch performed as Jerusalem was destroyed and the people were led into exile. The final comment concerning the bitter lament[55] is unusual, suggesting that the original conclusion has been lost and replaced by another of Christian origin. If, in the original Jewish text, Jeremiah died with the words of the prayer of 9:3–6, this would fit well with *4 Baruch*'s depiction of Jeremiah as the new Moses: just as Moses died before entering the promised land, so also Jeremiah dies, having led the people in the exodus from Babylon back to Jerusalem but before entering the "promised land" of *4 Baruch*'s eschatologically shaped hope: the heavenly Jerusalem. In contrast to Moses, however, who did not enter the promised land (Deut 34), Jeremiah goes on ahead. Jeremiah's death as the new Moses thus has eschatological significance for those who remain behind.[56]

---

55. See Judg 21:2; 2 Sam 13:36.

56. On the discussion on the death of Moses, see esp. *Midr. Petirat Moshe*. See J. Goldin, "The Death of Moses: An Exercise in Midrashic Transposition," in *Love and Death in the Ancient Near East* (ed. John H. Marks and Robert M. Good; Guilford: Four Quarters, 1987), 220, 240–41; S. E. Loewenstamm, "The Death of Moses," in *Studies on the Testament of Abraham* (ed. W. E. George; SBLSCS 6; Missoula, Mont.: Scholars Press, 1976), 192–208. Josephus bound together the two traditions of death and translation into heaven in an original way in *Ant*. 4.320–331; see James D. Tabor, "Returning to the Divinity Josephus's Portrayal of the Disappearances of Enoch, Elijah, and Moses," *JBL* 108 (1989): 225–38; Loewenstamm, "The Death of Moses," 197. See also *L.A.B.* 19:10–13: "And he [God] showed him the place from which the manna rained upon the people, even unto the paths of paradise … But neither angel nor man will know your tomb in which you are buried until I visit the world. And I will raise up you and your fathers … and you will come together and dwell in the immortal dwelling place that is not subject to time" (Nullus autem angelorum nec hominum scient sepulchrum tuum in quo incipies sepeliri, sed in eo requiesces donec visitem seculum. Et excitabo te et patres tuos…, et invenietis simul et inhabitabitis habitationem immortalem que non tenetur in tempore) (quoted from D. J. Harrington, "Pseudo-Philo (First Century A.D.): A New Translation and Introduction," *OTP* 2:327–28; Latin according to G. Kisch, *Pseudo-Philo's Liber Antiquitatum Biblicarum* [Publications in Medieval Studies 10; Notre Dame, Ind.: University of Notre Dame Press, 1949], 165; see further M. Wadsworth, "The Death of Moses and the Riddle of the End of Time in Pseudo-Philo," *JJS* 28 [1977]: 12–19).

The traditions concerning Jeremiah's death, which is not even mentioned in the biblical text, vary widely.[57] The tradition that he was stoned was widespread, but its secondary nature is demonstrated by its stylization of his death as that of a martyr. Older traditions concerning a natural death are found not only in *4 Baruch* but also in various other texts.[58] For example, *Cav. Tr.* 50:24ff. reports that Jeremiah died in Samaria twenty years after Jerusalem's fall and was buried in Jerusalem.[59] The Christian *Book of Adam* 130:31–32 and Jerome, *Comm. Isa.* 9.30.6 (see also *S. 'Olam Rab.* 26), both speak of Jeremiah's death in Egypt,[60] which is confirmed by and deduced from the report of his flight with the Jewish refugees in Jer 43:4–7. However, of greatest interest here is *2 Bar.* 85:3, in which Jeremiah's death is alluded to in Baruch's letter. Jeremiah's death is once again assumed to be in exile.[61]

The Christian Ending of *4 Baruch* (9:10–32)

The Christian conclusion neatly follows the ending of *4 Baruch* in 9:9 by speaking of the beginning of Jeremiah's burial ceremony (9:10). An unnamed voice prevents the burial by announcing that Jeremiah's soul will return to his body (9:11), which happens three days later (9:12). The raised Jeremiah then begins to praise God and Jesus Christ (9:13), praise that ends in an apocalyptic vision (9:14–18). The people are enraged by the vision (9:19) and decide to kill Jeremiah, making explicit reference to the death of Isaiah, who was condemned for uttering similar statements (9:20–21).[62] In the face of this threat, Jeremiah commands Baruch and Abimelech to bring him a stone, which takes on the form of Jeremiah and thus rescues him temporarily by receiving the brunt of the stoning (9:24–27). During this time, Jeremiah communicates "all the secrets he had seen" to Baruch and Abimelech (9:28). Eventually, however, the people become aware of their mistake and turn their rage on the "true" Jeremiah (9:30–

---

57. See Wolff, *Jeremia im Frühjudentum und Urchristentum*, 89–95. In the *Jeremiah Apocryphon* Jeremiah's death is probably intentionally left out; Harris, "Introduction I," in Mingana and Harris, "Jeremiah Apocryphon," 130; Wolff, *Jeremia im Frühjudentum und Urchristentum*, 91 n. 1.
58. Wolff, *Jeremia im Frühjudentum und Urchristentum*, 93. Many church fathers assume Jeremiah's natural death (92).
59. Wolff, *Jeremia im Frühjudentum und Urchristentum*, 60.
60. Theodor Schermann, *Propheten- und Apostellegenden nebst Jüngerkatalogen des Dorotheus und verwandte Texte* (TUGAL 31.3; Leipzig: Hinrichs, 1907), 124; Wolff, *Jeremia im Frühjudentum und Urchristentum*, 91–92.
61. Wolff, *Jeremia im Frühjudentum und Urchristentum*, 93.
62. That the manner of Jeremiah's death is to be different from Isaiah's demonstrates that traditions concerning Isaiah's death were known in the circles of the Christian redaction of *4 Baruch*.

31). In the end, the stone becomes Jeremiah's gravestone, inscribed "This is the stone, the ally[63] of Jeremiah" (9:32).

The most significant evidence that 9:10–32 is Christian is the mention of the name Christ in 9:13, but other clues point in the same direction. For example, Jeremiah's resuscitation after three days recalls the resurrection of Jesus Christ after three days.[64] In addition, the phrase μὴ κηδεύετε τὸν ἔτι ζῶντα (9:11) alludes to Luke 24:5. Certainly the concern in *4 Bar.* 9:10–18 is not the resuscitation of a dead man but the temporary separation of body and soul in order that heavenly things might be seen (9:22–23).[65] Finally, the title υἱὸς θεοῦ (9:13; see 9:20) for Jesus, his promised return (9:14), and the reference to the twelve apostles who will take the gospel to the nations (9:18) all speak for the Christian origin of the conclusion.

The subsequent story of Jeremiah's martyrdom (9:21–32), on the other hand, does not have an explicitly Christian message. Therefore, the conclusion to *4 Baruch* consists of two distinct parts: the introduction, praise, and vision of Jeremiah; and the report of his martyrdom. One may suspect that the Christian redaction of the second part includes further Jewish material.

JEREMIAH'S PRAISE AND VISION

Although Jeremiah begins by calling people to praise God, the true object of his praise and vision is the "Son of God ... Jesus Christ" (9:13). The first attribute of Christ listed, that he is the one "who awakens" (ἐξυπνίζω, ptc. pres. act.), makes Christ rather than God the agent of raising the dead and is thus unusual. Viewed tradition-critically, this hints at the environment of the Johannine literature, since Christ is also the subject of the raising of the dead there.[66] In addition, ἐξυπνίζω appears in the New Testament only in John 11:11 for Jesus' raising of Lazarus.[67] Further, the expression "light of all ages" uses a motif from John 8:12; 9:5; 12:46 (see John 1:9)—Christ as φῶς τοῦ κόσμου—though *4 Baruch* universalizes this expression by using αἰών. The

---

63. ὁ βοηθός is an apposition.
64. See Mark 8:31; 9:31; 10:34 par.; see 1 Cor 15:4; Acts 10:40. Schaller refers to *T. Job* 53:7a ("Paralipomena Jeremiou," 752).
65. Viewed differently by Schaller, referring to Ezek 37:10 ("Paralipomena Jeremiou," 752); however, *4 Baruch* reflects the idea of a journey of the soul to heaven; see 2 Cor 12:2–4. On this topic, see Gerhard Lohfink, *Die Himmelfahrt Jesu: Untersuchungen zu den Himmelfahrts- und Erhöhungstexten bei Lukas* (Munich: Kösel, 1971), 32–34, 51–53.
66. See John 2:19(21); 6:39, 40, 44, 54; 10:18; 11:25; 12:1, 17. Differing views are found in, e.g., Rom 4:17; 8:11; 1 Cor 6:14; 15:22; 2 Cor 1:9; 4:14.
67. Schaller refers to Christian reworking of Isa 26:19; 29:8; Job 14:12; and *T. Jud.* 25:4 ("Paralipomena Jeremiou," 752).

christological reference of φῶς thus stands in contrast to earlier uses of light language in *4 Baruch* (5:34; 6:9).[68]

Still other links with the Johannine literature can be observed. The term ἄσβεστος λύχνος reminds one of John 5:35, since the Gospel text uses λύχνος to refer to a real person.[69] In Rev 21:23, moreover, Christ is the λύχνος who lights the eschatological city. In the Christian closing of *4 Baruch*, therefore, a terminological continuation of this eschatological conception can be observed. Similar considerations apply to the last title for Christ, ζωὴ τῆς πίστεως.[70]

In contrast to the titles applied to Christ in 9:13, not all the motifs in Jeremiah's vision (9:14–18) derive from the Johannine tradition. The number 477, for example, is found neither in the Old Testament and Jewish literature nor in the New Testament. Thus, no interpretation of this number is free from speculation.[71] Yet another non-Johannine motif is the expectation of the coming of Christ (9:14),[72] which is determined apocalyptically.[73]

Harris understands the phrase ἐρχόμενον εἰς τὸν κόσμον in 9:18 as echo of John 1:9.[74] That is probable. However, John 1:9 refers to the incarnation of Christ, whereas *4 Bar.* 9:18 interprets it eschatologically. Thus, it is not obvious which coming of Christ is in view here: the first, earthly coming or the second for judgment. From Jeremiah's fictitious standpoint, the first is more likely to be in view, and the reference to John 1:9 also points in this direction. On the other hand, the eschatological dimension of Jeremiah's vision points to the final coming of the glorified Christ. A solution to this apparent dilemma is found

---

68. See Herzer, *Paralipomena Jeremiae*, 109–10 n. 351.

69. Philonenko sees a parallel to the Paris magical papyrus, without assessing this further ("Simples Observations," 172–73). On that, see Herzer, "Antwort," 37–38. Schaller picks up on this point and sees a reference to the seven-armed lamp of the temple ("Paralipomena Jeremiou," 752). This text does not, however, speak for the gnostic origin of the text, since 9:13 is part of the Christian conclusion and not the Jewish text.

70. See John 3:15–16, 36; 5:24; 6:40, 47, 68; 11:25; esp. John 20:31: "and that through believing you may have life in his name" (NRSV).

71. See the text of MSS A and B. The witnesses differ at this point. Codex Barberini, the Slavic versions T1 (see Wolff, *Jeremia im Frühjudentum und Urchristentum*, 235), and P have 377 years, the Slavic version T2 (ibid., 223) reads 677 years, S reads 387 times (ibid.), N 307 times (ibid.), the Ethiopic translation offers 333, 330, or 303 weeks (see on that König, "Rest der Worte Baruchs," 336 n. 1), and, finally, arm reads 375 years; see Issaverdens, *Uncanonical Writings of the Old Testament*, 203. Harris, *Rest of the Words of Baruch*, 17, refers to Josephus, *J.W.* 6.439 concerning the number 477 (477 years and six months after David the temple had been destroyed by the Babylonians), but this is not convincing, for it would suppose a direct reference to Josephus; see Herzer, *Paralipomena Jeremiae*, 161–62 n. 646. Paul Rießler (*Altjüdisches Schrifttum außerhalb der Bibel* [Freiburg: Kerle, 1975], 918) conjectures 365 (the number of days in a year) but offers no reason.

72. 1 Thess 4:15–16; Matt 24:30–31.

73. Dan 9:24–26; 12:11–12; Rev 20:2–6; *1 En.* 21:6; 90:5; 93:1–10; 91:11–17; *4 Ezra* 7:28; *2 Bar.* 28:2; *Mart. Ascen. Isa.* 4:14.

in the background of John's Gospel, which makes clear the eschatological significance of Christ's incarnation: "Very truly, I tell you, anyone who hears my word and believes him who sent me has eternal life, and does not come under judgment, but has passed from death to life. Very truly, I tell you, the hour is coming, and is now here, when the dead will hear the voice of the Son of God, and those who hear will live" (John 5:24–25 NRSV; see also John 16:11). The judgment motif plays a similar role in *4 Bar.* 9 (cf. 9:15–16): Christ who has come into the world will execute judgment (9:18).

According to 9:18, the place of Christ's coming will be the Mount of Olives. The Christian tradition (Acts 1:12) makes this the place of Christ's ascension,[75] so it gains importance for his return. The location of his return on the Mount of Olives is a christological interpretation of Zech 14:4,[76] which says of the Day of the Lord: "On that day his feet shall stand on the Mount of Olives, which lies before Jerusalem on the east; and the Mount of Olives shall be split in two from east to west by a very wide valley; so that one half of the Mount shall withdraw northward, and the other half southward" (NRSV). Thus, in the Christian conclusion to *4 Baruch*, the first and second comings of Christ are seen as elements of a single event that will culminate in judgment. The first coming of Christ has decisive significance for his eschatological coming, and the result of the judgment (9:15) is foreshadowed by his first coming. A similar connection is made in *Martyrdom and Ascension of Isaiah:* Isaiah sees the coming of Christ, whereby the descent of Christ from paradise begins (chs. 10–11); Christ's earthly activity (11:1–21) is then followed by his return into the seventh heaven to the right hand of God.

The "tree of life, planted in the middle of paradise" (9:14) as a picture of Christ is known from the vision of the new Jerusalem in Rev 22:2, 14, 19 (see also 2:7). Again, Old Testament and Jewish references can be found here.[77] In what follows, however, the links to the Johannine tradition are less clear. The motif of the sprouting trees (9:14), for example, may be compared to *1 En.* 26:1: "And from there I went into the center of the earth and saw a blessed place, shaded with branches which live and bloom from a tree that was cut."[78] In

---

74. Harris, *Rest of the Words of Baruch*, 26.
75. See further Schaller, "Paralipomena Jeremiou," 754.
76. See Bogaert, *Apocalypse de Baruch*, 1:214; Riaud, "Jérémie, martyr chrétien," 234. On the traditional significance of the Mount of Olives, see J. B. Curtis, "An Investigation of the Mount of Olives in the Judaeo-Chistian Tradition," *HUCA* 28 (1957): 137–80.
77. Gen 2:9; Prov 11:30; 13:12; 15:4; *1 En.* 24:8; 25:4–5; *4 Ezra* 8:52; *T. Levi* 18:11. See Delling, *Paralipomena Jeremiae*, 34; Riaud, "Jérémie, martyr chrétien," 234.
78. Quoted from Isaac, "1 Enoch," *OTP* 1:26. See also *Pss. Sol.* 14:3–4: "The Lord's devout shall live by it forever; the Lord's paradise [παράδεισος], the trees of life, are his devout ones. Their

spite of this shared motif, the intention in *4 Bar.* 9:14 is different. The trees that receive their fruitfulness from the tree of life and bring a crop leading to eternal life (9:14)[79] are contrasted with those that boast of their own fruitfulness and are given over by the "firmly rooted tree," the tree of life,[80] to judgment.[81] One may also compare the picture of the "crimson" that becomes "as white wool" (9:15) to Isa 1:18, which likewise uses the opposites crimson and white.[82] Finally, *4 Bar.* 9:17 offers a christological interpretation of Isa 42:4: "He will not grow faint or be crushed until he has established justice in the earth; and the coastlands wait for his teaching" (NRSV).[83] The election of the twelve apostles in *4 Baruch* is thus understood as one for Gentile mission.[84]

In summary, the praise and vision of Jeremiah combines Johannine motifs and christological interpretations of Old Testament ideas to form an apocalyptic vision concerning Christ's return. The literary placement of the vision before Jeremiah's martyrdom has parallels in Stephen's vision before his martyrdom (Acts 7:55) and that of Isaiah in *Mart. Ascen. Isa.* 5:7. The last verse of the vision (*4 Bar.* 9:18) underlines the links to the Johannine tradition with overtones of John 12:41; 17:5, 24 and 6:23.

---

planting is firmly rooted forever; they shall not be uprooted as long as the heavens shall last" (quoted from Wright, "Psalms of Solomon," *OTP* 2:663).

79. The words καὶ ὁ καρπὸς αὐτῶν μετὰ τῶν ἀγγέλων μενεῖ (Harris) are added according to the Ethiopic text and have an explanatory function; see Herzer, *Paralipomena Jeremiae*, 19. The Slavic translations do not have them either; see Wolff, *Jeremia im Frühjudentum und Urchristentum*, 223 (on N, T2 und S) and 235 (on T1).

80. Riaud interprets the "firmly rooted tree" as the Roman emperor ("Jérémie, martyr chrétien," 235). This view is connected with his dating of the Christian ending to the time of the persecutions of 155 C.E. This does not, however, fit with the vision of the returning Christ's triumph. On the term "tree of life," see Schaller, "Paralipomena Jeremiou," 753.

81. On the wording of *4 Bar.* 9:15, see Herzer, *Paralipomena Jeremiae*, 19. Eth alters the judgment word to fit the positive direction of 9:14. Harris considers the judgment in 9:15 to be concerned with "the extreme section of the Jews," so with those who do not follow the church's "Eirenicon" to the synagogue (*Rest of the Words of Baruch*, 46).

82. See Herzer, *Paralipomena Jeremiae*, 164. On the motif, see *Apocr. Ezek.* frg. 2 (= *1 Clem.* 8:3): "If your sins reach from earth to heaven, and if they are redder than scarlet or blacker than sackcloth, and you turn back to me with a whole heart and say, 'Father,' I will heed you as a holy people" (quoted from J. R. Mueller and S. R. Robinson, "Apocryphon of Ezekiel [First Century B.C.—First Century A.D.]: A New Translation and Introduction," *OTP* 1:494). Fresh water that becomes salty (*4 Bar.* 9:16) is rightly seen by Harris to be borrowed from *4 Ezra* 5:9, which speaks of salty water found in fresh (Harris, *Rest of the Words of Baruch*, 20; see also Stone, *Ezra*, 112–13).

83. Riaud thinks of Ps 72:10 (*Les Paralipomènes du Prophète Jérémie*, 201); this is unlikely, since *4 Bar.* 9:17 says "bearing fruit by the word of the mouth of his Christ," and this links well with Isa 42:4: "the coastlands wait for his teaching." It was shown that the judgment of 9:15 refers to the Gentiles not the Jews as early as Harris, *Rest of the Words of Baruch*, 45–46.

84. See Mark 3:14; par. Luke 6:13; Matt 10:2; also *Mart. Ascen. Isa.* 3:17; 4:3 ("Planting of the twelve apostles"); *Pre. Pet.* frg. 3b.

The Stoning of Jeremiah

The Christian version of Jeremiah's death differs significantly from the Jewish one in 9:7–9. For example, 9:19–21 narrates the reason for Jeremiah's death, recounts the decision to kill him, and describes the manner of his execution. As previously noted, 9:20 clearly refers to the martyrdom of Isaiah as reported in *Martyrdom and Ascension of Isaiah*. The accusation made against Isaiah is of specific interest: "Moses said, 'There is no man who can see the Lord and live.' But Isaiah has said, 'I have seen the Lord, and behold I am alive.'... And he [Balkira] brought many accusations against Isaiah and the prophets before Manasse" (3:9–10; see further 3:9–12; 5:1–14).[85] Likewise, the chief accusation in *4 Bar.* 9:20 is Jeremiah's claim to have seen God,[86] which is expanded by a Christian hand into a reference to the Son of God. This expansion could have been motivated by *Mart. Ascen. Isa.* 3:13–20, which also speaks of the "arrival of the beloved," namely, Jesus Christ[87] (3:13).[88] The mention of the twelve apostles (*4 Bar.* 9:18) also has its parallel in *Mart. Ascen. Isa.* (3:17; 11:22).[89] Finally, *Mart. Ascen. Isa.* 4:13 explicitly says that Isaiah saw the crucified one (cf. 11:19–20). The link between seeing God or the Christ and the execution of the prophet is in both texts the idea of a Christian redactor. Thus, the author of *4 Baruch* assumes that his readers know how Isaiah died,[90] which from a tradition-critical perspective implies a Jewish-influenced Christian background.

---

85. Quoted from Michael A. Knibb, "Martyrdom and Ascension of Isaiah (Second Century B.C.–Fourth Century A.D.): A New Translation and Introduction," *OTP* 2:160. Cf. Isa 6:5. On the problem of the production and writing of this document, see Knibb, "Martyrdom and Ascension of Isaiah," 2:143, 147–49; Emil Schürer, *The History of the Jewish People in the Age of Jesus Christ (175 B.C.–A.D. 135): A New English Version* (rev. and ed. Fergus Millar and Geza Vermes; 3 vols. in 4; Edinburgh: Clark, 1973), 3.1:335–41; Herzer, *Paralipomena Jeremiae*, 165–66 n. 663.

86. See *b. Yeb* 49b; Hans-Werner Surkau, *Martyrien in jüdischer und frühchristlicher Zeit* (FRLANT NS 36; Göttingen: Vandenhoeck & Ruprecht, 1938), 32; André Caquot, "Bref Commentaire du 'Martyre d'Isaie,'" *Sem* 23 (1979): 83.

87. A reference to *4 Bar.* 3:8 is unlikely; see Herzer, *Paralipomena Jeremiae*, 166 n. 668.

88. *Mart. Ascen. Isa.* 3:13–20 is part of the Christian redaction; see Eissfeldt, *Introduction*, 610; R. G. Hall, "The Ascension of Iesajah: Community, Situation, Date and Place in Early Christianity," *JBL* 109 (1990): 290–92; Knibb, "Martyrdom and Ascension of Isaiah," 2:147.

89. See Caquot, "Bref Commentaire," 84–85; Knibb, "Martyrdom and Ascension of Isaiah," 2:149.

90. According to *Mart. Ascen. Isa.* 5:1–16 (see 11:41), Isaiah is sawed in two; see *Liv. Pro.* 1:1; *b. Yeb* 49b; *y. Sanh.* 10:28c; *b. Sanh.* 103b; *Pesiq. Rab.* 14; Heb 11:37; *Cav. Tr.* 40:4; see H. A. Fischel, "Martyr and Prophet: A Study in Jewish Literature," *JQR* NS 37 (1946/47): 276–77; Hans Joachim Schoeps, "Die jüdischen Prophetenmorde," in *Aus frühchristlicher Zeit* (ed. Hans Joachim Schoeps; Tübingen: Mohr Siebeck, 1950), 128–29. Josephus, *Ant.* 10.38, seems not yet to know these legends. On the tradition in general, see Eli Yassif, "Traces of Folk Traditions of the Second Temple Period in Rabbinic Literature," *JJS* 39 (1988): 216–20.

It is further apparent that the author not only adopted the *reason* for the killing of Jeremiah from *Mart. Ascen. Isa.* 3:9 but also knew a tradition about the *manner* of Jeremiah's death, namely, by stoning. Such a tradition no doubt lies behind similar accounts such as *Liv. Pro.* 2:1 or Heb 11:37.[91] Concerning the location of Jeremiah's death, *Liv. Pro.* 2 offers the older tradition, suggesting Egypt as the place of his death. The author of *4 Baruch,* on the other hand, locates the events in Jerusalem for obvious narrative reasons.

Whereas 9:20–21 develops known traditions surrounding the deaths of Jeremiah and Isaiah, 9:22–32 is more legendary in style. The people's anger is first expressed against a stone that takes on Jeremiah's form,[92] giving Jeremiah a chance to tell Baruch and Abimelech his secrets (see *Mart. Ascen. Isa.* 5:7).[93] When the stone explains to the "foolish" people that the true Jeremiah still stands among them, they rush to finish their deadly work.[94] In contrast to *4 Bar.* 1:1–9:9, the Christian conclusion portrays the Jews quite negatively.[95] The association with Matt 23:37 is presumably intentional: "Jerusalem, Jerusalem, the city that kills the prophets and stones those who are sent to it! How often have I desired to gather your children together as a hen gathers her brood under her wings, and you were not willing" (NRSV). An originally Jewish accusation concerning the killing of prophets is here underlined from a Christian perspective.[96]

---

91. See Harris, *Rest of the Words of Baruch,* 23–24; Delling, *Paralipomena Jeremiae,* 15; Wolff, *Jeremia im Frühjudentum und Urchristentum,* 60, 95; Knibb, "Martyrdom and Ascension of Isaiah," 2:149; David S. Russell, *The Old Testament Pseudepigrapha: Patriarchs and Prophets in Early Judaism* (London: SCM, 1987), 116; and Herzer, *Paralipomena Jeremiae,* 167 n. 673.

92. On the protective miracle motif, see Adolf Schlatter, *Der Märtyrer in den Anfängen der Kirche* (Gütersloh: Bertelsmann, 1915), 35–37: "Dem kirchlichen Märtyrerbericht war das Schutzwunder von Anfang an eigen [From the beginning, the ecclesiastical martyr account was characterized by the motif of the protecting miracle]" (36).

93. Ina Willi-Plein, "Das Geheimnis der Apokalyptik," *VT* 27 (1977): 78–80.

94. Harris, *Rest of the Words of Baruch,* 20, rightly sees in the motif of the speaking stone *4 Baruch*'s dependence on *4 Ezra* 5:5 (see also 4:33): "Blood shall drip from wood, and the stone shall utter his voice; the people shall be troubled" (quoted from Metzger, "Fourth Book of Ezra," *OTP* 1:532). Bogaert, *Apocalypse de Baruch,* 1:214, refers to Hab 2:11 (see also Luke 19:40). Schaller, "Paralipomena Jeremiou," 756, further names *Sib. Or.* 3:804. See further *Liv. Pro.* 10:8–11.

95. Riaud sees in the conclusion open anti-Judaism ("Jérémie, martyr chrétien," 235); see Schoeps, "Die jüdischen Prophetenmorde," 143: "die Krone des 'Schriftbeweises' contra Judaeos [the crown of the scriptural proofs against the Jews]." On that, see Herzer, *Paralipomena Jeremiae,* 168–69 n. 683.

96. According to Odil Hans Steck, Neh 9:26 is the oldest reference for the Deuteronomistic tradition of the violent end of the prophets (*Israel und das gewaltsame Geschick der Propheten: Untersuchungen zur Überlieferung des deuteronomistischen Geschichtsbildes im Alten Testament, Spätjudentum und Urchristentum* [WMANT 23; Neukirchen-Vluyn: Neukirchner Verlag, 1967], 77–79). The tradition of Jeremiah's stoning developed presumably from Jer 43:8–10. See Richard

The inscription on Jeremiah's grave refers, surprisingly, not to Jeremiah and his deeds but to the stone itself and its miraculous function: "This is the stone, the ally of Jeremiah." In view of this clear etiological concern, Bogaert suspects that our author has adopted the etiological legend from 1 Sam 7:12 and inscriptions found in Palestine.[97] However, these references speak of God as the helper, not the stone, as in *4 Baruch*.[98] The origins of the etiology are thus not clear, though it refers to a monument that gives readers reason to think once again about the story of Jeremiah and the people.

Bernheimer, "Vitae Prophetarum," *JAOS* 55 (1935): 202; Steck, *Israel*, 249 n. 7; and Wolff, *Jeremia im Frühjudentum und Urchristentum*, 89.

97. Bogaert, *Apocalypse de Baruch*, 1:199–200; see Schaller, "Paralipomena Jeremiou," 756.

98. See Schaller, "Paralipomena Jeremiou," 756. See also the inscription from Caesarea (B. Lifshitz, "Inscriptions de Césarée en Palestine," *RB* 72 [1965]: 99): Εἷς θεὸς βοηθῶν Μαρίνῳ, cf. also 1 Sam 7:12 (LXX): καὶ ἐκάλεσεν τὸ ὄνομα αὐτοῦ Αβενεζερ λίθος τοῦ βοηθοῦ καὶ εἶπεν ἕως ἐνταῦτα ἐβοήθησεν ἡμῖν Κύριος.

SELECT BIBLIOGRAPHY

BIBLIOGRAPHIES

Denis, Albert-Marie. "Les Paralipomènes de Jérémie." Pages 70–75 in *Introduction aux Pseudépigraphes Grecs d'Ancien Testament*. Edited by Albert-Marie Denis. VTSup 1. Leiden: Brill, 1970.

Lehnhardt, Andreas. "Bibliographie zu den jüdischen Schriften aus hellenistisch-römischer Zeit." *JSHRZ* 6.2 (1999): 159–62.

Schaller, Berndt. "Paralipomena Jeremiou." *JSHRZ* 1.8 (1998): 659–777.

———. "Paralipomena Jeremiou: Annotated Bibliography in Historical Order." *JSP* 22 (2000): 91–118.

TEXTS AND TRANSLATIONS OF *4 BARUCH*

Ceriani, Antonio Maria. *Paralipomena Jeremiae Prophetae quae in Aethiopica Versione dicuntur Reliqua Verborum Baruchi*. Monumenta Sacra et Profana ex Codicibus praesertim Bibliothecae Ambrosianae. 5.1. Milan: Typis et impensis Bibliothecae Ambrosianae, 1868.

Dillmann, August. *Reliqua Verborum Baruchi, Chrestomathia Aethiopica*. Leipzig: Weigel, 1866.

Gebhardt, Oscar von. *Paralipomena Jeremiae: Abschrift aus dem Codex Petropolitanus XCVI fol. 78b–89: Aus seinem Nachlass XII/2*. Staatsbibliothek Preußischer Kulturbesitz zu Berlin, n.d.

Harris, J. Rendel. *The Rest of the Words of Baruch: A Christian Apocalypse of the Year 136 A.D: The Text Revised with an Introduction*. London: Clay, 1889.

Issaverdens, Jacques. Pages 252–304 in *The Uncanonical Writings of the Old Testament, Found in the Armenian MSS: Of the Library of St. Lazarus*. Venice: Armenian Monastery of St. Lazarus, 1901.

König, Eduard. "Der Rest der Worte Baruchs: Aus dem Aetiopischen übersetzt und mit Anmerkungen versehen." *Theologische Studien und Kritiken* 50 (1877): 318–38.

Kraft, Robert A., and Ann-Elizabeth Purintun. *Paraleipomena Jeremiou*. SBLTT 1, Pseudepigrapha Series 1. Missoula, Mont.: Society of Biblical Literature, 1972.

Prätorius, Franz. "Das Apokryphische Buch Baruch im Äthiopischen." *ZWT* 15 (1872): 230–47.

Riaud, Jean. "Paralipomènes de Jérémie." Pages 1733–63 in *La Bible: Écrits intertestamentaires*. Edited by A. Dupont-Sommer and M. Philonenko. Bibliothèque de la Pléiade 337. Paris: Gallimard, 1987.

———. *Les Paralipomènes du Prophète Jérémie: Présentation, texte original, traduction et commentaires*. Cahiers du Centre Interdisciplinaire de Recherches en Histoire, Lettres et Langues 14. Angers: Association Saint-Yves, 1994.

Rießler, Paul. Pages 903–19 in *Altjüdisches Schrifttum außerhalb der Bibel*. Freiburg: Kerle, 1975.

Robinson, Stephen E. "4 Baruch (First to Second Century A.D.): A New Translation and Introduction." *OTP* 2:413–25.

Thornhill, R. "The Paraleipomena of Jeremiah." *APOT*, 813–33.

Tichonravov, Nikolaj S. "Povoest o plenenii Jerusalima." Pages 273–97 in vol. 1 of *Pamjatniki otretschennoi russkoj literatury*. St. Petersburgh: 1863. Repr., Paris: Le Hague, 1979.

Turdéanu, Emile. "Les Paralipomènes de Jérémie en Slave." Pages 348–63 in *Apocryphes Slaves et Roumains de l'Ancien Testament*. Edited by Emile Turdéanu. SVTP 5. Leiden: Brill, 1981.

Vegas-Montaner, Luis. "Paralipomenos de Jeremias." Pages 353–83 in vol. 2 of *Apocrifos del Antiguo Testamento*. Edited by Alejandro Diez Macho et al. 2 vols. Madrid: Ed. Cristiandad, 1983.

Wolff, Christian. Pages 193–237 in *Jeremia im Frühjudentum und Urchristentum*. TUGAL 118. Berlin: Akademie, 1976.

Other Texts and Translations

Amélineau, Emile. *Contes et Romans de l'Égypte Chrétienne*. Vol. 2 of *Collections des Contes et Chançons populaires 13.14*. Paris: Leroux, 1888.

Beer, Georg, et al., eds. *Die Mischna: Text, Übersetzung und ausführliche Erklärung mit eingehenden geschichtlichen und sprachlichen Einleitungen*. 6 vols. Gießen: Töpelmann, 1912–91.

Bezold, Carl. *Die Schatzhöhle "ME'ARATH GAZZE": Eine Sammlung biblischer Geschichten aus dem sechsten Jahrhundert jemals Ephraem Syrus zugeschrieben: syrischer Text und arabische Version*. Amsterdam: Philo, 1981. Repr., 2 vols. Leipzig: Hinrichs, 1883–88.

Bogaert, Pierre-Maurice. *Apocalypse de Baruch : Introduction, Traduction du Syriaque et Commentaire*. 2 vols. Paris: Cerf, 1969.

Braude, William G. *The Midrash on Psalms: Translated from the Hebrew and Aramaic*. Yale Judaica Series 13. 2 vols. New Haven: Yale University Press, 1959.

Burchard, Christoph. "Joseph und Aseneth." *JSHRZ* 2.4 (1983): 577–735.

Charles, Robert Henry. *The Apocalypse of Baruch translated from the Syriac*. London: Black, 1896.

Charlesworth, James Hamilton, ed. *The Old Testament Pseudepigrapha*. 2 vols. London: Darton, Longman & Todd, 1983–85.

Cohn, Leopold, and Paul Wendland. *Philonis Alexandrini Opera quae supersunt*. 7 vols. Berlin: Reimerii, 1896–1926.

Correns, Dietrich, ed. *Seder 2 Moed, Traktat 9 Taanijot Fastentage: Text, Übersetzung und Erklärung nebst einem textkritischen Anhang.* Vol. 2 of *Die Mischna. Text, Übersetzung und ausführliche Erklärung.* Edited by Karl Heinrich Rengstorf and Siegfried Herrmann. Berlin: de Gruyter, 1989.

Denis, Albert-Marie. *Fragmenta Pseudepigraphorum quae supersunt Graeca.* PVTG 3. Leiden: Brill, 1970.

Dillmann, August. "Das christliche Adambuch des Morgenlandes." *Jahrbücher der biblischen Wissenschaft* 5 (1852–1853): 1–144.

Dimant, Devorah. Pages 91–260 in *Qumran Cave 4.XXI: Parabiblical Texts, Part 4: Pseudo-Prophetic Texts.* DJD 30. Oxford: Clarendon, 2001.

Diogenes Laertius. *Lives of Eminent Philosphers.* Translated by R. D. Hicks. LCL. 2 vols. Cambridge: Harvard University Press, 1966–70.

Doran, Robert. "Pseudo-Hecataeus (Second Century B. C.–First Century A.D.): A New Translation and Introduction." *OTP* 2:905–18.

Friedlander, G. *Pirkê de Rabbi Eliezer: The Chapters of Rabbi Eliezer the Great according to the Text of the Manuscript Belongig to Abraham Epstein of Vienna.* London, 1916.

García Martínez, Florentino, and Eibert J. C. Tigchelaar, eds. *The Dead See Scrolls Study Edition.* 2 vols. Leiden: Brill, 1997–98.

Goldschmidt, Lazarus. *Der Babylonische Talmud mit Einschluß der vollständigen Mishnah: Herausgegeben nach der ersten zensurfreien Bombergschen Ausgabe (Venedig 1520–1523) nebst Varianten der späteren von S. Lorja, Berlin J. Sirkes u.a. revidierten Münchner Talmudhandschrift möglichst sinn- und wortgetreu übersetzt und mit Erklärungen versehen.* Haag: Martinus Nijoff, 1933–35.

Gulkowitsch, Lazar. *Der kleine Talmudtraktat über die Samaritaner, übersetzt und erklärt.* Pages 48–56 in vol. 1.1.2 of *ΑΓΓΕΛΟΣ. Archiv für neutestamentliche Zeitgeschichte und Kulturkunde.* Edited by Johannes Leipoldt et al. 4 vols. Leipzig: Pfeiffer, 1925.

Gunneweg, Antonius H. J. "Der Brief des Jeremias." *JSHRZ* 3.2 (1975): 183–92.

Habicht, C. "2. Makkabäerbuch." *JSHRZ* 1.13 (1976): 167–285.

Hage, Wolfgang. "Die griechische Baruchapokalypse." *JSHRZ* 5.1 (1974): 15–44.

Harrington, D. J. "Pseudo-Philo (First Century A.D.): A New Translation and Introduction." *OTP* 2:297–377.

Henning, Max. trans. *Der Koran: Aus dem Arabischen.* Introduction by E. Werner und K. Rudolph. Text revision, notes, and indices by K. Rudolph. Leipzig, 1983.

Higger, Michael. *The Treatises Derek Erez: Masseket Derek Erez—Pirke Ben Azzai—Tosefta Derek Erez. Edited from manuscripts with an Introduction, Notes, Variants and Translation.* New York: Rabanan, 1935.

Holladay, Carl R. *Historians.* Vol. 1 of *Fragments from Hellenistic Jewish Authors.* SBLTT 20, Pseudepigrapha Series 10. Chico, Calif.: Scholars Press, 1983.

Irving, Thomas Ballantine. *The Qur'an: The First American Version, Translation and Commentary.* Brattleboro: Amana, 1985.

Isaac, E. "1 (Ethiopic Apocalypse of) Enoch (Second Century B.C.—First Century A.D.): A New Translation and Introduction." *OTP* 1:5–89.

Josephus, Flavius. *Flavii Iosephi Opera.* Edited by Benedikt Niese. 2nd ed. 7 vols. Berlin: Weidmann 1955.

———. *Works*. With an English Translation by Henry St. John Thackeray. LCL. 13 vols. Cambridge: Harvard University Press, 1997–98.
Kautzsch, Emil. *Die Apokryphen und Pseudepigraphen des Alten Testaments*. 2 vols. Hildesheim: Olms, 1962.
Kisch, G. *Pseudo-Philo's Liber Antiquitatum Biblicarum*. Publications in Medieval Studies 10. Notre Dame, Ind.: University of Notre Dame, 1949.
Klijn, Albertus Frederik Johannes. "2 (Syriac Apocalypse of) Baruch (early Second Century A.D.): A New Translation and Introduction." *OTP* 1:615–52.
Klijn, Albertus Frederik Johannes. "Die syrische Baruch-Apokalypse." *JSHRZ* 5.2 (1976): 107–84.
Klijn, Albertus Frederik Johannes. *Die Esra-Apokalypse*. Berlin: Akademie-Verlag, 1992.
Knibb, Michael A. "Martyrdom and Ascension of Isaiah (Second Century B.C.—Fourth Century A.D.): A New Translation and Introduction." *OTP* 2:143–76.
Krauß, S. "Sanhedrin (Hoher Rat)—Makkōt (Prügelstrafe)." Pages 4–5 in vol. 4 of *Die Mischna: Text, Übersetzung und ausführliche Erklärung mit eingehenden geschichtlichen und sprachlichen Einleitungen und textkritischen Anhängen*. Edited by Georg Beer and Oscar Holtzmann et al. Gießen: Töpelmann, 1933.
Kuhn, Karl Heinz. "A Coptic Jeremiah-Apocryphon." *Mus* 83 (1970): 95–135, 291–350.
Lehrman, S. M. *Exodus*. Vol. 3 of *Midrash Rabbah: Translated into English with Notes, Glossary and Indices*. Edited by H. Freedman, and M. Simon. 3rd ed. 10 vols. London: Soncino, 1983.
Lidzbarski, Marc. *Ginza: Der Schatz oder das große Buch der Mandäer*. Quellen der Religionsgeschichte 13. Göttingen: Vandenhoeck & Ruprecht, 1925.
———. *Mandäische Liturgien*. Hildesheim: Olms, 1962.
Lifshitz, B. "Inscriptions de Césarée en Palestine." *RB* 72 (1965): 98–107.
Mingana, Alphonse, and J. Rendel Harris. "A Jeremiah Apocryphon." Woodbrooke Studies I.2. *John Rylands Library Bulletin* 11 (1927): 125–233.
Mueller, J. R., and S. R. Robinson. "Apocryphon of Ezekiel (First Century B.C.—First Century A.D.): A New Translation and Introduction." *OTP* 1:486–95.
Nemoy, Leon, ed. *Pesikta Rabbati: Discourse for Feasts, Fasts and Special Sabbaths*. Translated by W. G. Braude. New Haven, 1968.
Neusner, Jacob. *The Mishnah. A New Translation*. New Haven: Yale University Press, 1988.
———. *The Talmud of the Land of Israel: A Preliminary Translation and Explanation*. Vol. 1: *Berakhot*. CSHJ. Chicago: University of Chicago Press, 1993.
———. *The Talmud of the Land of Israel: A Preliminary Translation and Explanation*. Vol. 14: *Yoma*. CSHJ. Chicago: University of Chicago Press, 1990.
———. *The Talmud of the Land of Israel: A Preliminary Translation and Explanation*. Vol. 16: *Rosh Hashanah*. CSHJ. Chicago: University of Chicago Press, 1988.
———. *The Talmud of the Land of Israel: A Preliminary Translation and Explanation*. Vol. 18: *Besah and Taanit*. CSHJ. Chicago: University of Chicago Press, 1987.
———. *The Talmud of the Land of Israel: A Preliminary Translation and Explanation*. Vol. 26: *Qiddushin*. CSHJ. Chicago: University of Chicago Press, 1984.
Oßwald, E. "Das Gebet Manasses." *JSHRZ* 4.1 (1974): 15–27.
Patrologia latina. Edited by J.-P. Migne. 217 vols. Paris: Migne, 1844–64.

Philo of Alexandria. Translated by F. H. Colson and G. H. Whitaker. LCL. 10 vols. Cambridge: Harvard University Press, 1929–39.

Philonenko-Sayar, B., and Marc Philonenko. "Die Apokalypse Abrahams." *JSHRZ* 5.5 (1982): 413–60.

Prijs, Leo. *Die Jeremia-Homilie Pesikta Rabbati Kapitel 26: Eine synagogale Homilie aus nachtalmudischer Zeit über den Propheten Jeremia und die Zerstörung des Tempels: Kritische Edition nebst Übersetzung und Kommentar*. Stuttgart: Kohlhammer, 1966.

Rabbinowitz, J. *Lamentations*. Vol. 7 of *Midrash Rabbah: Translated into English with Notes, Glossary and Indices*. Edited by H. Freedman and M. Simon. 3rd ed. 10 vols. London: Soncino, 1983.

―――. *Ta'anith: Translated into English with Notes, Glossary and Indices*. Vol. 9 of *The Babylonian Talmud*. Edited by Isidore Epstein. 35 vols. London: Soncino, 1935–52.

Rubinkiewicz, R. "Apocalypse of Abraham (First to Second Century A.D.): A New Translation and Introduction." *OTP* 1:681–705.

Saldarini, Antonio J. *The Fathers according to Rabbi Nathan (Aboth de Rabbi Nathan Version B): A Translation and Commentary*. SJLA 11. Leiden: Brill, 1975.

Schaller, Berndt. "Das Testament Hiobs." *JSHRZ* 3.3 (1979): 301–87.

Schenke, Hans Martin. "Das Evangelium nach Philippus: Ein Evangelium aus dem Funde von Nag-Hamadi." Pages 31–65 in *Koptisch-Gnostische Schriften aus den Papyrus-Codices von Nag-Hamadi*. Edited by Johannes Leipoldt and Hans Martin Schenke. Theologische Forschung 20. Hamburg-Bergstedt: Reich, 1960.

Schneemelcher, Wilhelm, ed. *New Testament Apocrypha*. Translated by R. Mcl. Wilson. 2 vols. Louisville: Westminster John Knox, 1991–92.

Septuaginta: Vetus Testamentum Graecum auctoritate Academiae Litterarum Gottingensis editum. Edited by Joseph Ziegler et al. Göttingen: Vandenhoeck & Ruprecht, 1931–.

Slotki, Israel W. *Sukkah: Translated into English with Notes, Glossary and Indices*. Vol. 8 of *The Babylonian Talmud*. Edited by Isidore Epstein. 35 vols. London: Soncino, 1935–52.

Spittler, R. P. "Testament of Job (First Century B.C.—First Century A.D.): A New Translation and Introduction." *OTP* 1:829–68.

Torrey, Charles Cutler. *The Lives of the Prophets: Greek Text and Translation*. JBLMS 1. Philadelphia: Society of Biblical Literature, 1946.

Turdéanu, E. *Apocryphes Slaves et Roumains de l'Ancien Testament*. SVTP 5. Leiden: Brill, 1981.

Violet, Bruno. *Die Apokalypsen des Esra und des Baruch in deutscher Gestalt*. GCS 32. Leipzig: Hinrichs, 1924.

Walter, Nikolaus. "Fragmente jüdisch-hellenistischer Historiker," *JSHRZ* 1.2 (1976): 89–163.

Wright, R. B. "Psalms of Solomon (First Century B.C.): A New Translation and Introduction." *OTP* 2:639–70.

Monographs and Articles on 4 Baruch

Baars, Willem. Review of G. Delling, *Jüdische Lehre und Frömmigkeit in den Paralipomena Jeremiae*. *VT* 17 (1967): 487–88.

Bogaert, Pierre-Maurice. Review of G. Delling, *Jüdische Lehre und Frömmigkeit in den Paralipomena Jeremiae*. *RB* 78 (1968): 345–46.

Coquin, René-Georges. "Quelle était la langue originelle du pseudépigraphe conservé en Copte sous le titre de *Paralipomènes de Jérémie* et en Arabe sous le titre *Captivité des fils d'Israel à Babylone*?" *Apocrypha* 6 (1995): 79–82.

Delling, Gerhard. *Jüdische Lehre und Frömmigkeit in den Paralipomena Jeremiae*. BZAW 100. Berlin: Töpelmann, 1967.

Denis, Albert-Marie. "Les Paralipomènes de Jérémie." Pages 70–75 in *Introduction aux Pseudépigraphes Grecs d'Ancien Testament*. Edited by Albert-Marie Denis. VTSup 1. Leiden: Brill, 1970.

Doran, Robert. "The Rest of the Words of Jeremiah." Pages 294–96 in *Early Judaism and Its Modern Interpreters*. Edited by Robert A. Kraft and George W. E. Nickelsburg. Philadelphia: Fortress, 1986.

Heininger, Bernhard. "Totenerweckung oder Weckruf (ParJer 7,12–20)? Gnostische Spurensuche in den Paralipomena Jeremiae." Pages 79–112 in *Studien zum Neuen Testament und seiner Umwelt* A 23. Edited by Albert Fuchs. Linz, 1998.

Herzer, Jens. "Alttestamentliche Traditionen in den Paralipomena Jeremiae als Beispiel für den Umgang frühjüdischer Schriftsteller mit 'Heiliger Schrift.'" Pages 114–32 in *Schriftauslegung im antiken Judentum und im Urchristentum*. Edited by M. Hengel and H. Löhr. WUNT 73. Tübingen: Mohr Siebeck, 1994.

———. "Direction in Difficult Times: How God Is Understood in the Paraleipomena Jeremiou." *JSP* 22 (2000): 9–30.

———. "Die Paralipomena Jeremiae—Eine christlich-gnostische Schrift? Eine Antwort an Marc Philonenko." *JSJ* 30 (1999): 25–39.

———. *Die Paralipomena Jeremiae: Studien zu Tradition und Redaktion einer Haggadah des frühen Judentums*. TSAJ 43. Tübingen: Mohr Siebeck, 1994.

Jonge, Marinus de. "Remarks in the Margin of the Paper 'The Figure of Jeremiah in the Paralipomena Jeremiae.'" *JSP* 22 (2000): 45–49.

Kohler, Kaufmann. "The Pre-Talmudic Haggada. B—The Second Baruch or Rather the Jeremiah Apocalypse." *JQR* 5 (1893): 407–19.

Licht, Jacob. ספר מעשי ירמיהו מן הספרים התיצונים (*Sefer ma'ase yirmiyahu–Paralipomena Jeremiae*). Annual of Bar-Ilan University, Studies in Judaica and Humanities 1. Jerusalem: Kiryath Sepher, 1963: xxi–xxii, 66–80.

Mallau, Hans Harald. "Baruch, Baruchschriften: Paralipomena Jeremiae." *TRE* 5:269–76.

Meyer, Rudolph. "Paralipomena Jeremiae." *RGG*[3] 5:102–3.

Nickelsburg, George W. E. "Narrative Traditions in the Paralipomena of Jeremiah and 2 Baruch." *CBQ* 35 (1973): 60–68.

Philonenko, Marc. "Les Paralipomènes de Jérémie et la Traduction de Symmaque." *RHPR* 64 (1984): 143–45.

———. "Simples Observations sur les Paralipomènes de Jérémie." *RHPR* 76 (1996): 157–77.

Riaud, Jean. "Abimélech, Personnage-Clé des Paralipomena Jeremiae?" *Dialoques d'histoire ancienne* 7 (1981): 163–78.

———. "La figure de Jérémie dans les Paralipomena Jeremiae." Pages 373–85 in *Mélanges bibliques et orientaux en l'honneur de M. Henri Cazelles.* Edited by André Caquot. AOAT 212. Kevelaer: Butzon & Bercker, 1981.

———. "The Figure of Jeremiah in the *Paralipomena Jeremiae Prophetae:* His Originality: His 'Christianization' by the Christian Author of the Conclusion (9:10–32)." *JSP* 22 (2000): 31–44.

———. "Jérémie, martyr chrétien. Paralipomènes de Jérémie 9:7–32." Pages 231–35 in *ΚΕΧΑΡΙΤΩΜΕΝΗ. Mélanges R. Laurentin.* Paris: Desclée, 1990.

———. "Paraleipomena Jeremiou." Pages 213–30 in *Outside the Old Testament: Cambridge Commentaries on Writings of the Jewish and Christian World 200 BC to AD 200.* Edited by Marinus de Jonge. 4 vols. Cambridge: Cambridge University Press, 1985.

———. "Les Paralipomena Jeremiae dépendent-ils de 2 Baruch?" *Sileno* 9 (1983): 105–28.

———. *Les Paralipomènes du Prophète Jérémie: Présentation, texte original, traduction et commentaires.* Cahiers du Centre Interdisciplinaire de Recherches en Histoire, Lettres et Langues 14. Angers: Association Saint-Yves, 1994.

———. "'Le Puissant t'emportera dans ta Tente': La Destinée ultime du Juste selon les Paralipomena Jeremiae Prophetae." Pages 257–65 in *Hellenica et Judaica: Hommage à V. Nikiprowetzky.* Edited by A. Caquot, M. Hadas-Lebel, and J. Riaud. Leuven: Peeters, 1986.

———. "Les Samaritains dans les 'Paralipomena Jeremiae.'" Pages 133–52 in *La Littérature Intertestamentaire, Colloque de Strasbourg 1983.* Edited by André Caquot. Paris: Presses Universitaires de France, 1985.

Rosenstiehl, J.-M. "Histoire de la Captivité de Babylone I–V." Ph.D. diss., Strasbourg, n.d.

Schaller, Berndt. "Is the Greek Version of the Paralipomena Jeremiou Original or a Translation?" *JSP* 22 (2000): 51–89.

Schürer, Emil. Review of J. R. Harris, *The Rest of the Words of Baruch: A Christian Apocalypse of the Year 136 A.D. TLZ* 15 (1890): 81–83.

Stone, Michael E. "Baruch, Rest of the Words of." *EncJud* 4:276–77.

———. "Some Observations on the Armenian Version of the Paralipomena of Jeremiah." *CBQ* 35 (1973): 47–49.

Turdéanu, E. "La Légende du Prophète Jérémie en Roumain." Pages 307–47 in *Apocryphes Slaves et Roumains de l'Ancien Testament.* Edited by Emile Turdeánu. SVTP 5. Leiden: Brill, 1981.

Wolff, Christian. "Irdisches und himmlisches Jerusalem—Die Heilshoffnung in den Paralipomena Jeremiae." *ZNW* 82 (1991): 147–58.

———. "Paralipomena Jeremiae." *RGG*[4] (forthcoming).

———. "Die *Paralipomena Jeremiae* und das Neue Testament." *NTS* 51 (2005): 126–36.

Other Works Quoted

Aalen, Sverre. *Heilsverlangen und Heilsverwirklichung: Studien zur Erwartung des Heils in der apokalyptischen Literatur des antiken Judentums und im ältesten Christentum*. Edited by K. H. Rengstorf. ALGHJ 21. Leiden: Brill, 1990.

Abel, Félix-Marie. "Deir Senneh ou le domaine d'Agrippa." *RB* 44 (1935): 61–68.

Ackroyd, Peter R. "The Temple Vessels—A Continuity Theme." Pages 166–81 in *Studies in the Religion of Ancien Israel*. Edited by Peter R. Ackroyd VTSup 23. Leiden: Brill, 1972.

Alon, Gedalia. "The Origin of the Samaritans in the Halakhic Tradition." Pages 354–73 in *Jews, Judaism and the Classical World*. Edited by G. Alon. Jerusalem: Magnes, 1977.

Arnold-Döben, Victoria. *Die Bildersprache der Gnosis*. Arbeitsmaterialien zur Religionsgeschichte 13. Köln: Brill, 1986.

Balentine, Samuel Eugene. "The Prophet as Intercessor: A Reassessment." *JBL* 103 (1984): 161–73.

Becking, Bob. *The Fall of Samaria: An Historical and Archeological Study*. SHANE 2. Leiden: Brill, 1992.

Ben-Chorin, Schalom. *Narrative Theologie des Judentums anhand der Pessach-Hagadda: Jerusalemer Vorlesungen*. Tübingen: Mohr Siebeck, 1985.

Berger, Klaus. *Synopse des Vierten Buches Esra und der Syrischen Baruchapokalypse*. Texte und Arbeiten zum neutestamentlichen Zeitalter 8. Tübingen: Mohr Siebeck, 1992.

Bergmeier, R. "Zur Frühdatierung samaritanischer Theologumena." *JSJ* 5 (1974): 121–53.

Bernhardt, Karl-Heinz. "ברא IV." *TDOT* 2:246–48.

Bernheimer, Richard. "Vitae Prophetarum." *JAOS* 55 (1935): 200–203.

Bertram. "ʹΙΚΑΝΟΣ in den griechischen Übersetzungen des Alten Testaments als Wiedergabe von schaddaj." *ZAW* 70 (1958): 20–31.

Betz, Otto. "Der Tod des Choni-Onias im Licht der Tempelrolle von Qumran: Bemerkungen zu Josephus, Antiquitates 14,22–24." Pages 59–74 in *Jesus: Der Messias Israels*. Aufsätze zur Biblischen Theologie I. Edited by Otto Betz. WUNT 42. Tübingen: Mohr Siebeck, 1987.

Beyer, Hermann Wolfgang. "κατηχέω." *TDNT* 3:638–40.

Blaß, Friedrich, Albert Debrunner, and Friedrich Rehkopf, eds. *Grammatik des neutestamentlichen Griechisch*. 15th ed. Göttingen: Vandenhoeck & Ruprecht, 1979.

Blenkinsopp, Joseph. *Ezra-Nehemia: A Commentary*. Philadelphia: Westminster, 1988.

Bogaert, Pierre-Maurice. "Le Nom de Baruch dans la Littérature Pseudépigraphique: l'Apocalypse Syriaque et le Livre Deutéronomique." Pages 56–72 in *La Littérature Juive entre Tenach et Mischna: RechBibl. IX*. Edited by Willem Cornelis v. Unnik. Leiden: Brill, 1974.

Böhl, Felix. "Die Legende vom Verbergen der Lade." *Frankfurter Judaistische Beiträge* 4 (1976): 63–80.

Böhlig, Alexander. "Der jüdische Hintergrund in gnostischen Texten von Nag Hammadi." Pages 80–101 in *Mysterion und Wahrheit: Gesammelte Beiträge zur spätantiken Religionsgeschichte*. Edited by A. Böhlig. AGSU 6. Leiden: Brill, 1968.

Böhm, Martina. *Samarien und die Samaritai bei Lukas: Eine Studie zum religionshistorischen und traditionsgeschichtlichen Hintergrund der lukanischen Samarientexte und zu deren topographischer Verhaftung.* WUNT 2.111. Tübingen: Mohr Siebeck, 1999.

Borowski, Oded. "Harvests, Harvesting." *ABD* 3:63–64.

Brockelmann, Carl. *Lexicon syriacum.* 2nd ed. Halle: Niemeyer, 1928.

Büchler, Adolph. *Types of Jewish-Palestinian Piety from 70 B.C.E. to 70 C.E.: The Ancient Pious Men.* Jew's College Publications 8. London: Gregg, 1922.

Caquot, André. "Bref Commentaire du 'Martyre d'Isaie.'" *Sem* 23 (1979): 65–93.

Cavallin, Hans C. C. *Life after Death: Paul's Argument for Resurrection of the Dead in 1 Cor 15: Part 1, An Enquiry into the Jewish Background.* Lund: Gleerup, 1974.

Charles, Robert Henry. "II Baruch. The Syriac Apokaypse of Baruch. Introduction." Pages 470–80 in vol. 2 of *The Apocrypha and Pseudepigrapha of the Old Testament in English with Introductions and Critical Explanatory Notes to the Several Books.* Edited by Robert Henry Charles. 2 vols. Oxford: Clarendon, 1913.

Coggins, Richard James. "The Old Testament and Samaritan Origins." *ASTI* 6 (1967–68): 35–48.

———. *Samaritans and Jews: The Origins of Samaritanism Reconsidered.* Atlanta: John Knox, 1975.

Cohn, Erich W. *New Ideas about Jerusalem's Topography.* Jerusalem: Franciscan, 1987.

Collins, Marilyn F. "The Hidden Vessels in Samaritan Traditions." *JSJ* 3 (1972): 97–116.

Curtis, J. B. "An Investigation of the Mount of Olives in the Judaeo-Chistian Tradition." *HUCA* 28 (1957): 137–80.

Dalgish, E. R. "Ebed-Melech." *ABD* 2:259.

Dalman, Gustaf. *Jerusalem und sein Gelände: Mit 50 Abbildungen und einer Karte.* BFCT 2.19. Gütersloh: Bertelsmann, 1930.

Delling, Gerhard. *Die Bewältigung der Diasporasituation durch das hellenistische Judentum.* Berlin: Evangelische Verlagsanstalt, 1987.

———. "Zum gottesdienstlichen Stil der Johannes-Apokalypse." Pages 425–50 in *Studien zum Neuen Testament und zum hellenistischen Judentum: Gesammelte Aufsätze 1950–1968.* Edited by Ferdinand Hahn, Traugott Holtz, and Nikolaus Walter. Göttingen: Vandenhoeck & Ruprecht 1970. Repr. from *NovT* 3 (1959): 107–37.

Denis, Albert Marie. *Concordance Greque des Pseudepigraphes d'Ancien Testament: Concordance, Corpus des Textes Indices.* Leiden: Brill, 1987.

———. *Introduction aux Pseudépigraphes Grecs d'Ancien Testament.* SVTP 1. Leiden: Brill, 1970.

Dexinger, F. "Samaritan Eschatology." Pages 266–92 in *The Samaritans.* Edited by Alan D. Crown. Tübingen: Mohr Siebeck, 1989.

Doering, Lutz. "Jeremia in Babylon und Ägypten: Mündliche und schriftliche Toraparänese für Exil und Diaspora nach *4QApocryphon of Jeremiah C**." Pages 50–79 in *Frühjudentum und Neues Testament im Horizont biblischer Theologie.* Edited by Karl-Wilhelm Niebuhr and Wolfgang Kraus. WUNT 162. Tübingen: Mohr Siebeck, 2003.

Donner, Herbert. *Geschichte des Volkes Israel und seiner Nachbarn in Grundzügen.* 2 vols. Göttingen: Vandenhoeck & Ruprecht, 1987.

———. *Pilgerfahrt ins Heilige Land: Die ältesten Berichte christlicher Palästinapilger (4.–7. Jahrhundert)*. Stuttgart: Katholisches Bibelwerk, 1979.
Dörrie, H. "Diogenes 12." *KlPauly* 2:45–46.
Dschulnigg, Peter. *Rabbinische Gleichnisse und das Neue Testament: Die Gleichnisse der PesK im Vergleich mit den Gleichnissen Jesu und dem Neuen Testament*. Judaica et Christiana 12. Bern: Lang, 1988.
Egger, Rita. *Josephus Flavius und die Samaritaner: Eine terminologische Untersuchung zur Identitätsklärung der Samaritaner*. NTOA 4. Fribourg: Universitätsverlag, 1986.
Ego, Beate. *Im Himmel wie auf Erden: Studien zum Verhältnis von himmlischer und irdischer Welt im rabbinischen Judentum*. WUNT 2.34. Tübingen: Mohr Siebeck, 1989.
Ehrmann, Michael. *Klagephänomene in zwischentestamentlicher Literatur*. BEATAJ 41. Frankfurt am Main: Lang, 1997.
Eissfeldt, Otto. *The Old Testament: An Introduction, Including the Apocrypha and Pseudepigrapha, and Also the Works of Similar Type from Qumran—The History of the Formation of the Old Testament*. Translated from the 3rd German edition by Peter R. Ackroyd. New York: Harper & Row, 1965.
Enßlin, W. "Theodosius 70." *PW* 2/10:1951.
Fabry, Hans-Jörg. "יָחַד." *TDOT* 6:40–48.
Falk, Zeev W. "Ehe/Eherecht/Ehescheidung III." *TRE* 9:313–18.
Felber, Heinz. "Horus." Pages 742–43 in vol. 5 of *Der Neue Pauly: Enzyklopädie der Antike*. Edited by Hubert Cancik und Helmuth Schneider. Stuttgart: Metzler, 1996–2003.
Fischel, H. A. "Martyr and Prophet: A Study in Jewish Literature." *JQR* NS 37 (1946/47): 265–80, 363–86.
Fischer, Ulrich. *Eschatologie und Jenseitserwartung im hellenistischen Diasporajudentum*. BZNW 44. Berlin: de Gruyter, 1978.
Fitzer, G. "σφραγίς κτλ." *TDNT* 7:939–53.
Fitzgerald, John T. *Cracks in an Earthen Vessel: An Examination of the Catalogues of Hardships in the Corinthian Correspondence*. SBLDS 99. Atlanta: Scholars Press, 1988.
———, ed. *Friendship, Flattery, and Frankness of Speech: Studies on Friendship in the New Testament World*. NovTSup 82. Leiden: Brill, 1996.
Freedman, David Noel, ed. *Anchor Bible Dictionary*. 6 vols. New York: Doubleday, 1992.
Freedman, David Noel, and B. E. Willoughby, (and H.-J. Fabry). "עָנָה." *TDOT* 11:253–57.
Gaster, Moses. "Beiträge zur vergleichenden Sagen- und Märchenkunde XI: Choni hamagel." *MGWJ* 30 (NS 13) (1881): 78–82, 130–38, 368–74, 413–23.
Gaster, Theodor H. *Festivals of the Jewish Year: A Modern Interpretation and Guide*. New York: Sloame, 1964.
Gese, Hartmut. "Der Name Gottes im Alten Testament." Pages 75–89 in *Der Name Gottes*. Edited by Heinrich von Stietencron. Düsseldorf: Patmos, 1975.
Ginzberg, Louis. *The Legends of the Jews*. 7 vols. Philadelphia: Jewish Pubication Society of America, 1909–38.

Goldin, Judah. "The Death of Moses: An Exercise in Midrashic Transposition." Pages 219–25 in *Love and Death in the Ancient Near East*. Edited by John H. Marks and Robert M. Good. Guilford: Four Quarters, 1987.

Goodenough, Erwin R. *Jewish Symbols in the Greco-Roman Period*. Princeton: Princeton University Press, 1992.

Görg, M. "Die 'ehernen Säulen' (1 Kgs 7:15) und die 'eiserne Säule' (Jer 1:18): Ein Beitrag zur Säulenmetaphorik im Alten Testament." Pages 137–54 in *Prophetie und geschichtliche Wirklichkeit im alten Israel*. Edited by Rüdiger Liwak et al. Stuttgart: Kohlhammer, 1991.

Gowan, Donald E. "The Exile in Jewish Apocalyptic." Pages 205–23 in *Scripture in History and Theology: Essay in Honor of J. Coert Rylaarsdam*. Edited by Arthur L. Merrill and Thomas W. Overholt. PTMS 17. Pittsburgh: Pickwick, 1977.

Grözinger Karl Erich, and Hartmut Hahn. "Die Textzeugen der Pesiqta Rabbati." *Frankfurter Judaistische Beiträge* 1 (1973): 63–104.

Gry, Léon. "La ruine du temple par Titus: Quelques traditions juives plus anciennes et primitives à la base de *Pesikta Rabbathi* XXVI." *RB* 55 (1948): 215–26.

Gunneweg, Antonius H. J. *Geschichte Israels bis Bar Kochba*. Stuttgart: Kohlhammer, 1972.

Hadot, Jean. "La Datation de l'Apocalypse Syriaque de Baruch." *Sem* 15 (1965): 79–95.

Haelewyck, Jean-Claude. *Clavis apocryphorum Veteris Testamenti*. Turnhout: Brepols, 1998.

Hall, Robert G. "The *Ascension of Isaiah:* Community Situation, Date, and Place in Early Christianity." *JBL* 109 (1990): 289–306.

Halpern, B. "Abimelech 3." *ABD* 1:21–22.

Harnisch, Wolfgang. *Verhängnis und Verheißung der Geschichte: Untersuchungen zum Zeit- und Geschichtsverständnis im 4. Buch Esra und in der syrischen Baruchapokalypse*. FRLANT 97. Göttingen: Vandenhoeck & Ruprecht, 1969.

Hartmann, Lars. "Survey of the Problem of Apocalyptic Genre." Pages 329–44 in *Apocalypticism in the Mediterranean World and the Near East: Proceedings of the International Colloquium on Apocalypticism, Uppsala 1979*. Edited by David Hellholm. 2nd ed. Tübingen: Mohr Siebeck, 1989.

Helderman, Jan. *Die Anapausis im Evangelium Veritatis: Eine vergleichende Untersuchung des valentinianisch-gnostischen Heilsgutes der Ruhe im Evangelium Veritatis und in anderen Schriften der Nag Hammadi-Bibliothek*. NHS 18. Leiden: Brill, 1984.

Heller, Bernard. "Éléments, Parallèles et Origine de la Légende des Sept Dormants." *REJ* 49 (1904): 190–218.

Hengel, Martin. *Die Zeloten: Untersuchungen zur jüdischen Freiheitsbewegung in der Zeit von Herodes I. bis 70 n.Chr*. 2nd ed. AGSU 1. Leiden: Brill, 1976.

———. *Judentum und Hellenismus. Studien zu ihrer Begegnung unter besonderer Berücksichtigung Palästinas bis zur Mitte des 2. Jahrhunderts v. Chr*. 3rd ed. WUNT 10. Tübingen: Mohr Siebeck, 1988.

Hermisson, Hans-Jürgen. *Sprache und Ritus im altisraelitischen Kult: Zur Spiritualisierung der Kultbegriffe im Alten Testament*. WMANT 19. Neukirchen-Vluyn: Neukirchener Verlag, 1965.

Herrmann, Siegfried. *Geschichte Israels in alttestamentlicher Zeit.* 2nd ed. Munich: Kaiser, 1983.

———. *A History of Israel in Old Testament Times.* Translated by John Bowden. 2nd ed. Philadelphia: Fortress, 1981.

Hobbs, T. Raymond. *2 Kings.* WBC 13. Waco, Tex.: Word, 1985.

Hofius, Otfried. *Katapausis: Die Vorstellung vom endzeitlichen Ruheort im Hebräerbrief.* WUNT 11. Tübingen: Mohr Siebeck, 1970.

Holladay, William Lee. *Jeremiah 1.2: A Commentary on the Book of the Prophet Jeremiah.* Hermeneia. Philadelphia: Fortress, 1986.

Holtz, Traugott. "Die Bedeutung des Apostelkonzils für Paulus." Pages 140–70 in *Geschichte und Theologie des Urchristentums. Gesammelte Aufsätze.* Edited by Eckhart Reimuth and Christian Wolff. WUNT 57. Tübingen: Mohr Siebeck, 1991.

Huber, Michael. *Die Wanderlegende von den Siebenschläfern: Eine literargeschichtliche Untersuchung.* Leipzig: Hinrichs, 1910.

Hünemörder, Christian. "Adler." Pages 115–16 in vol. 1 of *Der Neue Pauly: Enzyklopädie der Antike.* Edited by Hubert Cancik und Helmuth Schneider. Stuttgart: Metzler, 1996–2003.

Hunzinger, Claus-Hunno. "Babylon als Deckname für Rom und die Datierung des 1. Petrusbriefes." Pages 67–77 in *Gottes Wort und Gottes Land: Festschrift für Joachim Jeremias.* Edited by Henning Graf Reventlow. Göttingen: Vandenhoeck & Ruprecht, 1965.

———. "συκῆ κτλ." *TDNT* 7:751–57.

Jeremias, Joachim. "αἴρω." *TDNT* 1:185–86.

———. *Die Gleichnisse Jesu.* 7th ed. Göttingen: Vandenhoeck & Ruprecht, 1965.

Johnson, Norman Burrows. *Prayer in the Apocrypha and Pseudepigrapha: A Study of the Jewish Concept of God.* JBLMS 2. Philadelphia: Society of Biblical Literature & Exegesis, 1948.

Josepheanz, H. Sargis. *Ankanon Girk' Hin Ktakaranac: Uncanonical Books of the Old Testament.* Venice: Lazar, 1896.

Käsemann, Ernst. *The Wandering People of God: An Investigation of the Letter to the Hebrews.* Translated by Roy A. Harrisville and Irving L. Sandberg. Minneapolis: Augsburg, 1984.

Keel, Othmar. *Jahwe-Visionen und Siegelkunst: Eine neue Deutung der Majestätsschilderungen in Jes 6, Ez 1 und 10 und Sach 4: Mit einem Beitrag von A. Gutbub über die vier Winde Ägyptens.* SB 84, 85. Stuttgart: Verlag Katholisches Bibelwerk, 1977.

———. *Vögel als Boten: Studien zu Ps 68:12–14, Gen 8:6–12, Koh 10:20 und dem Aussenden von Botenvögel in Ägypten: Mit einem Beitrag von Urs Winter zu Ps 56:1 und zur Ikonographie der Göttin mit der Taube.* OBO 14. Fribourg: Universitätsverlag, 1977.

Kern, Otto. "Epimenides." *RAC* 6:173–78.

Kilpatrick, George D. "Acts VII.52 ΕΛΕΥΣΙΣ." *JTS* 46 (1945): 136–45.

Kippenberg, Hans G. *Garizim und Synagoge: Traditionsgeschichtliche Untersuchungen zur samaritanischen Religion der aramäischen Periode.* Religionsgeschichtliche Versuche und Vorarbeiten 30. Berlin: de Gruyter, 1971.

Kittel, Gerhard, and Gerhard Friedrich, eds. *Theological Dictionary of the New Testament*. Translated and edited by G. W. Bromiley. 10 vols. Grand Rapids: Eerdmans, 1964–1976.
Klijn, Albertus Frederik Johannes. "The Sources and the Redaction of the Syriac Apocalypse of Baruch." *JSJ* 1 (1970): 65–76.
Knittel, Thomas. *Das griechische "Leben Adams und Evas": Studien zu einer narrativen Anthropologie im frühen Judentum*. TSAJ 88. Tübingen: Mohr Siebeck, 2002.
Koch, John. *Die Siebenschläferlegende, ihr Ursprung und ihre Verbreitung*. Leipzig: Reissner, 1883.
Koester, Craig R. *The Dwelling of God: The Tabernacle in the Old Testament, Intertestamental Jewish Literature and the New Testament*. CBQMS 22. Washington, D.C.: Catholic Biblical Association of America, 1989.
Kosmala, Hans. "Jom Kippur." *Jud* 6 (1950): 1–19.
Kraft, Robert A., and George W. E. Nickelsburg, eds. *Early Judaism and Its Modern Interpreters*. Philadelphia: Fortress, 1986.
Krause, Gerhard, and Gerhard Müller, eds. *Theologische Realenzyklopädie*. 33 vols. Berlin: de Gruyter, 1976–2002.
Kuhn, Heinz-Wolfgang. "Die Kreuzesstrafe während der frühen Kaiserzeit. Ihre Wirklichkeit und Wertung in der Umwelt des Urchristentums." *ANRW* 33.1:648–793.
Langer, Birgit. *Gott als "Licht" in Israel und Mesopotamien: Eine Studie zu Jes 60,1–3.19–20*. OBS 7. Klosterneuburg: Österreichisches Katholisches Bibelwerk, 1989.
Le Déaut, Roger. *Introduction à la Littérature Targumique 1*. Rome: Pontifical Biblical Institute, 1966.
Lenhardt, Pierre, and Peter von der Osten-Sacken. *Rabbi Akiva: Texte und Interpretationen zum rabbinischen Judentum und Neuen Testament*. Berlin: Institut Kirche und Judentum, 1987.
Levi, G. B. "Abimelech." *EncJud* 1:62.
Liddell, Henry George, and Robert Scott, eds. *A Greek-English Lexicon*. Oxford: Clarendon, 1968.
Liwak, Rüdiger. *Der Prophet und die Geschichte: Eine literarhistorische Untersuchung zum Jeremiabuch*. BWANT 7. Stuttgart: Kohlhammer, 1987.
Loewenstamm, Samuel E. "The Death of Moses." Pages 185–217 in *Studies on the Testament of Abraham*. Edited by W. E. George. SBLSCS 6. Missoula, Mont.: Scholars Press, 1976.
Lohfink, Gerhard. *Die Himmelfahrt Jesu: Untersuchungen zu den Himmelfahrts- und Erhöhungstexten bei Lukas*. SANT 26. Munich: Kösel, 1971.
Lundbom, Jack R. "Jeremiah." *ABD* 3:684–98.
Magonet, Jonathan. "Der Versöhnungstag in der jüdischen und christlichen Liturgie." Pages 133–54 in *Versöhnung in der jüdischen und christlichen Liturgie*. Edited by Hanspeter Heinz. QD 124. Freiburg: Herder, 1990.
Maier, Johann. "Jüdische Faktoren bei der Entstehung der Gnosis?" Pages 239–28 in *Altes Testament, Frühjudentum, Gnosis*. Edited by Karl-Wolfgang Tröger. Gütersloh: Gütersloher Verlagshaus, 1980.

———. "Die Sonne im religiösen Denken des antiken Judentums." *ANRW* 19.1:346–412.

Malherbe, Abraham J. *Paul and the Popular Philosophers*. Minneapolis: Fortress, 1989.

Marmorstein, Arthur. "Die Quellen des neuen Jeremia-Apocryphons." *ZNW* 27 (1928): 327–37.

Maser, P. "Sonne und Mond: Exegetische Erwägungen zum Fortleben der spätantik-jüdischen in der frühchristlichen Kultur." *Kairos* 25 (1983): 41–67.

Masson, Denise. *Le Coran et la Révélation Judéo-Chrétienne*. 2 vols. Paris: Adrien-Maisonneuve, 1958.

Matthews, Victor. H. "Abimelech 1.2." *ABD* 1:20–21.

Metzger, Bruce M. "The Fourth Book of Esra (Late First Century A.D.) with the Four Additional Chapters: A New Translation and Introduction." *OTP* 1:516–59.

Michaels, J. Ramsey. "Jewish and Christian Apocalyptic Letters 1 Peter. Revelation, and 2 Baruch 78–87." Pages 268–75 in *Society of Biblical Literature 1987 Seminar Papers*. SBLSP 26. Atlanta: Scholars Press, 1987.

Milgrom, Jacob. *Leviticus 1–16: A New Translation with Introduction and Commentary*. AB 3. New York: Doubleday, 1991.

Milik, Jósef Tadeusz. "Le Rouleau de Cuivre de Qumrân (3Q15)." *RB* 66 (1959): 321–57.

Montgomery, James Alan. *The Samaritans, the Earliest Jewish Sect: Their History, Theology, and Literature*. New York: Ktav, 1968.

Mor, Menahem. "The Persian, Hellenisic and Hasmonean Period." Pages 1–18 in *The Samaritans*. Edited by Alan D. Crown. Tübingen: Mohr Siebeck, 1989.

Morawe, Günter. *Aufbau und Abgrenzung der Loblieder von Qumrân: Studien zur gattungsgeschichtlichen Einordnung der Hodajôth*. Theologische Arbeiten 16. Berlin: Evangelische Verlagsanstalt, 1960.

Morgenstern, J. "Two Prophecies from the Fourth Century B.C. and the Evolution of Yom Kippur." *HUCA* 24 (1952/53): 1–74.

Murphy, Frederick J. "The Temple in the Syriac Apocalypse of Baruch." *JBL* 106 (1987): 671–83.

Naumann, Weigand. *Untersuchungen über den apokryphen Jeremiasbrief*. BZAW 25. Gießen: Töpelmann, 1913.

Neusner, Jacob. "Akiba ben Joseph." *TRE* 2:146–47.

———. *Early Rabbinic Judaism: Historical Studies in Religion, Literature and Art*. SJLA 13. Leiden: Brill, 1975.

———. *Life of Rabban Yohanan ben Zakkai, ca. 1–80 C.E.* StPB 6. Leiden: Brill, 1962.

Nickelsburg, George W. E. *Jewish Literature between the Bible and the Mishnah: A Historical and Literary Introduction*. Philadelphia: Fortress, 1981.

Nitzan, Bilhah. *Qumran Prayer and Religious Poetry*. Translated by Jonathan Chipman. STDJ 12. Leiden: Brill, 1994.

Overholt, T. W. "King Nebuchadnezzar in the Jeremiah Tradition." *CBQ* 30 (1968): 39–48.

Philonenko, Marc. "La Littérature Intertestamentaire et le Nouveau Testament." *RSR* 47 (1973): 270–79.

———. "Un titre messianique de Bar Kokheba." *TZ* 17 (1961): 434–35.

Pummer, Reinhard. "Antisamaritanische Polemik in jüdischen Schriften aus der intertestamentarischen Zeit." *BZ* 26 (1982): 224–42.

———. "The Book of Jubilees and the Samaritans." *EgT* 10 (1979): 147–78.

Rad, Gerhard von. "οὐρανός." *TDNT* 5:497–509.

Rehm, Martin. *Das zweite Buch der Könige: Ein Kommentar.* Neue Echter Bibel. Würzburg: Echter-Verlag, 1982.

Reichmann, Victor. "Feige I (Ficus carica)." *RAC* 7:640–82.

Reinhartz, Adele. "Rabbinic Perceptions of Simeon Bar Kosiba." *JSJ* 20 (1989): 171–94.

Rössler, Dietrich. *Gesetz und Geschichte: Untersuchungen zur Theologie der jüdischen Apokalyptik und der Pharisäischen Orthodoxie.* WMANT 3. Neukirchen-Vluyn: Neukirchener Verlag, 1960.

Rost, Leonhard. *Einleitung in die alttestamentlichen Apokryphen und Pseudepigraphen einschließlich der großen Qumran-Handschriften.* Heidelberg: Quelle & Meyer, 1971.

Rudolph, Wilhelm. *Jeremia.* 2nd ed. HAT 1.12. Tübingen: Mohr Siebeck, 1958.

Russell, David S. *The Old Testament Pseudepigrapha: Patriarchs and Prophets in Early Judaism.* London: SCM, 1987.

Safrai, Shmuel. *Das jüdische Volk im Zeitalter des Zweiten Tempels.* Neukirchen-Vluyn: Neukirchener Verlag, 1978.

———. "Der Versöhnungstag in Tempel und Synagoge." Pages 32–55 in *Versöhnung in der jüdischen und christlichen Liturgie.* Edited by Hanspeter Heinz. QD 124. Freiburg: Herder, 1990.

Sallmann, K. "Plinius 1." *KlPauly* 4:928–36.

Sanders, Ed P. "The Genre of Palestinian Jewish Apocalypses." Pages 447–59 in *Apocalypticism in the Mediterranean World and the Near East: Proceedings of the International Colloquium on Apocalypticism, Uppsala 1979.* Edited by David Hellholm. 2nd ed. Tübingen: Mohr Siebeck, 1989.

Saylor, Gwendolyn B. *Have the Promises Failed? A Literary Analysis of 2 Baruch.* SBLMS 72. Chico, Calif.: Scholars Press 1984.

Schäfer, Peter. *Der Bar Kokhba-Aufstand: Studien zum zweiten jüdischen Krieg gegen Rom.* TSAJ 1. Tübingen: Mohr Siebeck, 1981.

———. "Die Flucht Johanan b. Zakkais aus Jerusalem und die Gründung des 'Lehrhauses' in Jabne." *ANRW* 19.2:43–101.

———. *The History of the Jews in Antiquity: The Jews of Palestine from Alexander the Great to the Arab Conquest.* Luxembourg: Harwood Academic Publishers, 1995.

———. "Prolegomena zu einer kritischen Edition und Analyse der Merkhava Rabba." Pages 17–49 in *Hekhalot-Studien.* Edited by P. Schäfer. TSAJ 19. Tübingen: Mohr Siebeck, 1988.

———. *Studien zur Geschichte und Theologie des rabbinischen Judentums.* AGJU 25. Leiden: Brill, 1978.

Schäfer, Peter, and Klaus Herrmann, eds. *Übersetzung der Hekhalot-Literatur.* TSAJ 17.2. Tübingen: Mohr Siebeck, 1987.

Schalit, Abraham. "Die frühchristliche Überlieferung über die Herkunft der Familie des Herodes: Ein Beitrag zur Geschichte der politischen Invektive in Judaea." *ASTI* 1 (1962): 109–60.

Schermann, Theodor. *Propheten- und Apostellegenden nebst Jüngerkatalogen des Dorotheus und verwandte Texte.* TUGAL 31.3. Leipzig: Hinrichs, 1907.
Schlatter, Adolf. *Jochanan Ben Zakkai, der Zeitgenosse der Apostel.* BFCT 3. Gütersloh: Bertelsmann, 1899.
———. *Der Märtyrer in den Anfängen der Kirche.* Gütersloh: Bertelsmann, 1915.
Schmid, Herbert. "Baruch und die ihm zugeschriebene apokryphe und pseudepigraphe Literatur." *Jud* 30 (1974): 54–70.
Schoeps, Hans Joachim. "Die jüdischen Prophetenmorde." Pages 126–43 in *Aus frühchristlicher Zeit: Religionsgeschichtliche Untersuchungen.* Edited by Hans Joachim Schoeps. Tübingen: Mohr Siebeck, 1950.
———. *Die Tempelzerstörung des Jahres 70 in der jüdischen Religionsgeschichte: Agadisches zur Auserwählung Israels.* Uppsala: Seminarium neotestamenticum Upsaliense, 1942.
Scholem, Gershom. *Die jüdische Mystik in ihren Hauptströmungen.* Frankfurt am Main: Metzner, 1957.
Schulte, H. "Baruch und Ebedmelech: Persönliche Heilsorakel im Jeremiabuche." *BZ* NS 32 (1988): 257–65.
Schur, Nathan. *History of the Samaritans.* BEATAJ 18. Frankfurt am Main: Lang, 1989.
Schürer, Emil. *The History of the Jewish People in the Age of Jesus Christ (175 B.C.–A.D. 135): A New English Version.* Revised and edited by Fergus Millar and Geza Vermes. 3 vols. Edinburgh: Clark, 1973.
Schützinger, Heinrich. "Die arabische Jeremia-Erzählung und ihre Beziehungen zur jüdischen Überlieferung." *ZRGG* 25 (1979): 1–19.
Schwartz, Daniel R. *Agrippa I. The Last King of Judaea.* TSAJ 23. Tübingen: Mohr Siebeck, 1990.
Schwemer, Anna Maria. *Studien zu den frühjüdischen Prophetenlegenden: Vitae Prophetarum I: Die Viten der großen Propheten Jesaja, Jeremia, Ezechiel und Daniel.* TSAJ 49. Tübingen: Mohr Siebeck, 1995.
———. "Die Verwendung der Septuaginta in den Vitae Prophetarum." Pages 62–91 in *Die Septuaginta zwischen Judentum und Christentum.* Edited by M. Hengel and A. M. Schwemer. WUNT 72. Tübingen: Mohr Siebeck, 1994.
Seitz, Christopher R. "The Prophet Moses and the Canonical Shape of Jeremiah." *ZAW* 101 (1989): 3–27.
Smith, M. S. "The Near Eastern Background of Solar Language for Yahweh." *JBL* 109 (1990): 29–39.
Snijders, L. A. "זָר/זוּר." *TDOT* 4:52–58.
Speyer, Wolfgang. "Mittag und Mitternacht als heilige Zeiten in Antike und Christentum." Pages 340–352 in *Frühes Christentum im antiken Strahlungsfeld.* Edited by W. Speyer. WUNT 50. Tübingen: Mohr Siebeck, 1989.
Stähli, Hans-Peter. *Solare Elemente im Jahweglauben des Alten Testaments.* OBO 66. Göttingen: Vandenhoeck & Ruprecht, 1985.
Steck, Odil Hannes. *Das apokryphe Baruchbuch: Studien zu Rezeption und Konzentration "kanonischer" Überlieferung.* FRLANT 160. Göttingen: Vandenhoeck & Ruprecht, 1993.

———. *Israel und das gewaltsame Geschick der Propheten: Untersuchungen zur Überlieferung des deuteronomistischen Geschichtsbildes im Alten Testament, Spätjudentum und Urchristentum.* WMANT 23. Neukirchen-Vluyn: Neukirchener Verlag, 1967.
Steiger, J. A. "Nathanael—Ein Israelit, an dem kein Falsch ist: Das hermeneutische Phänomen der Intertestamentarizität aufgezeigt an Joh 1:45–51." *BTZ* 9 (1992): 50–73.
Stemberger, Günter. *Der Leib der Auferstehung: Studien zur Anthropologie und Eschatologie des palästinischen Judentums im neutestamentlichen Zeitalter (ca. 170 v. Chr.–100 n. Chr.).* AnBib 56. Rome: Biblical Institute Press, 1972.
———. *Pharisäer, Sadduzäer, Essener.* Stuttgarter Bibelstudien 144. Stuttgart: Katholisches Bibelwerk, 1991.
Stemm, Sönke von. *Der betende Sünder vor Gott: Studien zu Vergebungsvorstellungen in urchristlichen und frühjüdischen Texten.* AGJU 45. Leiden: Brill, 1999.
Stone, Michael E. *Features of Eschatology of IV Ezra.* HSS 35. Atlanta: Scholars Press, 1989.
———. *Fourth Ezra: A Commentary on the Book of Fourth Ezra.* Hermeneia. Minneapolis: Fortress, 1990.
Strack, Hermann L., and Günther Stemberger. *Introduction to the Talmud and Midrash.* Translated by Markus Bockmuehl. 7th ed. Edinburgh: T&T Clark, 1982.
Strack, Hermann L., and Paul Billerbeck. *Kommentar zum Neuen Testament aus Talmud und Midrasch.* 6 vols. Munich: Beck, 1922–61.
Strecker, Georg. "Judenchristentum und Gnosis." Pages 261–82 in *Altes Testament, Frühjudentum, Gnosis.* Edited by Karl-Wolfgang Tröger. Gütersloh: Gütersloher Verlagshaus, 1980.
Stuhlmacher, Peter. *Das paulinische Evangelium I.* FRLANT 95. Göttingen: Vandenhoeck & Ruprecht, 1968.
Surkau, Hans-Werner. *Martyrien in jüdischer und frühchristlicher Zeit.* FRLANT NS 36. Göttingen: Vandenhoeck & Ruprecht, 1938.
Taatz, Irene. *Frühjüdische Briefe: Die paulinischen Briefe im Rahmen der offiziellen religiösen Briefe des Frühjudentums.* NTOA 16. Fribourg: Universitätsverlag, 1991.
Tabor, James. D. "Returning to the Divinity Josephus's Portrayal of the Disappearances of Enoch, Elijah, and Moses." *JBL* 108 (1989): 225–38.
Thoma, Clemens. "Gott III. Judentum." *TRE* 13:626–45.
———. "Jüdische Apokalyptik am Ende des ersten nachchristlichen Jahrhunderts." *Kairos* 11 (1969): 134–44.
Timm, Stefan. *Die Dynastie Omri: Quellen und Untersuchungen zur Geschichte Israels im 9. Jahrhundert vor Christus.* FRLANT 124. Göttingen: Vandenhoeck & Ruprecht, 1982.
Tissot, Y. "Les Prescriptions des Presbytres (Actes XV,41,D): Exégèse et Origine du Décret dans le Texte syro-occidental des Actes." *RB* 77 (1970): 321–46.
Tröger, Karl-Wolfgang. "Gnosis und Judentum." Pages 155–68 in *Altes Testament, Frühjudentum, Gnosis.* Edited by Karl-Wolfgang Tröger. Gütersloh: Gütersloher Verlagshaus, 1980.
Unnik, Willem Cornelis van. "Gnosis und Judentum." Pages 65–84 in *Gnosis: Festschrift für Hans Jonas.* Edited by Barbara Aland. Göttingen: Vandenhoeck & Ruprecht, 1978.

Vielhauer, Philipp. "ΑΝΑΠΑΥΣΙΣ: Zum gnostischen Hintergrund des Thomasevangeliums." Pages 215–34 in *Aufsätze zum Neuen Testament*. Edited by Peter Vielhauer. TB 31. Munich: Kaiser, 1965.
Volz, Paul. *Die Eschatologie der jüdischen Gemeinde im neutestamentlichen Zeitalter nach den Quellen der rabbinischen, apokalyptischen und apokryphischen Literatur*. 2nd ed. Tübingen: Mohr Siebeck, 1934.
Voss, M. Heerma van. "Horus." *DDD*, 808–9.
Wadsworth, M. "The Death of Moses and the Riddle of the End of Time in Pseudo-Philo." *JJS* 28 (1977): 12–19.
Walter, Nikolaus. "Hellenistische Eschatologie im Neuen Testament." Pages 335–56 in *Glaube und Eschatologie: Festschrift für Werner Georg Kümmel*. Edited by Erich Gräßer and Otto Merk. Tübingen: Mohr Siebeck, 1985.
———. *Der Thoraausleger Aristobulos: Untersuchungen zu seinen Fragmenten und zu pseudepigraphischen Resten der jüdisch-hellenistischen Literatur*. TU 86. Berlin: Akademie-Verlag, 1964.
Weiß, Hans-Friedrich. *Der Brief an die Hebräer*. KEK 13. 15th ed. Göttingen: Vandenhoeck & Ruprecht, 1991.
Wilkinson, John. "The Way from Jerusalem to Jericho." *BA* 38 (1975): 10–24.
Williamson, Hugh G. M. *Ezra, Nehemia*. WBC 16. Waco, Tex.: Word, 1985.
Willi-Plein, Ina. "Das Geheimnis der Apokalyptik." *VT* 27 (1977): 62–81.
Wolff, Christian. *Jeremia im Frühjudentum und Urchristentum*. TUGAL 118. Berlin: Akademie, 1976.
Wolff, Hans Walter. "Das Kerygma des deuteronomistischen Geschichtswerks." *ZAW* 32 (1961): 171–86.
Yassif, Eli. "Traces of Folk Traditions of the Second Temple Period in Rabbinic Literature." *JJS* 39 (1988): 212–33.
Zimmerli, Walther. *Ezekiel: A Commentary on the Book of the Prophet Ezekiel*. Vol. 1 translated by Ronald E. Clements. Edited by Frank Moore Cross et al. Vol. 2 translated by James D. Martin. Edited by Paul D. Hanson and Leonard Jay Greenspoon. Hermeneia. 2 vols. Philadelphia: Fortress, 1979–83.

INDEX OF BIBLICAL LITERATURE*
by Susanne Schuster

Hebrew Bible

Genesis		27:33	91 n. 48
1:1	96	28:16 (LXX)	90
2:9	153 n. 77	29:11	101 n. 3
2:21	84 n. 18, 91 n. 47	29:13	101 n. 3
5	124 n. 27	30:13	78 n. 25
8	xxviii, 122 n. 14	33:4	101 n. 3
8:7–11	122 n. 14		
8:10–11	121	Exodus	
8:21	146 n. 31	2:24	114, 114 n. 79
9:15	114 n. 79	3:2	125 n. 32
12:7	125 n. 32	3:3	48 n. 16
15:12	84 n. 18, 91 n. 47	3:13–15	108, 109
17:1	125 n. 32	3:14	109 n. 50
18:33	51 n. 25	3:18	123 n. 24
20–21	66 n. 35	4:27	101 n. 3
20:2	109 n. 50	5:1	123 n. 24
22	127	5:3	123 n. 24
22:2	127, 127 n. 43	6:4	114
22:12	127	6:5	114 n. 79
22:16	127	7:16	123 n. 24
24:3	95 n. 66	12:17	126 n. 35
26:1	66 n. 35	12:24	126 n. 35
26:8–11	66 n. 35	12:25	126 n. 35
26:16	66 n. 35	13:10	126 n. 35
26:26	66 n. 35	13:21	98, 144 n. 22
27:27	101 n. 3	14:2	111 n. 59

* Boldface marks a reference containing either a longer quotation, a broader discussion of an argument, or a deeper reflection on a certain subject.

Exodus (cont.)		11:25	144 n. 22
14:5	134	11:28	47 n. 6
14:15	111 n. 59	12:5	144 n. 22
15:26	115 n. 81	14:10	125 n. 32
16:10	123 n. 24, 125 n. 32, 144 n. 22	15:3	146 n. 31
		15:5	146 n. 31
18:7	101 n. 3	15:7	146 n. 31
19:1–24:8	123	18:5	126 n. 35
19:4	121, 125, 125 n. 29	29:7	142 n. 11
19:5	115 n. 84		
19:13	60	*Deuteronomy*	
19:16	60	1:1	123 n. 25
19:18	60	2:27	122 n. 17
19:19	60	4:40	115 n. 81
20:18	60	5:32	122 n. 17
23:13	126 n. 35	6:2	115 n. 81
33:9–10	144 n. 22	6:4	62
33:19	77 n. 21	7:3–4	114
		7:11–12	115 n. 81
Leviticus		8:1	126 n. 35
1:2	111 n. 59	13:14	76 n. 16
1:9	146 n. 31	13:19	115 n. 84
1:13	146 n. 31	15:5	115 n. 84
1:17	146 n. 31	17:11	122 n. 17
2:2	146 n. 31	17:20	115 n. 82
2:9	146 n. 31	24:15	101 n. 5
2:12	146 n. 31	26:15	96
3:5	146 n. 31	27:15	114
7:38	123 n. 25	28:1	115 n. 84
8:35	126 n. 35	28:2	115 n. 84
9:23	125 n. 32	28:9	115 n. 84
12:4 (LXX)	53	28:13	115 n. 84
16	xxix, 145	30:8	115 n. 84
16:2	144, 144 n. 22	32:11	121, 125, 125 n. 29
16:12–13 (LXX)	144, 145	32:15 (LXX)	63
16:13	144, 144 n. 22	32:16	129 n. 57
16:29	142 n. 11	33:5 (LXX)	63
18:2	111 n. 59	33:26 (LXX)	63
19:4	114		
23:27	142 n. 11	*Joshua*	
26:1	114	1:13	117
26:42–45	114 n. 79	3	117
		3:5	117
Numbers		5:2–9	118 n. 106
1:1	123 n. 25	6	60

INDEX OF BIBLICAL LITERATURE

6:8	60	10:8	78 n. 25
6:13	60	10:14	82
7:6	54 n. 4	16:25–26	136
7:9	108	17:4–6	121
Judges		2 Kings	xxviii, 136
2:11–13	113 n. 74	2:12	55
2:11–18	113 n. 74	6:21	55
2:14–15	113 n. 74	13:14	55
2:16	113 n. 74	16:24	135
2:18	113 n. 743	17	134 n. 17, 136, 137, 138
3:6	114	17:24	136
3:7–9	113 n. 74	17:24–41	135, 136
7:2	77 n. 18	17:26	136
8:31	66 n. 35	17:28	136
9:1–6	66 n. 35	17:29–32	136
9:16–56	66 n. 35	17:33	136
10:1	66 n. 35	17:34–41	136
11:34	127 n. 42	17:40 (NRSV)	136
19:16	92 n. 54	20:7	72 n. 64
21:2	149 n. 55	22:16	46
		23:26–36	46
1 Samuel		24:13	61 n. 13
2:3	77 n. 17	25:4	70 n. 56
2:8b–9	96 n. 68	25:13–15	61 n. 13
2:10 (LXX)	77 n. 18		
		Isaiah	
2 Samuel		LXX	44
7:12 (LXX)	157, 157 n. 98	1:18	154
11:21	66 n. 35	2:5	98
13:19	54 n. 4	5:16	101 n. 6
13:26	149 n. 55	5:19	101 n. 6
14:33	101 n. 3	6:3	144, 145
15:5	101 n. 3	6:3a	146
18:18	68	6:4	145
22:29	**98**	12:6	101 n. 6
		26:19	151 n. 67
1 Kings		29:1	133 n. 12
1–11	114	29:8	151 n. 67
4:25	84 n. 17	29:9	91 n. 48
7:15	48 n. 15	30:12	101 n. 6
8:10–11	144 n. 22	30:15	101 n. 6
8:30	96	38:21	72 n. 64
8:42	108	40:13 (LXX)	148 n. 52
8:56	95	40:31	121, 125

Isaiah (cont.)

42:1	47 n. 6	6:19	46 n. 5
42:4	154, 154 n. 83	6:26	127, 127 nn. 43 and 45
42:8	114	7:9	46 n. 5
43:1–7	121 n. 10	7:16	47
43:26	47 n. 6	7:23	115 n. 84
44:2 (LXX)	63	7:29	76 n. 14
44:24	121 n. 10	8:23 (LXX)	56, 57 n. 13
45:4	47 n. 6	9:1	56, 57 n. 13
47:4	101 n. 6	9:9	76 n. 14
49:16	50 n. 21	9:17	56 n. 12, 76 n. 14
52:6	109 n. 50	9:19	76 n. 14
52:7–12	107 n. 42	9:23	77
53:12	148, 149	10:2–4	46 n. 5
57:15	101 n. 6	10:16	121 n. 10
60:1–3	75 n. 11	11:4	115, 115 n. 84
60:19–20	98	11:7	115 n. 84
62:12	101 n. 6	11:14	47
63:15	96	13:14	77 n. 21
		13:22	46
Jeremiah		14	47
1–30	113 n. 74	15:1	47
1:1	74	15:11	47
1:18	47, 48, 48 n. 15	15:20	48
2:4–13	114	16:13	129
2:5	46 n. 5	16:19	107 n. 39
2:8	46 n. 5	18:20	47
2:11	72	21:7	77 n. 21
2:23	46 n. 5	21:10	115 n. 80
2:34	46 n. 5	22	62 n. 17
2:35	46 n. 5	22:13	101 n. 5
3:9	46 n. 5	22:29	62 n. 17, 65 n. 29
3:13	46 n. 5, 129 n. 57	23:18	148 n. 52
4:1–2	114	24	xxviii
4:5	60	24:1 (LXX)	72 n. 63
4:19	60	24:1–10	72, 90
4:21	60	25:11	82 n. 7
5:1	46 n. 5	26(33):13	115 n. 84
5:4–5	46 n. 5	27(50):34	147 n. 35
5:7	46 n. 5	28(35):3	61 n. 13
5:8	46 n. 5	28(35):6	61 n. 13
5:19	46 n. 5	28(51):19	121 n. 10
6:1	60, 73	28(51):39	90
6:7	46 n. 5	28(51):57	147 n. 35
6:17	60, 73	29:1–23	111, 113
		29:5	113

INDEX OF BIBLICAL LITERATURE 181

29:6	113	52:17–19	61 n. 13
29:6c	113		
29(36):10	82 n. 7, 114	Ezekiel	
29:14	114	1:3	74 n. 10
30–33	113 n. 74	1:4–28	74 n. 10
31:1–4	**123 n. 26**	3:1	111 n. 59
31(38):13–16	101 n. 5	8–11	70
31(38):35(36)	147 n. 35	8:1–18	74 n. 10
32:12–13	47	10:1–22	74 n. 10
32(39):36	115 n. 80	10:15	74 n. 2
30:15	46	11:23	70
31(38):1–4	123	17:3	121, 123
31:23	64	17:7	121
36:4	47	18:7	145 n. 27
36(43):4–18	92	18:12	145 n. 27
36:6	47, 65 n. 29	19:1	76 n. 14
36:6–18	110	20:10–20	**124**
36:10	47	20:13	123
36:32	47	20:21	123
37(44):17	115 n. 80	28:2	115 n. 82
38(45):6	66 n. 34	28:5	115 n. 82
38(45):7	66 nn. 34–35	28:17	115 n. 82
38(45):7–13	**66**	28:18	46
38(45):10–11	66 n. 35	36	118
38:10–13	65 n. 29	36:23	108
38:16	101 n. 5	36:24–25	118
39	67	37	65 n. 30, 89 n. 37
39:4	70 n. 56	37:10	151 n. 65
39(46):6	66 n. 35		
39:15–18	67	Hosea	
39(46):16	66 n. 35	2:16–25	123
39(46):16–18	xxvii, 67 n. 37		
39(46):16b–18	**67**	Joel	
42:14	60	1:1–2:11	113 n. 74
43(50):1–7	70	2:13	**56**, 57
43(50):6–7	70	2:12–17	113 n. 74
43:3	47	2:18–4:21	113 n. 74
43:4–7	150		
43:6	47	Amos	
43:8	156 n. 96	4:13	147 n. 35
44(51):26	108	5:1	76 n. 14
45:1	47	5:27	147 n. 35
48(31):29	115 n. 82	7:15	111 n. 59
51:27	60	8:10	127, 127 n. 45
52:7–8	70 n. 56	9:6	147 n. 35

Micah

4:4	84 n. 17
7:8	98
7:19	77 n. 21

Habakkuk

2:11	156 n. 94

Zechariah

1:12	82 n. 7
3:10	84 n. 17
4:1	90
7:5	82 n. 7
12:10	127, 127 n. 45
14:4	**153**
14:13	91 n. 48

Malachi

1:7	130 n. 66
1:11	108 n. 45
1:12	130 n. 66
3:20	75 n. 11

Psalms

1:1	78 n. 25
2	148
2:12	78 n. 25
4:7	98
11(12):4–5	77 n. 18
13(14):5	77 n. 17
17(18):2	107 n. 39
17(18):29	98
21:21	127 n. 42
22:12	127 n. 43
26(27):1	98
30:23 (LXX)	91 n. 48
31(32):1–2	78 n. 25
33	90 n. 39
33(34):9	78 n. 25
33(34):10	101 n. 6
34:1	66 n. 35
34:17 (LXX)	127 n. 42
37(38):17	77 n. 17
43(44):21	129 n. 57, 130
45(46):2	107 n. 39
54(55):8	123
56:8 (LXX)	105 n. 26
59(60)3	77 n. 21
59(60):7	63
62(63):5	95
67:7	127 n. 43
72:10	154 n. 83
72:17 (LXX)	53
73:7 (LXX)	53, **54**
75(76):2	108
77(78):52	123
80(81):13	115 n. 83
82:13 (LXX)	53, 54
83:13	54
84:12	75
85(86):14	76 n. 16
88(89):16	98
91(92):13–15	145 n. 23
93(94):3–4	77 n. 17
96:4–5	114
97:7	114
98(99):3	108
102(103):5	121, 125
104(105):39	98
105:8	114 n. 79
105:8–11	114
105(106):23	47 n. 6
106(107)	123
106:45	114 n. 79
107(108)	96 n. 68
107(108):2	105 n. 26
107(108):7	63
109 (LXX)	148
112(113):5–7	96 n. 67
113:23 (LXX)	96
115:2 (LXX)	91 n. 48
115:15	96
118(119):85	76 n. 16
118(119):105	98
120(121)	96 n. 68
120(121):2	96
122(123):1	101 n. 4
125(126)	xxviii, 84, 86
125(126):1	**83–84**, 87, 88
126(127):2	63

INDEX OF BIBLICAL LITERATURE   183

135(136):16	123	Daniel	
135(136):26	95 n. 66	1:2	61 n. 13
136:2 (LXX)	130 n. 62	1:8	130 n. 66
136(137):3–4	120, 120 n. 4, 129,	2:18–19	95 n. 66
	130 n. 62	5:2–4	61 n. 13
144(145):2	95	7:21	101 n. 6
145(146):5–9	96 n. 68	7:27	101 n. 6
146(147):5	148 n. 52	7:28	91 n. 48
		9:1	44
Proverbs		9:2	82 n. 7
4:27 (LXX)	122 n. 17	9:24–26	152 n. 73
6:9 (LXX)	90	10:7	91 n. 48
6:23	98	12:1	73
8:25	148	12:11–12	152 n. 73
11:21	101 n. 5		
11:30	153 n. 77	Ezra	xxviii
13:12	153 n. 77	1:7–11	61 n. 13, 144 n. 16
15:4	153 n. 77	3:4	143
18:10	108 n. 45	5:11	95 n. 66
		5:14	61 n. 13
Job		6:5	61 n. 13
2:11–13	53	7:19	61 n. 13
2:12	54	8:8	110
5:9	148 n. 52	8:9	110
5:17	78 n. 25	8:19	110
9:10	148 n. 52	8:26–30	61 n. 13
14:12	151 n. 67	8:31	94
15:8	148 n. 52	8:35	143 n. 15
15:25	115 n. 83	9–10	131, 137
		9:1–4	138 n. 34
Song of Songs		9:2	138 n. 34
2:14	146 n. 34	9:4	138 n. 34
		9:9–15	138 n. 34
Lamentations		9:11–12	138 n. 34
1:1	76 n. 14	9:39	110
2:7–10	**54**	9:42	110
3:32	77 n. 21	9:49	110
3:49–50	55 n. 7	10:3	138 n. 34
5:12	128		
		Nehemiah	xxviii
Esther		1:4–5	95 n. 66
4:1	54 n. 4	2:1	94
4:3	54 n. 4	3:15	70 n. 56
4:16	54 n. 4	8–9	143 n. 15
		8:13–18	143

Nehemiah (cont.)		2 Chronicles	
9:26	156 n. 96	3:1	133 n. 12
13:23–31	131, 137	5:13–14	144 n. 22
13:24	133 n. 9	6:32	108
13:27	138 n. 34	22:3	110 n. 58
13:28	137	30:27	96
		34:28	46
1 Chronicles		36:17	43
9:28 (LXX)	61	36:18–19	61 n. 13
18:16	66 n. 35	36:21	82 n. 7
		36:23	95 n. 66

NEW TESTAMENT

Matthew		3:15–16	77 n. 22, 152 n. 70
5:3–11	78 n. 25	3:16	127 n. 41
10:2	154 n. 84	3:18	127 n. 41
23:37	**156**	3:36	152 n. 70
24:30–31	152 n. 72	4:9	134 n. 17
25:6	50 n. 24	5:24	77 n. 22, 152 n. 70
		5:24–25	153
Mark		5:26	77 n. 22
3:14	154 n. 84	5:35	152
8:31	151 n. 64	5:39–40	77 n. 22
9:31	151 n. 64	6:39	151 n. 66
10:34	151 n. 64	6:40	77 n. 22, 151 n. 66, 152 n. 70
13:35	50 n. 24	6:44	151 n. 66
15:21	92	6:47	152 n. 70
15:33	50 n. 24	6:54	151 n. 66
		6:68	152 n. 70
Luke		6:7	77 n. 22
1:4	93 n. 58	6:53–54	77 n. 22
1:45	78 n. 25	8:12	151
6:13	154 n. 84	9:5	151
12:42	121 n. 8	10:10	77 n. 22
13:6	60 n. 4, 72	10:18	151 n. 66
17:18	135	11:11	151
19:40	156 n. 94	11:25	151 n. 66, 152 n. 70
24:5	151	12:1	151 n. 66
		12:17	151 n. 66
John		12:41	154
1:9	145 n. 28, 151, 152	12:46	151
1:14	127 n. 41	16:11	153
1:45–51	84 n. 17	17:5	154
2:19(21)	151 n. 66	17:6	109

INDEX OF BIBLICAL LITERATURE

17:24	154	6:10	121 n. 8
19:14	50 n. 24	12:4	103 n. 18
19:16	50 n. 24		
20:29	78 n. 25	1 Thessalonians	
20:31	77 n. 22, 152 n. 70	4:15–16	152 n. 72
Acts		Titus	
1:12	153	1:12	89 n. 34
7:55	154		
8:39	145 n. 27	Hebrews	
10:40	151 n. 64	11:37	xxix, 155 n. 90, 156
15:20	130, 130 n. 66		
15:28–29	130 n. 66	James	
16:25	50 n. 24	1:12	78 n. 25
17:23	108 n. 49		
17:28a	89 n. 34	1 Peter	
27:27	50 n. 24	4:10	121 n. 8
		4:14	78 n. 25
Romans			
4:17	151 n. 66	2 Peter	
8:11	151 n. 66	1:13–14	102 n. 8
11:34	148 n. 52		
		1 John	
1 Corinthians		3:15	77 n. 22
2:16	148 n. 52	4:9	127 n. 41
4:1	121 n. 8	5:12–13	77 n. 22
4:2	121 n. 8		
6:14	151 n. 66	Revelation	
7:10–11	131 n. 3	1:3	78 n. 25
9:2	116	1:8	49 n. 18
15:4	151 n. 64	2:1	111 n. 59
15:22	151 n. 66	2:7	153
		4:8	49 n. 18, 144 n. 18
2 Corinthians		8–10	60
1:9	151 n. 66	11:17	49 n. 18
4:14	151 n. 66	14:4	105
5:1	102 n. 8	14:13	78 n. 25
6:18	49 n. 18	15:3	49 n. 18
12:2	145 n. 27	16:7	49 n. 18
12:2–4	151 n. 65	19:6	49 n. 18
12:4	108 n. 49, 145 n. 27	20:2–6	152 n. 73
		21:2–4	99 n. 81
Galatians		21:22	49 n. 18
2:9	48 n. 16	21:23	152
6:6	93 n. 58	22:2	153

Revelation (cont.)
     22:14   153
     22:19   153

INDEX OF ANCIENT LITERATURE

APOCRYPHA AND SEPTUAGINT

Baruch	xv	1 Maccabees	
1:1–2	70	1:11	76 n. 16
1:1–3	xviii	1:15	131 n. 4
1:3–4	110	3:47	54 n. 4
1:4–6	xviii	10:61	76 n. 16
1:7–11	xviii	11:21	76 n. 16
1:8	61 n. 13		
2	115	2 Maccabees	
2:29	115 n. 84	2	xxii n. 42, xxiii
2:29–35	**114**	2:4–5	xxiii
3:1–4	49 n. 18	2:4–8	61 n. 13, 62
4:12	46	2:5	74 n. 8
5:6–8	98	2:7	xxii, xxiii, 62 n. 16, 63, 63 n. 23, 65 n. 31
5:9	98		
		3:30	49 n. 18
1 Esdras		5:14	47 n. 9
9:2 (Lxx)	46	5:22–23	xxviii n. 77, **138 n. 38**
		6:1–3	138 n. 38
Epistle of Jeremiah		7:11	104 n. 21
2	83 n. 15	8:2	77 n. 21
		14:12	84 n. 17
Judith			
4:11–15	**54**	3 Maccabees	
4:13	49 n. 18	2:2	49 n. 18, 147 n. 35
5:17	95 n. 66	2:7	147 n. 35
8:13	49 n. 18	2:9	108 n. 45
9:2–4	134 n. 17	2:17	76 n. 16
9:12	95 n. 66, 147 n. 35	5:51	77 n. 21
15:10	49 n. 18		
16:5	49 n. 18	4 Maccabees	
16:17	49 n. 18	9:3	110 n. 58

4 Maccabees (cont.)

17:5	98 n. 79

Sirach

2:8	101 n. 5
6:5	146 n. 34
17:24	142 n. 8
22:7	90
34:15	78 n. 25
39:15	108 n. 45
40:29	130 n. 66
42:16	75 n. 11
42:17	49 n. 18
46:1	108 n. 45
47:22	47 n. 6
48:15	142 n. 8
49:6	49 n. 19
50:7	75 n. 11
50:13	98
50:17	49 n. 18
50:25–26	134 n. 17
50:26	135

Tobit

3:15	127 n. 42
4:12	131 n. 4
6:11	127 n. 42
6:15	127 n. 42
8:15	101 n. 6
8:17	127 n. 42
12:7	95 n. 66
13:13	49 n. 19
14:7	101 n. 6

Wisdom of Solomon

3:1	97, 97 n. 73
3:1–3	**97 n. 73**
4:7	97, **97 n. 73**
4:10–11	145 n. 27
5:15	101 n. 5
9:15	102 n. 8
18:1–2	101 n. 6
18:4	98
18:5	101 n. 6
18:9	101 n. 6

Old Testament Pseudepigrapha

Apocalypse of Abraham

17:8–10	148 n. 50

Apocalypse of Moses

	101 n. 2

Apocryphon of Jeremiah

	xxv–xxvi, xxvii n. 73
14:2–4	47 n. 9
17:8	47 n. 9
30–31	70 n. 58
35–37	70 n. 58
39	70 n. 58
39:13	94
150:1–160:2	xxv
152:4–18	xxv
159:18–20	xxv
161:26–163:19	xxv
167	xxvi
167:3–30	xxv
167:8	xxvi
167:10	xxvi
167:11	xvi
167:23	xxvi
167:25–26	xxvi
167:28–29	xxvi
167:31–185:7	xxv
176:21–23	xxvi
185:8–187:26	xxv
185:10	xxvi
185:18	xxvi
185:21–22	xxvi n. 70
185:26–30	xxvi n. 70
188:12–14	144 n. 16
189:3–5	144 n. 16

Aristeas the Exegete

142	130 n. 66
185:2	147 n. 35

INDEX OF ANCIENT LITERATURE 189

Assumption of Moses
3:1   61 n. 13
3:14   82, 83, 83 n. 15

2 Baruch (Syriac Apocalypse)   xv n. 3, xvi–xxv, xxvii–xxx, xxxiv, 44, 57, 60, 61 n. 14, 62, 62 n. 17, 64, 65, 65 n. 29, 70 n. 59, 71 n. 60, 74, 75, 79, 81, 82, 98 n. 78, 102, 102 n. 11, 103, 104, 106, 107, 107 n. 37, 112 n. 70, 113, 120, 121, 122, 122 n. 14, 123, 125 n. 29

1–12	xvii
1:1	xviii
1:1–5	xvii
1:1–2:1	xvii
1:2–4	46
1:2–5	xviii, 50 n. 22
2	xviii
2:1	xviii, 48
2:1–2	xviii
2:2	xvii, 47 n. 9
3	xviii
3:1–9	xviii
3:6	130 n. 62
4	xviii
4:1–5	xviii
4:1–6	99 n. 81
4:2	xx, 50 n. 21
4:3	99 n. 81
5	xviii
5:1	xvii, xviii, 77 n. 18, 108
5:2–4	xviii
5:3	50 n. 22
5:5–6	xviii
6	60, 63, 64
6–8	xviii
6:1	xvii, 73, 74 n. 3, 82 n. 6
6:1–8:5	xviii
6:3	60 n. 7
6:3–9	60
6:3–10	xvii, xxiii
6:4	60
6:5	xvii, 73 n. 1
6:5–7	60
6:6	61 n. 14
6:7	xxiii, 61, 62
6:8	**62,** 62 n. 19, 65 n. 29, 147 n. 35
6:9	62, 64
6:10	64
7:1	147 n. 35
7:1–2	xvii
7:1–3	xix n. 14, 74 n. 3
7:1–8:1a	74 n. 4
7:2	77 n. 18
8:1	xix n. 14, 73 n. 2
8:1–5	xvii, 74 n. 3
10:1–5	xvii, xviii, 70
10:2	71 n. 60
10:3	70
10:5–19	xviii
10:6–77:26	xviii
10:18	xvii, xx, 74, **75**
11:4	78 n. 27.29
11:4–5	xvii
11:4–6	77
13:2	147 n. 35
13:3	xvii, 102
13:4	147 n. 35
21:1	xvii, 69 n. 54, 78 n. 29, 79
21:19	65
21:21	65
21:21–23	xxiii, **65,** 66
21:23	65
21:24	78 n. 27
25:1	xvii
28:2	152 n. 73
30:2	97 n. 77
33:2	xvii, 71 n. 60
35:2	xvii, 56, 56 n. 11, 57 n. 13
44:3–45:2	xvii
46:7	102
48:30	102
50:1–4	**104**
50:2	104
50:3	105
50:4	104 n. 24
51:1	104 n. 24
51:1–4	105
63:3–9	48 n. 15

2 Baruch (cont.)

67:2	77 n. 18
76:2	xvii, 102
77	xvii, 106
77–79	xviii
77:10	xvii, 50 n. 22
77:11–19	111
77:11–87:1	xviii
77:12	106
77:12–14	120
77:12–19	xvii
77:13	106
77:15–18	120
77:18	82 n. 6, 112 n. 70
77:19	106 n. 37, 120
77:20–26	xvii, xx, 106 n. 37, 120
77:21a	121
77:23	121
77:24	121, 122 n. 14
77:25	121
77:26	122
78–86	xxvii
78:1	106 n. 37
78:1–86:1	120
78:5	102, 113 n. 73
79:2	113 n. 73
80:1–6	113 n. 73
80:2	xvii, 61 n. 12
80:3	xvii, 77 n. 18
82:2–83:8	113 n. 73
84:1	102
84:2	113 n. 73
84:5	113 n. 73
84:6–85:4	113 n. 73
85:1–2	xvii
85:3	150
85:9–11	113 n. 73
85:11	98 n. 78
87:1	xvii, 106 n. 37, 120

3 Baruch (Greek Apocalypse)

	xv n. 3, 67 n. 38
1:3	147 n. 35

4 Baruch (Paraleipomena Jeremiou)

1	45, 50 n. 23, 53, 76
1–4	xvii
1:1	xvii, xviii, xlii, 44, 45, 46, 47, 53, 61 n. 11
1:1b	50
1:1–3	50, 51
1:1–9:9	xxxv, 156
1:2	xvii, 47, 55 n. 8
1:3	xvii, 44
1:4	46, 49, 51
1:4–6	xviii
1:5	xvii, 44, 49, 147
1:5–6	47
1:6	xx, 50 n. 21
1:6–7	49
1:7	xvii, 45, 46, 49, 50, 53, 55 n. 8, 76
1:7–9	50
1:7–11	xviii
1:8	50
1:8–9	50
1:9	50, 50 n. 23
1:10	45, 47, 50, 57
1:12	71
2	xvii, xviii, 45, 50, 50 n. 23, 53, 59
2–4	92
2:1	**53,** 76 n. 14
2:1–10	xviii
2:1a	57 n. 15
2:1a.c	57 n. 15
2:1b	53
2:2	46, 53, 76, 126
2:2–9	**55**
2:3	xvii, 47, 53, 55, 74, 76
2:4	xvii, 53, 55, 57, 126
2:5	**56**
2:6	44, 55, 126
2:6–7	**57**
2:7	49
2:8	55, **57,** 126
2:9	60
2:10	53, 60
3	xxvii, xxxiv, 45, 59, 60, 62 n. 19, 63, 73, 81, 144
3:1	74 n. 3, 87

INDEX OF ANCIENT LITERATURE

3:1–8 xvii, xxiii
3:1–4:5 xviii
3:1–8:14 60
3:2 71
3:3 **60**
3:4 49
3:4–5 46
3:5 49 60
3:6 49, 59, 61
3:7 59, 141
3:7–8 142
3:8 xxii, xxiii, 55, 57, 57 n. 16, 59, **61,** 62, 63, 63 n. 23, 65, 65 nn. 29 and 31, 66, 71 n. 61, 76, 76 n. 15, 99, 116, 116 nn. 91 and 94, 125 n. 29, 128, 128 n. 48, 142, 147, 155 n. 87
3:9 xxviii, 47, 59, 65 n. 29, 66, 66 n. 34, 67 n. 36, 120
3:9–10 59, 66, 81, 126
3:9–13 64
3:10 xxvi, 60, 67, 68, 69, 83, 87
3:10–11 59
3:11 xviii, 59, 66, 70, 93, 98 n. 80, 122, 122 n. 16
3:11–12 xvii
3:12 70, 71
3:13 51, 71
3:14 xvii, 57 n. 16, 59, 64, 71
3:15 xxvi, 59, 60, 68, 68 n. 41, 69, 71, 73, 82, 87, 90, 119, 130
3:15–16 81, 89
4 xviii, xxxiv, 73, 81, 144
4:1 44, 59, 73, 73 n. 1, 74 n. 3
4:1–2 xvii
4:1a 74 n. 3
4:2 74
4:3 74, 75, 141
4:3–4 xvii, xx, 74, 142
4:4 75, 76, 87
4:4a 121 n. 8
4:5 xvii, xviii, 76, 81
4:6 xvii, 45, 46, 55, 63, 74, **76,** 77 n. 19
4:6–7 46

4:6–11 xviii, 105
4:7 xvii, **76**
4:7c 77 n. 20
4:8 76, **77,** 106
4:9 xvii, 76, **77**
4:9–10 xxxiv
4:10 78
4:11 xvii, xxiii, 69 n. 54, **79,** 101
5 xvii, xxv nn. 64 and 65, xxviii, 45, 59, 59 n. 2, 67 n. 38, 81, 83 n. 15, 84 n. 20, 85, 85 n. 24, 87–90, 97, 101, 104, 149
5:1 xxvi, xxx, **82,** 84 n. 17, 87, 90, 94 n. 60, 95, 126
5:1–6:7 81
5:1–6:8 xxv, 87, 141
5:2 84, 89
5:3 xxxiii
5:4 84, 89
5:4–6 90
5:5 91
5:6 82, 99 n. 81
5:7 87, **91**
5:7–16 89
5:8 84, **91**
5:9 69, 87
5:9–16 91
5:10 84, 89, 91
5:12 xxxiii, xxxiv, 87, 91
5:14 84
5:16 84
5:17 89, **92**
5:17–18 92
5:17–34 87
5:18 47, 65 n. 29, 74, **92,** 92 n. 55, 110, 143
5:19–22 **92**
5:21 xvii, 43, 71, 71 n. 60, 93 n. 57, 122, 122 n. 16
5:22 98 n. 80
5:23 **93**
5:24 93
5:25 xxvi, 55, 68, 72, 126
5:25–26 93
5:26 89

4 Baruch (cont.)
- 5:27 — 93
- 5:28–31 — 93
- 5:28–34 — 89
- 5:30 — xxx, 82, 84, 87, 94, 95, 126
- 5:31 — 93
- 5:32 — 91, 94, 95, 97, 97 n. 73, 98, 99, 104, 125 n. 29, 126
- 5:33 — 93, **94,** 95
- 5:34 — xxxiv, 51, 87, 87 n. 29, 91, 94, **95,** 97, 98, 99 n. 81, 104, 107, 107 n. 42, 133, 141, 145, 152
- 5:38 — 78
- 6 — xxviii, 114, 117, 118, 119, 131, 148 n. 54
- 6–7 — xvii
- 6–9 — 63
- 6:1 — 101
- 6:1–7 — 101
- 6:2 — 79
- 6:2–7 — 101
- 6:3 — 72, **102–4,** 105, 105 n. 26, 110, 111, 114
- 6:3–6 — 145 n. 27
- 6:3–7 — 119, 125 n. 29
- 6:4 — 105, 120, 121
- 6:5 — xxx, 82, 105, 126
- 6:6 — 105, 135, 141, 142
- 6:7 — xvii, 82, 103, 104
- 6:8 — 106, 110, 120
- 6:8–10 — 106
- 6:8–12 — 120
- 6:8–23 — xvii
- 6:8–7:32 — xviii
- 6:9 — 106, 107, 108, 109, 145, 152
- 6:10 — 106, **110**
- 6:11 — 101, 110
- 6:12 — 106, 110, 120, 122
- 6:12–14 — 111
- 6:13 — 106, 111
- 6:13–14 — 111, 112, 113, 115, 129
- 6:13–15 — 120
- 6:13–22 — xxxiv
- 6:13–23 — 112
- 6:14 — 44, 106, 111, 113 n. 74, 131
- 6:15–16 — 112
- 6:16 — 120
- 6:17 — 102, 114
- 6:17–20 — 114
- 6:17–23 — 111, 112, 113, 120
- 6:18 — 114
- 6:19–20 — 111
- 6:20 — 115
- 6:20–21 — 125
- 6:21 — 46, 115
- 6:21–22 — 93 n. 57, 111
- 6:21–23 — 114
- 6:22 — 107, 111, 113 n. 74, 115, 126, 133
- 6:22–23 — 116, 132 n. 7
- 6:23 — 111, 116, 116 nn. 91 and 94, 118, 131, 133 n. 10, 154
- 7 — xxviii, 119, 122 n. 14, 124, 131
- 7:1 — 119, **120**
- 7:1–2 — 119
- 7:1–12 — xvii, 120
- 7:2 — 75 n. 13, 105, 110, 111 n. 60, 120, 121 n. 8
- 7:2–12 — 123
- 7:3 — 49, 121
- 7:4 — 123
- 7:8 — xvii, 81, 111, 119
- 7:8–12 — xx
- 7:9 — 121, 130
- 7:10 — 121
- 7:11 — 49, 121, 122
- 7:12 — 122, 122 nn. 14 and 17, 123
- 7:12–20 — 125 n. 29
- 7:13 — 119, 123
- 7:13–22 — 123
- 7:14 — 43, 74, 123 n. 19, 124
- 7:15 — 46, 49, 81, 120
- 7:15–16 — 124
- 7:15–18 — 119
- 7:17 — 111, 123, 125
- 7:18 — 106, 123, 125
- 7:20 — 126
- 7:21 — 126
- 7:22 — 98 n. 80, 107, 126
- 7:23 — 44, 48, 55

7:23–24	120	9:1–7	142
7:23–26	29, 119, 126 n. 36	9:2	92, 141
7:23–29	123, 126	9:3	102, 103, 144, 145, 145 n. 27, 146
7:23c	126	9:3–5	xxxiv
7:24	xxx, 55 n. 9, 56, 82, 126, 127	9:3–6	149
7:24–26	127	9:3–7	102
7:25	43, 128, 129, 130 n. 62	9:4	47, 146 n. 32
7:25–26	114, 128, 129	9:4–5	145
7:26	128, 129, 130	9:5	xxv, 73, 101, 141, 146 n. 30
7:28	48, 78, 81, 97 n. 72, 119, 120, 126, 129	9:6	96 n. 67, 146, 147, 148
7:29	120, 129	9:6b	147
7:30	xvii	9:7	64, 141, 148
7:30–32	130	9:7–9	102, 142, 155
7:32	xvii, 71, 74, 81, 93 n. 57, 98 n. 80, 107, 111, 113 n. 74, 119, 123, 129, 130, 130 n. 66, 131	9:7–32	81
		9:8	55, 126, 149
		9:9	141, 142, 149, 150
8	xvii, xxviii, 31 n. 10, 112, 131, 131 n. 1, 132, 133 n. 10, 135, 136, 137, 138	9:10	102, 142, 142 n. 4, 148, 150
		9:10–18	151
		9:10–32	xxix, xxxv, 47 n. 6, 150–51
8:1	131	9:11	142, 150, 151
8:1–2	xxxiv	9:11–32	90 n. 39
8:2	131	9:12	150
8:2–3	113 n. 74	9:13	150, 151, 152
8:2a	131	9:13–18	142
8:2b	131	9:14	151, 152, 153, 154, 154 n. 81
8:3	93 n. 57, 107, 132	9:14–18	150, 152
8:3–5	118 n. 108	9:15	153, 154, 154 n. 81.83
8:4	107, 133	9:15–16	153
8:4–5	131, 132	9:16	154 n. 82
8:4b	132 n. 8, 133	9:17	154, 154 n. 81
8:5	xxxvii, 44, 81	9:18	151, 152, 153, 154, 155
8:5–9	112	9:19	150
8:5b–7	112	9:19–21	155
8:6	133	9:19–32	142
8:6–8	132 n. 5	9:20	151, 155
8:7	44, 134, 135	9:20–21	150, 156
8:8	132, 134	9:21–32	151
8:9	xxviii, xxxv, 73, 113 n. 74, 133, 138, 142, 142 n. 7, 146	9:22–23	151
		9:22–32	156
8:12	142	9:24–27	150
9	xvii, xxix, xxxiv, 62, 90, 95, 145 n. 23, 153	9:28	150
		9:30–31	150
9:1	129, 141	9:32	151
9:1–2	xxxiv, 142		

Cave of Treasures
40:4	155 n. 90
50:24ff.	150

1 Enoch (Ethiopic Apocalypse)   109
1:8	145 n. 26
5:8	145 n. 26
21:6	152 n. 73
22	97 n. 77
22:1–3	97 n. 76
24:3–25:6	144 n. 21
24:8	153 n. 77
25:4–5	153 n. 77
25:6	144 n. 18
26:1	153
39:12	144 n. 18
51:1	105 n. 27
69:14	109
69:26	109
90:5	152 n. 73
90:28–36	99 n. 81
93:1–10	152 n. 73
91:11–17	152 n. 73

4 Ezra
4:25	108 n. 46
4:33	156 n. 94
4:35–37	97 n. 77
5:5	156 n. 94
5:9	154 n. 82
6:20	63 n. 25, 116 n. 93
6:58	127, 127 n. 42
7:32	97 n. 77
7:80	97 n. 77
7:5	97 n. 77
7:26	99 n. 81
7:28	152 n. 73
7:32	104 n. 21
7:54	62 n. 17
7:101	97 n. 77
8:52	99 n. 81, 153 n. 77
9:38–10:54	99 n. 81
10:22	108 n. 46
13:36	99 n. 81
13:40–41	50 n. 22
14:31	46

Joseph and Aseneth
7:5	131 n. 4
8:5	131 n. 4
8:7	131 n. 4
8:9–10	99 n. 81
8:10	97 n. 76
12	64
15:7	97 n. 76, 99 n. 81, 142 n. 8
17:6	99 n. 81
22:13	97 n. 76, 99 n. 81

Jubilees
20:4	131 n. 4
22:20	131 n. 4
25:1–10	131 n. 4
30	134 n. 17
30:1–3	131 n. 4
30:5	134 n. 17
30:7	134 n. 17
49	134 n. 17
49:16–21	134 n. 17

Liber antiquitatum biblicarum (Pseudo-Philo)
9:5	132 n. 4
18:13–14	132 n. 4
19:10–13	**149 n. 56**
21:1	132 n. 4
31:1	77 n. 18
43:5	132 n. 4

Life of Adam and Eve
9:5	132 n. 4
18:1314	132 n. 4
19:3	105 n. 32
19:10–13	149 n. 56
20:4	105 n. 32
21:1	132 n. 4
29:4–5	146 n. 31
31:4	148
37	103
37:5	103, 145 n. 29
37:6	103

37:31–32	103	*Psalms of Solomon*	
42:8	148	4:18	145 n. 27
43:5	132 n. 4	4:25	101 n. 6
		6:1	105 n. 26
Lives of the Prophets		6:6	101 n. 6
1	155 n. 90	8:1	60, 73
2	xxix, 156	10:3	101 n. 6
2:1	156	13:9	127 n. 45
2:3	47 n. 9	14:1	101 n. 6
2:9–11	xxiii, 61 n. 13	14:3	145 n. 23
2:11	xxii	14:3–4	**153 n. 78**
4:13	63 n. 25	18:4	127, 127 n. 42
10:8–11	156 n. 94		
		Sibylline Oracles	
Odes of Solomon		3:804	156 n. 94
3:10	77 n. 18	4:178–180	104 n. 21
12:1	49 n. 18		
12:3	107 n. 42	*Testament of Abraham*	
14:12–13	49 n. 18	2:7	98 n. 78
29:7	117 n. 104	A 3:3	144 n. 18
39:7	117 n. 104	A 8:3	49 n. 18, 147 n. 35
		A 15:12	49 n. 18, 147 n. 35
Martyrdom and Ascension of Isaiah	xxix,	A 16:2	147 n. 35
xxx, 153, 155		B 7	145 n. 27
3:9	156	B 7:6	145 n. 26
3:9–10	155		
3:9–12	155	*Testament of Asher*	
3:13	155	5:3	145 n. 26
3:13–20	155, 155 n. 88		
3:17	154 n. 84, 155	*Testament of Dan*	
4:3	154 n. 84	5:12	99 n. 81
4:13	155		
4:14	152 n. 73	*Testament of Gad*	
5:1–14	155	6:6	142 n. 8
5:1–16	155 n. 90		
5:7	154, 156	*Testament of Job*	
10–11	153	28:3	54 n. 4
11:1–21	153	43:7	102 n. 8
11:19–20	155	45:3	131 n. 4
11:22	155	53:7a	151 n. 64
11:41	155 n. 88		
		Testament of Judah	
Prayer of Manasseh		13:2	77 n. 18
1:1	49 n. 18	14:6	131 n. 4
6	148 n. 52	25:4	151 n. 67

Testament of Levi

5:3–4	134 n. 17
6:8–10	134 n. 17
7:2	134 n. 17, 135
8:15	63 n. 25
9:10	131 n. 4
14:4	145 n. 26
14:6	131 n. 4
18:11	153 n. 77
19:1	145 n. 26

Testament of Reuben

1:9	142 n. 8
3:1	84 n. 18
4:4	142 n. 8

Testament of Simeon

2:13	142 n. 8

Testament of Zebulun

9:8–9	145 n. 26

DEAD SEA SCROLLS AND RELATED TEXTS

1QH^a 4:5	145 n. 26	4Q266 (D^a)VIII:18c–20	126 n. 39
1QS 2:3	145 n. 26	4Q385a frg.18:I, a–b	xxvii n. 73
1QS 4:2	145 n. 26	4Q385a frg. 18:II	xxvii n. 73
1QS 4:21	118 n. 107	4Q385b	61 n. 13
1QS 11:7–8	101 n. 6	4Q389	xxvii n. 73
1QSIsa^b 1:5	101 n. 6	4QapocrJer	xxvii n. 73, 70 n. 58
3Q15	61 n. 12		

HELLENISTIC JEWISH AUTHORS

Josephus, *Against Apion*

1.187	83
2.167	108 n. 49, 147 n. 43

Josephus, *Antiquities of the Jews*

1.222	127, 127 n. 42
4.319	148
4:320–31	149 n. 56
7.243	69
8.191	132 n. 4
8.312	136 n. 24.25
9.278–79	136 n. 26, 137 n. 31
9.288	137 n. 31
9.289–90	136 n. 27
10.80	74
10.136	50
10:145–46	61 n. 13
10.184	82 n. 7
11.2	82 n. 7
11.84	134 n. 17
11.114–16	134 n. 17
11.187	102 n. 8
11.321–328	137
12:278	77 n. 20
14:22ff	84 n. 20
14.54–63	xix n. 14
18.340–42	132 n. 4
19.326–27	68
20.20	127 n. 42
20.166	50 n. 22
20.233	82 n. 7

Josephus, *Jewish War*

5.47–97	69
5.142–83	68
5:152	68 n. 47
5.172–83	68
5.389	82 n. 7
110.110	50 n. 22
6.299–301	73 n. 2
6.439	152 n. 71
7.202	128 n. 52
7.328	50 n. 22
7.332	46, 50 n. 22

INDEX OF ANCIENT LITERATURE 197

Philo, *Allegorical Interpretation*		Philo, *De vita Mosis*	
3.219	148	1.74–75	**108–9**
		2.114	108
Philo, *De fuga et inventione*		2.171	148 n. 51
141	148 n. 47		
165	148 n. 52	Philo, *On the Special Laws*	
		3.29	132 n. 4
Philo, *De mutatione nominum*			
15	148 n. 47	Philo, *Quis rerum divinarum heres sit*	
		249	84 n. 18
Philo, *De sacrificiis Abelis et Caini*		257	84 n. 18
57	147 n. 43		
60	147 n. 43	Philo, *Quod deterius potori insidari soleat*	
66	147 n. 43	124	147 n. 43
		158	147 n. 43

Rabbinic Literature

Mishnah		Babylonian Talmud	
Baba Batra		*Berakot*	
2:9	124 n. 28	9b	109 n. 50
		28b	48 n. 16
Kuttim			
2:28	xxviii n. 77, 139 n. 38	*Hagigah*	
		14b	103 n. 18
Qiddušin			
4:3	xxviii n. 77, 139 n. 40	*Qiddušin*	
		71	108 n. 48
Sanhedrin			
10:1C–G	**108 n. 48**	*Roš Haššanah*	
		32b	147 n. 41
Tamid			
7:2	108 n. 48	*Sanhedrin*	
		90b	xxviii n. 70
Yoma		103b	155 n. 90
5:1	143 n. 13		
		Sukkah	
Tosefta		55b	**143 n. 14**
Nega'im			
6:2	124 n. 28	*Ta'anit*	
		23a	xxvi, xxviii, 82 n. 7, **84–88**, 89 n. 37
Sotah			
138	108 n. 48	29a	74 n. 6

Yebamot		*Derek Eretz Rabbah*	103
49b	155 n. 86.90	1:18	103
Yoma		*Exodus Rabbah*	
39b	108 n. 48	2:6	48 n. 16
53b	143 n. 14	3:6	**109 n. 50**
Jerusalem Talmud		*Genesis Rabbah*	
Berakot		54:4	66 n. 35
2:5c	127 n. 40		
7:1	xxviii n. 77, 138 n. 38	*Lamentations Rabbah*	
		1:5	**48 n. 16**
Gittin			
1:4	xxviii n. 77, 138 n. 38	*Leviticus Rabbah*	
		19:6	74 n. 6
Qiddušin		20:3–4	143 n. 13
4:3	139 n. 40	35:8	75 n. 12
Roš Haššanah		*Merkabah Rabba*	117
1:3	143 n. 11		
1:15	143 n. 11	*Midrash Berakot*	
		3:5	91 n. 49
Sanhedrin			
10:28c	155 n. 90	*Midrash Haseroth we Yeteroth*	**143**
Šeqalim		*Midrash Psalms*	
7:2	74 n. 6	17	143 n. 11
		34	66 n. 35
Taʿanit	87, 88	102	143 n. 11
3	xxviii, 84 n. 20	126:1	82 n. 7, 84, 84 nn. 21–22, 86
3:9	xxvi, xxviii, 82 n. 7, **84–88,** 91 n. 50	*Pesiqta Rabbati*	xxiii–xxv
3:10	87 n. 28	14	155 n. 90
4:5	**xxxiii n. 96,** 69 n. 49	21:5	101 n. 2
		21:9	101 n. 2
Yoma		21:11	101 n. 2
3:7	108 n. 48	26	xxiii
5:2	143 n. 13	26:16	74 n. 6, 77 n. 18
6:2	108 n. 48	26:18	70 n. 58
8:7	**143 n. 13**		
8:9	143 n. 13	*Pesiqta de Rab Kahana*	
		26	143 n. 13
Other Rabbinic Works			
ʾAbot de Rabbi Nathan		*Pirke Rabbi Eliezer*	
B 31	**xxxii**	4	146 n. 32

Second Alphabet of Ben Sira
28b 103

Seder Olam Rabbah
26 150
26:1 70 n. 58

Sipra
16:12–13 144 n. 22

Sipre Numbers
39 108 n. 48

Sipre Zuta
15–16 108 n. 48
39 108 n. 48

Tanḥuma
B§4 143 n. 13

CHRISTIAN AUTHORS AND TEXTS

Apostolic Fathers
1 Clement
5:2 48 n. 16
8:3 154 n. 82

Shepherd of Hermas, *Similitude*
9:16.3–7 115 n. 87
9:17.4 115 n. 87
8:2.3–4 115 n. 87
8:6.3 115 n. 87
93:4 117 n. 104

Shepherd of Hermas, *Vision*
5:5 111 n. 59

Patristic Authors
Clement of Aleandria, *Eclogae propheticae*
21 148 n. 47
25:3 147 n. 46

Clement of Alexandria, *Excerpts from Theodotus*
45:1 147 n. 46

Clement of Alexandria, *Stromata*
2:5.4 147 n. 46
2:51.5 147 n. 46
5:82.3 147 n. 46
6:58.1 147 n. 46
6:165.5 147 n. 46

Eusebius of Caesarea, *Against Hierocles*
5.1.6.17 48 n. 16
9.39.5 61 n. 13

Eusebius of Caesarea, *Preparation for the Gospel*
8.9.13 130 n. 66
9.22.6 131 n. 4

Hippolytus, *Refutation of All Heresies*
5.7.41 117 n. 104
10.11.6 117 n. 104

Irenaeus of Lyon, *Against Heresies*
1.21.3 109

Jerome, *Commentariorum in Isaiam libri XVIII*
9.30.6 150

Jerome, *Commentariorum in Jeremiam libri VI*
6:1064–1065 on Jer 31(38):15 **112 n. 70**

Justin Martyr, *1 Apology*
14:1–2 147 n. 46
14:2 147 n. 44
25:2 147 nn. 44 and 46
49:5 147 n. 46
53:2 147 n. 46

Justin Martyr, *2 Apology*		283–284	117 n. 99
6:1	147 n. 46	310:15	117 n. 99
12:4	147 n. 46	326:3	117 n. 99
13:4	147 n. 46	360:35	117 n. 99

Justin Martyr, *Dialogue with Trypho*		*Gospel of Truth*	96 n. 70
5:1	147 nn. 44 and 46	36:35–39	97 n. 76
5:4–6	147 n. 46		
114:3	147 n. 46	New Testament and Later Christian Apocrypha	
126:2	147 n. 46		
127:1	147 n. 46	*Apocalypse of Paul*	
		14	145 n. 29
Christian-Gnostic Works		22	145 n. 29
Apocryphon of John		27	145 n. 29
53:11–17 (NHC II 23:27–31)	125 n. 29		
61:1–5 (NHC III 30:17–20)	125 n. 29	*Book of Adam*	
		130:31–32	150

Ginza	109, 117	*Preaching of Peter*	
I 5:15–16	125 n. 29	frg. 2	147 n. 46
I 6:3–5	125 n. 29	frg. 3b	154 n. 84
II 3	125 n. 29		
II 58:23–28	125 n. 29	*Pseudo-Clementines (Homilies)*	
19:24–25	117 n. 99	3.72.1–2	**96 n. 70**
39:23	116, 116 n. 97	16.19.2	117 n. 104
48:20	117 n. 99	17.7.4	117 n. 104
51:1–3	117 n. 99	17.10.1	96 n. 70
58:3	117 n. 99		
98:8–10	109	*Thomas, Acts of*	
184–186	117 n. 99	91	125 n. 29
190–193*	117 n. 99	11:49–54	125 n. 29

CLASSICAL GRECO-ROMAN AUTHORS

Dio Cassius, *Historia Romanum*		Pliny the Elder, *Natural History*	
69 12.113.2	xxxiii	7:53 [175]	88 n. 33

Diogenes Laertius		Plutarch, *Caesar*	
1.10.109–110	87, 88 n. 33, 91 n. 50	2.2	128 n. 52

Herodotus, *Histories*		Plutarch, *De Iside et Osiride*	
7.194.1–2	128 n. 52	16	123 n. 20
9.120	128 n. 52		

Plutarch, *Moralia*
357C 123 n. 20

Tacitus, *Histories*
5.13 73 n. 2

Theodosius, *De situ terrae sanctae*
5:6 **69,** 90 n. 39

OTHER WORKS

Qur'an
2:259 89 n. 37
18:8–25 89 n. 37
18:24 89 n. 37

Index of Modern Authors
by Thorsten Klein

Aalen, S., 97 n. 76
Abel, F.-M., 69, 89 n. 37
Ackroyd, P. R., xix n. 15, 61 n. 13
Alon, G., 135 n. 17, 137 n. 31, 138 n. 38
Arnold-Döben, V., 96 n. 70
Balentine, S. E., 47 n. 10
Becking, B., 136 n. 26
Ben-Chorin, S., **xxx n. 84**
Bergmeier, R., 61 n. 13
Bernhardt, K.-H., 121 n. 10
Bernheimer, R., 157 n. 96
Bertram, G., 101 n. 7
Betz, O., 84 n. 20
Beyer, H. W., 71 n. 60
Blaß, F., 144 n. 23
Blenkinsopp, J., 138 n. 34
Böhl, F., xxii n. 42.43, 61 n. 13.14
Böhm, M., 134 n. 17, 135 n. 17.20
Bogaert, P.-M., xvi n. 8, xvii, **xix, xx,** xxii n. 40, xxiv n. 56, xxvi n. 73, 20, 47 n. 11, 50 n. 21, **59,** 62 nn. 17–18, 66 n. 35, 68 n. 44, 69, 70 n. 57, 74 n. 7, 78 n. 29, **81,** 84 n. 21, 85 n. 24, 87 n. 27, 91 n. 44, 99 n. 81, 101 n. 7, 102 n. 10, 105 n. 29, 106 nn. 33 and 36, 107 n. 37, 108 n. 46, 112 nn. 66 and 70, 113 n. 70, 114 n. 77, 115 nn. 86–88, 116 nn. 89 and 91, 121 nn. 8 and 12, **122 n. 14,** 125 n. 29, 128, 129 n. 58, **130,** 141 n. 1, 142 n. 4.11, 144 n. 21, 147 n. 35, 148 n. 48, 153 n. 76, 156 n. 94, 157
Borowski, O., 93 n. 59
Brockelmann, C., 62 n. 17
Büchler, A., 84 n. 20

Caquot, A., xxi n. 22, 98 n. 79, 112 n. 64, 155 n. 86.89
Cavallin, H. C. C., 97 n. 77, 104 n. 21
Charles, R. H., xvii n. 8, xx n. 16.19
Coggins, R. J., 134 n. 17, 138 n. 38
Cohn, E. W., 70 n. 56
Collins, M. F., 63 n. 23
Coquin, R.-G., xxv n. 57
Curtis, J. B., 153 n. 76
Dalgish, E. R., 66 n. 35
Dalman, G., 68 n. 46, 69, 70 n. 56
Delling, G., xx n. 19, xxiii n. 45, xxxiv n. 103, 49 n. 18, 50 n. 22, 57 n. 15, 59 n. 3, 62 n. 18, 63 nn. 21–23, **64,** 66 n. 35, 67 n. 37, 71 n. 60, **82,** 87 n. 27, 92 n. 51, 93 n. 58, 96 n. 69, 97, 98 n. 80, 101 nn. 1 and 5, 102 nn. 12 and 15, 105, 107 nn. 39 and 44, 108, 110 n. 57, 112 n. 65, 116 n. 90, 117 n. 105, 125 n. 29, 126 n. 37, **127,** 128 n. 56, 129 nn. 56–58, 132 n. 4, 133 n. 11, 134 n. 15, 138 nn. 35–36, 139 n. 39, 141 nn. 1–2, 142 n. 8, 144 n. 18, 145 n. 26, 146 n. 31, **147,** 148 n. 47, 153 n. 77, 156 n. 91
Denis, A.-M., xx n. 19, xxxi n. 89, xxxiv n. 98, 103 n. 19
Dexinger, F., 139 n. 38
Doering, L., xxvii n. 73
Donner, H., 68 n. 47, 69 n. 52, 89 n. 37, 90 n. 39
Dörrie, H., 88 n. 33
Doran, R., xv n. 3, 83 n. 14
Dschulnigg, P., 127 n. 40

INDEX OF MODERN AUTHORS

Egger, R., 134 n. 17, 136 nn. 26 and 29, 138 nn. 35 and 38
Ego, B., 24 n. 55, 97 n. 77, 99 n. 81, 143 n. 14
Ehrmann, M., 49 n. 18
Eissfeldt, O., xix n. 15, 155 n. 88
Enßlin, W., 69 n. 52
Fabry, H.-J., 127 n. 44.45
Falk, Z. W., 131 n. 3
Felber, H., 123 n. 21
Fischel, H. A., 155 n. 90
Fischer, U., 97 n. 75
Fitzer, G., 116 n. 94
Fitzgerald, J. T., vii, 77 n. 18, 117 n. 97
Freedman, D. N., 48 n. 16, 109 n. 50, 144 n. 22
Gaster, M., 85 n. 24, 87, 88 n. 33, 90 n. 38
Gaster, T. H., 143 nn. 11 and 15
Gese, H., **109**
Ginzberg, L., 63 n. 23, 103 n. 18, 125 n. 30
Goldin, J., 149 n. 56
Goodenough, E. R., 125 n. 31
Görg, M., 48 n. 15.16
Gowan, D. E., 113 n. 73
Grözinger K. E., 24 n. 51
Gry, L., 21, 24 n. 54, 61 n. 14, 78 n. 29
Gunneweg, A. H. J., 83 n. 15, 136 nn. 24 and 26
Hadot, J., **19 n. 14**
Hall, R. G., 155 n. 88
Halpern, B., 66 n. 35
Harnisch, W., 102 n. 11
Hartmann, L., xxix n. 82
Heininger, B., xxxvi n. 106, 122 n. 15, 123 n. 22, **125 n. 29**
Helderman, J., 96 n. 70, 97 n. 76
Heller, B., 85 n. 24, 89 nn. 36–37, 90 n. 38
Hengel, M., xxiii n. 48, 56 n. 10, 68 n. 47, 74 n. 6
Hermisson, H.-J., 143 n. 14
Herrmann, S., 86 n. 26
Herzer, J., xvi n. 5.6, xix n. 10, xxiv n. 52, xxvii n. 75, xxix nn. 78–81, xxxvi n. 107, 11 n. 3, 29 n. 9, 43 n. 1, 45 n. 4, 48 n. 17, 50 n. 21, 56 n. 10, 57 n. 13, 60 n. 5.10, 63 n. 24, 64 n. 28, 68 n. 44, 72 n. 63, 74 nn. 4 and 6, 77 n. 23, 81 nn. 1–2, 82 n. 8, 83 n. 16, 84 nn. 19 and 21, 87 n. 30, 88 nn. 33–34, 90 nn. 39 and 42, 92 n. 53, 93 n. 57, 94 n. 61, 96 n. 70, 99 n. 83, 102 nn. 10 and 14, 103 nn. 16–17, 105 n. 28, 106 n. 33, 107 nn. 37, 38, 40 and 42, 110 nn. 55–56, 111 n. 61, 112 n. 64, 116 nn. 90, 92 and 95, 117 n. 104, 120 nn. 3 and 5, 121 n. 9, 122 nn. 17 and 18, 123 n. 22, 126 n. 36, 128 n. 56, 130 nn. 62 and 65–66, 133 n. 10, 134 n. 14, 135 n. 22, 137 n. 32, 139 n. 38, 141 n. 1, 142 nn. 5 and 9, 144 nn. 17, 19 and 22–23, 145 nn. 24–26 and 29, 146 n. 32, 147 nn. 35, 39–40 and 42, 152 nn. 68–69 and 71, 154 nn. 79 and 81–82, 155 nn. 85 and 87, 156 nn. 91 and 95
Hobbs, T. R., 70 n. 56
Hofius, O., 96 n. 69, 97 nn. 74–75
Holladay, C. R., 83 n. 14
Holladay, W. L., 70 n. 56
Holtz, T., 49 n. 18, 130 n. 66
Huber, M., 85 n. 24, 87 n. 31, 89 nn. 35–37, 90 n. 38
Hünemörder, C., 123 n. 23
Hunzinger, C.-H., 44 n. 2, 60 n. 4, 72 n. 62
Jeremias, J., 103 n. 17
Johnson, N. B., 48 n. 17
Jonge, M. de, xxxv n. 101, 47 n. 10
Josephanz, H. S., xxxvii n. 117
Käsemann, E., 97 n. 75
Keel, O., 122 nn. 13–14, 143 n. 14, 146 n. 32
Kern, O., 87 n. 31
Kilpatrick, G. D., xxxi n. 89, xxxv n. 99, 62 n. 18, **63**
Kippenberg, H. G., 134 n. 17, 136 nn. 26 and 28, 137 n. 33, 138 n. 35

Klijn, A. F. J., xix n. 15, xx n. 19, 60 n. 7, 73 n. 2, 74 n. 5, 104 n. 23, 106 n. 37, 108 n. 46, 122 n. 17, 127 n. 46
Knittel, T., 103 n. 19, 145 n. 29, 146 n. 31
Koch, J., 89 n. 36
Koester, C. R., xxiii n. 44, 63 n. 23
Kohler, K., xv n. 3, **xix,** xxix n. 83, 61 n. 13, 68, 78 n. 29, 82 n. 6, 99 n. 81, 133 n. 12, 138 n. 36
Kosmala, H., 143 n. 14
Kraft, R. A., xv n. 3, xxxvi, xxxvii, xxxviii n. 124, xli n. 128, xlii, 71 n. 60, 77 n. 20, 91 n. 43, 102 n. 9, 107 n. 41, 146 nn. 30 and 32, 147 n. 36
Kuhn, H.-W., 128 n. 52
Langer, B., 75 n. 11
Le Déaut, R., **xxx n. 84**
Lenhardt, P., xxxiii n. 96, 103 n. 18
Levi, G. B., 66 n. 35
Licht, J., xxix n. 83, xxxi n. 87, xxxvi n. 103, 84 n. 21, 128 n. 53
Liwak, R., 48 n. 15, 75 n. 10
Loewenstamm, S. E., 149 n. 56
Lohfink, G., 151 n. 65
Lundbom, J. R., 75 n. 10
Magonet, J., 143 n. 11
Maier, J., 75 n. 11.12
Malherbe, A. J., vii, 48 n. 15
Mallau, H. H., xxvi n. 73
Marmorstein, A., xxvii n. 73
Maser, P., 75 n. 12
Masson, D., 89 n. 37
Matthews, V., 66 n. 35
Metzger, B. M., 116 n. 93, 127 n. 46, 156 n. 94
Meyer, R., 138 n. 36
Michaels, J. R., 106 n. 34.35
Milgrom, J., 143 n. 11, 145 n. 23
Milik, J. T., 61 n. 12
Montgomery, J. A., 134 n. 17
Mor, M., 138 n. 38
Morawe, G., 95 n. 65
Morgenstern, J., 142 n. 11
Murphy, F. J., xix n. 15, 46 n. 5, 62 n. 19, 73 n. 2, 74 n. 7, 99 n. 81, 130 n. 62
Naumann, W., 83 n. 15
Neusner, J., xxvi n. 71, xxxii n. 91, **xxxiii n. 96,** 69 n. 49, 86 n. 25, 108 n. 48, 125 n. 31, 139 n. 38, 139 n. 40, 143 n. 14
Nickelsburg, G. W. E., xv n. 3, xvii n. 8, xx n. 20, xxi nn. 23 and 26–27, **xxii, xxiii,** xxxi n. 87, 47 n. 12, 62 n. 17, 73 n. 2, 116 n. 94, 118 n. 106
Nitzan, B., 95 n. 65
Overholt, T. W., 113 n. 73, 128 n. 55
Philonenko, M., xxix n. 80, xxx n. 86, xxxvii n. 113, 64 nn. 27–28, 72 nn. 63 and 67, 102 n. 8, 107 nn. 40 and 42–43, 109, 110 n. 58, 115 n. 86, **116,** 117, 120 n. 4, **122, 123,** 128 n. 48, 145 n. 25, 148 n. 50, 152 n. 69
Pummer, R., 132 n. 4, **134 n. 17**
Rad, G. von, 96 n. 67
Rehm, M., 70 n. 56
Reichmann, V., 72 n. 64
Reinhartz, A., **xxxiii n. 96**
Riaud, J., xvi n. 5, xvii n. 8, **xix,** xx, **xxi, xxii,** xxv nn. 58, 60 and 63, xxvi n. 66, xxvii n. 74, xxx n. 84, xxxi, xxxiv n. 98, xxxv nn. 99 and 101, xxxvi n. 105, xxxvii, xxxviii n. 124, xli n. 128, 47 nn. 6 and 10, 49 n. 20, 50 n. 21, 55 n. 6, 61 n. 13, 62 n. 18, 63 nn. 23 and 25, 64 n. 26, 66 nn. 32 and 34–35, 67 n. 37, 68, 69 n. 50, 71 n. 60, 74 nn. 6 and 9, 77 n. 20, 81 nn. 3 and 5, 82 n. 9, 83 nn. 11 and 16, 84 n. 21, 88 n. 34, 90 n. 39, 91 nn. 43 and 45, 97 n. 75, 98 nn. 79–80, 101 n. 1, **102,** 103 nn. 16 and 17, 105 n. 30, 107 n. 43, 110 n. 58, **112,** 116 n. 94, 125 nn. 29 and 33, 126 n. 37, 128 n. 54, 133 n. 9, 134 nn. 14 and 16, 135 n. 22, 136 n. 30, 138 nn. 35–36, **141,** 142 nn. 10 and 11, 144 n. 21, 145 n. 27, 147 n. 36, 153 n. 77, 154 nn. 80 and 83, 156 n. 95
Rössler, D., 71 n. 60

INDEX OF MODERN AUTHORS

Rosenstiehl, J.-M., xxi, xxvii n. 74, 88 n. 34
Rost, L., xx n. 16
Rudolph, W., 75 n. 10
Russell, D. S., 156 n. 91
Safrai, S., 32, 143 nn. 11 and 13–14
Sallmann, K., 88 n. 33
Sanders, E. P., xxix n. 82
Saylor, G. B., xx n. 16, xxxi n. 87
Schäfer, P., xxxii nn. 93 and 95, xxxiii nn. 96–97, 68 n. 47, 117 nn. 101–2
Schalit, A., 68 n. 47
Schaller, B., xxi n. 29, xxii n. 39, xxv n. 57–59, xxvi nn. 66 and 72, xxx n. 84, xxxv n. 102, xxxvi nn. 104–5, xxxvii, xxxviii n. 124, xli n. 125, 45 n. 3, 47 n. 7, 49 n. 18, 51 n. 25, 53 n. 3, 54 n. 4, **55,** 57 nn. 15–16, 60 n. 9, 62 n. 15, 64 n. 27, 66 nn. 33–35, 67 n. 40, 71 n. 60, 72 nn. 63 and 65, 75 n. 13, 77 n. 20, 78 n. 29, 82 n. 7, 84 n. 18, 87 n. 28, 91 nn. 43–44 and 46–47, 92 n. 52, 93 nn. 56 and 58, 94 n. 61, 95 n. 64, 101 nn. 2 and 7, 102 nn. 8–9, 105 nn. 29 and 31–32, 106 n. 33, 107 nn. 39 and 41, 112 n. 65, 113 n. 71, 114 n. 79, 116 nn. 90 and 94, 118 n. 108, 120 nn. 3–4, **121,** 123 nn. 20 and 22, 125 n. 33, 128 nn. 50–51, 129 n. 59, 130 nn. 63 and 65–66, 132 n. 8, 135 n. 18, 143 n. 12, 144 nn. 20–21, 145 nn. 23 and 28, 146 nn. 30 and 33, 147 nn. 37 and 44–45, 148 n. 53, 151 nn. 64–65 and 67, 152 n. 69, 153 n. 75, 154 n. 80, 156 n. 94, 157 nn. 97–98
Schermann, T., 150 n. 60
Schlatter, A., xxxii n. 91, 156 n. 92
Schmid, H., xix n. 15, 78 n. 29
Schoeps, H. J., 143 n. 14, 155 n. 90, 156 n. 95
Scholem, G., 117 n. 101
Schürer, E., xxxi, xxxvii nn. 120–21, 155 n. 85
Schulte, H., 67 n. 37
Schur, N., 136 n. 26
Schützinger, H., xxvii n. 73, 67 n. 37, 89 n. 37
Schwartz, D. R., 68 n. 48
Schwemer, A. M., xxiii n. 48, 61 n. 13, 129 n. 61
Seitz, C. R., 113 n. 74
Smith, M. S., 75 n. 11
Snijders, L. A., 129 n. 57
Speyer, W., 50 n. 24
Stähli, H.-P., 75 n. 11
Steck, O. H., 61 n. 13, 156 n. 96
Steiger, J. A., 84 n. 17
Stemberger, G., xxiv n. 51.53, xxxii n. 92, 84 n. 22, 104 nn. 21–22, 144 n. 22
Stemm, S. v., 49 n. 18
Stone, M. E., xxxvi n. 105, xli n. 126, 62 n. 17, 63 n. 25, 97 n. 76, 104 n. 21, 108 n. 46, 116 n. 94, 127 n. 46, 154 n. 82
Strack, H. L., xxiii n. 51, xxiv n. 53, 84 n. 22, 144 n. 22
Strecker, G., 96 n. 70
Stuhlmacher, P., 71 n. 60
Surkau, H.-W., 155 n. 86
Taatz, I., xx n. 17, 83 n. 15, 106 nn. 34 and 36, 111 n. 62, 112 n. 67, 113 nn. 72 and 76, 126 n. 38
Tabor, J. D., 149 n. 56
Thoma, C., xxiv n. 55, 108 n. 46, 109 n. 50
Timm, S., 136 nn. 23–25
Tissot, Y., 130 n. 66
Tröger, K.-W., 96 n. 70
Turdéanu, E., xxxi n. 89, xxxiv n. 98, xxxvi n. 105, xxxvii n. 118, xxxviii, xli n. 127, 68 n. 42
Unnik, W. C. v., xix n. 14
Vielhauer, P., 96 n. 70
Volz, P., 97 n. 77
Voss, M. H. v., 123 n. 21
Wadsworth, M., 149 n. 56
Walter, N., 49 n. 18, 83 n. 14, 99 n. 81
Weiß, H.-F., 97 n. 75
Wilkinson, J., 70 n. 56
Williamson, H. G. M., 138 n. 34

Willi-Plein, I., 156 n. 93

Wolff, C., vii, xvi n. 4, xx n. 19, xxii nn. 32–35 and 37, xxv nn. 57, 60 and 62, xxvi nn. 69 and 73, xxvii n. 73, xxix nn. 79 and 83, xxxvii, xli n. 127, 47 n. 10, 48 nn. 14 and 17, 59 n. 3, 61 n. 13, 62 nn. 17 and 19, 63 n. 23, 74 nn. 6 and 9, 78 n. 29, 82 nn. 7–8 and 10, **83,** 84 n. 21, 90 n. 41, 92 n. 54, 93 n. 58, 96 nn. 69 and 71, 97 n. 74, 98 n. 80, 99 n. 81, 101 n. 1, 102 nn. 8 and 12, 104 nn. 20–22, 111 n. 63, 115 n. 88, 116 n. 90, 117 n. 105, 119 n. 1, 121 n. 8, 125 nn. 30 and 33, 127 n. 47, 128 n. 50, 130 n. 66, 134 nn. 13 and 14, 141 nn. 1–2, 142 n. 10, 145 n. 29, 147 n. 38, 150 nn. 57–61, 152 n. 71, 154 n. 79, 156 n. 91, 157 n. 96

Wolff, H. W., 113 n. 74

Yassif, E., 155 n. 90

Zimmerli, W., 74 n. 10

Index of Ancient Names and Places

Names

Abba-Hilqija, 86 n. 26
Abimelech, xxviii, **66–67**
Abraham, 48 n. 16, 51 n. 25, **77–78,** 103, **114–15,** 127
R. Aqiba, xxviii n. 77, **xxxiii,** 108 n. 48, **138 n. 38**
Bar Kokhba, xix, **xxxi–xxxv,** 69 n. 49, **128 n. 48**
Chaldaeans, **43–45,** 50, 60, 70 n. 56, 73, 126 n. 36
Chutaens, 136 n. 26
Decius, 89
Dio Cassius, xxxiii
Ebed-melech, **66–67,** 103
Elijah, 103, 55, 121, 123 n. 14
R. Eliezer, 48 n. 16, 103, 146 n. 32
Epimenides, 87–89
R. Gamaliel II, xxxii–xxxiii
Hadrian, **xxxii–xxxv,** 45, 69 n. 49, 92, 112
Herodes Agrippa I, 68
Herodes Agrippa II, 68 n. 47
Hillel, xxxii
Honi the Circle Drawer, xxviii, 84–87, 88, 90
Jacob of Sarug, 89 n. 35
Jesus Christ, 50 n. 24, **92, 150–51,** 155
R. Johannan ben Toreta, xxxiii n. 96
R. Johannan ben Zakkai, xxxii–xxxiv, 48 n. 16, 143 n. 14
Josephus, 50, 68–69, 73 n. 2, 84 n. 20, 134 n. 17, 136 n. 26, 137, 149 n. 56
R. Joshua, 48 n. 16
Joshua, 47 n. 6, 117
R. Yudan Giria, 85
Manasse, 155
Moses, 47 n. 6, 108–9, 113 n. 74, 124 n. 27, 125, 133 n. 8, **149,** 155
Nebuchadnezzar, xxv, **43–44,** 70 n. 56, 92, **128,** 132 n. 8
Noah, xxviii, 121–22
Omri, 136
Onias (*see* Honi the Circle Drawer)
Pliny the Elder, 88 n. 33
Pompey, xix n. 14
Solomon, 68, 84 n. 17, 121
Sanballat, 137
Sargon, 136
R. Simon/Simeon ben Gamaliel, xxviii n. 77, 138 n. 38
R. Simeon ben Yochai, xxxiii n. 96
Simon of Cyrene, 92
Simon the Just, 108 n. 48
Theodosius, 69 n. 52, 91 n. 39
Theodosius the Younger (II), 89
Titus, 69
Trajan, xxxii
Vespasian, 48 n. 16, 112 n. 70
Zar, 128–29
Zedekiah, xxv, 70 n. 56, 74 n. 3, 106 n. 36
Zeus, xxxiii, 123

Places

Aelia Capitolina, xxxiii, 45
Bethlehem, 68, 112 n. 70
Cisterns of Solomon, 68
Egypt, 70, 94, 108, 115, 123–25, 134, 150, 156
Garizim, 137–38
Hermippo, 69
Hirbet ibk'dan, 69
Kidron Valley, 69 n. 54, 70 n. 56, 79 n. 29
Mamre, 112
Mount of Olives, 69–70, 153
Samaria, xxviii, 131–38, 150
Yavneh, xxxii, xxxiv
Zeus/Jupiter temple, xxxiii
Zion, 54, 83, 85, 86, 129, **133**

INDEX OF SUBJECTS

Abimelech (sleep of), xv, xxii, xxv, **xxvi,** xxviii, xxxiii, 25, 79, **81–99**
Abimelech (story of), **xxv–xxviii,** 59, 66 n. 35, 67, 71, 73, 79, **81–82,** 87, 111, 130
altar, 53–54, 57, **60,** 61 n. 12, 62, **64–65,** 71 n. 61, **141, 142,** 143 n. 14
angel of righteousness, 101, 133, 135, 138, **141,** 142
angels, 45, **60,** 71, 73, 79
apostle, 142, 151, 154, 155
archangel (*see* Michael)
ascension of Christ, 153
Atonement, Day of (*see also* Yom Kippur), xxix, 74, 108 n. 48, **143 n. 14**
baptism, 64 n. 28, 115–17
Bar-Kokhba War, xxxi, xxxiii–xxxiv, 69 n. 49, 128 n. 48
beauty, 62, 64–65
beloved (*see* people)
birds, 121–22
cave, 61 n. 13, 69 n. 54, 78 n. 29, 79, 82 n. 6, **86, 88,** 89, 97
circumcision, 116 n. 94, 118 n. 106
cleansing, 98 n. 80, 112 n. 65, 118, 132
creation, 63–65, 73, 75, 78 n. 27, **116–17,** 121 n. 10, 146–47, **148**
creation, new, 63–65, 148
date of *2 Baruch,* xix
date of *4 Baruch,* xix–xx, xxx–xxxiv
date of the Christian closing, xxxiv–xxxv
Day of Atonement (*see* Atonement, Day of)
death, 55 n. 9, 65, 79, 84 n. 20, 85, 87, 89 n. 37, 97–98, **101–4, 105,** 114, 145 n. 27, 148–49, 153

death of Isaiah, xxix, 151, 156
death of Jeremiah, xxii, xxix, 64, 102, 141–50
deeds, 46, 66, 109 n. 50, 114, 131, 157
defilement, 130, 131
desert, 118, 123–25
Diaspora, xxxii, xxxiii, xxxv, xxxvi, 97, 138 n. 34
dove, 121–22
dream, xv, xxviii, 83, 85, 86, 99
eagle, xxviii, 49, 106, 111, **119–25,** 130
enlightenment, 145
Epimenides Legend, 87–88
exile, Babylonian, **xv,** xviii, xxviii, xxxvii, **44,** 49, **55,** 59, **63–64,** 72, 76, 79, **81–83,** 84, 88, **90, 92, 95,** 98, 107 n. 42, 111, 113, 114, 118, 119, 122, **126,** 129–30, 131, **134,** 136–37, 141, 143 n. 14, 149, 150
exodus, 94, 96, 98, 115, 118, **125,** 134
exodus, new/second, 94, 134, 149
faith virginal, 105–6
father, 119, 126 n. 36
fathers, arch-, 76, 85, 132 n. 8, 149 n. 56
Feast of Unleavened Bread, 93 n. 59
field, 92
fifteen (figs/days), 112 n. 65
fig tree, 60 n. 4, 69, 72, **82, 84 n. 17,** 105 n. 32
figs, 60 n. 4, 72 n. 64, **82,** 84 n. 17, **90,** 93–94, 98, 105 n. 32
Gabriel, 110
gnosis/gnostic, xxix, 64 n. 28, **96,** 99 n. 83, 106, 107 n. 42, **109–10, 116–17,** 123 n. 22, **125 n. 29,** 148 n. 48, 152 n. 69

209

gods, foreign, **114,** 118, **129,** 136 n. 29
good news, 70, **93,** 119, **122**
grave, 65, **78–79,** 105, 157
gravestone of Jeremiah, 151
haggadah, xxix, **xxx n. 84,** xxxiv–xxxv, 43, **93–95,** 101, 104, 106–7, 119, 125 n. 29, 126, **128 n. 48,** 141, 144, 146, 149
high priest, 74, 83, 92, 109, 112, 137, 142, 143
holiness, 49, 146
hope, **xvi,** xxviii, xxxiv
immortality, 102, 126 n. 30
incense, 61 n. 12, 144–46
interpolations, Christian, 59, 77 n. 23, 131 n. 2
Isis, 123
Israel, xxviii, xxx, xxxi, 43, 45, 54, 65 n. 30, 67, **76–77,** 95, 98, 110, 113, 115, 123 n. 26, 124, 127, 128, 132 n. 8, 133 n. 9, 134, **137–38,** 143 n. 14, 143 n. 15, 156 n. 96
Jerusalem, destruction of, **xv–xviii,** xxiv, xxvii, xxx–xxxiii, xxxv, **45–46,** 50, 54–55, 59, 66, 67, 69, 70, 74, 76, 78, 89, 105, 108,
Jerusalem, heavenly, xxix, **xxxiv,** 49, 50 n. 21, 51, 63, 91, **95, 97–99,** 104, 125 n. 29, **133,** 144, **145–46,** 149
Jordan, 111, 112 n. 66, **115–18, 131–33**
joy, 72, 98, 110, 111, 114, 125
judgment, 115, 116, 127, **45–50,** 55, 56–57, 59, 60, 66, **71–72,** 73, 76–78, 82, 94, 97, 103, 104–5, 107, 109 n. 50, 113 n. 74, 114–15, 123, 127 n. 45, 133, 138, **147,** 152–54
knowledge (*see* γνῶσις)
language, original of *4 Baruch*, xxxv–xxxvi, 66 n. 35
law, xxxii, xxxiv, 46 n. 5, 70, 76, 85, 93, **98,** 105, **107, 110–11,** 115, 126, 133 n. 8, 136, 145
light (from God; *see also* φῶς), 95, **98, 106–7, 110,** 145, 151, 152
market of the Gentiles, 112

marriages, mixed, xxviii, 114, 131–38
martyrdom of Isaiah, 155
martyrdom of Jeremiah, 151, 154
Messiah, xxxii, xxxiii n. 96, xxxv, **63,** 103, 128 n. 48
Michael, xxv, 73, 101, 103, 141, **145–46**
mission, xxxv, 154
Moses, new, xxii, **149**
name (of God), 54, 65, 106, **107–10,** 124
Nisan, **93–94,** 95
obedience/disobedience, xxviii, 57, 105, **113,** 115, 126, 132, 135, **137–38**
Passover, 94–95
people, beloved, 46, 55–56, **62–63, 65,** 76–77, 79, 125 n. 29, **127,** 128 n. 48
people, gathering of, xxii, xxxiv, **62–63, 65,** 72
Pharisees, xxxi, xxxii n. 92
pillar, 47–48, 98
prayer, xviii, **xxix,** xxxiv, **47–48,** 54, 55, 79, 101, 110, **129,** 132 n. 8, **141, 143,** 144, 146, 148 n. 48, 149
raven, 122, 125 n. 30
repentance, 113 n. 74, 126, 134–35, 138, 143 n. 11
rest, 70, 91, **95–99,** 104, 124 n. 26
resurrection, xxxiv, xxxv, 99, 101–2, **104–5,** 111, 119, **123–25,** 149, 151
return of the people, xxv, xxvii, 59, 63, 67, 95, 98, 107, 125, 130, 135
reward, 101
Rosh Hashanah, 147
sacrifice, 143 n. 14
salvation, xviii, xxviii, **xxxiv–xxxv,** 44, 45, **49,** 51, 67, **71–72,** 73, 76, 77, 78, 87, 90, 93, **98–99,** 101, 106–7, 111, **113–16,** 119, 125, 128, 129, 135, 142, 144, 146–48
Samaritans, xxviii, **131–39,** 142, 146
Sanhedrin, xxxii
seal(s)/sealing, 62–65, 116–17, 147
separation, 44, 111–12, 118, 129–31, 135
seraphim, 146
seven, 60, 62–65, 83 n. 15, **89–90,** 108 n. 48, 112 n. 65, **116,** 152 n. 69

INDEX OF SUBJECTS

Seven Sleepers, legend of, 89–90
sin, xvii, 46, 49, 53, **55–57,** 59, **76,** 109 n. 50, **113 n. 73,** 115, 143 n. 15, 154 n. 82
sins, forgiveness of, 55, 143 n. 14
sixty-six, xv, **xxvi,** xxx, **81–83,** 88, 94–95, 105, 126
Son of God, 151, 153, 155
son, only, 56, 127–28
stewards of faith, 74, 105, 120 n. 6, 121
stoning of Jeremiah, xxix, 150, 155–57
sun, 74–75
syncretism, 114, 136
teaching (of the law), 71 n. 60, 119, **122,** 131
temple, xvi, xxvi–xxvii, xxxi–xxxiv, 47, 53–55, 64, 70, 73 n. 2, 74, 85–87, 91 n. 44, 94–95, 133 n. 12, **141–42,** 143 n. 14, 144

temple, keys of, xxii, **74–75, 141,** 144
temple, vessels of, xxii, xxiii, 57, **59, 61,** 63–64, 66, 70–71, 74 n. 3, 92, **141–42,** 144, 152 n. 69
tent, 54, 62 n. 13, **102,** 132 n. 8
translation, **102–3,** 145 n. 27, 149 n. 56
tree of life, 153, **154**
trees, living, 144–45, 153–54
Trishagion, 144
Unleavened Bread, Feast of, 93 n. 59
vineyard (of Agrippa), xv, xxvi, **60, 67–69,** 72
wisdom, 110
word of God, 62, 98, 65 n. 29, 70, **111–12,** 153
works (see also deeds), 48, 131
Yom Kippur (*see also* Atonement, Day of), xxii, 112, 142–44, 147

INDEX OF GREEK TERMS

ἀγαπητός, 127–28
ἀγέννητος, 147
ἁγιαστήριον, 53–54, 57 n. 15, 57 n. 16
ἀγρός, 92
αἴρειν, 103
ἀλισγήματα, 130 n. 66
ἀναλαμβάνεσθαι, 102–3, 145 n. 27
ἀνάπαυσις, 95–97
ἀνάψυξον, 105
ἀπερινόητος, 148
γνῶσις, 110
ἐξυπνίζειν, 151
ἐπιστρέφειν, 83
ἐπίτροπος ψεύδους, 75, 121 n. 8
εὐαγγελίζεσθαι, 70, 71 n. 60, 122
εὐωδία, 146
ζωή, 145 n. 23, 152
ἠγαπημένος, xxiii, 46, **62–63**, 128
θεὸς ἀλλότριος, 129
θυμίαμα, 144, 146
θυσιαστήριον, 57 n. 15, 57 n. 16, 62
ἱκανός, 101
καλὴ φάσις, 122

καρδία, 105 n. 26
κρίσις, 147
κτίσις, 147
λόγος, 93, 71 n. 60
λύχνος, 152
μετανοεῖν, 134, 142 n. 8
μισθαποδοσία, 101
μνημεῖον, 79 n. 29, 119
μονογενής, 56, 127–28
νόμος, 93 n. 57, 110
οἰκονόμος τῆς πίστεως, 105, 110, 120
πίστις, 105, 120, 152
παντοκράτωρ, 49, 146, 147 n. 35
παρθενικός, 105
σημεῖον, xxxiv, 91, 116
σκήνωμα, 54
σύμβουλος, 110
συνέλευσις, 62–63
σφραγίς, 63, 115, 116, 118 n. 106
υἱὸς θεοῦ, 151
φῶς, 98, 110, 151–52
φωταγωγεῖν, 98 n. 79, 99 n. 81

www.ingramcontent.com/pod-product-compliance
Lightning Source LLC
Chambersburg PA
CBHW021807220426
43662CB00006B/213